The Year 2000

The Year 2000

Essays on the End

EDITED BY

Charles B. Strozier

and

Michael Flynn

New York University Press

NEW YORK AND LONDON

NEW YORK UNIVERSITY PRESS
New York and London

Copyright © 1997 by New York University

Chapter 3. © The Society for the Comparative Study of Society

Chapter 4. Catherine Keller's article "The Breast, the Apocalypse, and the Colonial Journey" originally appeared in the *Journal of Feminist Studies in Religion* 10 (Spring 1994).

Chapter 5. © 1994 Charles B. Strozier. From *Apocalypse: On the Psychology of Fundamentalism in America* by Charles B. Strozier. Reprinted by permission of Beacon Press, Boston.

Chapter 6. © Paulist Press. Originally published as "Apocalyptic Spirituality" by Bernard McGinn in *Catholic World* (January, 1996).

Chapter 9. © Robert Jay Lifton

Chapter 16. Reprinted by permission of the Mid-American Studies Association. Originally published as "Racist Apocalypse: Millenialism on the Far Right" by Michael Barkun, in *American Studies*, vol. 31, no. 2, pp. 121–40.

Chapter 17. © Sara Diamond

Chapter 21. Reprinted from *The Illusion of the End*, by Jean Baudrillard, translated by Chris Turner, with the permission of the publishers, Stanford University Press. This translation © 1994 Polity Press

Chapter 22. © Sandra Schanzer

Chapter 24. © Peter von Ziegesar

Chapter 26. © Hillel Schwartz

Library of Congress Cataloging-in-Publication Data
The year 2000 : essays on the end / edited by Charles B. Strozier and Michael Flynn.
        p. cm.
Includes bibliographical references and index.
ISBN 0-8147-8030-X (alk. paper). — ISBN 0-8147-8031-8 (pbk. : alk. paper)
1. Two thousand, A.D. 2. Millennium. 3. End of the world.
    I. Strozier, Charles B. II. Flynn, Michael, 1962– . III. Title: Year two thousand.
CB161.Y39 1997
909.83—dc21   97-4786
                CIP

New York University Press books are printed on acid-free paper, and their binding materials are chosen for strength and durability.

Manufactured in the United States of America

For Alison and Olivia

Contents

Chapter One

Introduction

Charles B. Strozier

The year 2000 is at hand, calling forth varied responses. For some it further agitates their already frantic relationship to personal and collective death. Soothsayers and cult movements abound. But no one in our culture can entirely escape the millennial hysteria of the 1990s. Certainly, as a potent symbol, 2000 stirs the imagination of virtually all believing Christians at some level. Jesus, after all, announces in the first book of the New Testament (Matthew 24) that he is coming back, just as the Bible's last book, Revelation, twice plays with the evocative power of thousand-year cycles in its climactic chapter 20. *End time* means that moment (which is at the same time a process) of moving out of human history and into God's time. But as a cultural artifact 2000 connects as well with secular forms of the apocalyptic. In this sense many are drawn into generalized images of endings around this pervasively concrete and available symbol *for the end*. The year 2000 appears everywhere as a subtext, in literature and art; in all the media; in politics, especially at the extremes; in all religions, new or old; and in what might be called the American self. Often this concrete imagistic millennialism degenerates into the apocalyptic chic of the *National Enquirer*. But it is never absent. For many, and not just the semiliterate and weak at heart, 2000 suggests much about potential ultimate human endings and God's agency in creating new forms. The year 2000 is in our souls.

This book explores the meanings of the year 2000 both as an approaching event and as an evocative symbol in American life. The beginning section presents essays that explore 2000 in religious history, from its first millennium experience through Columbus to the Civil War and the New Age, along with arguments for a transformed Christianity inspired by apocalyptic spirituality. The second section features essays on the manifestations of apocalyptic violence that have been energized significantly by the year 2000, from Waco and Oklahoma City to Aum Shinrikyo in Japan, as well as in various other kinds of totalistic communities. The third section, on 2000 and politics, addresses in particular the preoccupation of right-wing extremism in America with millennial themes but includes as well discussions of the way 2000 works together with racial tensions and the reality of potential endings in nuclear catastrophe. The final section includes essays on 2000 and culture, from art to theater and deconstruction, and includes even the collapsing universe of computer programming, faced with the daunting challenge of a rollover of zeros.

It is astonishing that a mere date should work its way through a culture in so many different ways. Undoubtedly, death figures centrally. It is, after all, knowledge of our own death that distinguishes humanity and is an important part of the process in the creation of culture. We also know of the apocalyptic, or collective death, because we all die. Knowledge of our own death allows us creatively to extend that knowing into an imagining of universal endings. To think about such things is heavily weighted spiritually, for it pushes up against knowledge of the divine, however conceived. For the fundamentalists this involves the revelation of God's anger and forgiveness in defined stages, or "dispensations," the knowledge of which we have from "signs" of the end. The fundamentalist end time story line is a teleological narrative that is literal and violent, as well as being so stereotypically masculine as to almost mock the patriarchy (the rider on the horse in Revelation 19:21 appears with a suggestive sword sticking out of his mouth). But it would be a serious mistake to leave 2000 to the fundamentalists. The themes are too universal, too human, too rooted in images of collective death and renewal. In most millennial scripts, whether New Age or Baptist, apocalypse precedes redemption, indeed cannot happen without it. In such stories salvation requires violence, which in its very destructiveness cleanses. Time collapses in the fullness of the old dying and the new coming to life. In the end time, despair and hope merge. Endings become beginnings. As a female black parishioner once told me, "You cannot go over it, you cannot go alongside it, but you must go through it. You must go *through the blood.*"[1]

Biblical genocide is the dread. The book of Revelation plays out God's anger in cascading waves of violence linked with sevens of trumpets, seals, and vials. In the theology of literalized Christianity, as it emerged between the 1830s and the 1880s, a very specific version of the end time took shape that was a departure from earlier narratives. The key figure was a British theologian named John Nelson Darby (who was to make many evangelist trips to the United States) and his small group of Plymouth Brethren in the 1830s. Their ideas of "premillennial dispensationalism" included the now-familiar notions of the rapture, the tribulation, the timing of the return of Jesus, the interpretation of biblical history as divided into defined stages or dispensations, and the special role of the Jews in the end time process. This elaborate theory of the end was later given a certain panache in the theory of textual literalness as developed by Charles Hodge, his son, Archibald Alexander Hodge, and Benjamin Warfield, who were all professors at Princeton Theological Seminary in the 1870s and 1880s. This theory of "inerrancy" was uniquely pernicious, for it cast a long tradition of literalness into dogma and changed forever the loose meanings of the complex symbols of prophetic texts. A sacred end time sequence emerged. In it the ingathering of the Jews foreshadows the coming of Antichrist and the beginning of the seven-year sufferings of the tribulation. But first, in most scripts, Jesus appears in the clouds to rapture the faithful. The great battle of Armageddon between the forces of good and evil brings to a close the period of tribulation. Jesus returns to earth with the resurrected saints and rules for a thousand years from the site of present-day Israel. Satan is then "loosed for a season," which leads to another great battle between good and bad. At last, then, there is the final judgment, when the faithful enter the newly created heaven and the rest, along with most readers of this book, are cast into the lake of fire.

The timetable of this sequence is relentless once the process begins. Satan is loosed, for example, *exactly* 1,007 years after the beginning of tribulation, which in turn must follow the appearance of Antichrist. It is all ordained, indeed pre-existing, though God will reveal hints of what he is up to through signs; that is why close readers of biblical texts become such valued experts in the world of fundamentalism. The narrative is self-driven once set in motion. But what sets it off? For all contemporary fundamentalists the great prophetic moment of the twentieth century was the founding of the Israeli state in 1948 because it seemed to realize their own predictions about the "ingathering" of the Jews. The more agitated talk portentously of 1948 as starting the end time clock ticking and await with ambivalence the appearance of Antichrist. In such a rendition the climactic moment of the end time narrative must be the year 2000 as the inevitable moment for the rapture of the faithful and the beginning of the tribulation. Date setting, however, is proscribed ("But of that day and hour knoweth no man, no, not the angels of heaven, but my Father only," says Jesus in Matt. 24:36 [Authorized Version]), and so it can only be whispered in the collective dreams of the culture.

This relatively new story line has transformed Christianity and shifted the emphasis within it from the Sermon on the Mount to the book of Revelation. In the sermon (chaps. 5–7 of the book of Matthew), which assumes a human future, Jesus instructs that the poor are blessed, as are the meek, and those who mourn, and those who make peace, and those who are persecuted. Jesus insists on a strict morality (no divorce except for reasons of fornication), but his main concern is love and forgiveness: "Whosoever shall smite thee on thy right cheek, turn to him the other also" (5:39) and "Love your enemies, bless them that curse you, do good to them that hate you, and pray for them which despitefully use you, and persecute you" (5:44). In Revelation, on the other hand, the images are of the sun becoming black as sackcloth of hair and the moon like blood (6:12), for the "day of his wrath is come" (6:17); of a beast rising up out of the sea, "having seven heads and ten horns, and upon his horns ten crowns, and upon his heads the name of blasphemy" (13:1); of a "great whore that sitteth upon many waters" who is "drunken with the blood of the saints, and with the blood of the martyrs of Jesus" (17:1, 6); of a mighty angel casting a stone like a millstone into the sea ("Thus with violence shall that great city Babylon be thrown down" [18:21]); of blood everywhere and the remnant slain by him who rides the white horse with the sword proceeding out of his mouth (19:21); and the final violent death of Satan (20:10) and the death of death itself (20:14).

Such a transformation in the read of Scripture is of some consequence. Most of all, the new emphasis on Revelation (and other prophetic texts, especially Ezekiel and Daniel from the Old Testament) celebrates violence, which is a necessary correlate of the more immediate endism of fundamentalism. Both psychologically and spiritually, any prophetic narrative that brings the end closer at hand heightens its emphasis on collective death and destruction. Revelation is a bloody book. But so is the fundamentalist read of that and other texts. Fundamentalists bring something to it, a harsh dualism, that leads them to revel in and deepen the meaning of the violence they encounter. Fundamentalists, for example, make all important things happen twice, from their personally transformative experience of being reborn to the horrid second death that sinners must die for refusing to accept Jesus. Jews in this system bear a special taint. Their ingathering somehow forces the mystical return of Jesus, but then before it is all over they must all die (except for 144,000 in most accounts). A converted Jew cannot even be raptured.[2]

A frequently asked question is whether the millennial concerns with which we live are really new. Aren't the current faddish obsessions with the year 2000 simply a contemporary replay of very old themes? In the very asking, the smug become jaundiced. No one has been more confident about what I have called "eternal endism" than the critic Frank Kermode, who was one of the first many years ago to talk about some of these issues.[3] Kermode dismisses as "childish" any attempt to attach special significance to the terrors of our modern age, arguing that apocalyptic thinking is too firmly rooted in human experience. Only the naive, he argues, would privilege one's own time as uniquely dark and set it off as a cardinal point in time. The anxiety itself is not new. Cultures since the Mesopotamians have been grappling with it. Only the patterns of creative response to that anxiety, he argues, have been different.[4] Kermode would also dismiss as heated imaginings that brooding anxiety aroused by 2000. It would seem to him a form of "centurial mysticism" or, as Don DeLillo calls it, "millennial hysteria."[5] To the extent that we feel we now live in a state of perpetual transition, we elevate our period of ambiguous ending into an "age" in its own right.[6]

Much wisdom lies in such a deep appreciation for the enduring, human attachment to the end. Certainly it is true, for example, that there was a tremendous surge of cultural anxiety in the last half of the tenth century, evidenced by a general decline in cultural and artistic activity, especially in the French monasteries, where monks even stopped copying their Bibles. It was "an evening of the world" *(mundus senescrit)* in people's imaginings.[7] The conclusion of the first millennium seemed too precise a fulfillment of *millennial* anxiety. It took no elaborate calculations, or year-day equivalents, or any special knowledge to feel secure in the approaching end of history. The end (followed by renewal) had long been associated with thousand-year cycles and was in fact known to *all* the ancient peoples "as a basic element of their religion or philosophy." The only change Christianity introduced via John of Patmos was to be specific about the thousand years: "And I saw thrones, and they sat upon them, and judgment was given unto them: and I *saw* the souls of them that were beheaded for the witness of Jesus, and for the word of God, and which had not worshipped the beast, neither his image, neither had received *his* mark upon their foreheads, or in their hands; and they lived and reigned with Christ a thousand years" (Rev. 20:4). Tenth-century Europe was a thoroughly biblical culture, one that was brimming with superstition and general illiteracy. The apocalyptic had a kind of democratic flavoring. No experts were required to foretell the coming of the end. Most people (as least as far as one can tell from the fragmentary evidence available) assumed the world was about to come to its logical conclusion. A "nameless fear gripped mankind," a dark mood fell on the age.[8]

The complex intersection of politics and millennialism, as Norman Cohn showed long ago, became a familiar theme in the few centuries up to 1500,[9] and Hillel Schwartz has recently described the disarray and confusion at the ends of *all* centuries in the last thousand years, especially the tenth, the fifteenth, and the twentieth.[10] Another little-explored millennial topic is the anxieties surrounding the years ending in 33 of various centuries (recalling the death and resurrection of Jesus), not to mention the plethora of offbeat prophets like Nostradamus about whom we have heard much of late. And all that, of course, restricts the apocalyptic to the Christian narrative. There has long been a powerfully rich Jewish mystical tradition associated with the Zohar that engages in its own end time arithmetic. Native American (especially Hopi) stories forecast the end of this, the fourth, world in ways that end evil human culture but preserve the earth and enough human life to insure continuity. And there are always often-discredited traditions (such as those of William Blake and the Muggeltonians) that work at the margins of our psyches.

But in one very important sense apocalyptic preoccupations of all kinds in the late twentieth century are historically unique: they occur in the context of real, scientific possibilities of ultimate destruction.[11] In the past various cultures assigned the task of imagining the end of human history to mystics, artists, and psychotics. Before the modern period, the very notion of an end time was in such vivid contrast with the seeming certainties of daily life that only those with fertile (or disturbed) minds could open themselves up to such endist notions. For the last few hundred years those certainties have been increasingly eroded in the imperialistic expansion of the West, the vast new powers of industrialization, and the deadliness of wars. The nuclear age, however, brought about a qualitative shift in that process of altering human consciousness of collective death. It is now quite obvious and real that the human experiment could end. It is fatuous to pretend otherwise. We no longer need poets to tell us it could end with a bang, or a whimper, or in the agony of AIDS.[12] Consciousness of human endings haunts the psyches of quite ordinary people.[13] The psychological consequences are enormous. If once it took an act of imagination to think about the end time, now it takes an act of imagination, or a numbing, *not* to think about it. In such a world we all become end timers.

This general context heightens the immediacy of 2000 for literal Christians, just as 2000 emanates to a variety of constantly changing forms. Heaven's Gate, for example, in southern California combined a belief in UFOs with elements of Christian symbolism and a deep fascination with the year 2000. When the entire group committed suicide just before Easter in the spring of 1997, each body was meticulously covered with a purple shroud, suggesting, among other things, Lent. The goup's founders, Marshall Herff Applewhite and Bonnie Lu Nettles, originally (in the 1970s) referred to themselves as "The Two" after the two witnesses "clothed in sackcloth" in Revelation 11:3–14 who are slain by the Beast and then rise from the dead. Such eclectic theologies typify cult movements.

Consider, as well, Aum Shinrikyo, the Japanese cult with aspirations to Armageddon. The leader of Aum, Shoko Asahara, put together a theology of esoteric Buddhism that blended elements of yoga and Hinduism and symbols from Christianity. At one time Asahara was thus a close student of the book of Revelation and, as is so often the case with such involvements, he came to talk about Armageddon in the year 2000. Later, the end was pushed ahead to 1997 for obscure reasons and then hurried along by releasing sarin gas because of a fear the police were about to raid the Aum compound. Another example is David Koresh, who was intensely apocalyptic in the early years of the decade leading up to 2000. In 1992 Koresh renamed the Mount Carmel compound near Waco, Texas, "Ranch Apocalypse" and died in a fiery Armageddon that has since inspired much radical millennialism in others.

Imagery of 2000 reaches deeply into extreme political movements. Timothy McVeigh, the accused Oklahoma City bomber, was himself transformed psychologically by his pilgrimage to Waco during the standoff there between the Branch Davidians and government officials. Later, he allegedly chose the anniversary of the fire as the date on which he and others would bomb the federal building in Oklahoma City. The far Right in America in general locates theological themes centrally in its ideology. They talk loosely of ZOG (Zionist Occupied Government), for example, which has its basis in the Christian Identity idea of Jews as the literal children of Satan. They read the rapture differently from Pat Robertson. Identity movements believe Jesus only returns in the middle of or after tribulation. It might seem strange that so much passion could be wasted on such a seemingly obscure piece of theology. But it makes much political and psychological sense. Followers of Identity theology want to experience the violence of the end times directly. They want to shoot it out with the beast of Revelation, to fight true evil with their Uzis.

But extremism and 2000 are not restricted to the Right. The greening of apocalypse is upon us. Earth First! began among those passionately committed to saving the environment. Few noted at first how dominated their rhetoric was by a kind of phallic millennialism. The male-dominated leadership called themselves "warriors" out to protect "mother earth" who needed to be saved by their martial tactics before total destruction wiped out our future. And indeed Earth First! became the most aggressive of all environmental groups in its fight with loggers and others whom they saw as despoilers of the sacred ground of our being. The ends of preservation came to justify the means of violence, and some were injured in tree-spiking and other tactics. Politically, it was extreme; spiritually, it was a desperate effort to stave off the end time and a hauntingly odd rendition of Revelation 11:18, that he "shouldest destroy them which destroy the earth."

Perhaps the most obvious and visible emanations of 2000 are in films. At times the apocalyptic is treated in its literal religious context, as in *The Seventh Sign* or *The Rapture* (too sexy a movie for believers and too biblical a one for the raunchy). In most cases, however, Hollywood secularizes the end time story, while retaining echoes of 2000. *Twelve Monkeys,* for example, dates human endings through an environmental plague in the 1990s, whereas virtually every movie Arnold Schwarzenegger has made in recent years either has a nuclear or a postnuclear theme. Viruses have proved a potent end time theme (*Ebola, Outbreak, The Hot Zone*). In literature as well, especially the novel, 2000 is everywhere. Among serious writers Don DeLillo may be currently the most explicitly and brilliantly apocalyptic, but he is hardly alone. The theme of collective endings is often mocked or exploited in the novel, but it is seldom forgotten. How could it be otherwise?

In other words, 2000 reverberates with our deepest psychological dread. It becomes a metaphor for collective death, an unseemly euphemism. Through it we speak in code, whereby one thing substitutes for something else and itself, irrationally, at the same time. The year 2000, for example, deepens our fears of disease and contamination and makes AIDS an end time plague. It is, of course, the end for those who get it, but it becomes end time in the minds of the faithful and all others open to such metaphors as the kind of plague that will ravage the land during the tribulation. Even the trivial deepens in contemporary America, as shown by the culture's recent preoccupation with the weather. Cable channels everywhere talk weather twenty-four hours a day, and then people go to a theater to see a movie about it (*Twister*). Many Americans are much better informed about the rain than about world events. Behind such preoccupations lie the earthquakes of Matthew 24 that mark the signs of the return of Jesus and the ecological devastation of Revelation. In such a world of underlying dread, nothing is trivial.

And so somehow an introduction to a book about the end must itself end. Concluding is the central dilemma for anything touching end time. That is why, as an art form, autobiography, whether told by Benjamin Franklin or Colin Powell, never reaches a satisfactory conclusion. Death, the only appropriate culmination of a life, is yet to come. Francis Ford Coppola discovered this millennial coda when filming *Apocalypse Now*. The only real end to the movie may have been the blight brought to the corner of the Philippines where the movie was shot. Martin Sheen showed up on the set in the midst of a nervous breakdown and was in fact dead drunk in his opening scene; that night he had a heart attack and was hospitalized for seven weeks. Coppola had to shoot around him, not knowing for sure whether Sheen would die on him and the whole project would have to be abandoned. Marlon Brando as Kurtz refused to adjust his limited time commitments to the movie, despite the madness on the set. By the time shooting was under way Coppola gave up the literal story line from "Heart of Darkness" and filmed several possible endings while he still had Brando at hand. Costs spiraled out of control and chaos reigned supreme. Like a great work of art, *Apocalypse Now* was never properly finished, just abandoned and later resurrected in the editing room.

The real question about 2000 is what follows. Will we go with a bang or a whimper? Will there be a human future?

NOTES

1. Charles B. Strozier, *Apocalypse: On the Psychology of Fundamentalism in America* (Boston: Beacon Press, 1994), 89.

2. Ibid., chap. 9, 194–208.

3. Frank Kermode, *The Sense of Ending: Studies in the Theory of Fiction* (New York: Oxford University Press, 1967), 16. Compare, however, Paul Boyer, *When Time Shall Be No More: Prophetic Belief in Modern American Culture* (Cambridge: Belknap Press of Harvard University Press, 1992), ix, 337. Boyer by no means mocks the contemporary popular concern with prophecy (as does Kermode); he tends to stress that its current emphasis blends "age-old themes" that will keep prophecy belief alive well into the next century.

4. Kermode, *Sense of Ending*, 95–96.

5. Don DeLillo, *Mao II* (New York: Viking, 1991), 80.

6. Kermode, *Sense of Ending*, 28.

7. Henri Focillon, *The Year 1,000* (New York: Frederick Ungar, 1969), 53. Lincoln Burr, "The Year 1000 and the Antecedents of the Crusades," *American Historical Review* 6 (1900): 429–44, argues that the "panic of terror" in the latter part of the tenth century actually originated in the mind of the fifteenth-century abbot Johannes Trithemuis, is entirely legendary, and now exists only as a "nightmare" of modern scholars. The evidence Burr rightly discounts, however, is of a popular panic that some nineteenth-century historians used to explain the crusades. He does not address the more interesting evidence that Focillon used from the monasteries. Burr, of course, wrote a half-century before Focillon.

8. Focillon, *The Year 1,000*, 40.

9. Norman Cohn, *The Pursuit of the Millennium* (New York: Oxford University Press, 1957).

10. Hillel Schwartz, *Century's End: A Cultural History of the Fin de Siècle from the 990s to the 1990s* (New York: Doubleday, 1990).

11. The scholar who has most intelligently opened up this line of inquiry is Robert Jay Lifton, whose major conceptual and empirical studies are *Thought Reform and the Psychology of Totalism: A Study of "Brainwashing" in China* (1961; reprint, Chapel Hill: University of North Carolina Press, 1989); *Death in Life: Survivors of Hiroshima* (New York: Vintage Books, 1967); *Home from the War: Vietnam Veterans, Neither Victims nor Executioners* (New York: Simon and Schuster, 1973); *The Nazi Doctors: Medical Killing and the Psychology of Genocide* (New York: Basic Books, 1986); *The Genocidal Mentality: Nazi Holocaust and Nuclear Threat* (with Eric Markusen) (New York: Basic Books, 1990); *Hiroshima in American: Fifty Years of Denial* (with Greg Mitchell) (New York: Putnam's Sons, 1995). Lifton's most popular book about the nuclear threat is *Indefensible Weapons: The Political and Psychological Case against Nuclearism* (New York: Basic Books, 1982) (co-authored with Richard Falk). His most important theoretical study is *The Broken Connection: On Death and the Continuity of Life* (New York: Basic Books, 1979), though note as well *The Life of the Self: Toward a New Psychology* (New York: Basic Books, 1983). The only collection of his essays is *The Future of Immortality and Other Essays for a Nuclear Age* (New York: Basic Books, 1987).

12. Susan Sontag, *AIDS and Its Metaphors* (New York: Farrar, Straus, and Giroux, 1988).

13. Besides my own *Apocalypse,* a number of empirical studies over the years have studied the effect of nuclear threat on people. See Thomas R. Tyler and Keith M. McGaw, "The Threat of Nuclear War: Risk Interpretation and Behavioral Response," *Journal of Social Issues* 39 (1983): 186; Thomas A. Knox, William G. Keilin, Ernest L. Chavez, and Scott B. Hamilton, "Thinking about the Unthinkable: The Relationship between Death Anxiety and Cognitive/Emotional Responses to the Threat of Nuclear War," *Omega* 18 (1987–88): 53–61; Raymond L. Schmitt, "Symbolic Immortality in Ordinary Contexts: Impediments to the Nuclear Era," *Omega* 13 (1982–83): 95–116; Scott B. Hamilton, Thomas A. Knox, William G. Keilin, and Ernest L. Chavez, "In the Eye of the Beholder: Accounting for Variability in Attitudes and Cognitive/Affective Reactions toward the Threat of Nuclear War," *Journal of Applied Social Psychology* 17 (1987): 927–52; Jerome Rabow, Anthony C. R. Hernandez, and Michael D. Newcomb, "Nuclear Fears and Concerns among College Students: A Cross-National Study of Attitudes," *Political Psychology* 11 (1990): 681–98. See also the collection of essays in Lester Grinspoon, ed., *The Long Darkness: Psychological and Moral Perspectives on Nuclear Winter* (New Haven. Conn.: Yale University Press, 1986). Another interesting—and controversial—area of research on nuclear threat in the 1980s was done on children. See Sybil K. Escalona, "Children and the Threat of Nuclear War," in *Behavioral Science and Human Survival*, ed. Milton Schwebel (Palo Alto, Calif.: Science and Behavior Books, 1965), 201–9. See also Milton Schwebel, "Nuclear Cold War: Student Opinion and Nuclear War

Responsibility," in *Behavioral Science and Human Survival,* ed. Milton Schwebel, 21–240. But the most important work on children and nuclear threat, much of which was conceptual and clinical, was done by John Mack, William Beardslee, and their colleagues at Harvard: John Mack and William Beardslee, "The Impact on Children and Adolescents of Nuclear Developments," in *Psychosocial Aspects of Nuclear Developments,* ed. Richard Rogers, Task Force Report no. 20 (Washington, D.C.: American Psychiatric Association, 1982); John E. Mack, William R. Beardslee, Robert M. Snow, and Lawrence A. Goodman, "The Threat of Nuclear War and the Nuclear Arms Race: Adolescent Experiences and Perceptions," *Political Psychology* 4 (1983): 501–30; William R. Beardslee, "Perceptions of the Threat of Nuclear War: Research and Professional Implications," *International Journal of Mental Health* 15 (1986): 242–52; and John E. Mack, "Resistances to Knowing in the Nuclear Age," *Harvard Educational Review* 54 (1984): 260–70. The most bitter (and polemical) criticism of this work was Charles E. Ginn and Joseph Adelson, "Terrorizing Children," *Commentary* 79 (1985): 29–36. Note also Fox Butterfield, "Experts Disagree on Children's Worries about Nuclear War," *New York Times,* Oct. 16, 1983.

Part I

Religion

Chapter Two

The Apocalyptic Year 1000
Millennial Fever and the Origins of the Modern West

Richard A. Landes

The year 1000. What a host of images it calls forth. Signs and wonders in the heavens; ghastly plagues and famines on earth; the populace—from the highest to the lowest—on their knees in dread, in churches, in fields, terrified at the coming Judgment when this Day of Wrath would turn into a Day of Doom, and man would confront his eternal destiny. With such brushstrokes did the Romantic historians of the mid–nineteenth century paint their lurid pictures of a world febrile with expectation in the tenth century and energized with relief in the eleventh.[1] To this day the guides who take us through the churches of France tell us that the *potentes* of those years, fearing for their souls, gave large portions of land to the clergy, especially to the monks, thus triggering the great explosion of church building that Radulfus Glaber, the historian of the millennium, describes in such poetic terms: "It was as if the whole world had shaken off the dust of the ages and covered itself in a white mantle of churches."[2]

No! said the new professional school of historians at the end of the nineteenth century: nothing of the sort; 1000 was a year like any other. There is no scriptural basis for the year 1000: it represents not a date, but a period of time (Rev. 20:7). We have almost no evidence for such a picture: half the lurid texts about 1000 are either outright fakes from the sixteenth century, or they describe events at a different date: 909, 950, 1010, 1033. Indeed, given how rarely documents even use Anno Domini, it seems that contemporaries neither knew nor cared about the date. And if, perchance, some few did evince an interest, they could not be certain when it came due—there were at least three competing A.D. systems in use at the time. Moreover, there is no corroborating evidence of a populace "paralyzed by the terror" of the coming Day of the Lord in the year 1000.[3] The overwhelming impression of the contemporary documentation suggests that the famous "terrors" spring not from the documents of 1000, but from the fevered brains of the Romantic historians, who have contaminated our understanding of our past with their unrestrained imaginations, leaving us not real history but legends.[4] Positivists depicted a year 1000 that passed amid widespread indifference, in many places unnoticed . . . a year like any other.

And yet, the positivists are part of a process I call capstone historiography—that is, a widespread tendency among medievalists to succumb not only to the quantitative impression of the sources (as Ferdinand Lot put it: few texts, few beliefs), but also to accept the texts at their face value: to believe, for example, what a writer says about the way he (far more rarely she) and fellow contemporaries interpreted events. What escapes us when we take this approach is that in most cases our texts are written retrospectively, with the same knowledge that we have (i.e., the apocalyptic expectations proved false). This neglect of the temporal perspective in considering our sources—no belief is more subject to dramatically different interpretation than one about the immediate future (what we call 20/20 hindsight and what I call the fallacy of the historically correct) leads us to neglect the fact that the retrospective narrative is not only not historically accurate, but also (in terms of our exclusively clerical composers) politically correct.[5] Those scribes who preserve, copy, compose, erase, and edit the wealth of manuscripts they inherit are not scientists dedicated to preserving the record; they are committed believers, trained in the Augustinian tradition, which says that one cannot know the end, must not interpret current events in terms of an apocalyptic scenario, and must interpret 1000 as an allegorical number symbolizing perfection, not as a fixed number of years before the Parousia.[6]

With their knowledge of what should have been, they could and did "correct the record," sparing their heroes—the founders and benefactors of the institutions they lived in—the embarrassment of so grievous a transgression of the Augustinian norm. These men were no more likely to preserve evidence that the great figures of the day—King Robert, Emperor Otto, Pope Gerbert, Abbot Odilo of Cluny, William of Dijon, Abbo of Fleury—were subject to apocalyptic concerns than historians of modern science are eager to dwell on Isaac Newton's fascination with apocalyptic calculations based on the book of Revelation.[7] Their work as composers and archivists is not to be taken at face value. If there were a brief moment when some of the leaders of Christendom openly embraced an apocalyptic year 1000, sponsoring the kinds of extraordinary and often dangerous or (retrospectively) ridiculous behavior that such beliefs entail, it would be too much to expect them to tell the story faithfully. It would be like arriving the day after the emperor had paraded naked before the entire city and asking the courtiers what happened. You might get the real story in the taverns; but historians, unfortunately, are primarily stuck with the "official record" of the courtiers.[8] Starting from this revised record, Henri Focillon (one of the few historians of the period to grant significance to the approach of 1000) made a key distinction between the enlightened elites and the superstitious commoners. These latter may have been swayed by such foolish fears, but certainly not the great figures who built Europe. They were almost like two different races of men.[9]

This approach has a number of characteristic analytic tendencies that, in the case of apocalyptic beliefs, tend to (dis)miss any evidence of such expectation. Thus, they interpret the relatively few documents from the period around 1000 that are actually dated Anno Domini as a sign of indifference among contemporaries and consider the learned discord over the date as a sign of that age's limited scientific abilities and general confusion. But one can read this data in precisely the opposite fashion and draw a picture of a generation acutely aware of the date, whose (relative) silence in certain documents indicates anxiety rather than indifference. First, consider the Easter Tables then in use: every single religious establishment that owned even half a dozen codices would have tables first drawn up by Bede (724) and adopted in the following generation by the Carolingians. These tables all used A.D. dating in their first column, followed by all the information necessary to determine when to celebrate Easter that year.[10] In other words, the assumed knowledge, the point of entry into the Easter material, was the date. No one could make the most vital liturgical determination in Christendom without knowing the year. Whether or not clerics were indifferent to the meaning of 1000, there is no possibility of arguing ignorance of the date.

But, we are told, the year 1000 had no eschatological meaning.[11] It appears in the famous (and explosive) passage of Revelation in reference to a future period of time, a millennium to begin at some point, rather than a period to end. This is true, and would hold as an argument were we dealing with the millennial expectations of the early Christian centuries. But starting in the third century, the coming millennium was linked to a scheme of seven millennia from creation: the sabbatical millennium of peace and justice and plenty would come at the end of this sixth and last millennium of travail and darkness.[12] The year 6000 was variously dated to 500 and 801 A.D. by successive generations of Christian chronographers; and at the approach of each date, some chronographers engaged in a "countdown" of years from their day "to the completion of this millennium." Moreover, with the passage of this second millennial date, evidence suggests that the new focus of the end of the millennium was retargeted to 1000.[13] Finally, and perhaps most ironically, this millennial calculation, which Augustine had done so much to drive out of the church and whose "marginal" appearance in the documentation led the specialists of Christian chronology to miss its significance, was reinforced by Augustine's own insistence that the current millennium, since the time of Christ, marked the period of the (invisible) millennial reign of the saints, thus giving either 1000 or 1033 a different, but no less eschatological, significance: rather than awaiting the beginning of the millennium of Revelation 20:1–6, mankind awaited its end (20:7–14) in a cosmic battle between good and evil.

The widespread knowledge of A.D. among clerics, along with the eight-centuries-old tradition of counting down to an eschatologically significant "fin-du-millé-naire," sheds a different light on the scholarly "confusion" concerning the precise date of 1000. To the contrary, all of the dates offered by the "anti-terreur" historians as "alternative" dates for 1000—968, 979, or 1033—reflect not a variety of equally plausible dates in circulation, but a series of efforts either to speed up the millennium's arrival,[14] to postdate it,[15] or to salvage a coming millennium after its passage.[16] The disagreement over which system of calculation for A.D. to use, then, which crops up only in the final generation before the year 1000, is not a sign of confusion, but of either anxiety or enthusiasm about an approaching eschatological deadline. Nor did it have any serious impact on the widespread acceptance of the common date A.D., still in use.[17]

As for whether the lay populace also knew the date, that is obviously a matter of sheer conjecture. We have precious little information on what they knew, and that is so spotty that it would be hard to confidently generalize from it. But conjecture we must, and it is better to do so in an informed manner than merely by asserting conclusions based on the principle that peasants are illiterate, stupid, and insignificant (what our clerical sources call "dumb" or "hornless" oxen). The first issue, then, is to ask whether they wanted to know or not. If the date were meaningful to them (a question to which we shall return), then there were certainly ways to find out—the sources are full of stories about wandering holy men, pilgrims of all stripes, monks who jumped the monastery walls or were expelled (like Glaber), religious leaders who rejected any kind of ecclesiastical discipline. Like children without watches, the rustics may have wanted to know just how much longer to wait. If Bede could complain of rustics who importune him over how many years remain in the millennium (i.e. at the approach of 6000 A.M. II [Anno Mundi II]),[18] one can easily imagine that the crowd in Paris who, in 970, heard that Antichrist would come in the year 1000, might be equally insistent on knowing when that date might come.

Having questioned the basis of an "insignificant year 1000," one needs to go further. What are the historiographical consequences of the kind of capstone historiography that has given us this "year like any other" and effectively atrophied our ability to think about an apocalyptic year 1000? Above all, such a view disconnects the year 1000 from any discussion of the great issues—millennial or social—of the past thousand years of Western civilization. Indeed, it has even disconnected it from developments in the very century it inaugurated, those revolutions of agriculture, of commerce, of urban and rural freedoms, of church reform, of law, of knightly piety, those mutant forms of behavior that produced, by the end of the eleventh century, the communes, the Investiture Conflict, the Crusades.[19] However he or she cuts it, the medieval historian describing the large sweep of the story must somehow start the tale of the High Middle Ages around 1000 (950–1050). Those who start their tale in 950 invoke slow, imperceptible changes and begin discussing the visible changes in the mid–eleventh century;[20] many simply start ca. 1050, or a year before, when the reforming Pope Leo IX had the relics of Saint Remi placed on the altar and demanded that all simoniac bishops (i.e., all of those assembled) come and resign their office for having polluted it with lucre. None of this, generally, is associated with the year 1000.

I would argue the opposite. Looking at the documentation in a longer trajectory of apocalyptic thought and preaching within the church—from its origins in the Galilean and Judean hills, through the conversion of the Roman emperor himself, to the conversion and ascendance of these barbaric tribes to the true faith and, under the name Charlemagne, to the imperial title—the year 1000 stands out as a year of outstanding eschatological importance to high and low alike, and its passage, far from exposing some foolish fantasy that soon dissipated, had immense consequences for the shape and direction of European culture. As the end of the second Christian millennium approaches, we are in a position to understand what happened at the approach and passage of the first.

Background to 1000: On the Nature of Christian Apocalyptic Thought

Christianity begins with the announcing of the good news, that is, "The kingdom of heaven is at hand." Whether that kingdom was meant as the chiliastic reign of the saints in this world, or some eschatological Last Judgment, it promised an imminent and public release from all the pain and suffering that the righteous suffer in this world where power is wielded by the brutal and immoral. It is important to keep in mind that for the believer, the promise of this final deliverance from evil lay at the core of much Christian thought: the Day of the Lord was, for the true believer, not one of fear but one of hope, not one of terror but one of vindication. One has only to read the Book of Revelation to get a sense of how powerful—indeed violent—the dreams of final deliverance might become.[21] However often Christians might cite the principle that "the kingdom of heaven is within," they continued to look for the Parousia. Bishop Hesychius, convinced that the end had come, and criticizing Augustine for his insistence that we cannot know the time, argued that the hope of the imminent Parousia was the food with which he nourished his flock.[22] Especially for the meek, who waited to inherit the earth, the moment was eagerly awaited.

But it never came. (Or has not yet . . . for the historian this is the key.) And in the meantime, each generation had to deal with both its hopes and its disappointments. In time there emerged two different positions: the Augustinian and the Hesychian, or what I would call the owls and the roosters. The roosters crow about the imminent dawn of redemption, of a public settling of accounts, exciting their flocks to extraordinary efforts of self-sacrifice, to the white-hot fervor of a full-blown Sermon on the Mount; the owls try to hush the roosters, arguing that only mischief, disappointment, and loss of credibility can come from such hastiness, emphasizing that in this perduringly fallen world the kingdom of heaven can only lie within, and that precious few are capable of a full embrace of ethics so glorious as those Jesus enjoined upon the faithful. At times of great uncertainty and unrest—when the sky filled with signs and wonders, when famines, plagues, and wars devastated the countryside, when rumors of prodigies and marvels spread, when long-awaited eschatological dates reached their term—the roosters crowed loudly and the owls were helpless to resist. When, as they always did, things quieted down, the owls gained the upper hand. And it is they who control our documentary record.

Thus, the capstone historians who dismissed 1000 as a "year like any other" overlooked a key variable: the end is not merely paralyzing terrors; it is also extravagant hope: hope to see an end to the injustice of suffering in this world, hope for a life of ease and delight, hope for the victory of truth and peace. Some of the very things that in one argument appear as "life as usual" appear in this perspective rather differently. The massive effort and success of imperial missionaries from Germany and Byzantium to convert the pagan peoples—Scandinavian, Slav, Hungarian—is not "proof" that people did not just freeze in terror; it is, on the contrary, an illustration of millennial enthusiasm: at once massive in scope and successful in endeavor. Similarly (a point to which I shall return), when the high aristocracy began to gather the commoners into large open-field assemblies to establish a social peace, this was not the sign of a confidently determined church keeping the social machine finely tuned, but of a fundamental social crisis and a (shocking) appeal to the most profoundly chiliastic hopes of the masses to resolve it.[23]

Let us approach the year 1000. In 741 the Carolingians adopted Bede's Anno Domini in historiography, computus, and some diplomatics, thus enabling them (as Bede had intended) to avoid mentioning the approaching of the year 6000 Anno mundi.[24] Thus on the first day of A.D. 801 (= 6000 A.M.), Charlemagne received the imperial crown in Rome. Everyone knew; no one wrote about it. Did anyone speak openly about 6000? Were references to this date in the ceremony? Did anyone pass from seeing the coronation as a *continuatio imperii Romani* (Rome stands, the Antichrist cannot come) to understanding something about a messianic emperor, a new and final Christian millennium?

We are forced to conjecture, because for the second time Christian scribes have proved capable of maintaining a strict and disciplined silence about an apocalyptic year. Using A.D. permitted them not only to blanket with silence the ever-more-apocalyptic year 6000; it also permitted them to focus on a date still comfortably far off in the future: 1000. When Thiota the pseudoprophetess (note, her very title is retrospective) came to Mainz in 847 announcing the end of the world for the following year and gathering a large and devoted following of commoners and even clerics,[25] the official rejoinder to her apocalyptic calculation could be (as it had been for the last 600–700 years) that still over a century (here 152 years) remained until the year A.D. 1000.

The Approach of 1000:
The First Millennial Generation (960–1000)

About 950 Adso of Montier-en-Der wrote a politically conservative treatise on the Antichrist addressed to the West Frankish queen, Gerberga, in which he made three key points about the contemporary scene: First, although the great Antichrist would be born in the East of the tribe of Dan, he would be preceded by many antichrists, who would rebel against their place in the social order. Second, the Antichrist could not come until the Roman Empire had fallen, and as long as there were Frankish kings who "ought to be emperor," that empire was still "standing." And third, one variant current among our "learned ones" *(doctores)* foresaw a mighty emperor who would unite the entire world in his Christian peace for a century or more and then go on a pilgrimage to Jerusalem, where, in laying down his crown, he would voluntarily put an end to the Roman empire and inaugurate the final, eschatological scenario.[26]

Adso's text became immensely popular, read, copied, and sent as a present to Heribert, archbishop of Cologne (999–1024) with a new preface, advising him to read it carefully as a guide to the times.[27] It was attached to a treatise, *Vices and the Virtues,* which urged a deep and abiding penitence and a struggle with one's old ways. Although capstone historians are likely to read the manuscript history of the text as evidence of a purely literary phenomenon, the likelihood is greater that behind every written text lay ever-widening gyres of readers, auditors, reciters, and embellishers. If so erudite an apocalyptic calculation as "the years in which the Annunciation and Crucifixion coincided" (i.e., March 25) could spread "throughout almost the entire world," then the mythical narrative that Adso gave voice to could easily move from the world of written to that of oral discourse. If Brian Stock can speak of "textual communities" in the early eleventh century that take the apostolic verses as their source of bonding,[28] then one can certainly imagine that communities, drawing on Revelation and Adso's *Vita Antichristi,* could have formed in the generation before the year 1000. The immense impact of Adso's work on the subsequent eschatological imagination of the West for two centuries attests precisely to such oral popularity in circles both high and low.

Let us, then, read the treatise as a roman à clef. To Adso in 950, the line that "ought to" produce a Frankish emperor was that of Gerberga's husband Louis IV of the western Franks, the last direct descendent of Charlemagne's royal (millennial) line. Adso was not thinking of her brother, King Otto of the East Franks, a Saxon from a dynasty whose royal pretensions had arisen only in the course of the tenth century. Within a generation all would change: by 962 Otto had become emperor, and by 987–91, Louis's descendants had lost the throne to a new and local aristocratic dynasty, the Capetians. As we approach the year 1000, therefore, Germany and France go in exactly opposite directions in playing out the eschatological scenario Adso had laid out. In the East, the Ottonians pursued a grand and triumphal strategy in which all the symbols of apocalypse and empire were combined: converting the pagans (far more successfully than Charlemagne), renewing the Roman empire in Rome, reforming the papacy (by the appointment of Gerbert the peasant scientist), and opening the tomb of Charlemagne (emperor of 6000) on Pentecost of 1000. Although he was not of the imperial blood, Otto III was nonetheless emperor; and a close look at his "over-heated mysticism" suggests that he conceived of himself as that messianic emperor spoken of by those *doctores* Adso mentioned.[29]

In the West, everything fell apart. The new dynasty began with a crisis of illegitimacy and impotence.[30] The constant pressure of local strongmen to assert their dominion over the population *(potentes* vs. *pauperes),* already strong under the last Carolingians, broke its bounds. In every place where the ruler did not assert constant vigilance, new castles went up, not to protect against invaders, but to dominate the countryside. Castellans and their bullyboys, the milites, asserted a new kind of peace, one in which the difference between an armed fighter and an unarmed worker was clear; and the advantage went to the one with arms, walls to hide behind, and control over the local courts. Not only was the church helpless to reign over these newly powerful, these *nouveau puissants,* not yet socialized to the exercise of that to which they so ruthlessly laid claim; she was often enough their victim. To the victims of this revolution in social relations, the new men could not help but seem like so many antichrists, rebelling against their place, intensifying warfare and pillage, embittering the already wretched life of the peasants whose produce fed them. Nor could regional aristocrats turn to the king for support; the new dynasty was, especially in the south, a nonentity. In the year 1000, accused of incest by the church, excommunicated by his own teacher, Gerbert, now Pope Sylvester II, King Robert stood as the symbol of royal impotence. Whereas the Ottonians rode the top of the wave of apocalyptic hopes and fears of 1000, the Capetians wiped out early.[31]

Sign and wonders, disasters and omens gave rich body to this apocalyptic political and social picture: famines, plagues, invasions by the Danes, beached whales, monstrous births, a bright Halley's comet in 989, widespread outbreaks of ergot poisoning (called, significantly, *sacer ignis* [holy fire] by contemporaries), earthquakes, eclipses of the sun and the moon. It would defy all the data on apocalyptic behavior to imagine that the roosters were *not* crowing continuously. Despite the assurances of the "anti-terrors school," the evidence is ample: indeed, in a passage that they dismiss as an insignificant text, indicating primarily the victory of "orthodoxy," we find evidence of several powerful roosters crowing.[32] As early as the 960s, Lotharingian computists were predicting the end for the year 970, when the Annunciation and the Crucifixion coincided: Friday, March 25, when Adam was created, Isaac sacrificed, the Red Sea crossed, Christ incarnated, and Christ crucified, and when the archangel Michael would defeat Satan. Against this rumor a Paris preacher urged the classic Carolingian response: "not now, in the year 1000." Abbo, a very smart and energetic young man, who would have to live with that balloon mortgage payment only three decades away, objected strenuously, emphasizing Augustine's radical agnosticism. "We cannot know," he would have argued; "these texts are not to be taken literally; we must look within and do penitence." The fact that Abbo was right did not put an end to the issue: the coincidence happened again in 981 and again in 992.[33]

However big or small we imagine them (Abbo spoke of a rumor spreading through almost the entire world), these waves of date-based apocalyptic expectation were only dress rehearsals for the year 1000.[34] Here the evidence seems quite powerful: we have a half-dozen chroniclers and annalists who specifically speak of the passage of 1000 (again retrospective), another dozen surviving examples of Easter Tables that either end in or begin in 1000 (i.e., most unusually in the middle of a nineteen-year cycle), another half-dozen texts that explicitly link the year 1000 A.D. or A.P. (Anno Passionis) to apocalyptic behavior. Perhaps the single most spectacular text, written in a contemporary hand in the margins of a Bedan Easter Table, describes a tremendous worldwide earthquake, "sign of the sure completion of all the prophecies and the imminent fulfillment of all our hopes."[35] We also know how Christians met these moments of crisis: public processions, often with relics, gathering the entire populace in acts of penitential contrition. Such moments may not last, but their memory does (they are, I would argue, depicted on the bottom stratum of the tympanum at Autun); and it is up to us to figure out how they influenced events. One can, therefore, with little difficulty, draw a text-based picture of an apocalyptic year 1000, one filled with both long-term eschatological projects (Otto III) and specific and public apocalyptic moments when, as the Romantics claimed and the Positivists mockingly dismissed, people literally stood in fear and trembling. The important point for the historian is to go on. What happened after? After the catharsis of public penitence? After (even the most committed began to realize that) the end did not come? After normal time resumed?

The Aftermath of 1000, the Approach of 1033:
The Second Millennial Generation

Things did not, I would argue, return to "normal." Capstone historians, with their unidimensional caricature of terror-filled apocalyptic beliefs, tend to look for relief, a sentiment one might well expect from ecclesiastical leaders like Abbo who had been saddled with this volatile eschatological promise by their Carolingian predecessors. And indeed we find it: Adam of Bremen, writing a chronicle on the northeastern frontier of Christendom, gratuitously noted that the year 1000 from the incarnation had been completed *feliciter*.[36] But I think the more significant sentiment for the historian to track is *hope* and its postapocalyptic sister, *disappointment*. Here one finds some of the most pregnant activity—the first and vigorous stirrings of a popular Christian culture of vast movements, of radical dissent and reform, of widespread pilgrimage, of collective actions.

Perhaps the single most enduring effect of this millennial generation was the development of a process of apocalyptic reform, in which movements like *Pax Dei*, which were launched at times of intense apocalyptic expectations, become, upon "reentry" into normal time, institutionalized as "reform" movements. Thus, the entire eleventh century is known as a time of fervent reform, beginning the with monastic orders (especially Cluny) and moving into the secular clergy with the reform of the canonical houses, finally becoming a full-fledged church reform in the second half of the century under the tutelage of the popes. Behind these clear and well-documented movements lie a more charismatic impulse, that of the apostolic life, that of the effort to live the ethics of the Sermon on the Mount in a committed community. One can detect all these elements clearly in the millennial generation— from the popular heresies, which were apostolic movements too radical for the clergy, to the vast movement of church building and parish organization. Indeed, Radulfus Glaber's famous passage about Western Christendom "shaking off the dust of the ages and covering itself with a white mantle of churches" specifically in 1003 suggests that within the millennial generation church reformers like his patron William of Volpiano viewed the remarkable renewal of Christian life as a sign of a new age.[37] Thietmar, bishop of the German town of Meerseburg in the north, wrote about a new dawn spreading over Europe.[38] Both of these exceptional characterizations of an optimistic future-oriented Europe are written around 1020 and refer specifically to the year 1003/4, the period immediately after Antichrist's reign. Reform is the postapocalyptic form of the spiritual renewal that the advent of the millennium brought.

And of course, when the apocalyptic date of 1000 passed without the advent of God's kingdom (indeed, there is a notable drop in the mention of peace councils in the first two decades of the new millennium), people who were aroused from their patient suffering by the hope of a new dawn hardly went gently into the new night. On the contrary, in a pattern well attested to in the annals of modern apocalyptic movements, they would have redated. And according to Radulfus Glaber, so they did, setting their sights on the millennium of the Passion (1033). As Glaber put it: "After the passage of all the wonders and prodigies around 1000, there were no lack of able men or penetrating intellect who predicted no less for the millennium of the Passion."[39]

These prognosticators proved correct. The Peace movement once again gained momentum, starting in the 1020s, this time in both north and south and under the auspices of the king of France. Even the German emperor met with King Robert in 1023 to declare a universal peace.[40] In 1028 a rain of blood fell on the Aquitanian coast, prompting a worried exchange of letters between the duke, the king, and two of his most trusted ecclesiastical advisors about what it might portend.[41] Soon thereafter, a devastating famine struck the entire land for three years and an exodus of pilgrims to Jerusalem began to swell. Glaber describes how in the year 1033 both of these gathering waves of popular religious activity—the pilgrimage to Jerusalem and the Pax Dei—reached their peak. Innumerable pilgrims made their way to Jerusalem and the Mount of Olives (traditional site of the Parousia), prompting wonder among their neighbors and disapproval from the ecclesiastical hierarchy.[42] Meanwhile, those who stayed were not idle: the Peace swept France from the south to the farthest reaches of the north, gathering people in vast assemblies.[43] Some bishops even claimed that they were instructed to proclaim a universal peace by a letter sent from heaven.[44]

Glaber's description of these councils will serve as a good basis for reflection on both the meaning of the millennial generation and its subsequent impact on European culture right up to the present. At the height of the enthusiasm aroused by these peace assemblies, he describes how the entire people raised their palms skyward and shouted "Peace, Peace, Peace." They believed, he tells us, that they were making (Glaber uses *spondo* [to marry]) a covenant *(pactum perpetuum)* with God. This is an extremely rare passage, one that tells us how commoners thought (such data are so rare, most medievalists have given up even guessing what commoners thought), how they perceived their actions, how they identified themselves; and it is no accident that it describes the peak moment of millennial expectations associated with the year 1000. Rather than a church filled with quaking and superstitious fools, we find the advent of the millennium energizing the entire culture, leading them to a full-hearted acceptance of a Christian covenant with God. This marks the moment when the commoners became genuinely enthused about Christianity (it had previously been largely an imposition from above), when Europeans first thought of themselves as God's new Chosen People. I would compare this moment with the previous case of a Chosen People, the covenant at Mount Sinai; the Peace, in its two millennial decades of the 990s and the 1020s–1030s, constituted the defining moment in European cultural identity, the key moment when European Christians first developed a sense of mission and of religious unity.

From the millennial generation onward, one can trace a continuous, if periodic, presence of widespread apocalyptic expectations that repeatedly ignite European culture and often, as in the millennial generation, are linked to an eschatological date: 1065, 1096–1100, 1147–50, 1166, 1179–86, 1200, 1212, 1233, 1260, 1290, 1300–1304, 1333, 1356–60, and so on. Indeed, preliminary investigation suggests that each century's end is marked by an apocalyptic generation that stretches from the final 90s to the 30s (this is especially true of 1200–1233, 1300–1333, and 1500–1533). Once we have paid attention to these moments, all of which elicit vast outpourings of social and religious activity among the common folk, we will begin to restore to our own history this vital dimension. In the process I think we will find that much of what we call modern is actually a phenomenon that started out apocalyptic and, in mutating to adjust to the failure of expectations, took on its more stable and recognizable forms. As opposed to the capstone historiography that affirms—even finishes—the work of our distorting sources, I propose a genealogical approach, one that restores the mistaken but powerfully consequential apocalyptic origins of much that makes us what we are today.

The (apocalyptic) year 1000 stands as an unusually stark case of the problems historians face when they try to penetrate beyond the simple meaning of their documentation, when they try to understand the minds of a vast majority, whose voice, no matter how loud it might have been at the time, rarely reaches our ears. Whereas the "middle path" is often an easy escape for the historian—both sides have merit—the issue of the year 1000 has no real middle ground: for those who take a document as reasonably transparent on reality, there is little or no evidence of apocalyptic belief; for those who attempt to compensate for the avowedly owlish spin that marks our every text, who look beneath the retrospectively Augustinian surface to the conversations that filled the less disciplined but unrecorded halls of verbal interaction, the traces of roosters crowing multiply rapidly. To the former such traces are insignificant marginalia; to the latter, the beginning of a thread that connects to a broad span of cultural phenomena, from pilgrimages to Jerusalem and Peace assemblies to heresies, communes, and crusades. To the one these are ice cubes floating meaninglessly on the surface of historical processes; to the other, the tip of an iceberg whose far greater mass and presence lies beneath the surface of a textual membrane that systematically throttles the voices of the roosters. To the former Charlemagne's coronation took place in the meaningless year 801; to the latter, on 6000 Anno mundi. To the former the year 1000 was a year like any other; to the latter the decades preceding 1000 and 1033 defined millennial generations, whose momentous deeds, high and low, were done under the sign of a Janus-faced cosmology of destruction and renewal. To the former the insignificance of 1000 prefigures the media hype of 2000; to the latter the power of the last millennial passage since Jesus offers both hope and fear for the coming millennium. This is not the millennium delivered in a package by a God who erupts into history, but one perceived by people who, believing that they are living at the turning point of cosmic time, dare the noblest and vilest feats of which they are capable.

We are part of an intellectual culture peculiarly given to both prospective unmasking and retrospective disguise. Christianity is only the first, paradigmatic, example of such apocalyptic revelation and revision; and modernity and "post-religious modernity" are only the most recent examples of its protean ability to take secular as well as religious shapes. The fact that in our own days volume upon volume denying the apocalyptic origins of Christianity can be written by the most sophisticated practitioners of all the latest intellectual techniques of deconstruction and sociology, illustrates the point with special poignancy: our apocalyptic past and future remain dangerously threatening territory.[45] As exegetes like Derrida have argued, much of our discourse denies through an eloquence that masks a silence: our most agile narratives and analyses impart a systematic spin, a brilliant cloth with which to cover our nakedness.

At a time when one culture critic after another speaks of Western and global culture as having reached profound and urgent social, technological, natural, and political crises, we need not only the genius to find solutions, but also the social will to implement such solutions. Those who try to mobilize large numbers to accept new paradigms of social interaction (like the environmentalists and the Pope) will inevitably use apocalyptic rhetoric, even when they might deny any apocalyptic intention. Not to do so would be to neglect a major force of social transformation, and those owls who chastely restrain themselves will likely be drowned out by those roosters who do not hesitate to act.

It can be argued that hope is one of the quintessential human emotions, one that sets us squarely in the time of past and future, one that sublimates our passions by reorienting us from present gratification to future enjoyment.[46] It has been shown that optimists are wrong more often than pessimists but accomplish more.[47] Apocalypticism is "merely" the most explosive of forms that hope takes, and it resides at a very deep level of our cultural psyche. Despite its innumerable disappointments, it has always arisen anew, energized and momentarily mighty, in every generation. We are, I would argue, a particularly accomplished and vigorous culture—and a particularly violent and paranoid culture—precisely because of our roosters.[48] Should we disown them? Not at all. On the eve of the third Christian millennium, we should acknowledge such impulses as a fundamental part of our world and seek ways to help those "ridden" by these passions to reenter "normal time" with irenic contributions to civil society, rather than with the savage violence of suicidal destruction.

NOTES

1. Christian Amalvi, "L'historiographie française face à l'avènement d'Hugues Capet et aux terreurs de l'an Mil: 1800–1914," in De l'art et la manière d'accommoder les héros de l'histoire de la France: Essais de mythologie nationale (Paris: Albin Michel, 1988), 116–45.

2. Radulfus Glaber, Quinque libri historiarum, 3.4.13; for a translation of this work, see John France, ed. and trans., Rodulfus Glaber, opera omnia (Oxford: Clarendon Press, 1989), 114–17.

3. This is the main theme of articles "debunking the terrors," from Dom Plaine ("Les prétendues terreurs de l'an mille," Revue des Questions Historiques 13 [1873]; 145–64) to Ferdinand Lot ("Le mythe des 'Terreurs de l'an mille,'" Mercure de France 300 [1947]; 639–55) to the most recent repetition of this argument by Peter Stearns, Millennium III, Century XXI: A Survivor's Guide to the New Millennium (Denver: Westview, 1996), chap. 2.

4. The distaste of the "positivists" for the "romantics" is almost palpable; indeed, one might even argue that it is a matter of "taste." Ferdinand Lot had nothing but contempt for the older school: "This scholarly rhetoric [referring to the writing of Emile Gebhart], no less

than the delirious ramblings of Michelet, which one could even suspect of insincerity provoke in us nothing more than an overwhelming disgust." "Le mythe," 413.

5. This will be one of the main themes of my forthcoming, *While God Tarried: Disappointed Millennialism and the Genealogy of the Modern West* (Houghton Mifflin), which, in its currently planned format, will have an appendix giving, for each chapter, a detailed analysis of at least one historian's treatment of the material with the characteristic rhetorical and analytic approaches that I term "capstone." For a preview of this kind of critique, see Richard A. Landes, "On Owls, Roosters, and Apocalyptic Time: A Historical Method for Reading a Refractory Documentation," *Union Seminary Quarterly* 49 (1996): 165–85.

6. For the best treatments of Augustinian eschatology, see Robert Markus, *Saeculum: History and Society in the Theology of Augustine* (Cambridge University Press, 1970), and Paula Fredriksen, "From John of Patmos to Augustine," *Vigiliae Christianae* 45, no. 2 (1991): 151–83. Augustine's impact on subsequent scribal production was so immense that historians have concluded that millennialism disappeared in Christianity from his day to that of Joachim of Fiore (the end of the twelfth century); I argue that his impact was primarily on scribal production and not on Christianity as a whole. See Richard A. Landes, "Millenarismus absconditus: L'historiographie augustinienne et le millénarisme du Haut Moyen Age jusqu'en l'an Mil," *Le Moyen Age* 98, nos. 3–4 (1992): 355–77 and 99, no. 1 (1993): 1–26.

7. On Newton, see Frank E. Manuel, ed., *The Religion of Isaac Newton* (Oxford: Oxford University Press, 1974); on Focillon, see below, note 9.

8. For an excellent analysis of the multiple layers of "transcripts" that emerge from various elements within a culture, see James C. Scott, *Domination and the Art of Resistance* (New Haven, Conn.: Yale University Press, 1991). Briefly put in his terms, the historian almost always has access only to some variant of the public transcript.

9. Focillon, one of the few historians in this century to argue that the year 1000 did have apocalyptic significance to contemporaries, is aware of the Augustinian tendency to repress apocalyptic documents. He followed through only the implications for activity among commoners, drawing the line at the unthinkable suggestion that the elites might have been subject to such superstitions: "It may be said that there are two races of men at work, at the same time and in the same places, but working wholly different lines. . . . [These years around the millennium] show the most energetic builders of the West at work, sound and clear minds filled with ideas that are both large and concrete . . . great princes, great prelates, heads of religious order. . . . below it there are shadowy zones, enormous strengths and weaknesses, waves of faith, courage, despair and fear." Henri Focillon, *L'an mil* (Paris, 1952; reprint, Paris: Denoël, 1984), 67 (reprint edition); a translation is Henri Focillon, *The Year 1000* (New York: Harper Torchbooks, 1971), 63.

10. See the long list of manuscripts in Charles W. Jones's edition of the *De temporum ratione* for the Corpus Christianorum Series Latina, including his remarks on the number of worn fragments that bear eloquent witness to how often and how hard ecclesiastics used these tables (241). *Bedae venerabilis, opera, pars VI, 2: Opera didiscalica*, ed. Charles W. Jones, Corpus Christianorum Series Latina, 123B (Turnhout: Brepols, 1977) 241–56.

11. Lot, "Le mythe," 398 and n.1. This argument is taken one step further by George Lincoln Burr, who, in 1901, first introduced the antiterrors argument to the American historical community. He argues that not only did the date lack any religious significance, but it also lacked the kind of meaning that the Arabic numeral system, then unknown, gives such "round numbers" in our day, "with its I's, V's, X's and C's." "The Year 1000 and the Antecedents of the Crusades," *American Historical Review* 6 (1901): 436. But a glance at the Easter Tables of the day suggests that in Roman numerals 1000 was actually more dramatic as a round number: from DCCCCLXXXXVIIII to M.

12. See Richard A. Landes, "Lest the Millennium Be Fulfilled: Apocalyptic Expectations and the Pattern of Western Chronography, 100–800 CE," in *The Use and Abuse of Eschatology in the Middle Ages*, ed. W. Verbeke, D. Verhelst, and A. Welkenhuysen (Leuven: Leuven University Press, 1988), 137–211.

13. See below. A particularly nice example comes in the work of a ninth-century copyist, working in the first century of the seventh millennium by the Anno mundi of the Carolingians, who, copying a manuscript written in 738 (i.e., 5937 A.M. II), changed the figure in the countdown from "63 years to the completion of this millennium" (i.e., 6000 A.M. II), to "263 years" (A.D. 1000). See Landes, "Lest the Millennium," 196.

14. In annals written in Anjou, shortly after recording a set of apocalyptic prodigies for 965, a chronicler wrote "mille anni a nativitate Christi" in the margin opposite 968, attesting to a (mistaken) belief that the Easter Tables he was dealing with started with the Passion, not the Incarnation. Louis Halphen, *Recueil d'annales angevines et vendômoises* (Paris: Picard, 1903), 58 n. 2, 116 n. 6.

15. Abbo of Fleury, in the thick of a series of battles with apocalyptic preachers, tried— with no success whatsoever—to correct Dionysus and Bede's dating of A.D., placing the Incarnation some twenty-one years earlier, thus redating the then-present year (983) to after the millennium (1004); see Landes, "Millenarismus absconditus," part 2, 21–22. This is characteristic of conservative chronographers at the approach of a millennial date; see Landes, "Lest the Millennium," 163, 174. Every time some pedant writes a letter to the newspaper pointing out that the new millennium starts in 2001, not 2000, we have a modern example of a similar effort: the technical millennium may begin in 2001, but the psychological (and computer) millennium begins in 2000.

16. According to a pattern long familiar among students of modern apocalyptic movements, the failure of a date leads to resetting the calendar; in the millennial generation of 1000, the obvious Augustinian target was 1033, attested to by a contemporary chronicler in almost explicit terms: "After the many prodigies which had broken upon the world before, after, and around the millennium, of the Lord Christ, there were plenty of able men of penetrating intellect who foretold others, just as great, at the approach of the millennium of the Lord's Passion, and such wonders were soon manifest." Glaber, *Quinque libri*, 4.1, 170–71.

17. Glaber, speaking in the name of Cluny, opened his book with a direct challenge to any such tinkering: "Although in the Greek and Hebrew versions of the Old Testament the number of years which have passed since the moment of creation is different, we can be certain that the year of the Incarnation of our Lord . . ." Ibid., 2–3). Similarly, when the southern houses refused to recognize the first Capetians, they dated their charters no longer "in year x of the reign of y," but "*anno domini* [987–94] with Christ reigning" or "in the expectation of a king" or "with Hugo usurping the throne." Not using a dating system in a particular sphere (here diplomatics) does not necessarily mean either ignorance of it or indifference to it. See below, notes 30, 33.

18. Landes, "Lest the Millennium," 176.

19. George Lincoln Burr specifically presents his nonapocalyptic year 1000 as a means of disconnecting the early eleventh century from the Crusades at the end. "The Year 1000," 438–39. For one of the most sweeping interpretations of the revolutionary nature of the eleventh century (the beginning of the age of European revolutions [Papal, eleventh; German Protestant, sixteenth; English Puritan, seventeenth; American and French secular, eighteenth; Marxist, twentieth]), see Harold Berman, *Law and Revolution: The Formation of the Western Legal Tradition* (Cambridge: Harvard University Press, 1983).

20. This is particularly true of economic and social historians from Roberto Lopez, *The Commercial Revolution in the Middle Ages, 950–1350* (Englewood Cliffs, N.J.: Prentice-

Hall, 1971), to Robert Bartlett, *The Making of Europe: Conquest, Colonization and Cultural Change, 950–1350* (Princeton, N.J.: Princeton University Press, 1993).

21. For two of many historians' readings of the book that are sensitive to its appeal, see John Gager, *Kingdom and Community* (Englewood Cliffs, N.J.: Prentice-Hall, 1964), chap. 3; Adela Y. Collins, *Crisis and Catharsis: The Power of the Apocalypse* (Philadelphia: Eerdmans, 1984). For one of the best treatments of the topic of apocalyptic violence, see Arthur P. Mendel, *Vision and Violence* (Ann Arbor: University of Michigan Press, 1992).

22. Hesychius, Letter to Augustine, edited in Augustine, *Epistolae,* 199; *Correspondence,* ed. and trans. Sister Wilfrid Parsons (Washington, D.C.: Catholic University of America Press, 1964–89), vol. 4, 384–402.

23. Note the contrast between the "romantic" Michelet's invocation of an aristocracy whose sword arm, paralyzed by fear of imminent judgment, swore to uphold the peace at these assemblies where all came in a penitence born of God's afflictions and Lot's listing of the assemblies as proof that the church was engaged in business as usual.

24. Landes, "Lest the Millennium," 186–211.

25. Rudolf of Fulda, *Annales fuldenses,* ad an. 847, Monumenta Germaniae Historica, Scriptorum (*MGH SS*) 1.365; for a translation of this, see Timothy Reuter, trans., *The Annals of Fulda* (New York: Manchester University Press, 1992), 26–27.

26. Daniel Verhelst, ed., *Libellus de Antichristo,* Corpus Christianorum continuatio medievalis (Turnhout: Brepols, 1976), 45. On the apocalyptic atmosphere to which Adso was responding, see Daniel Verhelst, "Adso van Montier-en-Der en de angst voor het jaar Duizend," *Tijdschrift voor Geschiedenis* 90 (1977): 1–10, also to be published in English translation in *The Apocalyptic Year 1000,* ed. Richard Landes and David Van Meter (New York: Oxford University Press, 1998). Antiterror historians consider the nonpolemical tone of this letter, "addressed to the theological curiosities of the queen rather than to refuting some error that had seized her in its grip," a "devastating silence that voids all relevance of this letter for the argument about the year 1000." Edward Pognon, *L'an mille* (Paris, 1949), xiv; similar arguments have come from Plaine, "Les prétendues," 152; Lot, "Le mythe," 400; and others.

27. See Verhelst, *Libellus,* 55–88.

28. Brian Stock, *The Implications of Literacy* (Princeton, N.J.: Princeton University Press, 1983), chap. 2.

29. For the basic details, see any study of the period, e.g., Christopher Brook, *Europe in the Central Middle Ages* (1964; London: Longman, 1987); for an elaboration of the thesis here, see Landes and Van Meter, *The Apocalyptic Year 1000.*

30. See comments above, note 17, on the use of A.D. dating by houses that refused to recognize the Capetians.

31. The larger issues are hotly debated as I write. I give a narrative summary of the "castellan revolution" with references to the larger debate in *Relics, Apocalypse, and the Deceits of History: Ademar of Chabannes, 989–1034* (Cambridge: Harvard University Press, 1995), chap. 2. For a rebuttal, see the article by Dominique Barthélemy, "La paix de Dieu dans son contexte," *Cahiers de Civilisations Médiévale* (1997): 3–35.

32. The text has been translated by Bernard McGinn, *Visions of the End: Apocalyptic Traditions in the Middle Ages* (New York: Columbia University Press, 1979) 89–90. McGinn here and elsewhere dismisses any apocalyptic concerns in this period as unexceptional; see, most recently, Bernard McGinn, *Antichrist: Two Thousand Years of Human Fascination with Evil* (San Francisco, Harper, 1994), 97–103.

33. See Landes, "Millenarismus absconditus," part 2, 19–21; Landes, *Relics,* 292–94.

34. Whereas capstone historians assume the belief faded with its first failure (as per Lot and others), the historian alert to the significance of 1000 and the dynamic of apocalyptic

expectation would expect believers to place still greater hope in the next one, especially as it approached the year 1000 (i.e., 981, 992). The fact that the coincidence continued to arouse massive apocalyptic expectation in 1065 (the first time after 1000 that it occurred) suggests that this was the case (see Landes, *Relics*, 321, n. 48). There is an interesting analogy here: on June 6, 1996, there was a panic in Bogota that involved parents seeking to baptize their children because on that date (6-6-96) the Antichrist would rise to power. Obviously 6-6-66 would have been a more appropriate date, but the proximity of 2000 gave the 1996 date its significance (three and one-half years to 2000). Note also the sophistication of this rustic and superstitious population: 6-6-96 is an urban form of annotation. The presence of highly successful evangelical (and apocalyptic) Christians in Latin America, again at the approach of 2000, must be considered a key here, just as clerics who leaked the date to commoners must be taken into account when one speculates on illiterates' knowledge of the date.

35. Annals of Saint-Amand, *Annales Elnonenses,* ad an. 1000; Bibliothèque de Valenciennes, 343, f.47v (contemporary hand); ed. *MGH SS* 5.12; a more recent edition is Philippe Grierson, ed., *Les Annales de Saint-Pierre de Gand et de Saint-Amand* (Brussells, 1910), 153.

36. Adam of Bremen, *Gesta Hammaburgensis ecclesiae pontificum,* 2, 40; ed. *MGH SS* 7:320; for a translation, see Franc Tschan, trans., *History of the Archbishops of Hamburg-Bremen* (New York: Columbia University Press, 1959), 83. Bremen was writing in the late eleventh century.

37. In his *Vita Guillelmi,* Glaber tells us that his patron had set him the task of writing "the story of the events and prodigies which happened around and after the millennial year of the Incarnation of the Savior" (chap. 13, 294–95); see Landes, *Relics,* 296–96.

38. *Chronicon* 6.1; see Robert Holtzman and Werner Trillmich, eds., *Thietmar von Merseburg, Chronik* (Darmstadt, Germany: Wissenschaftliche Tsuchgesellschaft, 1957), 243 and n. 7.

39. Glaber, *Quinque libri,* 4.preface, 170–71.

40. Ibid., 3.2.8, 108–9.

41. See the discussion, with references, in Landes, *Relics,* 178–79.

42. Glaber, *Quinque libri,* 4.6.18; France, *Rodulfi Glabri,* 199–205; for an analysis of this passage, see Landes, "On Owls, Roosters, and Apocalyptic Time," 181–85.

43. Glaber, *Quinque libri,* 4.5; France, *Rodulfi Glabri,* 194–99.

44. The text referring to the letter is the *Gesta episcoporum Cameracensium,* 3.52; *MGH SS* 7.585; for a translation of the text, see Thomas Head and Richard Landes, eds., *The Peace of God: Social Violence and Religious Response in France around the Year 1000* (Ithaca: Cornell University Press, 1992), 336–37; the date of the council has recently been placed specifically in 1033 by David Van Meter in "The Peace of Amiens-Corbie and Gerard of Cambrai's Oration on the Three Functional Orders: The Date, the Context, the Rhetoric," *Revue Belge de Philologie et d'Histoire* 75 (1997), forthcoming. On the millennial themes of the Peace of God, see also David Van Meter, "St. Adelard and the Return of the Saturnia Regna: A Note on the Transformation of a Hagiographical Tradition," *Analecta Bollandiana: Revue Critique d'Hagiographie* 113 (1995): 297–316.

45. See Paula Fredriksen, "What You See Is What You Get: Context and Content in Current Research on the Historical Jesus," *Theology Today* 52 (1995): 75–97.

46. Norman O. Brown, *Life against Death: The Psychoanalytic Meaning of History* (1959; reprint, Middletown, Conn.: Wesleyan University Press, 1985); Henri Desroches, *Sociologie de l'espérance* (Paris: Calmann-Levy, 1973).

47. Lionel Tiger, *Optimism: The Biology of Hope* (New York: Simon and Schuster, 1979), chap. 1.

48. The theme of my current work, *While God Tarried: Disappointed Millennialism and the Genealogy of the Modern West,* is that the longer God tarried, the more we substituted human effort for divine intervention in the millennial scenario until, finally, we "needed" no divine intervention. The "modern world" is the millennial Frankenstein, and the "postmodern" came when we looked in the mirror. For a summary of the thesis, see "While God Tarried: Modernity as Frankenstein's Millennium," *Deolog* 6 (1996): 6–9, 22–27, 41–45, as well as posted on website of the Center for Millennial Studies: www.mille.org.

Chapter Three

Medieval Millenarianism
*Its Bearing on the Comparative Study
of Millenarian Movements*

Norman Cohn

A necessary preliminary is to determine what meaning is to be given to the word *millenarian*. Its original meaning was narrow and precise. It referred to the belief held by some Christians on the authority of Revelation 20:6 that after his Second Coming, Christ would establish a messianic kingdom on earth and would reign over it for one thousand years before the Last Judgment. According to the book of Revelation, the citizens of that kingdom will be the Christian martyrs, who are to be resurrected for the purpose one thousand years in advance of the general resurrection of the dead. In general, Christian millenarians have interpreted that part of the prophecy in a liberal rather than a literal sense: they have equated the martyrs with the suffering faithful—themselves—and have expected the Second Coming in their lifetime.

It is natural that Christian theologians should in general insist upon this traditional sense of the term *millenarian*. We are concerned, however, not with classifying beliefs from the standpoint of any Christian orthodoxy but with analyzing certain types of behavior in a variety of societies, not all of them even nominally Christian. The term millenarian is clearly intended to be understood here in that wider sense which in recent years has become customary among anthropologists and sociologists, and to some extent among historians, too. Understood in this sense, millenarianism becomes simply a convenient label for a particular type of salvationism.

It remains to define that type. At least for the purpose of this chapter, I propose to regard as millenarian any religious movement inspired by the fantasy of a salvation that is to be

- collective, in the sense that it is to be enjoyed by the faithful as a group;
- terrestrial, in the sense that it is to be realized on this earth and not in some otherworldly heaven;
- imminent, in the sense that it is to come both soon and suddenly;
- total, in the sense that it is utterly to transform life on earth, so that the new dispensation will be no mere improvement on the present but perfection itself; and
- accomplished by agencies that are consciously regarded as supernatural.

It may be thought appropriate to give particular attention to comparatively recent movements, for only these have been studied, in detail and at first hand, by social scientists. It is nevertheless important to bear in mind that movements such as the Ghost Dance among the Indians of the American Southwest, the Cargo Cults in Melanesia, Sematism in Java, and the Jehovah's Witnesses in the United States, Europe, and Africa are but new installments of a story that began more than two thousand years ago.

The oldest form of millenarianism of which much is known is the messianic hope of the Jews. Chapter seven of the book of Daniel, which was composed about 165 B.C., at the height of the Maccabean revolt, is a millenarian manifesto that foretells how Israel will overthrow the Greek empire and thereafter dominate the whole world for all eternity. Similar fantasies abound in the militant apocalypses composed during the struggles that the Jews waged against the Romans from 63 B.C. to 72 A.D. Thus, the Apocalypse of Baruch tells how the Messiah will shortly break the power of Rome, exterminate all nations that have ever ruled over Israel, and establish a kingdom that will last to the end of the world. Then pain, disease, untimely death, violence and strife, want and hunger will be unknown and the earth will yield its fruits ten-thousandfold. There is evidence that the party of the zealots, who precipitated and led the wars of 6–72 A.D. and of 131 A.D., was a truly millenarian movement, obsessed by such fantasies as these and convinced of the imminent coming of a supernatural Messiah.

Those wars resulted in the destruction of the temple, the annihilation of political nationality, and the final dispersion of the Jews; and the messianic hope changed its form accordingly. The Messiah was no longer expected to lead Israel to military victory or to establish a world empire under Jewish domination, but only to reassemble the scattered communities and reconstitute the national home. Nevertheless, this was still a millenarian belief, for the messianic reign was still thought of as a new Golden Age in which God's plan for the world was to find its consummation. That Jewry has been able to survive after enduring an unparalleled series of catastrophes has undoubtedly been due in part to the hold exercised by this collective fantasy. And it is most significant that, whereas usually the coming of the Messiah was relegated to some vague and distant future, it became a matter of tense, urgent expectancy whenever some major disaster occurred. It was during the massacres that ran from the eleventh to the fourteenth century that European Jewry first produced pretenders to the role of Messiah; each time the result was a wave of millenarian enthusiasm that often expressed itself in a sudden mass migration toward Palestine. The great expulsion from Spain and Portugal at the close of the fifteenth century was followed by the appearance of several messiahs who attracted large followings. Up to the seventeenth century Polish Jewry, which enjoyed a uniquely favorable position, was immune to messianic excitement; but during that century it was subjected to persecutions that culminated in the massacre of some three hundred thousand and resulted in permanent ruin—and at once we find Polish Jewry supplying the most enthusiastic followers of the most celebrated of Jewish messiahs, Shabbetai Zvi.

More than any other, the Jewish religion centers on the expectation of a future golden age; Christianity, developing out of Judaism, inherited that expectation. Moreover, in the time of Jesus the Jews were much given to millenarian movements; for many of its early adherents, Christianity was just such a movement. Whatever Jesus himself may have meant when he talked of the imminence of the kingdom of God, it is certain that many Christians from the first to the fourth century, including such eminent fathers of the church as Papias, Irenneus, and Lactantius, expected a dispensation in which the earth would without cultivation produce unheard-of abundance of wine and corn and milk and in which the heathen would be handed over to servitude under the faithful. Such fantasies are indistinguishable from those in the Jewish apocalypses; even the very notion that the age of bliss will occupy the last thousand years before the end is of Jewish origin. And for Christians as for Jews, the Messiah was to be an avenger, annihilating the wicked, casting down the mighty, exalting the faithful. The one point of difference was that, whereas the Jews were awaiting the coming of such a deliverer, the Christians were awaiting his return.

Millenarianism remained powerful in the Christian church so long as Christians were an unpopular minority threatened with persecution. When in the fourth century Christianity attained a position of supremacy in the Mediterranean world and became the official religion of the Roman empire, the church set out to eradicate millenarian beliefs. Little was heard of them for many centuries. Then suddenly they reappeared, held now in more or less explicit opposition to the teaching of the church. This new millenarianism was far more complex than the old, drawing on a variety of ideological traditions and inspiring a variety of movements. Out of the proliferation of such movements in western Europe during the later Middle Ages and the Reformation period, it is possible to identify a few principal types.

The earliest movements form as it were a Christian counterpart to the mass migrations of Jews toward Jerusalem. To medieval Christians Jerusalem was not only the scene of the passion and resurrection of Christ—it was also a symbol of that heavenly Jerusalem "like unto a stone most precious," which, according to the book of Revelation, was to replace it at the end of time. Even the learned referred to it as "the navel of the world, the land fruitful above all others, like another paradise of delight"; and simple folk did not easily distinguish between the celestial and the terrestrial city. This fantasy of a miraculous realm, abounding both in spiritual and in material blessings, played a large part in many of the Crusades that were launched between the end of the eleventh and the beginning of the fourteenth century—not so much, however, in the official Crusades of professional warriors under the auspices of the Pope as in the unofficial crusades of the poor. These movements arose from recurrent waves of popular excitement in which masses of men and women and young folk would follow some ascetic, miracle-working preacher on a wild, desperate expedition across unknown lands and seas until they perished. Ideologically these movements owed much to the works known as the medieval Sibylline Oracles, with their prophecy of a great emperor who is to arise before the Second Coming, massacre all Muslims, establish a golden age of plenty, and make his way to Jerusalem. At least some of the leaders of the Crusades assumed this role, but their hordes, seldom able to reach the Muslims, massacred Jews instead, and by the thousands.

These crusades of the common people constituted an enterprise that was carried on for generations in conscious rivalry with the official Crusades. The poor claimed that their very poverty made them God's elect and ensured them the success denied to the knights; and they were apt to be set in motion by the news either that an official Crusade was in preparation or else that it had failed. What is most striking, however, is the part played in these movements by mass insecurity. The areas that saw the rise of popular crusades were always those areas north of the Alps that had a relatively dense population, including landless peasants: Flanders, northern France, and the Rhine valley. In these areas many people, because they found themselves in such an insecure position, reacted all the more sharply to any sudden, overwhelming threat. It is significant that at the time of the first Crusade of 1095, the areas that were swept by mass enthusiasm had for ten years been afflicted by famine and drought and for five years by plague; the crusades of 1146, 1309, and 1320 were all preceded by famines. Nor must it be assumed that famine was a normal condition. In the long period 1225–1309, for instance, there were only three major famines in the Low Countries and along the lower Rhine; each of these was accompanied either by a people's crusade or by some mass movement of a similar kind.

Flourishing at first in the shadowy margins of orthodox Catholicism, in the thirteenth century the popular crusades turned against the church, which they condemned for its wealth and worldliness. In this they pointed forward to the next wave of millenarianism, the movement known as Joachimism. The twelfth century had seen a rapid increase in the economic prosperity of western Europe, and this affected the way of life of the higher clergy. Abbots turned their monasteries into luxurious establishments, while bishops built palaces in which they could live in the same magnificent style as other great feudal lords. The greater circulation of money and the revival of trade enabled the papacy to develop a vast fiscal system, which in turn enabled it to fight political battles, to hire armies, and to maintain a court of the utmost splendor—in fact, to behave just like a particularly powerful secular monarchy. Joachimism developed as a protest against this state of affairs.

Around the middle of the thirteenth century, certain of the so-called Franciscan Spirituals—rigorous ascetics who had broken away from the main body of the Franciscan order over the issue of absolute poverty—began to produce their commentaries on the prophetic writings of the Calabrian abbot Joachim of Fiore, who had died half a century earlier. In these works Joachim was made to tell how in 1260 the Spirituals would inaugurate the third and last age, the age of the Holy Spirit, which would abrogate the Christian dispensation in the same way as that had abrogated the dispensation of the Old Testament and the Law. This would mark the beginning of the millennium, in which all men—including Jews, Muslims, and other heathen, now converted—would be united in prayer, mystical contemplation, and voluntary poverty. Other forged prophecies attributed to Joachim foretell how, as preparation for the millennial church, the existing church is to be chastised and the clergy massacred by the German emperor. When the year 1260 came in without bringing the awaited transformation, the date was postponed again and again. In one form or another, the Joachimite faith persisted down to the Reformation and even beyond, and it provided the ideology for various millenarian movements.

Inevitably, the Joachimite Spirituals were condemned as heretics and persecuted accordingly; this in turn increased their fury against the church. They came to see it as the Whore of Babylon and the Pope as Antichrist and the Beast of the Apocalypse; at the same time they came to expect a savior from their own ranks to mount the papal throne as the "angelic Pope" chosen by God to convert the whole world to a life of voluntary poverty. In the conviction that this was on the point of happening, a certain Fra Dolcino collected, about the year 1300, a following of over a thousand armed men. Entrenched in the mountains of Piedmont, the band waged ruthless war against the papal armies until, as was bound to happen, it was defeated and massacred. Dolcino was burned as a heretic, but so great was his prestige that years later followers of his still chose to perish at the stake rather than deny their master.

Marxists have sometimes tried to interpret the millenarianism of the Spirituals, and particularly the militant movement around Dolcino, as a protest by poor peasants against a church that was exploiting and oppressing them. This interpretation is certainly mistaken. Research shows that the Spirituals were drawn mainly from the more privileged strata of society, notably from the mixture of noble and merchant families that formed the dominant class in the Italian towns. Far from belonging to the poor peasantry, many of them had renounced great wealth in order to become poorer than any beggar. And when they condemned the wealth and worldliness of papacy and church, they were protesting not against economic exploitation but against a defection of spiritual authority—indeed of the one divinely ordained authority that with its prescriptions and demands embraced the life of every Christian and which alone, through its sacraments, could offer him or her hope of salvation after death. Medieval men, accustomed to seeing in asceticism the surest sign of grace, naturally questioned the validity of a church that was manifestly unascetic. But uncertainty on so vital a matter was bound to engender intolerable anxieties. It was in response to these anxieties that the Spirituals elaborated their fantasy of the millennium as one vast, all-embracing, poverty-loving church. And as in all millenarian fantasies, the imperfect existing order was to be replaced not by one less imperfect but by perfection itself. The age of the Holy Spirit was to be an age of supernatural bliss and harmony, and its denizens were to enjoy a knowledge of God superior to that of Christ himself.

The church was the chief agency traditionally charged with the task of regulating relations between men and the powers ruling the cosmos—but it was not the only one, for supernatural authority pertained also to the national monarchy. Medieval kingship was still to a large extent a sacred kingship; however restricted in his political powers, the monarch was a representative of divinity, an incarnation of the moral law and the divine intention, a guarantor of the order and rightness of the world. Joachimism was an international movement, but according to the interpretation advanced above, its appeal in a given country might reasonably be expected to be in inverse ratio to the prestige of the monarchy. And it would seem that this was indeed the case. Joachimism flourished most vigorously in Italy, where there was no national monarchy and where the Pope was himself a great territorial potentate. In France and England, where the prestige of the monarchy stood high, Joachimism had relatively little influence. In Germany, on the other hand, where there was a monarchy but one that was falling into ever greater impotence and discredit, Joachimism took a peculiar form. There the fantasy of the coming angelic Pope was sometimes accompanied, sometimes even replaced, by that of the coming supernatural German emperor, a poverty-loving monarch sent by God to institute a worldwide messianic empire.

The Joachimites held that in the third age mankind would become a community of perfected beings, rejoicing in divine insight and needing guidance from neither church nor state; and they believed themselves to be inaugurating that dispensation. A very similar fantasy underlay the heterodox mysticism known as the Free Spirit, which flourished from the thirteenth century onward and inspired a number of millenarian sects. But, whereas for the Joachimites perfected beings were ipso facto ascetics, for the adepts of the Free Spirit they were ipso facto moral anarchists—total amoralists who could do whatever they chose without disquiet of conscience. Typically, a sect of the Free Spirit would be headed by a man claiming to be the second Adam, engaged in establishing on earth a third age, which would be at the same time a recreation of paradise as it existed before the fall. In theory the members of such a sect were free to commit murder or robbery, and indeed every conceivable crime. In practice they seem merely to have practiced free love among themselves and occasionally, by way of dramatizing the restoration of primal innocence, to have performed communal ceremonies in a state of ritual nakedness.

Although the individual sects were small, collectively they formed an underground movement that ramified across vast areas of Europe and preserved a certain ideological continuity over some five centuries. Like other heretical and millenarian doctrines, the Free Spirit was disseminated by wandering prophets who included many former monks and priests—but with this peculiarity, that they disseminated it chiefly among unmarried women and widows in the upper strata of urban society. In medieval Europe, with its constant wars and its celibate clergy, the number of women always far exceeded the number of possible husbands; and whereas spinsters and widows in the lower strata could always work, and those in the aristocracy could always become nuns, in the prosperous merchant class they often found themselves both idle and despised. It was common for such women to become experimenters in religious experience, practicing extreme mortifications and developing mystical ecstasies; and unlike nuns, they were little supervised by the clergy. It was among such women that adepts of the Free Spirit would make their way, in the guise of miracle-working holy men, inspired confessors, and preachers. In this manner the adepts built up, in conspiratorial secrecy, their millenarian groups dedicated to the reconquest of total innocence. The millennium of the Free Spirit was an invisible empire, held together by the emotional bonds—which of course were often erotic bonds—between men and women.

The adepts of the Free Spirit were not social revolutionaries and did not normally seek followers among the poor—but as part of their creed of total emancipation they did conserve the one thoroughly revolutionary social doctrine known to the Middle Ages. That human beings had at first lived as a community of equals holding all things in common and knowing nothing of "mine" or "thine" was a commonplace in the ancient world. The fathers, too, held that such was the original intention of God, and from them the notion was taken over by the medieval scholastics and canonists. But it was certain adepts of the Free Spirit who, toward the end of the fourteenth century, first tried to call the egalitarian state of nature out of the depths of the past and to present it as an attainable ideal. In doing so they provided the basis for a new form of millenarianism. The millennium could now be imagined as a recreation of that lost Golden Age, which had known nothing of social classes or of private property. During the great social upheavals that accompanied the close of the Middle Ages, various extremist groups were inspired by the conviction that at any moment the egalitarian, communistic millennium would be established by the direct intervention of God.

It was always in the midst of some great revolt or revolution that the revolutionary millenarian group first emerged into daylight. This is equally the case with John Ball and his followers in the English peasants' revolt of 1381; the extreme Taborites during the early stages of the Hussite revolution in Bohemia, 1419–21; Thomas Muntzer and his "League of the Elect" in the German peasants' revolt of 1525; and the Radical Anabaptists, who, in the midst of a wave of revolts in the capitals of the ecclesiastical states in northwest Germany, established the New Jerusalem at Munster in 1534–35. What is seldom realized—and what Marxist and right-wing historians have united in concealing—is how little these groups had in common with the mass uprisings they tried to exploit. Yet, to appreciate the contrast, one has only to consider what kind of objectives the mass movements set themselves. Thus, the English peasants, seeing new possibilities opened up by the labor shortage after the Black Death, wanted to have manorial dues commuted for cash rents and villeinage replaced by wage labor. The Hussites envisioned expropriating the church in Bohemia (and incidentally the German aliens who governed it) and, in varying degrees, increasing the status and independence of the laity as against the clergy. The German peasants, a prosperous and rising class, desired to increase the autonomy of their communities and to defend their traditional rights against encroachments by the new territorial states. In the ecclesiastical states of northwest Germany, the powerful and wealthy guilds of the capital cities were concerned to restrict the economic privileges and immunities of the local clergy. These were all limited and realistic aims. On the other hand, the aims of the millenarian group in each case corresponded not to the objective social situation and the possibilities it offered, but to the salvationist fantasies of a handful of freelance preachers; and they were accordingly boundless.

A millenarian revolt never formed except around a prophet—John Ball in England, Martinek Hauska in Bohemia, Thomas Munster in Thuringia, first Jan Matthys and then Jan Bockelson at Munster. Wherever the career of such a prophet can be traced, it turns out that he had been obsessed by apocalyptic fantasies for years before it occurred to him, in the midst of some social upheaval, to address himself to the poor as possible followers. What he then offered them was not simply a chance to improve their material lot. It was also, and above all, the prospect of carrying out a divinely ordained mission of stupendous, unique importance. On the strength of supernatural revelations, the social conflict of the moment was presented as essentially different from other struggles known to history, a cataclysm from which the world was to emerge totally transformed and redeemed. A movement fighting such a battle under a divinely inspired leader inevitably regarded itself as an elite set infinitely above the rest of mankind, infallible and incapable of sin. Avowedly dedicated to purifying the world of sin in preparation for the coming of the millennium, these movements commonly showed themselves very bloodthirsty indeed.

It has sometimes been argued that a revolutionary millenarian group fulfills the function of preparing the way for more realistic social movements. This was not the case with the movements that have just been described, for each of these appeared only when an organized insurrection of a decidedly realistic kind was already under way. The spectacle that presents itself is, rather, of a band of a few hundred dedicated enthusiasts struggling to master, in the interests of its own apocalyptic fantasy, a vast popular movement numbering tens or hundreds of thousands. And if the millenarian group differed vastly from the mass movement around it in aim and outlook and strategy, it differed just as much in social composition. The prophet himself was not normally, any more than in other millenarian movements, a manual worker or even a former manual worker, but an intellectual or half-intellectual. Ball, Hauska, and Muntzer were all former priests turned freelance preachers; of Muntzer it is known that he was born to modest comfort and became a graduate with a voracious appetite for reading. Of the prophets at Munster, Matthys was indeed a master baker, but Bockelson was the bastard son of a village mayor, literate, and a failed cloth merchant; their manifestos were composed for them by Rothmann, another former priest. As for their following, it is significant that all these movements flourished in areas where there existed a population that had no institutionalized means of defending or furthering its interests.

The life of a settled peasant or a skilled artisan in medieval Europe was often a hard one, but it did not normally lack a certain basic security. On the land the manorial regime was by no means a system of uncontrolled exploitation. The custom of the manor that bound the peasants also bound their lord; and in the village group, peasants possessed an organization that was highly efficient in defending traditional rights and even on occasion in extending them. The guilds into which the skilled artisans in the towns were organized were formidable bodies, perfectly capable of planning and leading a successful revolt against an obstinate overlord or an extortionate patriciate. But in the most populous and economically advanced areas of Europe, there existed numbers of poor folk who had no such organizations behind them: in the countryside landless peasants and farmhands, in the towns journeymen (who were forbidden to organize), unskilled workers (who had no guilds), and a floating population of beggars and the unemployed. It was such people as these who provided the revolutionary prophets with their following.

In social composition not so very different from the popular crusades of earlier centuries, these last millenarian movements of the Middle Ages took place in a very different context. The society that bred them was a society profoundly disoriented by the defection of the traditional relationships, a society crumbling under the pressure of the new capitalist economy. In more than a purely chronological sense, these movements stand at the threshold of the modern world.

The future miraculous age of bliss can be imagined in many very different ways. And being themselves so various, millenarian fantasies can appeal to people of the most varied kinds and in the most varied situations. The present survey of medieval millenarianism deals with only a few of the immense number of variations revealed by historical, anthropological, and sociological research. Even so, it may prompt some general reflections that are relevant to the comparative study of millenarian movements.

It seems certain that the rise of millenarian movements is favored by certain specific circumstances—and all the more strongly when two or more of those circumstances are present together. It is possible to identify some of the circumstances that so operated in medieval Europe, and it is legitimate to enquire whether they have operated elsewhere, too.

1. *Catastrophe or the fear of catastrophe.* Examples include the famines and plagues that preceded several popular crusades and similar movements and the massacres that preceded the mass movements of dispersed Jews toward Jerusalem. Is catastrophe or the fear of catastrophe particularly favorable to millenarian movements of a migratory kind?

Have we a related phenomenon in the recurrent migrations of the Apapokuva-Guarani of Brazil in search of the Land without Evil? It appears that such migrations were occurring already before the arrival of the Portuguese and are dictated by sudden panic fears, based on Guarani mythology, of the impending destruction of the whole world save only the Land without Evil. It is significant that medieval Christians accepted catastrophes as "signals" for the Second Coming and the Last Judgment, and for the Jews intensified persecution was traditionally expected to herald the coming of the Messiah.

2. *Supposed defection of the authority traditionally responsible for regulating relations between society and the powers governing the cosmos.* Italian Joachimite movements around or in expectation of the last, "angelic" Pope and German Joachimite movements around or in expectation of the final world-emperor—these have their counterparts in various Russian sects, which from the time of the Raskol (1666) regarded the czar as the Antichrist, who had ruined the church as an agency of salvation. Some of these sects were millenarian, for example the Skoptsi, who in the nineteenth century numbered tens of thousands scattered all over Russia and included nobles, officials, army officers, and rich merchants, as well as peasants. The basic rule of the Skoptsi was that within their organization (a clandestine but highly efficient one) all men must be castrated and all women must lose their breasts. The leader of the Skoptsi, Selivanov, was regarded as a reincarnation of Christ—but also as Czar Peter III, saved from his murderers and now biding his time to mount the imperial throne, hold the Last Judgment, and establish a worldwide millennial kingdom of sexless beings. The case has its importance, for here is a millenarian movement that clearly cannot be interpreted in terms of class conflict, or indeed of anything except religiously motivated anxiety.

It would be worthwhile to examine what part the defection of a ruler as cosmic dictator may have played in non-Christian millenarian movements, for example, after the collapse of the Burmese monarchy and the desecration of the Golden Palace at Mandalay. This could perhaps be treated as part of a more general question: Can one not detect in the genesis of a great number of millenarian movements, from medieval Europe to Java and from the Guarani of Brazil to the Taiping rebels in China, the workings of mass anxiety concerning the stability and orderly functioning of the cosmos?

3. *Emotional frustration in women of means and leisure but without social function or prestige.* Throughout the history of Christianity this circumstance has contributed to the rise of revivalist movements, and it still does so today. What ideal such a movement sets itself seems to depend chiefly on personal factors: in the first place on the particular personality of the prophet, which will appeal only to certain types of women. The antinomian and erotic millenarianism of the Brethren of the Free Spirit does, however, indicate one recurrent possibility. Nineteenth-century France, for instance, saw similar sects spring up—for example, the transformation of the Saint-Simonian movement under Barthelemy-Prosper Enfantin, in 1831–33, and the clandestine sect that built up around Jean-Antoine Boullan in the 1880s.

Do comparable movements occur in societies where the sexual life is less guilt-ridden than it has usually been in Christendom?

4. *The existence, in a society that recognizes that the relative power and prosperity of different sections (classes, ethnic groups) can change, of elements that cannot organize for the purpose of defending and furthering their interests by secular means.* This circumstance, which in Europe so greatly assisted revolutionary prophets from Ball to Bockelson, seems also to have provided the stimulus for many of the anti-European millenarian movements that have flourished in Africa and Asia and the Americas during the last century. Central to this form of millenarianism is the belief that the oppressors are about to be cast down, even annihilated, with the help of supernatural beings. Whereas medieval sectarians expected the return of Christ as judge and avenger, many of the "primitive" peoples of today and yesterday have awaited the return of their long-dead ancestors. It is not, incidentally, only "nativistic" movements that imagine the millennium as the restoration of a lost golden age—medieval millenarians did so too.

Has there ever been a millenarian movement that can confidently be attributed to this circumstance alone, or is this always reinforced by circumstances making for cosmic anxiety, as described above?

It remains to ask whether these observations are helpful in developing a general sociological interpretation of millenarian movements. They would seem at any rate to invalidate, as inadequate to the complexity of the matter, those current quasi-teleological interpretations (not all of them Marxist) that see millenarian movements as necessarily contributing to cultural evolution. As one's mind ranges from the Skoptsi to the Apapokuva Guarani, one is impelled, rather, to consider the psychic prerequisites for these movements, that is, the common emotional needs of those who participate in them.

With all due tentativeness, I shall now advance, as a topic for further study, a general sociopsychological hypothesis concerning the causation of millenarian movements. Of course, to suggest that all millenarian movements arise in situations that have certain identifiable features is not to suggest that wherever such situations exist millenarian movements must infallibly arise. Whatever other value it may or may not have, the following hypothesis has certainly no predictive value at all.

It is suggested, then, that the decisive causative factors are these:

1. Many traditional religious worldviews include a promise of a future age of bliss to be enjoyed by the faithful. This traditional promise provides the indispensable basis for a millenarian faith. It seems that in societies—such as that of ancient Greece—where the religious worldview has no place for such a fantasy, millenarianism cannot develop. But where such a fantasy is familiar, it can sometimes be given the immediacy and particularity necessary to convert it into an effective millenarian ideology.

2. It is the prophet who carries out this adaptation of traditional lore and who becomes the bearer of the resulting ideology. If in addition the prophet possesses a suitable personality and is able to convey an impression of absolute conviction, he is likely in certain situations of emotional tension to become the nucleus of a millenarian movement.

3. It is perhaps possible to indicate how such situations of emotional tension arise. It seems that there is in many, perhaps in all, human psyches a latent yearning for total salvation from suffering; that yearning appears to be greatly intensified by any frustration or anxiety or humiliation that is unaccustomed and that cannot be tackled either by taking thought or by any institutionalized routine. Where a particular frustration or anxiety or humiliation of this nature is experienced at the same time and in the same area by a number of individuals, the result is a collective emotional agitation that is peculiar not only in its intensity, but also in the boundlessness of its aims.

4. Such a situation provides the perfect opportunity for a prophet promising a collective salvation that is to be both immediate and total. It is the discharge of accumulated emotional tension that gives such energy to the resulting millenarian movement.

There remain many problems that this hypothesis, even if it proved correct, would do nothing to clarify. Why, for instance, has Indian society been almost free from millenarian movements—even though in the prophecy of Vishnu's avatar as Kaiki, Hinduism has its own millenarian myth? Is it perhaps because a series of reincarnations ending infallibly in Nirvana offers the individual a more convincing prospect of total salvation than does the Christian hope (which must remain most uncertain) of heaven? And in general what are the factors, historical or immediate, that militate against the growth of millenarian movements? Is one such factor, operating in the West today, that strengthening of the ego that is said to be a characteristic modern trend?

Again, what relationship can be established between a given millenarian ideology and its underlying religious worldview? Is it true, for instance, that those worldviews (such as the Christian, the Jewish and the Muslim) that include the notion of a divine will working through history toward a preordained end provide a better climate for millenarianism than worldviews that know nothing of a divine purpose and see history as an unending series of cycles? Or is such a climate better only for some kinds of millenarianism? In particular, is the fantasy of a "chosen people," divinely appointed to inaugurate and enjoy the millennium, confined to movements of Christian, Judaic, or Muslim origin? Such movements often show signs of collective megalomania; would the same be true of millenarian movements that spring from other types of worldviews?

And finally, to what extent can millenarianism be self-generating? The Greek and Roman empires, normally so tolerant in matters of religion, persecuted Jews and Christians. Have we here examples of religious communities that, precisely because they regard themselves as agents of the divine will and predestined heirs to the millennial kingdom, call down persecution—and then, in response, develop still more strongly the millenarian aspects of their religions?

These are difficult problems indeed, and if we could solve them all we should no doubt find others as difficult confronting us. But consideration of such problems may, nonetheless, advance a little in the direction of producing a sociology of millenarianism.

Chapter Four

The Breast, the Apocalypse, and the Colonial Journey

Catherine Keller

I know only the bright hunger
in my belly,
centered and true
as a child's question; it leads
me on in this motherless geography.
If History calls me
I may return, but not
As I was. This time
I will not so easily
throw away my good name.
  —Elaine Orr, *In This Motherless Geography*

Here at the end of the millennium, we find ourselves also marking, or perhaps wishfully declaring, the end of modernity. How one announces its end depends upon where one locates its origin. What trajectory of assumptions, energies, and values are we relegating to the past? This is, in terms of chronology, somewhat arbitrary: where one situates the alpha and the omega of an age remains an exercise in eschatological mythmaking. This is no reason not to do it. Such historical periodizing reflects the "history of the present" (Foucault) in a particular context, charged with its own desires and hopes. There are many figures—Descartes, Bacon, Newton—in whom the intellectual history of the modern period can be seen originating. But no single event better combines in its force field the politics and economics, eros and animosity, spirit and spatiality of the time of the modern West than the invasion of the Americas. So let me suggest, before postquincentennial letdown renders the matter placidly passé, that we identify the beginning of the modern period with the journeys of Cristobal Colon (the name later anglicized as Christopher Columbus). In so doing we join Hegel, who dates the modern era from the Renaissance, the Reformation, and the "discovery of the New World."[1]

Encoding modernity in the person of Cristobal Colon allows us to link the passage of the five hundred years with the end of modernity. At the same time we thus join with third- and fourth-world survivors of the five hundred years of colon-ization in announcing an end to this aging "new world" order, denouncing its astonishing aggressions, and pronouncing it, if not dead, at least deadly. Reinvestigating Colon himself may therefore contribute a Euramerican feminist fragment to the postcolonial project—perhaps to what Gayatri Spivak calls "decolonizing the mind."[2] It allows us to pose questions from the belly of feminism. What do the Colonian expeditions, responsible for more massive alteration of the planet's social, cultural, and ecological arrangements than any other single event in human history, have to do with Western gender formation? If it turns out that a distinctive evolution of masculinity can be witnessed here—not just a continuation of premodern gender norms—then we may learn something about the androcentrism of colonialism. Indeed, I will argue that the transition into modern manhood is not only flagrantly secular but irreducibly religious. The evidence for this claim will become most vivid in the bizarre theological confluence of two metaphors during Colon's third journey: those of the apocalypse and of the breast. But just what they reveal makes sense only within the context—the motherless geography—established by his first two expeditions.

Who, or perhaps more to the point, what is Christobal Colon? What does he embody that is not already common knowledge after the year of celebration and anticelebration? Each of us has some version of the discredited narrative. I remember the image from some grammar school text of a blue-eyed boy Columbus gazing out across the matching blue sea, making his astonishing induction from ships coming and going over the horizon. But the horizon-as-edge-of-the-world is itself a retroactive myth of modern science. Every sailor of Colon's time knew they did not fall off the edge. His own crew is never reported in his journals to have been concerned about that, and the hypothesis of a round globe was common among the educated. Now I look back and notice the look itself: the young male gaze of the modern age. Unlike the androcentric vision of its premodern fathers, which radiated along the vertical axis, this masculinity looks *forward,* penetrating its own future, piercing horizons. Its eschatology will render the planet endlessly available to cartography, to conquest, to control, to commodification. But a particular masculinity and a particular apocalypse will energize this colonial work, indeed manifest themselves as constitutive of its selfhood, its subjectivity.

Colon referred to the newly encountered land as "otra mondo"—the "other world" (the nomenclature "new world" came later). That world across the seas turned out to be populated with "others." The voices of those others, refusing their alterity, refusing to remain objects of the colonial subject, have in the passing of this five-hundred-year mark turned the narrative around, exposed its own "otherness." The story has itself become alien to the childhood deposits and now leads us back to the actually recorded events, hitherto veiled by densely layered romanticizing, beginning already with the biography written by Colon's son. We find in Colon's and other contemporary journals a clear and startling progression: it moves steadily from a honeymoon phase, in which the natives are depicted as good, loving, and generous; to scorn of them for just such attributes; to plans for their conversion and exploitation; and on swiftly to enslavement, wanton mayhem, and genocide.

Let me suggest, however, that without attending to the gender code structuring the entire colonial enterprise, its complexity, its passion, and its persistence, represented in Colon himself, cannot be understood. Simple condemnation of Colon as genocidal aggressor is true as far as it goes, but it does not account for the ambiguous motivations that inform any credible counternarrative.

This masculinity is uninterrupted—which is exactly not a reason to take it for granted. The subjects of all four Colonian expeditions, including that of the seventeen-ship colonizing fleet of the second voyage, is all male. Nor is this masculinity a matter of historical accident. Patriarchy itself, or the arrangement of society according to male priorities and privileges, is arguably, from its late Neolithic or early Bronze Age establishment, produced by circumstances of long-distance migration and conquest.[3] However much one credits the hypothesis of patriarchal invaders, it is clear that the Bronze Age civilizations, which codify as the law of the state father-right over women's and children's bodies and female submission, also militarize the male population and colonize aggressively.[4] At the same time, these early Mesopotamian city-states spawn a social order based on the enslavement of whole peoples—usually those tribal and agrarian peoples who had no defenses against the weaponry and the systematized aggression of the "men of Bronze" (Hesiod). Only such possession of the surplus productive and reproductive capacities of captive peoples and of their land made possible the qualitative leap into what those same abovementioned textbooks taught us to recognize as "civilization." But the strongman elites could forge this new world order of gender, class, and slave control only on the anvil of a new androcentric religion.[5] State, military, and religious patriarchy went hand in hand.

At the dawn of the modern period, this same configuration seems to regroup itself with a vengeance. It depicts itself in the iconography of the first contact, in which Colon is portrayed with upraised standard, sword, and cross. He is there to enact the written mandate of his sovereigns "to discover and acquire."[6] At the first moments of contact, and even more in its endless reinscription in subsequent narratives, the *otra mondo*—as both land and people—presents itself as feminizable Other. Yet, it does so not first in the mode of enmity and assault, but of a paradise of gratified desire.

A layered pair of historians' comments says it well: Morison, the leading authority on Columbus, writes of the early scenes rhapsodically: "Never again may mortal men hope to recapture the amazement, the wonder, the delight of those October days in 1492 when the New World gracefully yielded her virginity to the conquering Castilians."[7] Kirkpatrick Sale, the revisionist historian, replies: "This the watching Indians would have known, as they did come to know it, as rape."[8] In what follows, I rely upon *The Conquest of Paradise,* Sale's rereading of the Colonian story.

Actually, despite Morison, one does not in Colon's wooden prose sense "amazement" or "wonder" in the face of the "other world," so much as a kind of admiring assessment. From the longboat of the *Santa Maria,* the admiral reports the vision of the island edged by coral sands, with "very green trees, many streams, and fruits of different kinds . . . the whole of it so green it is a pleasure to gaze upon." And at that distance he recognizes a group of "naked people . . . of very handsome bodies and very fine faces . . . all of good stature, very handsome people" (October 12). Here begins the projection onto the natives of the old European fantasy of the lost paradise.[9] Then the landing party. Having "discovered" the land, he moves straightaway to "acquire" it. Of the event Sale writes, "It is quite curious how casually and calmly the Admiral took to this task of possession, so much that he gave only the most meager description of the initial ceremony on San Salvador."[10] Certainly this rite of possession seems to belie the tradition emphasizing Colon's mistaken hope that this was India—which would already have been "possessed." Also, he brought trinkets such as those used in trade with Africans, not the treasures that would be offered to oriental potentates.

Colon tells us that "many natives were assembled there," but he seems to have seen therein no obstacle to the "planting" of the standards of Spain and the cross of Christ. This unambiguously phallic act inaugurates the power of the modern world—at least at the level of representation—with the inseminating of the new world, coded as virgin innocence. Generations of North American school children have had implanted in their imaginations these potent penetralia, conceived as the instruments of an originative act of manly possession that would result, in due time, in the "birth of a nation." Not only will the dark woman provide, like the dark soil, the Other for these adventurers. The entire Other World, mysterious and fertile, lies before them as woman.

On October 12, still very much in the honeymoon mode, he writes:

> I in order that they might develop a very friendly disposition towards us, because I knew that they were a people who could better be freed and converted to our Holy Faith by love than by force, gave to some of them red caps and to other glass beads, which they hung on their necks, and many other things of slight value, in which they took much pleasure. They remained so much our friends that it was a marvel. . . . Finally they traded and gave everything they had, with good will. (October 12)

A month later he is reporting that they are "very gentle and without knowledge of what is evil, neither murder nor theft" (November 12). Then, "Your highnesses may believe that in all the world there can be no better or gentler people . . . for a better people there cannot be on earth, and both people and land are in such quantity that I don't know how to write it. . . . all show the most singular loving behavior and speak kindly" (December 24). "I assure your Highnesses that I believe that in all the world there is no better people nor better country. They love their neighbors as themselves, and they have the sweetest talk in the world, and are gentle and always with a smile" (December 25).

As in all abuse relationships, this honeymoon phase carries within it the seeds of its own demise.[11] The Tainos, as Colon named the Arawaks, after their own word for "good," continue to astound the invaders with their gracious and happy demeanor. And yet, in the same phase of the journal, this "goodness" is already receiving its definitive interpretation: in exchange for their gold, "they even took pieces of the broken hoops of the wine casks and like beasts [como bestii], gave what they had" (Santangel letter).[12] Their perceived goodness, their ability to fulfill the love commandment, fills the Europeans not only with wonder but also with disdain—the Tainos appear as children, as "they ought to be good servants and of good skill. . . . I believe that they would easily be made Christians, because it seemed to me that they belonged to no religion. I, please Our Lord, will carry off six of them at my departure to Your Highnesses, that they may learn to speak"[13] (October 12).

Just as he declares for the first time his intention to enslave, he suddenly describes their "sweet talk" as no language at all; this inconsistency speaks worlds. In this phase the aliens seem to talk and love, yet with no discernible language or religion. They seem to drift altogether into what Julia Kristeva calls the "semeiotic," the realm of the poetic, the sensual, rhythm, the maternal—as the conquerors gather themselves back into the "symbolic," the realm of language and the law of the Father.[14] In their unarmed vulnerability, their hospitable generosity, the Tainos are now perceived as childish, ignorant, inferior, vulnerable, and therefore fit to be enslaved. Infantilization and racism coalesce in a set of attributes precisely mirroring the intense ambivalence of European medieval and early modern stereotypes of femininity. This honeymoon could only consummate itself in rape.

Soon after, the admiral sent his crew ashore to capture "seven head of women, young ones and adults, and three small children." Here are the first captives of the new world order. Does the lack of any evidence of moral misgivings in this brief description seem bizarre in the light of the original paradise fantasy? Hardly. Perhaps an archetypal projection can actually establish, with its idealizing pressure, the distance needed for objectification. That the first victims there at the origin of European global colonialism are women and children is far less surprising, conforming precisely to the original gestalt of patriarchal civilization. Colon did not need to specify their use for a boat of sex-deprived sailors. It puts the paradise paradigm of early modernity in proper perspective.

Indeed, the first garrison left on Hispaniola (present-day Haiti and Dominican Republic) of forty Spaniards was found destroyed, all its men killed, when Colon returned a year later.[15] Coma, a member of the second journey, gives the most likely explanation: "Bad feeling arose and broke out into warfare because of the licentious conduct of our men towards the Indian women, for each Spaniard had five women to minister to his pleasure," and "the husbands and relatives of the women, unable to take this, banded together to avenge this insult and eliminate this outrage . . . and attacked the Christians in great force."[16] In their attempt to literalize paradise in the form of endlessly available women's bodies, not to mention laborers and land, the first orgy backfired. But only temporarily.

On the first journey Colon had already learned to distinguish from the good Tainos the "fierce Caribs," supposedly cannibalistic, darker, and warlike. Although the Caribs were a separate group, he caricatured and exploited their difference. The myth (and it is historically almost without foundation outside of medieval legends) of the "man-eating Caribs" served to justify the evolution of the colonizing policy from self-described generosity to unmitigated genocide. It also facilitated the policy toward women, as appears in the first narration of a sexual encounter in the other world. Sale cites Cuneo, an Italian nobleman who came on the second voyage and who enjoyed, as a class privilege, the generosity of Admiral Colon:

> While I was in the boat I captured a very beautiful Carib woman, whom the said Lord Admiral gave to me, and with whom having taken her into my cabin, she being naked according to their custom, I conceived desire to take pleasure. I wanted to put my desire into execution but she did not want it and treated me with her finger nails in such a manner that I wished I had never begun. But seeing that . . . I took a rope and thrashed her well, for which she raised such unheard of screams that you would not have believed your ears. Finally we came to an agreement in such manner that I can tell you that she seemed to have been brought up in a school of harlots.[17]

Again, Sale responds precisely: "It is every rape fantasy ever penned, dripping with ugly macho triumph. One longs to know the young woman's version."[18]

We encounter here not just a narrative of the relation of a set of invading white males to a number—which would dramatically increase shortly—of captured women and children of color and their feminized-infantilized men. We begin to discern the contours of the inaugural relationship of European culture to both a people and a land. In its force field, discovery, acquisition, and mastery depict themselves as male adult conquest of feminized and infantilized space. Space itself had long been subject to feminization under androcentric possession (e.g., Virgin New Jerusalem, Earth Mother) especially in an eschatologically inspired history that privileges time. But we are here beginning to trace the effects of a new literalization of paradise as the space of an eroticized commodification.

The second journey has the admiral leading an immense imperial fleet back to Hispaniola. He is equipped—except for the noteworthy lack of any women, who can be procured locally—for colonization in earnest. He has promised gold and slaves for Spain in return for the ships. So the conquerors arrive, dreaming of this paradise in which Spaniards will do no work for themselves—a garden existence to be derived from the abundance of natural resources and Indian labor (the latter to be repaid by Christianization). The free gifts of nature and natives mean their enslavement, their exploitation, and in the case of both the human population and the natural ecology of Hispaniola, their annihilation.

De Las Casas, a member of the second expedition and one of the rare voices dissenting against Spanish treatment of the Indians, gives an example of early colonial life. He was accompanying some Spanish troops who had that morning sharpened their swords on stones in a riverbed and were eager to test them out. The opportunity presented itself as the contingent entered the plaza of a village of Tainos:

> A Spaniard . . . suddenly drew his sword. Then the whole hundred drew theirs and began to rip open the bellies, to cut and kill those lambs—men, women, children and old folk, all of whom were seated, off guard and frightened, watching the mares and the Spaniards. And within two credos, not a man of all of them there remains alive. The Spaniards entered the large house nearby, for this was happening at its door, and in the same way, with cuts and stabs, begin to kill as many as they found there, so that a stream of blood was running, as if a great number of cows had perished. . . . To see the wounds which covered the bodies of the dead and dying was a spectacle of horror and dread.[19]

Such spectacle was not merely a matter of spontaneous aggression; it symptomatizes the daily violence of a colonial military settlement, a system that seems to encourage spontaneous mayhem. From the outset, the violence of this second phase was institutionalized through the gallows, the pyres, the chopping blocks that marked all of the Spanish island settlements. Five hundred Tainos were rounded up as slaves in 1495, but two hundred died before they reached Spain, and the rest rarely survived European conditions. "Let us in the name of the Holy Trinity go on sending all the slaves that can be sold."[20] Is Colon's trinitarian exclamation merely an expletive, or, as seems more likely, a model for modern Western piety? At any rate, the admiral had to repay his dividends. By now the dualistic distinction between the good Tainos and the fierce Caribs had blurred in his vocabulary—all the natives read out as savages for the taking.

The quest for gold became desperate. The islands only contained enough gold to whet the insatiable appetite of the Europeans, an appetite that could be satisfied only through the next wave of conquistadores marching into the mainland: Las Casas describes the system of gold quotas as "impossible and intolerable." Tainos over fourteen years old had to supply the rulers with a hawk's bell of gold every three months, for which they received a copper token. Without the token around their necks, they would have their hands cut off and bleed to death. Then the horrors of the mines:

> Mountains are stripped from top to bottom and bottom to top a thousand times; they dig, split rocks, move stones, and carry dirt on their backs to wash it in the rivers, while those who wash gold stay in the water all the time with their backs bent so constantly it breaks them, and when water invades the mines, the most arduous task of all is to dry the mines by scooping up pans full of water and throwing it up outside."[21]

Normally a third of the men died within their required yearly time. In the meantime, the women were dying at home.

> Thus husbands and wives were together only once every eight or ten months and when they met they were so exhausted and depressed on both sides . . . they ceased to procreate. As for the newly born, they died early because their mothers, overworked and famished, had no milk to nurse them, and for this reason, while I was in Cuba 7000 children died in three months. Some mothers even drowned their babies from sheer desperation. . . . In this way, husbands died in the mines, wives died at work, and children died from lack of milk . . . and in a short time this land which was so great, so powerful and fertile . . . was depopulated. . . . My eyes have seen these acts so foreign to human nature, and now I tremble as I write.[22]

The presence of this single empathetic Spanish subjectivity strips away the ambiguity in which some notion of barbaric heroism might be tucked away. If he recognized the force of evil, at some level they all did.

On Hispaniola, half of the 250,000 Arawaks (Tainos) died in two years through "murder, mutilation or suicide," after their sorrowful attempt at resistance; then, worked in slave labor, the population shrank to 50,000 by 1515, 500 by 1550, and by 1650—none.[23] Ironically, 1650 is the date set by Colon, in the apocalyptic speculations still to come, for Armageddon. The end of the world proved, as ever, more local, more specific, than had been predicted. The end of *whose* world? becomes the counterapocalyptic question for those of us reading history from the vantage point of its shattered worlds.

The uncontained destructiveness of the colony, freed from any of the restraints that their own landscapes and families might have imposed, quickly engulf the Spaniards themselves. The admiral and the appointed governor, his brother, attempt to control fellow Spaniards with such gross levels of violence and capital punishment that, as word filtered back, even the rulers of Spain find it excessive. Leaving his brother in charge, Colon returns to Spain and nonetheless finally wins the funding for a third expedition. Six small ships set sail in 1498. Perhaps precisely because of the disappointments to his grandiosity and the desperate need to succeed this time, a new discourse enters the Colonian text. It is on this trip that the startling metaphors of apocalypse and breast will emerge, will merge, and will quite literally *map* themselves—and our world as well.

He has been warned not to go back to Hispaniola and so heads southward. At this point he finds the land mass of South America. After encountering the evidence of a continent—*tierra firme*—at the mouth of the Orinoco River and its four tributaries, he sails into a "state of disarray."[24] He pivots in the waters, leaving suddenly and swiftly and sailing, surprisingly, back to Hispaniola, giving various practical reasons in his journal. But the real reason announces itself in a journal entry of August 17, on his way north. For he has decided that the land he found was in fact the lost Eden: "I am completely persuaded in my own mind that the Terrestrial Paradise is in the place I have said."[25] He now admits that his reason for leaving was fear of entering paradise itself without a directive from God.

The titillating fantasy of the terrestrial paradise bursts into prominence. No doubt his illnesses of the period contribute to his new visionary condition. But at any rate he finds that these rivers match all too well the four biblical rivers flowing out of Eden. Moreover, he finds there, as tradition predicted, around the fringes of Eden, people "whiter than any others I have seen in the Indies" and "more intelligent." The racist note harmonizes with the tones of early capitalism, even at this moment of unfathomably important discovery: these also would have "plenty of gold."

On the basis of this quaint cosmological speculation, reinforced by various astrological and legendary calculations, the new geography for the modern world begins to unfold. Colon's citings of the North Star, and the mountainous panorama, together convince him that the earth after all is not round. He infers that the earth "has the shape of a pear, which is all very round, except at the stem, where it is very prominent, or that it is as if one had a very round ball, and one part of it was placed something *like a woman's nipple [una teta de mujer]*.[26]

The world shaped like a woman's breast culminating at its nipple in paradise: so Cristobal Colon articulates the object, the aim, of the colonial adventure. He repeats the images both of the pear and of the breast: this is no casual analogy. Here we find arising a graphic—indeed as we shall see, cartographic—vision of this new world. It looms as forbidden fruit, the virgin body ripe for the plucking, the mother breast ready to suckle death-ridden, oppressed, and depressed Europe into its rebirth.[27] The renaissance of its ultimate hopes now merges in infantile intensity with material desire. Gaia's nipple arises in the sterility of the all-male world of the conqueror, promising not relationship but suckle. Having come infantilizing the natives, this great emblem of manhood, of the maturation of "man" into secular modernity, reveals the most infantile of desires.

Yet what is of note is the ambivalence, indeed the symbolic matriphobia. Renewal through the nourishing breast fails—he flees. The very sacrality of the fantasy of the oral paradise of the Mother presents itself at the same time as a powerful taboo, as forbidden by the Father. Colon's fearful retreat calls to mind what Julia Kristeva calls "abjection." "There looms within abjection," she writes, "one of those violent, dark revolts of being, directed against a threat that seems to emanate from an exorbitant outside or inside, ejected beyond the scope of the possible. . . . that leap is drawn toward an *elsewhere* as tempting as it is condemned."[28] The *abject* roots in the pre-oedipal situation, prior to the formation of the (m)other as *object*.

And "instead of sounding himself as to his 'being,' 'the abjector' does so concerning his place. '*Where* am I?' instead of 'Who am I?'"[29] Like Columbus, he is also characterized as a perpetual exile—"the more he strays, the more he is saved." The subject constituting himself in relation to the abject is twisting and turning in relation, always, to the Mother. Seeking "the desirable and terrifying, nourishing and murderous, fascinating and abject inside of the maternal body"—yet always "the hoped rebirth is short-circuited."[30] He cannot but flee, scheming immediately to return, to conquer, to keep his boundaries clear and yet at the same time transgress them.

The breast of a maternal continent, swelling to the Edenic nipple, becomes the subject not only of lengthy epistolary outpourings back on Hispaniola on the Terrestrial Paradise but also regarding his plans for its conquest. The mother, at a distance, can be turned into the virgin to be taken. But the virgin is colored by the dark aura of the sacred and the bestial, the taboo and the threat. The cycle of abuse can begin again. The breast of paradise, which Colon immediately lays plans to colonize, is of course always the Savage Breast as well. This ambivalence, alternating between repulsion and fascination, characterizes his bifurcation of the indigenous peoples as well into good Indians and cannibals—which in Europe would constitute the complementary traditions of the Noble Savage and the Savage Beast. Good breast and bad, in Karen Horney's parlance.[31]

But the point is not his psychological motives so much as their contribution to the modern project. So we recall that at the dawn of the epoch of high rationalism, the unconscious of its wandering hero, having now erupted into the vision of the breast, becomes manifest in the mode not of a dream, a story, an art work, or a ritual, but of a map. For all his confabulatory preoccupations, the product is a quite precise chart of the coast line of Paria in relation to Cuba and the other islands. Indeed, this is the map that made possible the work of Cortes in less than two decades.

What's in a map? "Map" presents itself as an apt trope of the modern. Early modernity required new—literal—maps, maps literalizing the space of conquest. "The [modern] map is, in effect, a homogenization and reification of the rich diversity of spatial itineraries and spatial stories."[32] From a postmodern vantage point, the map appears as a "totalizing device" that "eliminates little by little" all traces of "the practices that produce it."[33] That is, maps were charmingly illustrated with bits of history and myth, exotic persons and wild beasts, with no more interest in exact geometric proportions than medieval art exhibited. Around this time the abstract mathematicizing of maps made its appearance, erasing the lives and deaths of the strange peoples and lands, and obviating the accountability of expressive, interpretive proportions. Those who reconstruct the histories of all that has been eliminated are thereby reconstituting the "spatial story" purged by the map but essential to its production.

But we have so far omitted discussion of an ancient story that may provide the most important dimension of Colon's motivational force field—or rather, that symbolism which infused the cartography of the colonized breast with its spiritual force.

> Of the New Heaven and Earth which our Lord made, as
> St John writes in the Apocalypse, after He had spoken it
> by the mouth of Isaiah, He made me the messenger
> thereof and showed me where to go.
> —Cristobal Colon, letter to Torres

These words were written in October 1500, while he was busy mapping out the nipple of paradise. It was my prior interest in apocalypticism as constitutive of late modernity that led me to them, and thence to my concern with Colon. I found the text stunning. We are not accustomed to hearing of his apocalyptic self-understanding. Isn't he, after all, the initiator of a new age of "man," the age of discovery and rationality, the renaissance hero of the endlessly receding horizon, the brilliant navigator and cartographer of the horizontal? Somehow his maternal fantasies, which feel typically patriarchal, come less into conflict with the propaganda image. Colon himself, who played to the hard-headed interests of the state and indeed, through his successful discoveries and acquisitions, would make possible its development into its modern form, nonetheless seems to have positioned himself as the realization of surprisingly premodern expectations.

But what sort of apocalypse is this? The exegesis implied in the above epigraph betrays a startling sleight of hand. The biblical hope of a future new creation by God the Creator is here read as having been already fulfilled. The new creation is therefore available to "discovery." *Apokalyptein,* meaning etymologically "to unveil," that is, "to discover" in the sense of "to disclose," now functions as a self-fulfilling prophecy. As was amply confirmed by later outpourings, the admiral's words do not read like some casual Christian convention of the time. If anything, his messianic self-designation risks blasphemy in a culture that has just mastered the art of burning heretics. Nor is his reading of "apocalypse" as "discovery" any simple mistake. He is no biblical illiterate, as his correct alignment of Isaiah and John demonstrates. A fateful exegetical conflation has taken "place": that of the two creations, the first and the final one. In other words, Colon has collapsed the expectation of the new creation into the tradition of the leftover paradise, the garden east of Eden denied to humanity since the fall.

In this temporal inversion, the symbolic future has been remade as a literal past. A new approach to space became possible: the symbolic place of the new heaven and the new earth now reduces to a geographic literalism. That is, to acquire and possess the paradisiacal nipple at the center of space, he must find himself at the center of biblical prophecy about time. And in order to accomplish this, he will bend *time* backward, making of it a commodifiable *place*.

Surely this move expedited the "discover and acquire" project. When the new heaven and the new earth lie "before" in space rather than in a numinous space-time, the possibility of human control of space and what lies "in" it gains force. We note the coalescence of such early modern theology with cartography: regarding maps, Harvey argues that "since space is a 'fact' of nature, this meant the conquest and rational ordering of space became an integral part of the modernizing project. The difference this time was that space and time had to be organized not to reflect the glory of God, but to celebrate and facilitate the liberation of 'Man' as a free and active individual."[34]

But this celebration could be conducted only through the redirection of the spiritual energies of the culture. "The liberation of Man" from the constraints of feudal theocracy required with it a potent eschatological charge. Imagery of the first and the coming paradise have readily mingled at the edges of the eschatological imagination. But the identification of a historic geographic discovery with "the Terrestrial Paradise," and at the same time with the new creation, turns the apocalypse pattern to unprecedented use. To accomplish his ends, Colon draws deeply on an old tradition. In his possession was Pierre d'Ailly's fanciful *Imago Mundi*. This text intertwines legends of Eden and of the adjacent land of blessed peoples with the eleventh-century chiliast prophecies of Joachim da Fiore.[35] Colon had pored over this book, making at least 848 marginal notes and calculations in his copy. And he had consistently underlined and annotated the Joachimite prophecies of a new age. Among other things, Colon concluded that "the world will come to an end" around 1650. Since the new heaven and the new earth had already been created (contrary to any Joachimite view), it followed that this end of history did not signal a new beginning. In this sort of mood he showed himself fully in sync with what Huizinga called "the confessed pessimism" and "the violent tenor of life"[36] of late medieval Europe, a kind of general feeling of impending calamity hanging over Europe. This apocalypticism seems to have meant for Colon that little time remained for the Christianization of the earth, of which he would understand himself, with some justification, as the indispensable agent.

Actually, there is a massive historical irony about Colon's selective use of apocalyptic prophecy. Joachim did not focus upon the end of the world but rather upon the coming millennium, or rather the "third age," of the free spirit—free also of private property. The movements associated with the heresy of the Free Spirit and with Joachim included not only the Radical Franciscans but also the Beguines, the first major European women's movement.[37] In this sense the medieval rebirth (after a millennium of quiescence) of apocalyptic creativity expresses fidelity to the economic communism and the anti-imperialism of the biblical Apocalypse. After all, the biblical apocalyptic tradition constitutes one long protest on the part of a colonized people against the world colonizer, Rome as "whore of Babylon." The book of Revelation itself is radically anti-imperialist, opposed to precisely the concentration of colonizing power and wealth that Rome represented and Spain was emulating. But the Crusades, as an apocalyptically inspired movement against dark, unchristian peoples, had already provided the transitional inversion of the Apocalypse into imperial aggression.

In Colon's version there will be no residue of the actual content Joachim ascribed to the coming period, no recourse to the hope for a communism of spiritually mature love. Au contraire: the identification of the "third age" with legends of paradisiacal lands allows a rather less subtle set of hopes to supervene, hopes well summarized in the constant refrain of Colon's journals: "There may be many things that I don't know, for I do not wish to delay but to discover and go to many islands to find gold."[38] The passion for gold answered, of course, to the promises made to his patrons.[39] He never could turn up the fabulous quantities he tirelessly sought, but those who followed immediately in his wake would so flood Europe with the gold and silver of America that a new economic system would arise. The rise of the capitalist world economy is directly indebted to the native peoples and the silver, gold, and resources their slave labor yielded for Europe.[40] The new heaven and the new earth of which Colon was the messenger would liberate Europeans not *from* private property but *for* its limitless pursuit.

The ironic inversion of the apocalyptic tradition reveals, however, a profound structural continuity. Whatever else is true of the apocalyptic tradition—and there is much to be said for its inspiration of anti-imperialist and ultimately revolutionary "protest and comfort"[41]—it is militantly patriarchal. The Book[42] has dire consequences. As we see in Colon's self-understanding, the apocalyptic contortion sanctifies a genocidal mission. This is not the first time, and perhaps it is after all not so surprising. The book of Revelation can with accuracy—and without prejudging theopolitical motivations—be described as "biblical genocide."[43]

From its beginning the apocalypse tradition participates uncritically in the androcentric myth of the holy warrior. Thus, it contains already the seeds implanted from the earliest military empires of the Middle East, whose social orders were formed, as suggested above, through the codification of patriarchal family rule and gender roles. These empires were sacralized in such hymns to divine warriors as the *Enuma elish,* with its gynocidal Marduk. Apocalypse shares common ground with that which it wishes to overcome.

It appears as no coincidence that Colon's messianic self-concept, unchecked by intimate relationships with women who could be his peers, blends with a vision of the breast of Paradise. This fantasy of feminine abundance writes itself with the purity of a text, like the New Jerusalem, only already there, available as the land and the women of the unveiled, the dis-covered, continent for those heroic enough to possess them. In the holy warrior mythology lie the premodern roots for the modern colonizing man and the corollary subjectivity of conquest and control, expelling body from consciousness and abjecting the loathsome/fascinating and overwhelmingly feminized bodies of the colonized. I submit that the anti-imperialist impulses of apocalypticism were able to be transformed into energy for colonization and its subsequent missions precisely because of its spiritual warrior-fixation.

When Colon returns to Spain again, desperate to get his glory and his money, he writes two books, whose titles already signal the complementary motives of heroic journeying. The first, *Las Privilegias,* cites arguments and accounts of all that he has achieved for Spain and all that is owed him and his descendants. But the twin book, *Las Profecias,* is virtually unknown. It was not published in English until 1991[44] and indeed was published only a few years earlier in the original Spanish.

Here is the plot line: the Lord chose Colon as the divine instrument for the fulfillment of the ancient prophecies. He would be the one to rescue Christianity before the Apocalypse (only 155 years away) by spreading Christianity to the unsaved pagan populations around the world, and to provide the gold for financing the Crusade to recapture the Holy Sepulchre from the infidels. This is why God led Colon to the *otro mondo,* where by providential coincidence so many heathens and so much gold were to be found. To this end he not only bestowed upon his herald the requisite marine talents, but also endowed him with special illumination: a "light, which comforted me with its rays of marvelous clarity . . . and urged me onward with great haste continuously without a moment's pause."[45]

Certainly this man and the armies and epochs that followed have not lacked their own luminosity, a clarity here depicted as spiritual, the paraclete comforting and guiding, indeed lending speed to the prophetic mission in the face of the imminent end of history. Thus, he addresses Ferdinand and Isabel, "You may rejoice when I tell you by the same authorities [his prophetic precedents] that you are assured of certain victory in the enterprise of Jerusalem if you have faith."[46] They, more protected by their machiavellian secularism from vision, were not thus assured.

Colon has thus consolidated his secular and his sacred claims. Sale takes an original stance among historians when he stresses that "bizarre though [the claim of the *Profecias*] was, to disparage it as simple madness or dismiss out of hand the apocalyptic vision and religious zeal that gave rise to it would be a mistake."[47] The direct influence of Colon's own apocalypticism, in other words, may have been slight—except that it seems to have provided, at least as much as greed for gold, the passionate intensity, the "rays of marvelous clarity" directing his endlessly influential voyages. Left there, the apocalyptic construction of the Other World might be accounted for as mere biography, as the personal motivations of a gigantic historical figure. But the point is that even if his own apocalyptic ramblings were ignored, they encode and enact a pervasive mood of late medieval Europe and therefore shed light on its movement into the subsequent period— indeed, they provide a religious passage from patriarchal past to patriarchal future. So Sale rightly argues that

> it was an authentic expression of that deeply embedded millenarianism we have seen in medieval European culture, and Colon would not be the only colonist motivated by this passion in the subsequent conquest of the New World. The apocalyptic vision, with its holy biblical foundation and ecclesiastic elaboration, provided many with the essential justification for—the overarching *rightness* of—the Christian mission of

expansion, as it was appealed to as often by the Puritan English and the evangelical French as by the Catholic Spanish in the decades to come.[48]

Starting in 1493 Colon had adopted a new identity device: using the abbreviation in Greek letters for Christ, he signed his name XRO-ferens, "Christ-carrier." One thinks of adolescent preoccupations with their signatures. He had cunningly amplified the cipher of Saint Christopher, whose name he bore and who had borne Christ across the river as now Colon bore him across an ocean. Thus he fashioned of himself, choosing the single name in the style of saints and royalty, a messianic sign, reworking, as do all self-made messiahs, the traditional symbols.

Colon's apocalypse not only gathers in itself a massive European mood of the fifteenth century, but also announces, like a dream, the hope for rebirth, renascence, for Europe itself.

His personal myth changes the collective myth structures of the Western world. The motif of the Crusade against an unchristian people, of the reconquest of Jerusalem as a means to the New Jerusalem—these old medieval myth themes, already with a brutal history of political actualization and theological marginality, undergird the new conquest. Indeed, they prepare the way for Colon's startling literalization of the apocalypse and the assault upon paradise. The images spring forth in Colon's desperation to provide a total story, a totalistic vision of the future opening up only in order to shut down for good. Or perhaps: opening violently, urgently, under the pressure of the ultimate deadline.

Feminist theory has already well identified the structural parallelism of the early modern white man's ambivalence toward women and toward "savages." "Animal passions believed to govern the Indian and to be present in all human beings were also symbolized by the lust of women and the disorder wrought by the witch."[49] I have sought to link this interplay of desire and disgust to a kind of collective male abjection of the female; I have suggested that its explosive charge, well stoked by the ambitions of the imperial nation state, has the explosive force of apocalypse—a force harnessed, corrosively and dangerously, as the very horsepower of modernity.

Although the International Monetary Fund, the World Bank, and free trade work to continue to keep dependency relations well-nigh total between colonizer and colonized, it is the dependency of the colonized that is conscious and therefore resisted. The dependency of the colonizer, mixed of endless oral gratifications (of coffee, sugar, fruit, meat), is repressed and therefore lethal. Hidden like the mother beneath Colon's map, it perpetuates the cycle of desire and loathing. And the breast of paradise threatens still to elude the grasp of the conqueror—it churns up revolution; its exotic *exuda* turn bitter, its spaces inhospitable.

But the paradise paradigm keeps the conquerors coming. "The paradises of western men—and of their wives, mostly sent for later—are their colonies," writes Christina Thurmer-Rohr in her critique of Bloch, who even as a Marxist rhapsodized the spirit of Columbus and who "describes them not as the sites of robbery, of oppression, or presumption, of rape and murder, but rather as 'geographic utopias,' earthly paradises, since heavenly paradise had proved unattainable." The bodies of colonized women—at home and abroad—absorb the full force of the sexualized and racialized apocalypse. One need only think of the quest for the dark breast of paradise pursued by millions of average white men in the sexual tourism and traffic in "third world" women. Thus, perhaps "we should let paradises alone. . . . We should try to live in our time *hope-lessly* and *in the present*."[50]

This may be a healthy "first world" discipline. Modernity has hoped against hope—against the hope of most of the planet's peoples. And protest movements, even feminist ones, have drawn energy from the charge of apocalyptic dualisms. Yet without hope the present collapses into paralysis. Rather than mere antiapocalypse, I would suggest counterapocalypse: a hope grounded in our mutual presences, in what Ada Mariz Isazi-Diaz defines as "solidarity": "a praxis of mutuality."[51]

Feminist experiences of solidarity with other decolonizing peoples partake of the peculiar postmodern hope of the force field of connecting differences, differences between, among, and within ourselves. As we come to understand ourselves in context, the motherless maps of modernity, writ over with the messianic signatures of pen, sword, and flag, become sites of horror and possibility, disrupting their own homogenization.

The post-colon-ial map is a cartographic collage. Journeying heroes and corporate executives who try to follow it south will fall off the edge of the world. It is pieced together of the old maps, worn and bloody, looking like medieval maps with story pictures painted all over them, and some current graffiti, too; I see bits of feather and beadwork, and of a premillenialist tract displaying its Sunday School porno queen, the Whore of Babylon; a Chiquita banana label; and a bas relief of Gaia, dark, rumbling, and chuckling from the belly, sporting a dirty nursing bra over her volcanoes. . . . You add your own pieces.

NOTES

1. Georg W. F. Hegel, *Lectures on the Philosophy of History* (New York: Dover, 1956), 442.

2. Gayatri Charkravorty Spivak, *The Post-Colonial Critic: Interviews, Strategies, Dialogues*, ed. Sarah Harasym, (New York: Routledge, 1990), 67.

3. Marija Gimbutas, *Goddesses and Gods of Old Europe* (Berkeley: University of California Press, 1982); Riane Eisler, *The Chalice and the Blade: Our History, Our Future* (San Francisco: Harper, 1987).

4. Gerda Lerner, *The Creation of Patriarchy* (New York: Oxford University Press, l986).

5. Cf. especially the Sumerian *Enuma elish*; the Babylonian *Epic of Gilgamesh*.

6. Kirkpatrick Sale, *The Conquest of Paradise: Christopher Columbus and the Columbian Legacy* (New York: Plume/Penguin, 1991), 12.

7. Samuel Eliot Morison, trans., *Journals and Other Documents on the Life and Voyages of Christopher Columbus* (New York: Heritage Press, 1963), 64–67 (journal entries for Oct. l2, l3). Journal entries are taken from this source and will be identified by date in the text.

8. Sale, *Conquest of Paradise*, 95.

9. Frank E. Manuel and Fritzie P. Manuel, *Utopian Thought in the Western World* (Cambridge: Harvard University Press, Belknap Press, 1979), 33ff.

10. Sale, *Conquest of Paradise,* 94.

11. Conversation with Sharon V. Betcher, October 10, 1993.

12. Morison, *Journals,* 182.

13. Ibid., 65.

14. Julia Kristeva, *The Kristeva Reader,* ed. Toril Moi (New York: Colombia University Press, 1986), 62ff.

15. Not (as in the 1992 film, named, interestingly, *The Conquest of Paradise* and touted for its balance) crucified—a nice touch, to turn a bunch of enslaving rapists into martyrs. But in harmony with the symbolism of the colonial cross.

16. Morison, *Journals,* 239–40, Coma letter.

17. Ibid., 212, DeCuneo's letter on second voyage.

18. Sale, *Conquest of Paradise,* 140.

19. Bartolomé de las Casas, *History of the Indies* (New York: Harper & Row, 1971).

20. Quoted in *A People's History of the United States: 1492–Present,* by Howard Zinn (New York: Harper & Row, 1980), 4.

21. Las Casas, quoted in *Conquest of Paradise: Christopher Columbus and the Columbian Legacy,* by Kirkpatrick Sale (New York: Knopf, 1990), 157.

22. Las Casas, quoted in *A People's History,* by Zinn, 6.

23. Ibid., 6–7.

24. Manuel and Manuel, *Utopian Thought,* 60.

25. Sale, *Conquest of Paradise,* 175.

26. Ibid., 176. See also Morison, *Journals,* 286: "But as for this other hemisphere I maintain that it is like a half of a very round pear which had a long stem, as I have said, or like a woman's teat on a round ball."

27. Johan Huizinga, *The Waning of the Middle Ages* (Doubleday-Anchor Press, 1954), 138.

28. Julia Kristeva, *Powers of Horror: An Essay in Abjection,* trans. Leon Roudez (New York: Columbia University Press, 1982), 1.

29. Kristeva, *Powers of Horror,* 8.

30. Ibid., 54

31. Naomi Goldenberg has done especially fine work making Horney's metaphors available for feminist theory today. See *Returning Words to Flesh* (Boston: Beacon, 1990).

32. David Harvey, *The Condition of Postmodernity* (Cambridge: Oxford University Press, 1989), 253.

33. Michel de Certeau, *The Practice of Everyday Life* (Berkeley: University of California Press, 1984), quoted in *Condition of Postmodernity,* by Harvey, 253.

34. Harvey, *Condition of Postmodernity,* 249.

35. From Joachim emanated that historicized apocalypse—the first great alternative to Augustine's theology of history—that fired the hopes of many countercultures of Europe. These movements were finally quelled only with the radical reformation a couple of decades after Colon's work.

36. Huizinga, *Waning of the Middle Ages,* 1.

37. Norman Cohn's *Pursuit of the Millennium* (Oxford: Oxford University Press, 1970) is the classic history of these movements from the twelfth through the sixteenth century. Indeed, the successful hereticizing and squelching of these countercultures required the production of the inquisitorial church. The apocalyptic gloom of the fifteenth century seems to reflect something of the shutdown of millennialist hopes. See esp. p. 30.

38. Sale, *Conquest of Paradise,* 137.

39. Jack Weatherford, *Indian Givers: How the Indians of the Americas Transformed the World* (New York: Fawcett Columbine, 1988).

40. Weatherford, *Indian Givers,* chap. 1.

41. Cf. Allan Boesak's *Comfort and Protest,* and Elisabeth Schüssler Fiorenza's *Book of Revelation,* two excellent readings of the book of Revelation as text, in its context and in similar contexts of oppression and persecution, of resistance and liberation.

42. Cf. Fiorenza, *Revelation,* chap. 7.

43. Charles B. Strozier, *Apocalypse: On the Psychology of Fundamentalism in America* (Boston: Beacon, 1994).

44. Christopher Columbus, *Prophecies* (Gainesville: University Press of Florida, 1991).

45. Sale, *Conquest of Paradise,* 190.

46. Ibid.

47. Ibid., 191.

48. Ibid.

49. Carolyn Merchant, *The Death of Nature: Women, Ecology, and the Scientific Revolution* (San Francisco: Harper & Row, 1980), 132.

50. Christina Thurmer-Rohr, *Vagabonding: Feminist Thinking Cut Loose,* trans. Lise Weil (Boston: Beacon, 1991), 24.

51. Ada Maria Isazi-Diaz, "Solidarity: Love of Neighbor in the 1980's," in *Lift Every Voice,* ed. Susan Thistlethwaite and Mary Potter Engel (San Francisco: Harper & Row, 1990), 39.

Chapter Five

God, Lincoln, and the Civil War

Charles B. Strozier

In America the psychohistorical shift in consciousness that in time created the contemporary forms of the apocalyptic that dominate our age began around 1820, though, of course it had antecedents: the colonists' struggles to create the city on a hill in the seventeenth century encountered truly great odds,[1] our own revolution was more radical than most people realize,[2] and as Catherine Keller notes in the previous paper in this volume, the very discovery of America began in the fierce and phallic apocalyptic of Christopher Columbus, who harbored extravagant dreams about the Americas and his relation to them.

But the apocalyptic began to take clearer shape in the early nineteenth century. Antebellum America was obsessed with apocalyptic anxieties. This era of rapid social and economic change seemed to spawn great confidence, and yet, as de Tocqueville and many other European visitors noted, the boisterous claims made for the superiority of American life and land and democratic institutions had a distinct note of insecurity.[3] Underneath everything lay the great moral blot of slavery that at last began to push many whites to feel that radical social change was necessary (or at least inevitable, even if regrettable). The sensitive founders, especially a Virginian like Thomas Jefferson, had recognized the immorality of slavery and the contradictions of their slave-owning lives as they wrote impassioned documents of human freedom. After the 1820s such tortured hypocrisy was a thing of the past, as the institution of slavery itself changed in the first half of the nineteenth century, gaining a new economic vitality and bringing vast wealth into the South. Its apologists became increasingly brittle. In the North the voice of dissent gained new moral ground, connected in part to the spirit of intense revivalism and religious fervor that swept the land from the 1820s on. Preachers like Charles Grandison Finney had remarkable evangelical successes in upstate New York, and whole new religions (such as Mormonism) appeared in the country. It was also a time of widespread apocalyptic predictions. William Miller, the most famous such prophet, had fifty thousand devoted followers and may have had as many as a million people more loosely associated with his movement in the early 1840s, though after his failed prediction of the return of Jesus on October 22, 1844—called the Great Disappointment—his movement rapidly disintegrated.[4]

The wait for some kind of dramatic resolution to the crisis affected peoples' minds and souls and profoundly influenced the shape of politics. The antislavery movement, for example, beginning in earnest in the 1830s, reacted with moral outrage and a mounting sense of frustration to the continued existence of slavery. With the identification of slavery as a national sin, the antislavery movement brought a new earnestness and zeal to the political process.[5] During the 1830s a strong religious fervor encouraged abolitionists to commit themselves to a variety of reform movements (especially temperance) and remain peaceful, even pacifist, in their means.[6] But after the war with Mexico and the huge land grab in 1848 seemed to open up the country to domination by a white-led South based in slavery, abolitionists felt the struggle for radical but peaceful social change was being lost. Moral persuasion was not working. The old pacifism gave way to accommodation to violence as the only way to end slavery. For example, John Brown's attack on some proslavery settlers in 1856 at Pottawatomie in Kansas reshaped attitudes and prepared the ground for his attempted raid on Harper's Ferry in 1859. That raid, said the leading African American intellectual, Frederick Douglass, "has attacked slavery with the weapons precisely adapted to bring it to the death. . . . Like Sampson, he [Brown] has laid his hands upon the pillars of this great national temple of cruelty and blood, and when he falls, that temple will speedily crumble to its final doom, burying its denizens in its ruins."[7]

An underlying dread pushed the culture to extremes. There was almost a war in 1850, especially over the return of fugitive slaves. Some, like Lincoln, reluctantly accepted the great compromise measures of that year ("I confess," he said, "I hate to see the poor creatures hunted down . . . but I bite my lip and keep quiet."). Others, however, were much more vehement in their denunciation. "Let the President drench our land of freedom in blood," said Joshua Giddings of Ohio, "but he will never make us obey *that* law."[8] Throughout the rest of the decade there was much apocalyptic rhetoric about the "irrepressible conflict" (William H. Seward), the "impending crisis" (Hinton R. Helper), more loosely of the great fight to come, and of course Lincoln's own imagery of the "house divided" in 1858 (which resonated so widely partly because it was imagery drawn from three of the four Gospels):[9] "It will become *all* one thing, or *all* the other," Lincoln said from the floor of the House of Representatives in Springfield, prophesying a climactic end to the great issue facing the nation.[10]

As the crisis over slavery deepened in the next three years, so did the sense of inevitability, North and South, about the approaching war. For the first time in the country's history, voters faced stark presidential choices regarding secession and slavery: the Southern wing of the Democratic party openly favored secession; the Republican candidate, widely perceived as an active enemy of the South was determined to abolish slavery. Even the centrist Stephen A. Douglas blamed the Harper's Ferry raid on the "doctrines and teachings" of the Republican party.[11] Nevertheless, as Don Fehrenbacher has recently noted, it remains surprising that the South should have taken such an apocalyptic view of the perfectly legal election of Abraham Lincoln. Somehow Southerners had come to feel that the Republican party was a "hostile, revolutionary organization bent on total destruction of the slaveholding system."[12] And so, mysteriously it seems to me, the Confederate States of America squandered whatever moral authority they might have possessed in their attempt to build a new nation and fired the first shot at Fort Sumter.

Arthur Schlesinger, Jr., has said that the end of slavery in America is a good example of the triumph of the rational in our history.[13] If true, it is an odd characterization of the rational. Slavery itself was grounded in wild fantasies on the part of Europeans about Africans;[14] the antislavery movement, from the moment of its active beginnings in the 1830s, drew its entire inspiration from biblical images of moral reform, and when it turned toward an accommodation with violence in the 1850s, it generated apocalyptic (and sometimes mad) leaders like John Brown, whereas even its moderates, like William Lloyd Garrison, thundered with Mosaic certainty: "Ardently as my soul yearns for universal peace, and greatly shocking to it as are the horrors of war, I deem this a time when the friends of peace will best subserve their holy cause to wait until the whirlwind, the fire and the earthquake are past, and then 'the still small voice' may be understandingly and improvingly heard."[15] The forces that the war set loose pushed the sluggish system toward radical change;[16] and the great jubilee of emancipation itself inspired apocalyptic rhetoric in almost all observers, including in that seemingly rational man of action whom history pushed to actually free the slaves.

The Civil War shattered the dream of infinite progress that Americans had long nourished. De Tocqueville noted, with grudging respect but more than a little irritation, that Americans possessed a complete confidence that they rode the wave of the future and that their democratic institutions would eventually triumph over the tired monarchies of Europe. Ideas about American millennial purpose reached a kind of apotheosis in the notion, first formulated in 1845, of our "manifest destiny" in the world. Such exuberance in both the North and the South cloaked imperialistic (and often genocidal) motives while at the same time expressing a genuine sense of chosenness. The South felt entitled to create a nation in its own image, whereas the North felt virtuous in its condemnation of the extension of slavery and its commitment to keeping the Union intact. Perhaps clashing forms of self-righteousness were required for such a bloody civil war to result. The special forms of our mission had been taking shape since the seventeenth century, when some ministers began calling their congregations "our Israel," and culminated in the Northern idea of the Civil War as "ennobling."[17] Such attitudes led a man like Matthew Simpson, a confidant of Lincoln and a champion of the Union, to comment during the war, "If the world is to be raised to its proper place, I would say it with all reverence, God cannot do without America."[18]

War also gave reality to images of apocalyptic horror. Americans before the 1860s, to a large degree, had been insulated from the violence of war. The Indians were uprooted and pushed west with relatively small contingents of regular troops and only rarely engaged in actual battles. On the edges of American life, an edge that kept pushing west, of course, there was some experience of violence and fighting. Otherwise, despite the violence of slavery, in our systematic destruction of Native American life and culture, in the newly emerging cities, and, one might say, in our souls,[19] Americans had been pampered with regard to war before the 1860s. We simply had no idea what it meant for hundreds of thousands of people to die in vast battles on our own soil. The Civil War prompted powerful yearnings among whites and, as far as one can tell without a written record, blacks as well, for an apocalyptic cleansing in the fires of war. War would purge the virus of rebellion and remove the blot of slavery. This idea was clearest among abolitionists, who talked of American sin in slavery with every breath and urged the battalions onward to redeem the land. Lydia Maria Child said that she abhorred war, "yet I have become so desperate with hope-deferred, that a hurra goes up from my heart, when the army rises to carry out God's laws."[20] And George Ide, a noted preacher, seemed to justify any destruction as part of the war's higher purpose: "The cause of our country and the cause of religion, the cause of humanity, the cause of eternal Right and Justice, are so intimately blended in this crisis, that you cannot separate them. The triumph of the Government will be . . . the triumph of pure Gospel."[21] Some, such as Lincoln and a few of his more timid or humane generals, were appalled at the carnage, but most seemed to revel in it.

An extraordinary number of Civil War generals, most notably Stonewall Jackson, were self-defined as Christian soldiers marching onward, and only slightly more secular types, such as William T. Sherman, often sounded like Old Testament prophets.[22] In general, as Charles Royster has noted, Northern military, political, and spiritual leaders talked loosely of a policy of extermination and repopulation of the South that would have to precede any regeneration of it in a way that set no limits on the destruction necessary to accomplish such goals. Both sides descended into

> visions of purgation and redemption, into anticipation and intuition and spiritual apotheosis, into bloodshed that was not only intentional pursuit of interests of state but was also sacramental, erotic, mystical, and strangely gratifying. This process of taking the war to heart, believing that it would change everyone, worked as strongly as any other influence toward making it more inclusive and more destructive.[23]

Even Robert E. Lee worked from within an apocalyptic script. Lee's misplaced sense of "honor" led him to pursue the war long past the time he was personally convinced it was lost. As Alan Nolan has thoughtfully argued, Lee despaired more than has been recognized in the summer of 1863 after the defeats at both Gettysburg and Vicksburg, though he could reasonably cling to a shred of hope in Northern opposition to the war. After the siege of Petersburg began in June 1864 (a full ten months before Appomattox), Lee characterized the certainty of Southern defeat as "categorical" and "unqualified." He then lost even the remotest hope for the Confederates States of America with the reelection of Lincoln in November 1864, which was still five months before the final surrender. As Nolan points out, military leadership is not just a private matter. To continue a lost cause means that thousands more must die, or be maimed, or suffer.[24] Why did Lee keep fighting when he knew it was hopeless? Certainly he was insensitive to his obligations as a general not to waste lives. But in all other ways Lee seemed to care greatly for the welfare of his soldiers, who reciprocated with a blind worship of him. The issue would appear to be a more complicated one psychologically, one that is common to leaders—military, political, business, whatever—in many situations of looming defeat, namely the enlargement of their own grandiosity so that they can no longer distinguish between their own failure and that of the world (or army, or government, or business); indeed, that if they go down to defeat the world ends in an apocalyptic sense. For those with a paranoid cast, like Hitler, suicide is the preferred route at such a final moment. Lee, being sensible, instead built a protective myth of the "Lost Cause" that shielded him and the South in general from facing the moral and political consequences of his disastrous leadership in the bloody war.

But perhaps only defeat could satisfy the South, which not only lacked the morale to win, because of their uncertainty about their identity and because of the peculiar circumstances that created secession, but which also harbored doubts about the validity of their cause. They were economically and militarily ill-equipped for a long war; but much more importantly, they were not spiritually or ideologically ready to fight one. There was much bravado. Alexander Stephens, vice president of the Confederate States of America, said at the outset of the war: "Lincoln may bring his 75,000 troops against us. We fight for our homes, our fathers and mothers, our wives, brothers, sisters, sons and daughters! . . . We can call out a million of peoples if need be, and when they are cut down we can call another, and still another."[25] But in fact most white Southerners "could not persuade themselves," as Kenneth Stampp has argued, "that slavery was a positive good, defensible on Christian and ethical principles." Abolitionism, as they recognized at some level, was the "echo of their own conscience." It was a $2 billion investment and white Southerners dreaded the consequences of living with four million free blacks in their region. But they also knew it was basically wrong to keep Africans enslaved. It was an impossible dilemma. Only defeat served their purposes, something they embraced, probably unconsciously, on the road to Appomattox.[26]

Lincoln, in turn, was not always helpful in taming the apocalyptic impulses in the culture. In his first inaugural address he talked loosely about secession as the "essence of anarchy," and soon after, he characterized the firing on Fort Sumter as an attempt to "end free government upon the earth" (July 4, 1861), which became, by the end of 1862, a war to defend our fragile democracy as the "last, best hope on earth." The apocalyptic was everywhere in Lincoln's rhetoric: in military strategy (seen in his statement, "I think to lose Kentucky is nearly the same as to lose the whole game"[27] and in his ready embrace of unconditional surrender as the goal of the fighting),[28] in his transmutation of individual soldiers' mortality for the nation's immortality in the Gettysburg Address,[29] and in his characterization of the war as a "fiery trial" through which we must pass.[30] As David Hein has noted, Lincoln surely used this phrase in conscious knowledge of its biblical origins in 1 Peter 4:12–13, where the experience of the fiery trial is that of martyrdom, or participation in the sufferings of Christ.[31]

Americans moved easily and quickly into this imagery of a purging through violence. As James H. Moorhead has noted, for example, the Civil War was the first time (and I would add the last) in our history that there was a virtually unanimous feeling among Northern ministers that war was hastening the day of the Lord and was a "climactic test of the redeemer nation and its millennial role."[32] By the second year of the war, soldiers were singing that apocalyptic favorite, "Mine eyes have seen the glory of the coming of the Lord," who is "trampling out the vintage where the grapes of wrath are stored," not to mention the implicit theme of sacrifice in their song, "We are coming Father Abraham, We are coming, We are coming." Horace Greeley spoke from within the violence of the apocalyptic when he wrote on July 7, 1864, "Our bleeding, bankrupt, almost dying country longs for peace—shudders at the prospect of fresh conscriptions, of further wholesale devastations, and of new rivers of human blood."[33]

Many thoughtful observers have been mistaken in their strenuous efforts to rationalize Abraham Lincoln and take him out of this cultural apocalyptic in which he thrived and to which he gave such powerful voice. He was himself undogmatic, cautious, forgiving, ambiguous, and always sensitive to the inscrutable ways of God. One has to be impressed by the subtle irony of someone who could call Americans the "almost chosen people."[34] Furthermore, Lincoln's avowed use of apocalyptic rhetoric is always tempered with a human touch of doubt and forgiveness. The stark choices for the country that he lays out in the first inaugural address culminate in an appeal for us all to be touched by the better angels of our nature. His passionate commitment to democracy was grounded in his belief that only free government can insure justice. He talked of fiery trials but moved quickly toward compromise about reconstruction in Louisiana as early as 1862. He insisted on the defeat and surrender of Southern armies in the field but strictly avoided, himself, using the rhetoric of unconditional surrender and never talked of purging any land with blood.

And yet, Lincoln defined the policies that created the war and formulated the specific apocalyptic language that gave it meaning for a Bible-drenched culture, from the image of the "fiery trial" in 1862, to that of the sacrificial redefinition of the nation's purpose at Gettysburg in 1863,[35] to his reference to God's purposes in ending slavery, in his second inaugural address:

> If we shall suppose that American Slavery is one of those offences which, in the providence of God, must needs come, but which, having continued through His appointed time, he now wills to remove, and that He gives to both North and South, this terrible war, as the woe due to those by whom the offence came, shall we discern therein any departure from those divine attributes which the believers in a Living God always ascribe to Him? Fondly do we hope—fervently do we pray—that this mighty scourge of war may speedily pass away. Yet, if God wills that it continue, until all the wealth piled by the bond-man's two hundred and fifty years of unrequited toil shall be sunk, and until every drop of blood drawn with the lash, shall be paid by another drawn with the sword, as was said three thousand years ago, so still it must be said "the judgments of the Lord, are true and righteous altogether."[36]

The most extraordinary development of the apocalyptic in the Civil War, however, occurred in connection with the death of Abraham Lincoln. Shot on Good Friday and dead the following morning, Lincoln immediately became, in those 1865 Easter morning sermons, a modern Jesus whose blood sacrifice fulfilled prophecy.[37] This "terrible tragedy," said the Reverend C. B. Crane of Hartford, Connecticut, was the "blackest page save one" in the history of the world and was an "after-type" of the passion of Jesus. It was "meet" that Lincoln should have been shot on Good Friday.

"Jesus Christ died for the world; Abraham Lincoln died for his country."[38] The Reverend Rolla Chubb, in turn, noted,

> On that sacred day, made holy and consecrated to the freedom of our race, by the crucifixion of Him, who died to redeem mankind from the thraldom of Sin and the slavery of the Devil, we were called as a nation to mourn the martyrdom of the great emancipator of four millions of slaves from the vilest bondage that ever saw the sun.

The parallel was not exact, he recognized. And yet the spiritual joining of Jesus and Lincoln was virtually complete: "Those who thought to crucify the spirit of Freedom, will behold it roll away the stone from the sepulchre, and visit with a pentacostical effusion its disciples, inspiring them with a faith that shall revolutionize the world."[39]

The analogy with Jesus helped explain God's purposes in the war. The "serene Providence" gave us Lincoln, said Ralph Waldo Emerson, to direct the country through the war.[40] And Henry Ward Beecher added, "His life now is grafted upon the Infinite, and will be fruitful as no earthly life can be."[41] In the minds of at least his Northern contemporaries, including some of the North's intellectual and moral leaders, Lincoln thus carried out divine intention. This keen sense of American mission in the immediate wake of both Lincoln's death and Lee's surrender at Appomattox was cast in millennial terms. "In blessing our Abraham," Theodore L. Cuyler said, "God blessed our regenerated country, and the whole household of humanity." And the noted historian, George Bancroft, opined in his sermon that "heaven has willed it that the United States shall live. The nations of the earth cannot spare them."[42] Through Lincoln God revealed his plan. "The great battle of Gog and Magog," said Chubb, "is being fought on the gory field of Armageddon, which is the American Republic— a contest between freedom and oppression, liberty and slavery, light and darkness— and O how that conflict has raged during the past four years!"[43]

The sanctification of the Union was essential in constructing the Lincoln/Jesus myth. On the day Lincoln was shot, but without knowledge of the assassination, the Reverend George Dana Boardman, speaking at the "re-establishment of the flag at Fort Sumter," described the American Republic as not a league but a nation, not a confederacy but a people, not a congeress of states but a Union. He said it was a "vital, throbbing, indivisible organism" and that secession was more than subtraction or amputation but a "vivisection, suicide, murder, a death." And now with peace "a millennium await[ed] the groaning, travailing creation" called the Union. The celebration at which Boardman spoke marked the return of the fort where the fighting began and, by extension, of the Union itself. At the ceremony the actual tattered flag that had been lowered in defeat four years earlier was raised to the salute of one hundred guns.[44] It was a moment of great significance for the Union; and within hours Lincoln lay dying. This eerie, almost mystical, sequence of events was hardly lost on contemporaries, which is why the Boardman sermon on April 14 was published together with his Easter Sunday sermon on the assassination two days later, why the Reverend Theodore L. Cuyler talked of the "resurrection" of the flag at Fort Sumter in his Easter sermon,[45] and why the Reverend S. S. Guthrie could say, "His [Lincoln's] soul took its flight amid the echoes of solemn praises which accompanied the raising of the old flag over Sumter. Both are significant. The nation has completed its atonement; let the New Man and the People see to it that the New Dispensation shall come."[46]

There was, of course, a good deal of variety in the sermons and many regional and denominational idiosyncrasies. The eastern as opposed to the western sermons, and the Unitarian and Congregational as opposed to the Baptist and Methodist sermons, tended to be more literate and less likely to fall into extravagant comparisons of Lincoln with Jesus, except by allusion and context. But in the end the *common* themes in the sermons are more striking than the variations. A great American secular and religious myth took shape almost instantly in the pews that Sunday morning. The historian and minister William E. Baron noted in the 1920s that there probably had not been a Sunday in American history when as many people attended church.[47] "Certainly history," noted a Boston preacher, "furnishes no case in which death has so instantly invested its victim with the sanctity of an approval more spontaneous and universal."[48] The Reverend W. E. Guthrie noted that Lincoln's death was his "apotheosis" and that he was now "The American Martyr."[49] "These trappings of sorrow," noted a Massachusetts minister, "this sable, fringing and shadowing the nation's flag—these wailing Misereres that rise in the place of the joyful Easter Jubilates that we thought to sing—they are but poor symbols of the grief that lies too deep for tears. What has he not been to us—this high priest of Freedom—murdered at the altar."[50]

The most hopeful version of the apocalyptic was explicitly joined to images of Lincoln's own generosity and spirit of forgiveness[51] and expressed the transformative power of the bloody sacrifices of the war. The war, said one minister, "baptized our land with blood."[52] But God caught the nation up short in their moment of victory, he went on, and took Lincoln. The minister said God hoped that Lincoln's death would bring Americans to their knees in a pious sense of their dependence on the Almighty, making them, through the sacrifice of Lincoln, fully aware of God's gift.[53]

Many sermons also developed transformative images of Lincoln as Moses, leading blacks out from slavery and glimpsing the promised land but not actually inhabiting it. Lincoln's identity as the Great Emancipator made such a comparison almost inevitable. Furthermore, the rhetoric of most preachers when they did refer to Lincoln as Moses slipped almost unconsciously, and sometimes unbiblically, into images of Jesus. The Reverend Charles S. Robinson said blacks expected Lincoln and had been waiting for him, as the Israelites did Moses. "They prayed he would come. They waited for him to come. And then he came. . . . He seemed to them and their children a second Messiah." This "world's Redeemer" became then for blacks "*their* Messiah" (though one has to wonder about the patronizing way Robinson speaks so grandly for African Americans), "the seed of the woman [Mary], appointed to bruise the head of the serpent, in whose folds so many generations of their race had been crushed." In the end Robinson adopted an explicit note of apocalyptic hope: "Over the sad pall that covers our buried hopes bloom the bright flowers of resurrection."[54]

But for all the bright and hopeful—if extravagant—images in these sermons, there was as well a violent and vindictive theme that expressed the passions of a country just emerging from four long years of civil war. The assassination itself

(America's first of a president) was darkly evil in the minds of many ministers. The Reverend James Douglas noted, "We mourn, in our deepest humiliation, the disgrace inflicted on our national character, in the most odious crime known, not only to civilization, but to barbarism."[55] No one doubted where ultimate responsibility lay for the assassination. A relatively unknown but quite typical minister, the Reverend James DeNormandie, rhetorically asked, "Who killed Lincoln?" He replied to himself that it was said a man named Booth had done it, but that that man was only an instrument. According to DeNormandie, the true cause lay in those who had supported slavery for two hundred years.[56] In most cases, in fact, the sermons glossed over the person of John Wilkes Booth, who on that Sunday was still at large. All felt that Booth would surely be caught and he and his coconspirators hanged. The larger issue was whether the South would somehow reassert itself and restore slavery, which, some darkly noted, was by no means fully eradicated since the Thirteenth Amendment, though passed in Congress, had not been adopted in a number of states.

This vindictive endism erupted in the sermons even though most ministers recognized it was out of character with Lincoln himself, as well as with the spirit of renewal and joy in the resurrection of Jesus on Easter morning. Those who developed this theme searched biblical texts for a rationale that would ground the theme of retribution. The Reverend John Chester, for example, quoted 1 Samuel 15:23, which equates rebellion with witchcraft, and Exodus 22:18, which says that witches should not be allowed to live. His conclusion was that the South had a "sinful complicity with slavery," was then rebellious, and like witches would have to die. Now they had murdered Lincoln. In dealing with their crime, he said there should be no "undue leniency," especially with the leaders of the Confederacy. "If this people let this sin of rebellion go unpunished, they will repent it in sackcloth and ashes."[57] The Reverend William Chaffin emphasized as well that those who murdered Lincoln were seeking to restore slavery. "Not to punish them with memorable penalties, is to set a premium on treason and bid for a recurrence of rebellions in the future. It is but right that we should be roused to a state of terrible indignation, for our uncompromising severity will, in the end, be the greatest mercy."[58]

There are those, said Charles Robinson, who were

> nurtured under the hot debasements and vile luxuries of the slave system, sojourning here on our charitable sufferance, in order meanly to escape the perils of the ruinous war they have helped to incite, who clap their hands in applause of this murder! I think, in serious self-defense, we are to see that this thing is ended. This wickedness clamors for retributive judgment, and invokes the wrath of God.

Although Lincoln himself demonstrated forgiveness in much of his life, Robinson thought that forgiveness was inappropriate in light of what the nation faced at this moment. "Let it be said, in reply [to the call for forgiveness], that the tidings of this murder, going into the ranks of rebellion, will be hailed with a howl of gladness and satisfaction, equal to the yell of Pandemonium, when Satan seduced Adam, and buried a race in ruin." Ultimate issues were at stake. The very existence of the Union, indeed of humanity, seemed in the balance. The North did not want revenge but retribution, he concluded: "Let judgment follow on as implacable as doom."[59]

"Strange (is it not?)," wrote Walt Whitman, "that battles, martyrs, blood, even assassination should so condense—perhaps only really, lastingly condense—a Nationality."[60] There is no question that the war, however terrible, brought some good and perhaps had to be fought; the end of the obnoxious institution of slavery has to be judged as a positive outcome of the war. But what is the nature of that millennium for which all those people, black and white, died? And what is the meaning today of having forged, but not discarded, the apocalyptic as the core experience of our nationality?

The great disappointment of it all was the huge letdown when it was over. The American character had been "tempered in the furnaces of war"[61] without much to show for it except missing limbs and a broken heart. The expectations of freedmen were dashed in the wake of a white Southern backlash and a feeble national effort to protect the gains of the war.[62] Whole cities were destroyed, families were broken, social and political institutions were in chaos. The apocalypse had not brought the millennium. The story remained unfulfilled, the script only partially enacted. The Union was secure, but the war had shattered the dream of infinite American progress. We could no longer fully trust a human future—and this loss of faith in the ground of our being was to find deeper resonance in the ultimate threats of the twentieth century. It is a haunting past that lives still very much in the present.

NOTES

1. The most interesting discussion of the underlying psychological tensions in seventeenth-century America is John Demos, *Entertaining Satan: Witchcraft and the Culture of Early New England* (New York: Oxford University Press, 1982). Note also Richard Slotkin, *Regeneration through Violence: The Mythology of the American Frontier, 1600–1860* (Middletown, Conn.: Wesleyan University Press, 1973).

2. Gordon Wood, *The Radicalism of the American Revolution* (New York: Knopf, 1992).

3. Edward Pessen, *Jacksonian America: Society, Personality, and Politics* (Homewood, Ill.: Dorsey Press, 1969), chap. 1.

4. Ronald L. Numbers and Jonathan M. Butler, eds., *The Disappointed: Millerism and Millenarianism in the Nineteenth Century* (Bloomington: Indiana University Press, 1987). Note also Malcolm Bull and Keith Lockhard, *Seeking a Sanctuary: Seventh-Day Adventism and the American Dream* (New York: Harper and Row, 1989); and Paul Boyer, *When Time Shall Be No More: Prophetic Belief in Modern American Culture* (Cambridge, Mass.: Belknap Press of Harvard University Press, 1992), 80–86.

5. Hazel Catherine Wolf, *On Freedom's Altar: The Martyr Complex in the Abolition Movement* (Madison: University of Wisconsin Press, 1952), ix.

6. Lawrence Friedman, however, persuasively argues that the degree of genuine pacifism that infused the abolitionists in the 1830s is open to some question. See Lawrence Friedman, "Antebellum American Abolitionism and the Problem of Violent Means," *Psychohistory Review* 9 (1980): 26–32. The basic question the abolitionists failed to grapple with was whether violence was acceptable if used defensively. The test case was the shooting of Elijah

Lovejoy in Alton, Illinois. See Charles B. Strozier, *Lincoln's Quest for Union: Public and Private Meanings* (New York: Basic Books, 1982), 188.

7. Frederick Douglass, *Life and Writings of Frederick Douglass*, ed. Philip Foner, 5 vols. (New York: International Publishers, 1950), 2:460–63.

8. Quotations from Geoffrey C. Ward with Rick Burns and Ken Burns, *The Civil War* (New York: Knopf, 1990), 19.

9. Matthew 12:22–28; Mark 3:22–26; Luke 11:14–20.

10. Strozier, *Lincoln's Quest for Union*, 182–87; compare Don Fehrenbacher, *Prelude to Greatness: Lincoln in the 1850s* (Stanford, Calif.: Stanford University Press, 1962).

11. Stephen B. Oates, *To Purge This Land with Blood: A Biography of John Brown* (New York: Harper and Row, 1970), 310.

12. Don Fehrenbacher in Ward, *The Civil War*, 84.

13. Arthur Schlesinger, Jr., "The Opening of the American Mind," *New York Times Book Review,* July 23, 1989.

14. Some of the large number of studies that have dealt with this issue are Joel Kovel, *White Racism: A Psychohistory* (New York: Pantheon Books, 1970); Robert Jay Lifton, *Death in Life: Survivors of Hiroshima* (New York: Vintage Books, 1967); and Robert Jay Lifton, *The Broken Connection: On Death and the Continuity of Life* (New York: Basic Books, 1979).

15. Peter J. Parrish, "The Instruments of Providence: Slavery, Civil War and the American Churches," *Studies in Church History* 20 (1983): 299.

16. Barbara Jeanne Fields, *Slavery and Freedom on the Middle Ground: Maryland during the Nineteenth Century* (New Haven, Conn.: Yale University Press, 1985). Note also Fields's short and provocative essay in Ward, *The Civil War.*

17. Ernest Lee Tuveson, *Redeemer Nation: The Idea of America's Millennial Role* (Chicago: University of Chicago Press, 1968), 195, 208.

18. Parrish, "The Instruments of Providence," 294.

19. Slotkin, *Regeneration through Violence*; Richard Slotkin, *The Fatal Environment: The Myth of the Frontier in the Age of Industrialization, 1880–1890* (Middletown, Conn.: Wesleyan University Press, 1986); Richard Slotkin, *Gunfighter Nation: The Frontier Myth in Twentieth-Century America* (New York: Macmillan, 1992). One could also note the famous President's Commission, *Violence in America: Historical and Comparative Perspectives: A Report to the National Commission on the Causes and Prevention of Violence,* June, 1969, ed. Hugh Davis Graham and Ted Robert Gurr (New York: Signet Books, 1969).

20. Parrish, "The Instruments of Providence," 299.

21. Ibid., 304.

22. Sherman said it was all hell as he and Grant crossed some perilous lines that have led others to make total war in the twentieth century. Note Charles B. Strozier, "Unconditional Surrender and the Rhetoric of Total War: From Truman to Lincoln," Occasional Paper of the Center on Violence and Human Survival, John Jay College, City University of New York, 1987 (republished in *Military History Quarterly* 2 [1990]: 8–15). Compare William Tecumseh Sherman, *Memoirs of General W. T. Sherman,* ed. Charles Royster (New York: Library of America, 1990); Ulysses Grant, *Personal Memoirs of U. S. Grant and Selected Letters,* ed. Mary Drake McFeely and William S. McFeely (New York: Library of America, 1990). Two recent books on Sherman are quite useful in terms of these issues: John F. Marshalek, *Sherman: A Soldier's Passion for Order* (New York: Free Press, 1993); and the extraordinarily interesting study by Charles Royster, *The Destructive War: William Tecumseh Sherman, Stonewall Jackson, and the Americans* (New York: Knopf, 1991).

23. Royster, *Destructive War,* 82, 241.

24. Alan T. Nolan, *Lee Considered: General Robert E. Lee and Civil War History* (Chapel Hill: University of North Carolina Press, 1991), 112–33, esp. 119, 126.

25. Ward, *The Civil War*, 55.

26. Kenneth Stampp, "The Southern Road to Appomattox," in Stampp, *The Imperiled Union: Essays on the Background of the Civil War* (New York: Oxford University Press, 1980), 246–69, quotations from 252, 260–61. Note also two recent books edited by Gabor S. Boritt that deal with the question of Lincoln's war-time leadership and why the South lost: *Lincoln, the War President* (New York: Oxford University Press, 1992) and *Why the Confederacy Lost* (New York: Oxford University Press, 1992).

27. Don Fehrenbacher, ed., *Lincoln*, 2 vols. (New York: Library of America, 1989), 1:220, 250, 415, 269.

28. Note Strozier, "Unconditional Surrender." Cf. James M. McPherson, "Lincoln and the Strategy of Unconditional Surrender," in *Lincoln, the War President*, ed. Boritt, 29–62; this paper was first published in pamphlet form at almost the same time as my own. McPherson and I have overlapping but also quite different perspectives on the issue of unconditional surrender during the Civil War.

29. Royster, *Destructive War*, 151.

30. "The fiery trial through which we pass, will light us down, in honor or dishonor, to the latest generation." Fehrenbacher, *Lincoln*, 1:415.

31. Hans J. Morgenthau and David Hein, *Essays on Lincoln's Faith and Politics*, ed. Kenneth W. Thompson, 4 vols. (New York: Lanham, 1983), 4:145.

32. James H. Moorhead, *American Apocalypse: Yankee Protestants and the Civil War, 1860–1869* (New Haven, Conn.: Yale University Press, 1978), x.

33. James M. McPherson, "American Victory, American Defeat," in *Why the Confederacy Lost*, ed. Boritt, 40.

34. Fehrenbacher, *Lincoln*, 2:209.

35. See Garry Wills, *Lincoln at Gettysburg: The Words That Remade America* (New York: Simon and Schuster, 1992).

36. Fehrenbacher, *Lincoln*, 2:687.

37. Moorhead, *American Apocalypse*, 174–75. I speak of Easter morning sermons rather loosely in this analysis. I am particularly interested in those given that Sunday morning, April 16. In some cases, however, I draw on sermons from Lincoln's Washington funeral on April 19 and even from those of Sunday, April 23, when some ministers, such as Henry Ward Beecher and Theodore L. Cuyler, gave their sermons because they had been at a ceremony at Fort Sumter on Friday, April 14, and had been unable to return to their churches for Easter by April 16. In the larger body of "assassination sermons"—though I avoid quoting from them—there were also many sermons on May 4, the date of the Lincoln funeral in Springfield, and June 1, the national day of mourning proclaimed by President Johnson. The further one gets from the actual death of Lincoln, the more conventional and "canned" become the sermons.

38. C. B. Crane, *Sermon on the Occasion of the Death of President Lincoln* (Hartford, Conn.: Case, Lockwood, 1865), 3. Unless otherwise indicated, i.e., as separately published in a book, the sermons I read were from the archives of the Illinois State Historical Library. I used as a key to the collection Jay Monaghan's *Collections of the Illinois State Historical Library: Bibliographical Series, Vol. 4, Lincoln Bibliography, 1839–1939, Vol. 1* (Springfield: Illinois State Historical Library, 1943). I also benefited from the assistance of Thomas Schwartz, the Lincoln curator at the library, and Mark Johnson, a research historian with the Illinois Preservation Agency. As far as I can tell, some three hundred sermons survive in various collections around the country (though the Illinois State Historical Library has by far the greatest number of the sermons). I read about one hundred of them.

39. Rolla H. Chubb, "A Discourse upon the Death of President Lincoln Delivered at Greenwich M. E. Church, June 1, 1865," Illinois State Historical Society, 3.

40. Ralph Waldo Emerson, "A Plain Man of the People," in *Building the Myth: Selected Speeches Memorializing Abraham Lincoln,* ed. Waldo W. Braden (Urbana: University of Illinois Press, 1990), 33–34.

41. Henry Ward Beecher, "A New Impulse of Patriotism for His Sake," in Braden, *Building the Myth,* 37.

42. Theodore L. Cuyler, "And the Lord Blessed Abraham in All Things. Gen. 29:1," in *Our Martyr President, Abraham Lincoln: Voices from the Pulpit of New York and Brooklyn* (New York: Tibbals and Whiting, 1865), 2; George Bancroft, "Oration," in *Our Martyr President,* 389.

43. Chubb, "A Discourse," 7.

44. Abraham Lincoln, *The Collected Works of Abraham Lincoln,* ed. Roy P. Basler et al., 8 vols. plus appendix and supplement (New Brunswick, N.J.: Rutgers University Press, 1953), 8:375 n, 375–76. There was some confusion in the hectic weeks toward the end of March about the actual date Fort Sumter had fallen. On March 27 Secretary of War Edwin Stanton telegraphed Lincoln at City Point detailing the problem, namely that the surrender had been agreed to on April 13, 1861, but that the Northern troops had not filed out of the fort until the next day. Lincoln replied that he thought there was "little or no difference" which day was selected to hold the ceremony. Stanton obviously chose April 14, which came to have much more meaning than he ever could have imagined.

45. Cuyler, "And the Lord Blessed Abraham," 159.

46. S. S. Guthrie, *In Memoriam: Abraham Lincoln* (Buffalo, N.Y.: Matthews and Warren, 1865), 6.

47. William E. Baron, "The American Pulpit on the Death of Lincoln," *The Open Court* 37 (Oct. 1923): 514.

48. A. A. Littlejohn, "Know Ye Not There Is a Prince and a Great Man Fallen This Day in Israel. 2 Sam. 3:38," in *Our Martyr President,* 2.

49. W. E. Guthrie, *Oration on the Death of Abraham Lincoln* (Philadelphia: John Pennington and Sons, 1865), 9.

50. E. S. Atwood, *Discourses in Commemoration of Abraham Lincoln,* April 16 and June 1, 1865 (Salem, Mass.: Salem Gazette, 1865), 4.

51. Lincoln was noted for his pardons of deserters who had been condemned to death by his harsher secretary of war, Edwin Stanton. Lincoln also did things like moving quickly to prevent retaliation after the Southern massacre at Fort Pillow on April 12 and 13, 1864, with the comment that "blood can not restore blood." Lincoln, *Collected Works,* 7:345.

52. Chubb, "A Discourse," 9.

53. Henry W. Bellows, "Sorrow Hath Filled Your Heart . . . John 16:6, 7," in *Our Martyr President,* 59–60, 62.

54. Charles H. Robinson, "He Was a Good Man, and a Just. Luke 23:50," in *Our Martyr President,* 91–92.

55. James Douglas, *Funeral Discourse on the Occasion of the Obsequies of President Lincoln,* April 19, 1865 (Pulaski, N.Y.: Democrat Job Press, 1865), 2.

56. James DeNormandie, "The Lord Reigneth: A Few Words on Sunday Morning, April 16, 1865, after the Assassination of Abraham Lincoln," Illinois State Historical Library. See also Isaac E. Carey, "Discourse on the Death of Abraham Lincoln, April 19, 1865," Illinois State Historical Library; John Chester, *The Lessons of the Hour. Justice as well as Mercy. A Discourse Preached on the Sabbath Following the Assassination of the President* (Washington, D.C.: Washington Chronicle Print, 1865).

57. Chester, *The Lessons of the Hour*, 11, 13.

58. William L. Chaffin, *A Discourse on Sunday Morning, April 23d, 1865* (Philadelphia: King and Baird, 1865), 9.

59. Robinson, "He Was a Good Man, and a Just," 97, 99, 100.

60. Ward, *The Civil War*, 393.

61. Parrish, "The Instruments of Providence," 318.

62. Eric Foner, *Reconstruction: America's Unfinished Revolution, 1863–1877* (New York: Harper and Row, 1988). Note also Albion W. Tourgee, *A Fool's Errand, by One of the Fools* (New York: Fords, Howard, and Hulbert, 1879).

Chapter Six

Apocalyptic Spirituality
Approaching the Third Millennium

Bernard McGinn

> Watch, then, praying at all times, that you may be
> accounted worthy to escape all these things that are to
> be, and to stand before the Son of Man.
>
> —Luke 21:36

Not all Christians have put much faith in the attitude of living in the shadow of the Second Coming enjoined in these words. Pope Boniface VIII, beleaguered by the attacks on his papacy by the Spiritual Franciscans in the name of an imminent end of the age of the carnal church, once testily exclaimed: "Why are these fools awaiting the end of the world?" Some great thinkers, such as Augustine and Thomas Aquinas, although never denying that Christ would one day return to judge heaven and earth, were strongly opposed to attempts to predict the timing of the event and suspicious of making the expectation of his return the center of Christian living.

In recent centuries the split between apocalyptic and nonapocalyptic views of Christianity has grown greater. All we need do is look around us. The major Christian denominations often seem to have little room for the apocalyptic message of the Scriptures. Historians of Christianity and theologians attempt reinterpretations of apocalyptic hopes, but these rarely cross over into the life of their communities. When was the last time you heard a good sermon on the Second Coming? On the other hand, millions of fervent Christians, those usually called fundamentalists, still make literal apocalypticism the center of their belief. The ways in which they express this literalism and the ends to which they direct it, however, are often abhorrent to fundamental Christian values, at least as conceived of by other Christians. Apocalypticism is a sword of division.

Talk about the End is definitely on the rise. One does not have to be a prophet to predict that it is likely to continue to increase until January 1, 2000, which is the date when the numerically challenged think the third millennium A.D. begins. Millennial madness already promises to be one of the media events of the next few years—it may even eclipse the Dead Sea Scrolls and the Shroud of Turin as hot-button items when reporters need something to say about religion. Still, this growing concern with the dawning new millennium may bring more than the satisfaction of idle curiosity, especially if renewed attention to the apocalyptic element in Christian belief allows us to take up once again the issue of how important waiting for the return of the risen Lord should be for Christians.

We can give this issue a name—apocalyptic spirituality—but in order to understand what it means we have to begin by investigating the two ambiguous words that make up the name. *Apocalypse,* a Greek word meaning "revelation, or unveiling," was originally used to describe a genre of text invented by Jews in the last centuries before Christ. These Jewish apocalypses contained a wide variety of heavenly secrets given to seers through the mediation of angels. The revelations often concerned the celestial realms and their inhabitants; indeed, some of the seers speak of ascending to heaven to receive their message. Other apocalypses involved revelations of the course of history (at times including enumerations of the ages of the world), and especially messages about approaching divine judgment on evildoers and the definitive triumph of the just in a new and final age to come. The intermingling of a *vertical* aspect connecting heaven and earth and a *horizontal* one disclosing God's control over the course of history has been characteristic of apocalypticism from its beginnings, though most modern uses of the term emphasize the horizontal, or historical, pole.

The first Jewish apocalypses, like the second part of the book of Daniel, were written by pious Jews at a time when they were undergoing persecution for their faith. The message given is one of encouragement and consolation through the conviction that God is the Lord of history and that he will soon vindicate his lordship in a final way. In some apocalyptic texts the actual date of this vindication is revealed, often in a highly symbolic way (all apocalypses feature rich symbolic language); other apocalypses oppose literal prediction, though still encouraging the believer to persevere because God will soon reveal his dominion over the powers of evil.

Various forms of apocalypticism can be found in late Second Temple Judaism, the world that formed the historical context for the beginning of Christianity. Without getting into the vexed question of to what extent Jesus himself was an apocalyptic preacher (there is no agreement on this among biblical scholars after a century of debate), no one doubts that those who wrote the New Testament were all deeply influenced by apocalypticism in various ways. The first Jews who confessed that Jesus was Messiah and Son of God viewed his Resurrection as the beginning of the apocalyptic new age and looked forward to the imminent return, or Parousia, which would establish his definitive rule on earth. One powerful strain in early Christianity, best reflected in the twentieth chapter of the Revelation of John, saw the Parousia as inaugurating the thousand-year rule of Christ and the saints on earth—the original meaning of the term *millennium*.

One still sometimes hears the argument that consciousness of the delay of the Parousia in second-century Christianity led believers to abandon apocalypticism, or at least to leave it to a lunatic fringe. Historical evidence, however, demonstrates that

Christianity has never been without a strong element of apocalypticism, though this has been expanded, reinterpreted, and transformed in many ways. For every major Christian thinker, such as Augustine and Thomas Aquinas, who turned against literal views of an imminent return of Jesus, there were others, for example, Bonaventure or Martin Luther, for whom the sense of the imminence of the End was a vital part of Christian spirituality, even though they often resisted exact predictions of the time of its coming.

But what is apocalyptic *spirituality*? It is not my intention to try to provide any easy definition of this often misused word, or even to review its history. It does seem safe to say, though, that spirituality can no longer be understood according to an exclusive emphasis on inner experience—the soul versus the body. The growing popularity of the term over the past few decades, despite the often vague ways in which it is employed, reveals a range of meanings based on the conviction that Christian belief contains more than just intellectual and institutional dimensions—it also demands the engagement of the whole person through a commitment to transformative living in the world. Few forms of Christian spirituality—for good or for ill—have been more total than those rooted in apocalypticism.

Just as the term *apocalypse* was taken over by Christians from Jews, the New Testament teaching on the role of the Holy Spirit, or Spirit of Jesus, has its background in the Jewish notion of the breath, or spirit *(ru'ah)* of God. The Pauline doctrine of the spiritual person "who judges all things" (1 Cor. 2:15) helps us understand spirituality (the word first appears in the fifth century) as the lived experience of the Christian who is totally rooted in the life-giving presence of the Spirit of the risen Lord. From this perspective one might argue that all Christian spirituality is, or should be, apocalyptic spirituality. I am using the term here, however, to indicate those forms of Christian belief that emphasize a conviction of Christ's imminent return and the effect this should have on daily life and practice.

Should Christian spirituality be apocalyptic as we approach the third millennium? When we look at the many forms of apocalyptic spirituality found among fundamentalist Christians, with their literal predictions of the imminence of Christ's Second Coming and the public stances this leads them to adapt, many may be inclined to think that apocalypticism produces an inauthentic, even dangerous, type of spirituality. Investigation of the literalist forms of apocalypticism in the history of Christianity tends to support these misgivings. The story of the followers of Joachim of Fiore, of the Dolcinists, of the Hussites, of the Munsterites, of the more radical forms of English Puritanism, of the Russian Old Believers, to name but a few of the more important groups, is troubling to say the least. Though we may admire some of the ideals for which these groups struggled and be appalled by the suffering they underwent for their beliefs, we are dismayed by their often ludicrous literalism, their exclusivity and opposition to all who disagreed with them, and especially the heartless savagery they at times unleashed in their conviction that they thus contributed to the advent of the kingdom of God on earth. Apocalyptic spirituality often appears as a projection of the least noble aspects of human hopes and fears onto history, and critics have pointed out that this does not necessarily result only from perverse understandings of the New Testament message, but that it has strong roots in the book itself, especially in the call for the just to rejoice in divine vengeance found in the book of Revelation (e.g., Rev. 6:10, 11:15, 16:5–6, 18:5–6, 21:8).

On the other hand, we can also ask whether it is possible to reject the apocalyptic elements in Christianity without rejecting something that is essential and has been essential to it from the beginning. Given the historical misuses of apocalypticism, the narrowness of present-day fundamentalism, and vapid media speculation about the new millennium, some will say that this is not only possible but necessary. Others will insist that essential aspects of Christian belief were formed in apocalypticism and it may be difficult to remove them totally from this foundation without doing serious damage. It is more challenging, though certainly more difficult, to consider what it might mean to try to uncover the spiritual resources still to be found in the Christian apocalyptic tradition.

I have no simple formula for how to recover an authentic and enriching apocalyptic spirituality. I will, however, suggest some possible starting places and strategies. In order to explore the issue of the renewal of apocalyptic spirituality, I think we need to begin with an honest appreciation of the ambivalences of apocalypticism. One of the most striking facts about the history of fervent expectation of the End is the way in which it has always had both positive and negative sides, that is, capacities for use and misuse. A consideration of some of these polarities raises central questions for any contemporary apocalyptic spirituality.

A primary factor in apocalypticism's broad appeal is how it answers to the anxiety we all face in the midst of the confusion of history, both the history of our own lives and the wider story of the race. Where have we come from? Where are we going? Do our lives belong to some meaningful whole? Apocalypticism introduced the concept of universal history, first into Judaism and then into Christianity and Islam. This alone makes it a worthy topic for study, even if it is difficult for contemporary believers to feel totally comfortable with traditional ideas of universal history in the light of our current global perspective and modern scientific cosmology. Despite these difficulties, Christian faith does entail the conviction that history has meaning, a meaning derived from the conviction that all things will reach completion in Christ. Though this sense of the universal significance of history found in Christ has been one of the positive elements in apocalyptic traditions, its negative side has been equally obvious in the claims of apocalyptically-minded Christians that they have been given control over history, even a blueprint allowing them certainty regarding the signs of the times and the approach of the End. The sad history of even the best-intentioned representatives of literalist apocalypticism indicates the power of this delusion.

One way of avoiding this danger has been to replace the sense of the imminent End of history with an immanent, or inward, expectation of Christ's coming into each person's life, especially at the moment of death. But this has often led to a privatizing of the apocalyptic sense of universal history to such an extent that hope for the Lord's return becomes a purely individual experience (as suggested by some of the demythologizing eschatologies of the mid–twentieth century). This seems to rob history of a collective dimension that is integral to Christian belief.

Apocalyptic confidence in God's control over the course of history and its End is the ground for other significant aspects of apocalyptic spirituality, each of which, however, has a corresponding dark side. Apocalyptic expectations form an intricate combination of optimism and pessimism—pessimism about the current state of the world under the control of the forces of evil and optimism about the coming era when God will triumph. Even though most apocalyptic scenarios of the End see evil increasing until the final showdown between Christ and Antichrist, the summation of all human opposition to goodness, the deepest current in apocalypticism is optimistic in its conviction regarding the eventual triumph of justice.

Apocalyptic pessimism can be a powerful force for good, especially when it empowers believers to identify and combat the demonic elements of injustice and oppression found in social, political, and ecclesiastical structures. But apocalyptic groups have often channeled their pessimism into withdrawal from the world to await divine destruction of the tainted order. At other times their opposition to evil has been the source of violent revolutionary action. To what extent can such reactions be legitimated, even within dire situations of injustice and persecution? This is one of the essential questions that an authentic apocalyptic spirituality must address.

Hope is one of the three theological virtues. No tradition of Christian spirituality has done more to cultivate this virtue, especially in its universal dimensions, than apocalypticism. Against those forms of Christian thought that hold out no expectation for any *real* improvement on earth, but place all our hope in heaven, early Christian millennialism and its subsequent revivals, especially the tradition dependent on the twelfth-century visionary Joachim of Fiore's predictions regarding a coming third age of the Holy Spirit, have looked forward to a new divine action leading to a higher stage of salvation history. The many forms of such optimistic millenarianism have two things in common—none has yet been realized, and the desire they represent refuses to die. Important theological voices have judged them to be dangerous innovations based on merely human aspirations, but this has done little to lessen their appeal.

Apocalyptic spirituality's emphasis on the importance of moral decision presents a comparable ambiguity. Though apocalypticism views world history as already determined by God from all eternity, it insists on the necessity for personal choice in the midst of the crisis of the present struggle between good and evil. Such decision is given heightened importance by seeing it in the light of the final choice between good and evil that determines the whole course of history. This feature of apocalyptic spirituality can work both for good and for ill.

Patience and endurance, as the expression of an inner decision to remain faithful to the divine command in the face of temptation, persecution, and death, have been hallmarks of apocalypticism in Judaism and Christianity from the beginning. This faithfulness to God is not individualistic—apocalyptic spirituality has always insisted that the saving decision is made in and with the body of believers, even if these are conceived of as the persecuted few who have refused the mark of the Beast (see Rev. 13:16–17). We are not saved alone; nor are we damned alone. Nevertheless, stress on the importance of a definitive decision for God in the light of what is perceived as the last time for choosing has often led to black and white judgments about *what* is right and wrong and (more tragically) *who* is right and wrong. From this flow other consequences. Fear of sin among apocalypticists has often entailed hatred of sinners; willingness to undergo persecution based on the conviction of ultimate vindication has at times facilitated a transition from the status of persecuted to that of persecutor. To deny that smugness and vindictiveness have often been part of apocalyptic spirituality is to deny the record of its history.

So perhaps it may be best after all to jettison apocalyptic spirituality as we approach the new millennium—to think of it as part of the childhood of Christianity: a neurosis we are endeavoring to overcome. There are, however, reasons why such a simplistic solution may involve as much loss as gain. In large part these reasons rest on two elements central to apocalyptic spirituality that do not, I believe, involve the kinds of ambivalences discussed above.

The first of these aspects is the apocalypticist's sense of the majesty of God. There are few places in the Old and the New Testaments where more effective witness is given to divine transcendence than in the apocalyptic texts in Daniel, the Synoptic Gospels, Paul, and especially in John's Revelation. While there are certainly other parts of the Bible that present pictures of God's absolute sovereignty over creation, it is not by accident that the most effective pictorial representations of divine majesty, such as the shining mosaics of early Christian basilicas and the impressive sculptured portals of medieval cathedrals, drew their inspiration from the portrayals of divine majesty in Revelation, especially in the fourth and fifth chapters.

The second reason involves apocalypticism's stress on the transcendence of death. Apocalyptic literature, at least from the time of the book of Daniel (see Dan. 12:2–3), insisted that God, in his goodness, majesty, and justice, will give his faithful ones a reward beyond human hope, the gift of overcoming death itself. The survival promised in apocalyptic texts was more than just the immortality of the soul that pagan philosophers had taught; it centered on the resurrection of the body—a belief difficult, even absurd, to human reason. The confession that Jesus had indeed risen from the dead in bodily fashion was the beginning of Christianity. Paul's ringing statement, "If Christ has not risen, vain then is our preaching, vain too is your faith" (1 Cor. 15:14), underlines the bond between apocalyptic teaching regarding the resurrection of the dead and the Resurrection witness of the earliest Christians. Although the Resurrection of Jesus, as well as that of his followers, has been understood in many ways over almost two millennia, it is hard to separate this fundamental Christian confession from its roots in apocalypticism.

If essential elements in Christianity were born in apocalyptic expectations and have continued to be shaped by them in varying ways over almost two millennia, this suggests that abandoning apocalypticism is perhaps not the best answer. A return to literal apocalypticism is equally misguided, because such a perspective fails to appreciate the ambivalences of apocalyptic spirituality discussed above. Purely immanent and private reinterpretations of apocalyptic beliefs also have their problems, especially their tendency to eviscerate the commitment to justice and the hope for renewed divine action in the world that are among the essential positive values of apocalypticism. The social critique implied in biblical apocalypticism is important for keeping Christians honest (or at least nervous) about how far they can ever commit themselves to accommodation with injustice in the present world order, as well as for empowering a hope for the future that is more than just world-denying. It is in the midst of such positions and counterpositions that the search for an authentic apocalyptic spirituality must be conducted.

This difficult task needs both honesty and discretion. It also needs good examples. So I would like to close by noting three creative reappropriations of apocalyptic spirituality in recent decades, though the fact that these choose different aspects of apocalypticism to emphasize will indicate how complicated the question of apocalyptic spirituality remains.

The power of apocalypticism to galvanize protest against demonic forces in history is not dead in our day. Consider two cases, one poetical, the other exegetical. Ernesto Cardenal, the revolutionary Nicaraguan poet, published his "Apocalypse" in 1965 when the threat of nuclear world-destruction was at its height. Cardenal's poem explodes the traditional symbols of the book of Revelation and then reassembles them in combination with contemporary technological images to create a potent critique of a society gone mad in its quest for self-destruction. I quote from the opening lines:

> AND BEHOLD
> I saw an Angel (all his cells were electronic eyes)
> and I heard a supersonic voice
> saying: Open up the typewriter and type.

The message typed by the electronic seer is a dire one:

> and the third Angel set off the warning siren
> and I beheld a mushroom cloud above New York
> and a mushroom cloud above Moscow
> and a mushroom cloud above London
> and a mushroom cloud above Peking
> (and Hiroshima's fate was envied).[1]

Like his biblical model, though, Cardenal concludes his account of world destruction with an expression of hope for a new heaven and a new earth, conceived of as a higher stage in human evolution.

Twenty years later, the South African pastor Allan Boesak, in solitary confinement in a South African prison, received what he called an "angelic visitation" that allowed him to put the finishing touches on a commentary on the book of Revelation he had been working on since 1980. Published in 1987, his *Comfort and Protest: The Apocalypse from a South African Perspective* uses John's revelation to challenge readers to choose once again between God and Caesar and utterly reject "those powerful and mighty men in top hats, sashes, and uniforms who threaten and maim, kill and destroy, and then go to prayer breakfasts and call upon the name of God."[2]

Finally, and to some surprisingly, I would point to Pope John Paul II. In his apostolic letter *Tertio Millennio Adveniente* (November 10, 1994), the pope proclaims that "preparing for the Year 2000 has become as it were a hermeneutical key of my Pontificate" (par. 23), noting that he had referred to the millennium in his first encyclical (*Redemptor Hominis*, 1979) and in the long encyclical he devoted to the

Holy Spirit (*Dominum et Vivificantem*, 1986). If Cardenal and Boesak appeal primarily to the power of apocalyptic spirituality to strengthen opposition to the appalling evils disregarded by so many Christians, the Pope, though never slow to point to what *Dominum et Vivificantem* called "the signs and marks of death" found in contemporary technological and scientific culture, primarily seeks to harness the optimistic aspects of the apocalyptic vision to encourage a new openness to the Holy Spirit and the evangelization of the entire world. While cautioning against any return to a crude millennialism, Pope John Paul clearly believes that hope for a future "more spiritual" age is an integral part of Christian teaching.

Each of these contemporary witnesses provides us with an example of the power still present in apocalyptic spirituality and the word of prophecy upon which it is founded. They have heeded the message of 2 Peter—"And we have the word of prophecy, surer still, to which you do well to attend, as to a lamp shining in a dark place, until the day dawns and the morning star rises in your hearts" (2 Pet. 2:19).

NOTES

1. Ernesto Cardenal, *Apocalypse and Other Poems* (New York: New Directions, 1971), 33–34.

2. Allan A. Boesak, *Comfort and Protest: The Apocalypse from a South African Perspective* (Philadelphia: Westminster, 1987), 127–28.

Chapter Seven

The Other Is Ourselves
A Feminist Spirituality for the Year 2000 and Beyond

Marie L. Baird

It was while reading Jean Améry's unforgettable chapter on torture[1] that I realized the necessity of focusing on women's struggle against the cultural and theological devaluation of their bodies, such a struggle forming the basis for new forms of feminist spirituality that might help to nourish and sustain women in the coming millennium. As I reflected upon Améry's characterization of the torturer's domain as "dominion over spirit and flesh, orgy of unchecked self-expansion" into the body of the tortured,[2] I could not help but notice a rather apt description, unintended to be sure, of the effects of patriarchal structures on women's bodies. For not only have traditional patriarchal philosophical and theological anthropologies delineated the binary opposition between "spirit" and "flesh" that Améry's characterization of torture upholds; they have also constructed and perpetuated consistently sexist practices of "unchecked self-expansion" into women's bodies. Such invasion preserves patriarchal superiority in religious traditions while continuing to constitute women's bodies as the "battlefields" upon which "men fight their ideological-religious wars."[3]

The purpose of this essay is threefold. First, I will provide a topography of women's-bodies-as-battlefield in the traditional cultural and religious domain, mapping at least some of the terrain where women lie injured, tortured, and slain. Next, I will show that this battlefield is not doomed to become merely a cemetery—the ironic sanctification as "holy ground" and ultimate reversal of women's bodies as givers of life. Finally, I will suggest the provisional lineaments of new forms of spiritual praxis for the year 2000 and beyond in which the battlefield—and all metaphors of violence used in relation to women—is to be replaced by an ethics of responsibility. I will show that such an ethics must be rooted in the inviolability of women's bodies as *full* participants in an order of life in which divinity manifests itself most immediately in and through relational acts of sustenance and care.

In the realm of spirituality, a project such as this one is immediately faced with problems of naming. For example, the idea of an article on "feminine spirituality and the year 2000" that might introduce new forms of women's spirituality for the coming millennium is hampered at the outset by the terms *feminine* and *spirituality*, terms that have lost their innocence but lack adequate synonyms as replacements.

Elisabeth Schüssler Fiorenza is certainly correct in pointing out the ambiguity surrounding the use of the term feminine in theological and church circles, because it conjures up the image of "the 'good woman' who respects male scholarship and expertise—against the feminist theologian—the 'bad woman' who radically questions them."[4] And of course the term spirituality perpetuates the spirit-flesh opposition already alluded to; it also takes the inferior position in the theology-spirituality dualism found in many academic theological circles.[5] And so, I find myself addressing a topic whose very delineation is suffused with problems of patriarchal origin: the debate between the use of *feminine* versus *feminist,* a debate with clear political overtones in many theological and church milieus; and the use of the term *spirituality,* which seems to automatically discount the body and its realities as being unworthy of theological consideration. My response will be to use the term feminist in a way that seeks to address as many aspects of women's embodied experience as possible and to explore new forms of spirituality that remain firmly rooted in this same embodied experience.

Women's-Bodies-as-Battlefield: Signifiers of Exploitability

The second half of this century has seen a rapid proliferation of feminist voices across the humanities; this development has occurred also in theological and religious circles. Mary Ann Hinsdale, for example, has distinguished between feminist scholars in religion who are "theologians," "thealogians (goddess feminists)" and "biblical" and "post-biblical" feminists.[6] One may also distinguish between feminist theologians whose primary concern is with women's subordination and devaluation and those ecofeminists who contribute that same concern to an analysis of the link between women's exploitation and that of all forms of nonhuman nature—an exploitation that is spawning the current ecological nightmare.[7] In listening to these various voices within feminist theology, as well as feminist voices in other disciplines, I have been struck by the consistency with which concern for the health and well-being of bodies—women's, children's, men's, animals', plants', the earth's—has been articulated. Indeed, here is an obvious starting point for the elaboration of a feminist spirituality for the coming millennium that seeks to redress potentially all women's experiences of devaluation,[8] typically inflicted upon their bodies, without finding itself necessarily tied to any one theological vision, or for that matter to any specifically religious vision at all.

Such a quasi-foundationalist view of women's cultural—and hence religious—subordination to men is supported first of all by cultural anthropological research such as that articulated in Sherry Ortner's classic article, "Is Female to Male as Nature Is to Culture?"[9] There, she demonstrates that biological determinism is not enough to explain the "universal devaluation of women" because the physiological differences between males and females take on significations imbued with "superior" versus "inferior" connotations only in the context of the "culturally defined value systems" within which women and men live.[10] In her estimation, women are universally devalued because every culture identifies women's bodies as taking up an intermediary position between "nature" and "culture," "nature" constituting that culturally based conceptual category that culture as such is precisely designed to control and trans-form. More specifically, women's procreative functions are seen as being closer to nature than are men's, and their social roles as mother and keeper of the hearth are thought to place them on a lower cultural rung than men. Because of their more restricted social roles, women also tend to be socialized in ways that are then inter-preted as being closer to nature than men: "The feminine personality tends to be involved with concrete feelings, things, and people, rather than with abstract entities; it tends toward personalism and particularism."[11] All in all, Ortner's anthropologi-cal analysis provides us with a first explanation of how it is that women, largely on the basis of their bodily functions, come to be culturally constituted as a sign of sub-ordination, of intermediacy between nature and culture.[12] On a more ominous note, however, she asserts that "woman's intermediate position may have the implication of greater symbolic ambiguity"[13] because woman's in-between status enables her to function as a sign capable of accommodating a much wider range of possible mean-ings than those typically assigned to men. If Ortner's thesis is correct, it seems prob-able that women's bodies come to be symbolically constituted as signs of exploitability to the extent that they continue to be regarded as more "natural" than "cultural," therefore as one more thing to be conquered and controlled.

The conferral of status as natural or cultural is, of course, itself a cultural phe-nomenon that has been dependent historically upon the "oculocentrism" of "phall-ogocentric" systems.[14] I would identify the "orgy of unchecked self-expansion" into women's bodies as the phallogocentric gaze that "knows" what it "sees," the gaze that "expands" into women's bodies and "knows" these bodies by naming them, by constituting them as signifiers imbued with a constellation of significations that imply a "natural" subordination to men because of the more "natural" functioning of women's physiological processes with their attendant social roles. As an example of such oculocentrism, patriarchal religious traditions have penetrated women's bodies with their phallogocentric gaze and have utilized this gaze as the basis for a theological "knowing" of women's bodies that continues to place disproportionate value on women's procreative possibilities as doctrinally and ontically definitive of women's essential social role as human beings. This doctrinal valuation is so radi-cally certain of its rightness in the eyes of "God and man" that many religious lead-ers can repeatedly and with impunity relegate women to a status that is currently called "complementarity," a status that Anne Carr asserts "really means subordina-tion or inferiority of one in relation to the other."[15] Since women's bodies have already been disposed of doctrinally, their faces need not be seen and their voices need not be heard.[16] As things disproportionately valued for their procreative capa-bilities, women's bodies are utterly "absorbed in the sign system"[17] that constitutes them as such.

It is, of course, but a short step from the nature-culture dualism, in which culture constitutes itself as superior to nature, to the spirit-flesh opposition in which spirit comes to be identified with a striving for what is beyond the world of "mere" mate-riality, which is then devalued on account of its capacity to seduce the spirit away from otherworldly contemplation of divinity. Geraldine Finn characterizes this opposition, and its effects, as follows:

The differentiation of "spirit" from "matter," for example, both mystifies and falsifies the complex reality of material being by splitting off from it its most creative and potentially subversive possibilities and effects and syphoning them off into and for some "transcendent" space of otherworldliness, of the *immaterial:* of God, the soul and/or the human spirit. This postulate of an immaterial and "transcendent" soul, spirituality or "Otherness" secures the "quiddity" of the material world *as it is* and at the same time the safety of the political status quo which organizes it. (Emphasis hers).[18]

Once again women are the losers, as the disproportionate value placed upon their reproductive capacities has the effect, *in women's concrete experience,* of defining the "essence" of their being in "fleshly" terms, all theological anthropological discourse on "soul" and "spirit" notwithstanding. Social subordination and devaluation are the inevitable outcomes of such a definition.

The historical antecedents of the spirit-flesh dualism that lies at the heart of traditional Christian theological anthropologies are unmistakable. For example, Molly Myerovitz Levine analyzes the "gendered grammar of ancient Mediterranean hair"[19] and concludes that women's hair, as metonymically signifying the whole person and metaphorically signifying "nature in an ahistorical synchronic dialectic with culture,"[20] was often perceived fearfully when men in ancient Mediterranean culture felt threatened by female sexuality:

> Since decapitation is a workable expedient only in myth, the universal sign of the transformation of virgin to wife among Greeks, Romans, and Jews early becomes hair—bound, tamed, braided, or covered, the token of matronly modesty and chastity. The social tolerance of female sexuality usually ends with marriage in patriarchal societies that value and need wives primarily for reproduction.[21]

Likewise, Amy Richlm's study of "the face of Roman gender"[22] examines Roman women's makeup practices as "crafts or skills aiming at a certain kind of control over the body and its surroundings."[23] And Howard Eilberg-Schwartz shows that "the eroticization of the female mouth in ancient Judaism"[24] led to a virtual equation of conversation between a man and a woman to an act of sexual intercourse.[25]

The traditional Christian theological anthropological distinction between spirit and flesh inevitably linked spirit with male and flesh with female as typically—both explicitly and implicitly—interpreted.[26] To be spiritual thus became an affair of the (male) mind with its capacities of intellect and will, "responsibility" and "freedom"; to be fleshly was to succumb to the (female) irrationality of carnal desire, which was intrinsically evil and in need of strict surveillance. As flesh must always be subordinated to spirit, so women must always be subordinated to men, a position that is upheld by the New Testament.[27]

For example, Mary Rose D'Angelo examines the apostle Paul's injunction that women must always cover their heads (1 Cor. 11:2–16) and concludes that "[woman's] relation to God as source is second to the man's; she is (only) the glory of a man, who is the image and glory of God."[28] Indeed, this passage from the New Testament has been interpreted traditionally in ways that have been so damaging to women's social status and personal well-being that Brazilian mujerista theologian Maria Clara Bingemer has called for theology to "go beyond traditional theological concepts that see a woman as God's image only in her rational soul and not in her sexed female body."[29] Yet it is precisely because women have not been traditionally regarded as the image of God with the degree of perfection that men are believed to exhibit that their bodies become available for cooptation by sexist practices promulgated by patriarchal religious structures. Patricia Klindienst Joplin, for example, notes that the woman taken in adultery (John 8:1–11) is so completely coopted by the sexist practice of ritual female exchange (in which her adulterous act leads to her transmission from husband's to patriarchs' jurisdiction) that she is forced to stand silent before the elders' murderous intent:

> Commentators . . . presume to know how to read the text of the silenced female body: she is silenced by her *shame*. This ignores the text's clear emphasis on the relationship between where one stands in the structure of violent exchange and whether or not one can speak and be heard. The woman cannot speak so long as she is exploited as sign/word, occupying the place of the surrogate victim, her voice stilled by the ventriloquism of the men who would speak through her. (Emphasis hers)[30]

And so, her status as a signifier of exploitability remains unchanged because the "dominion of spirit over flesh, orgy of unchecked self-expansion" practiced by the phallogocentric gaze that "knows" what it "sees" is perpetuated in patriarchal theological/doctrinal discourse and praxis.

Unfortunately, current cultural and theological practice has brought about insufficient improvement in women's situation. For the overwhelming majority of the women of the world, it has brought about virtually no change at all, enabling Rebecca Chopp and Mark Lewis Taylor to assert that "women bear in their bodies and lives the marks of sexist practice."[31] Indeed. In a distressing and all too frequent confirmation of the effects of traditional theological teaching on women's bodies, Susan Brooks Thistlethwaite has noted that

> most social workers, therapists, and shelter personnel view religious beliefs as uniformly reinforcing passivity and tend to view religion, both traditional Christianity and Judaism, as an obstacle to a woman's successful handling of abuse. Unfortunately, they also say that many strongly religious women cease attending shelters and groups for abused women when these beliefs are attacked.[32]

And so, the traditional theological interpretations of passages from the Hebrew Scriptures such as Gen. 2:21–24, Gen. 3:1[33] and New Testament passages such as 1 Cor. 11:2–16, all of which stress women's subordinate status in relation to men, help enable men to abuse their wives, girlfriends, daughters, and other females—acts of violence that they can then justify in religious terms. Elisabeth Schüssler Fiorenza's metaphorical characterization of women's bodies as "battlefield" thus takes on a distressingly literal signification, which she intends, over and above the ideological and religious connotations mentioned earlier:

> Bodily existence is not detrimental or peripheral to our spiritually becoming *ekklesia* but constitutive and central to it. Not the soul or the mind or the innermost self but the body is the image and model for our being church. How can we point to the eucharistic bread and say "this is my body" as long as women's bodies are battered, raped,

sterilized, mutilated, prostituted, and used for male ends? How can we proclaim "mutuality with men" in the Body of Christ as long as men curtail and deny reproductive freedom and moral agency to us?[34]

Such forms of extreme physical violence against women are practiced around the world in the forms of dowry deaths and bride burning in Sri Lanka[35] and prostitution in the Philippines, Sri Lanka, Indonesia, and Thailand,[36] to cite just a few examples occurring in Asia. The plight of women under fundamentalist Islamic regimes is well known. And womanist theologian Shamara Shantu Riley notes that black women "are not limited by issues defined by our femaleness but are rather often limited to questions raised about our very humanity"[37] wherever white supremacist ideologies are explicitly or implicitly enforced. Ursula King asserts that "spiritual strength" is capable of enabling women to withstand these violent assaults upon their bodies:

> It will strengthen women to struggle against sexism, and against the crimes committed—as in India, bride burning, sati, female infanticide, female foeticide, and dowry deaths. Spiritual strength will enable women in Pakistan to eradicate evil traditional practices like the tattooing of women's faces, and to safeguard the rights and privileges of young girls who are sexually exploited by rich men and hence deprived of marriage.[38]

The task before us now is to discover how women's overall experience—cultural, theological, religious—of the body as signifier of exploitability and thus as "battlefield" might form the basis for a recovery of the "spiritual strength" that King points to, as well as the basis for new forms of spiritual praxis that might nurture and sustain women in their ongoing struggles in the year 2000 and beyond.

Redemption through Suffering? An Alternative Approach

The traditional notion in many forms of spirituality that redemption is to be achieved by undergoing the requisite amount of suffering is dangerous in the extreme when facilely applied to women's lives. Ivone Gebara notes the "growing suspicion" that such an approach to redemption simply "might not be true."[39] She, and others, are therefore critical of a liberation theology that perpetuates the notion of redemption through suffering when the suffering of indigenous and third world peoples never seems to result in the liberation so desperately hoped for.[40] In a similar vein, Naomi P. F. Southard points out that women

> have too often sacrificed for the wrong reasons—because of a patriarchal system that forced women to suffer unwillingly, or that told them they had to sacrifice in order to overcome their "unacceptable" female (created) nature. Women must not allow themselves to fall into the trap of suffering because they have accepted the patriarchal dictum that it is "their lot" to suffer.[41]

If a traditional understanding of "redemption through suffering" is not appropriate to women's experience, especially when they find their bodies disproportionately exposed to the "unchecked self-expansion" of myriad aggressors in the forms of physical, cultural, and theological violence, how might we begin to explore women's bodily experience as a signifier of exploitability, utilizing such experience as the basis for the discovery of new forms of spiritual praxis?

The beginning of a provisional response to this question is to be found in Marjorie Hewitt Suchocki's confirmation of many feminists' view that all cultural and theological discourse, even though ultimately rooted in experience, nevertheless finds its articulation in and through a socially constructed language system that reflects the "universalization of the masculine experience."[42] Women might thus begin to explore the ways in which their bodies have been constituted as signifiers of exploitability by examining their own experiences of suffering at the hands of patriarchal systems, androcentric discourses, and sexist practices[43] and by bringing a hermeneutic of suspicion to bear on the traditional religious beliefs that seemingly sanction their concrete experiences of suffering. Specifically, I am suggesting a provisional interrogation of women's experiences of suffering that is based on a very simple premise: *By virtue of their very existence women are full participants in an order of life-as-such that in no way sanctions their positioning as the inferior member of any binary opposition that would posit men as superior in any form whatsoever.*[44] This is a premise that flies directly in the face of what women have been traditionally, and hence ideologically and theologically, socialized to believe about themselves and their relation to men. It is also a premise that underlies much of feminist thought across the disciplines, all of which questions the seemingly immutable nature of cultural institutions that would continue to promulgate women's "inferiority" as a perhaps publicly inadmissible yet "natural" given and hence as the basis for "infallible" pronouncements that perpetuate their inferior status. Sherry Ortner reminds us that "the whole scheme is a construct of culture rather than a fact of nature. Woman is not 'in reality' any closer to (or further from) nature than man—both have consciousness, both are mortal."[45] And cultural institutions that would parade their anthropological vision of women as somehow "true" in an infallible way must allow their ontological and moral "truth" about women to be interrogated and challenged by the concrete, all too often violent effects produced by their teachings. Truth must now become an "interactive deliberation of a multiple, polyvalent assembly of voices" understood as the democratic "alternative to torture"[46] instead of the infallible given handed down from on high by hierarchically structured institutions whose leaders remain safely insulated from witnessing the effects of their pronouncements on women's bodies and lives.

By attending to their concrete experiences of suffering and making an honest and certainly at times personally difficult and courageous effort to identify the sources of their suffering, women can begin to claim personal autonomy away from dependent forms of heteronomy often encouraged by religious traditions that equate "virtuous" with "passive"[47] and toward a more mature sense of independence and responsibility for personal well-being. By attending to their bodies' ways of knowing and speaking, women can begin to dismantle the spirit-flesh opposition by noticing and locating the ways in which spirit is constituted in and through bodily experience.[48] By confronting the fear that Grace Jantzen asserts originates "with an alienation of the bodily dimension of male selfhood that has not been welcomed" and that constitutes women as "others" to be feared,[49] women can institute a more comprehensive dismantling of the traditional binary oppositions that oppress them by renouncing such oppositions in and through concrete acts of sustenance and care for the "others," the "poor, and weak and despised," that hold us "accountable not to the powerful but to the powerless."[50] To that list must be added the "others" of nonhuman nature whose growing rate of extinction lies upon human heads. Finally, by identifying the basis for new forms of spiritual praxis in "the ethical encounter with others" as body and life-sustaining acts rooted in personal responsibility, women are challenged "to think and be anew, to risk being 'otherwise than being' what we have already known and become."[51] The following discussion of new forms of spiritual praxis for the coming millennium seeks to take up this challenge.

A Feminist Spirituality for the Year 2000 and Beyond: The Other Is Ourselves

I have identified the basis for new forms of spiritual praxis as the ethical encounter, in personal responsibility, for all "others" who have been constituted as the "inferior" members of traditional binary oppositions. Rather than a "naive reversal of the hierarchies inscribed in such binary couplings,"[52] I believe that such an ethical encounter reacquaints women with their full participation in the order of life itself, a participation that chooses not to invest patriarchal structures with the power of naming women's "essences" as social beings or delineating the range of their personal and communal possibilities.

The ethical encounters that many of us envision are already occurring and will continue to occur in the interstices between, and the spaces outside of, traditional conceptual categories. For such categories have a dismal and often violent history of governing women's concrete experiences by superimposing upon them various grids of representability that delineate "truth" from "falsehood" and "right" from "wrong" as a means of insuring their own "legitimacy" and "superiority" while at the same time constituting the "illegitimacy" and "contingency" of "others":

> This space between representation and reality, text and context, expression and experience, language and being is the necessary and indispensable space of judgement and critique, creativity and value, resistance and change. It is the ground of the critical intentions and originating experiences which enable us to call the political status quo into question and challenge the already-known universe and its organization into and by the predicative and prescriptive categories of "practical reason." As such, it is *the* ethical space—the space of the specifically ethical relation with others—and the only place from which the conventionality, the contingency (the "arbitrariness") of reality (of political positivities and identities) can be seen and challenged. (Emphasis hers)[53]

This new ethical space thus mandates encounters with the "other" that do not seek to reduce this other to a regulated, and thus readily identifiable, conceptual category that may be used to predict, control, and then prescribe "appropriate" treatment of the other on the basis of the category invoked.[54] Such an ethical space also constitutes a basis for resistance that will enable women not only to "think anew" but also to name reality anew[55] by constructing their own interpretive strategies, ever mindful, however, of the danger that "a 'feminist successor science' (development of epistemology free from gender bias) may provide 'yet another set of rules for the policing of thought.'"[56]

One of the most important spiritual practices women can engage in is the act of "naming and reclaiming the female body" in order to rescue it from anthropological visions that remain dualistic despite their assertions to the contrary.[57] Sandra Schneiders asserts that

> feminist spirituality is deeply concerned with the reintegration of all that has been dichotomized by patriarchal religion. . . . Thus, feminist spirituality is concerned with giving voice to and celebrating those aspects of *bodiliness* which religion has covered with shame and silence, particularly those feminine experiences associated with life-giving which have been reduced to sex and those aspects of sexuality which have been regarded as unclean. (Emphasis hers)[58]

As a theoretical support for this new spiritual practice of naming and reclaiming the female body, Sallie McFague calls for a new "theology of embodiment"[59] predicated on *all* bodies' legitimate need for the kind of space that can sustain their lives and on the realization that the earth is our home, our place, and not just a way station on the path to immortality.[60] She invites us to consider all bodies, and the earth itself, as "part of the body of God, not as separate from God (who dwells elsewhere), but as the visible reality of the invisible God."[61] Mujerista theologian Maria Clara Bingemer also stresses the "redeemed bodiliness" of women in Matt. 9:20–22, in which Jesus of Nazareth risked ritual impurity allowing the woman with the issue of blood to touch his garment and thus cured the woman of her hemorrhage.[62]

Another important spiritual practice from which women's bodies stand to benefit is the ongoing struggle to "break the structures of silencing and exclusion" that will unfortunately persist for the foreseeable future in many hierarchically based cultural and ecclesial institutions.[63] Feminist theologians and spiritual writers must continue to formulate alternative theological and spiritual questions and modes of inquiry that continue to expose the ongoing violence done to women's bodies by traditionally patriarchal forms of biblical interpretation, androcentric doctrinal formulation, and sexist practice.[64] Patricia Klindienst Joplin, whose revisioning of the woman taken in adultery (John 8:1–11) was cited earlier, notes, for example, that Jesus of Nazareth's obstruction of the ritual female exchange that reduced the woman to silent victim leads to "the *withdrawal* of false meaning from her flesh: no longer a sign/word, she comes into view as a speaker of words, a woman" (emphasis hers).[65] Here is the kind of biblical interpretation that provides a salutary alternative to traditional readings that would highlight the woman's sinfulness while ignoring her oppression. Joplin's interpretation also offers Christian women yet another example of Jesus' remarkable refusal to conform to patriarchal religious standards and practices in relation to women, thus encouraging them to struggle against those aspects of patriarchal domination that continue to haunt many Christian denominations.

As yet another form of spiritual praxis for the coming millennium, third world feminist theologian Aruna Gnanadason recounts Asian women's reclamation of

Shakti, divine feminine power, as the basis for their rediscovery of God.[66] By imaging divinity in terms of the female body as primal source of life, women everywhere stand to value anew their bodies and bodily processes that traditional religious visions have typically denigrated as ritually impure. Similarly, mujerista theologian Maria Clara Bingemer has reclaimed women's bodies by identifying them as a sacrament:

> God's compassion, as flowing from female and maternal organs, takes on itself the hurts and wounds of all the oppressed. A woman who does theology is called to bear witness to this God with her body, her actions, her life. . . . It is women who possess in their bodiliness the physical possibility of performing the divine eucharistic action. In the whole process of gestation, childbirth, protection, and nourishing of a new life, the sacrament of the Eucharist, the divine act, happens anew.[67]

In this way traditional religious symbols are reconceptualized in ways that affirm women's bodies as full participants in the order of life and as bearers of divinity in their roles as source and nurturer of life. Women are then encouraged to view themselves as fully participating agents in the act of sustaining creation rather than as passive recipients of patriarchal pronouncements concerning their "appropriate" status and range of personal and communal possibilities.

As will be readily apparent, full participation in the sustenance of creation requires activity over and above that traditionally associated with women's roles as mother, keeper of the hearth, and subsistence farmer. Ecofeminist voices, however, provide the crucial theoretical link by demonstrating how such traditional women's roles may function as models for a radically new commitment to *all* of creation in and through relational acts of sustenance and care for all forms of life. This too constitutes a form of spiritual praxis for the coming millennium that is concerned with a properly millennial topic: eschatology.[68]

Catherine Keller situates the current ecological crisis under "the theological topic of 'apocalyptic eschatology'"[69] because of her belief that "the ecological trauma apocalyptically encoded in the weather may clue us into our eschatological missions as theological practitioners—our missions not to a life *after* life but to life itself" (emphasis hers).[70] Obviously, such a commitment is not restricted to the theoretical discourse of theologians but also belongs, in concrete praxes of sustenance and care for creation, to all individuals. Women in particular can offer a valuable corrective, I believe, to a traditional Christian eschatological vision that focuses on the "final things"—the end of history, Christ's second coming, and the resurrection from the dead—to the exclusion of a this-worldly concern for the "mere" survival of the planet. It is particularly in women's capacities for *relational* forms of action that the necessity for their full participation becomes apparent, as women grasp the profound interconnectedness among all forms of life and understand that the sustenance of life requires the sustenance of the planet as a whole: "We humans are not the 'Lords of Creation.' Instead, we are the Earth's thought, the Earth's reflection of itself; one type of consciousness present on the planet."[71] It is this kind of attitude, and concrete acts flowing forth from this kind of attitude, that all new forms of feminist spirituality must actively promote if we are ultimately to survive at all.

In my estimation, all new forms of feminist spiritual praxis for the coming millennium must be committed to the eradication of patriarchal "dominion over spirit and flesh, orgy of unchecked self-expansion" into the bodies of women. Spiritual praxis for the year 2000 and beyond must be committed to the preservation and sustenance of all bodies—all forms of life, whose interdependence cannot allow us to think of them as existing separately from one another. I believe that the basis for such spiritual praxis is to be found in the ethical encounter in which I take an active responsibility for the "other" by the sheer fact of her, his, or its existence: "When we behold the sick body of the poor, and see the injustice they suffer, we see it as our own body. *There is no other. The other is myself.* We are part of one immense, pulsating body that has been evolving for billions of years—and is still evolving" (emphasis added)."[72] This radical commitment to the other, in and through concrete acts that sustain life and simultaneously relieve suffering, is embodied in the figure of the Bodhisattva, the Mahayana Buddhist saint whose compassion for the suffering of the world is expressed in her or his postponement of nirvana and commitment to the deliverance of all creation. This "embodiment of complete and unconditional compassion" is the iconic representation of new forms of feminist spiritual praxis for the coming millennium; she is the one whose merciful and compassionate action in the world rests in her knowledge that "there is no other. The other is myself."[73] If divinity can be said to manifest itself in this postmodern milieu as we approach the year 2000, it manifests itself most emphatically here.

NOTES

1. Jean Améry, *At the Mind's Limits: Contemplations by a Survivor on Auschwitz and Its Realities,* trans. Sidney Rosenfeld and Stella P. Rosenfeld (New York: Schocken, 1986), 21–40.

2. Ibid., 36.

3. Elisabeth Schüssler Fiorenza, *Discipleship of Equals: A Critical Feminist Ekklesialogy of Liberation* (New York: Crossroad, 1993), 204.

4. Ibid., 259.

5. There is also the question, which limitations of space forbid exploring here, whether the term *spirituality* necessarily requires a theological or religious backdrop for its functioning.

6. Mary Ann Hinsdale, "Ecology, Feminism, and Theology," in *Readings in Ecology and Feminist Theology,* ed. Mary Heather MacKinnon and Moni Mcintyre (Kansas City, Mo.: Sheed and Ward, 1995), 198.

7. See MacKinnon and Mcintyre, *Readings,* for many articles that discuss not only these distinctions but others as well.

8. See Betty Govinden, "No Time for Silence: Women, Church, and Liberation in Southern Africa," in *Feminist Theology from the Third World: A Reader,* ed. Ursula King (Maryknoll, N.Y.: SPCK/Orbis, 1994), 283–98. Govinden warns feminist theologians of all stripes against taking Western feminist theories as normative for all women's experience.

9. Sherry Ortner, "Is Female to Male as Nature Is to Culture?" in MacKinnon and Mcintyre, *Readings,* 36–55.

10. Ibid., 39, 40.

11. Ibid., 49.

12. Ortner offers an important qualification to the insight in quoting Lévi-Strauss:"Woman could never become just a sign and nothing more, since even in a man's world she is still a person, and since insofar as she is defined as a sign she must [still] be recognized as a generator of signs." Ortner, "Is Female to Male?" 44.

13. Ibid., 52.

14. Philippa Berry, introduction to *Shadow of Spirit: Postmodernism and Religion,* ed. Philippa Berry and Andrew Wernick (London: Routledge, 1992), 2. She defines "oculocentrism" as "a perspective which, as Michel Foucault pointed out, was based on a naive yet extremely dangerous equation between seeing and knowing." 2. She quotes Foucault's *Birth of the Clinic: An Archeology of Medical Perception,* trans. Alan Sheridan (New York: Random House, 1975), 89, where he writes of "the sovereignty of the gaze . . . the eye that knows and decides, the eye that governs." 7.

15. Anne Carr, "On Feminist Spirituality," in *Women's Spirituality: Resources for Christian Development,* ed. Joanne Wolski Conn (New York: Paulist, 1986), 51.

16. To cite but one brief example: Elisabeth Schüssler Fiorenza reports that "during the last visit of Pope John Paul II to the Netherlands Professor Catharina Halkes, the Roman Catholic "dean" of feminist theology in Europe, was forbidden to address the pontiff." *Discipleship,* 251.

17. Mark C. Taylor, "Reframing Postmodernisms," in Berry and Wernick, *Shadow of Spirit,* 19.

18. Geraldine Finn, "The Politics of Spirituality: The Spirituality of Politics," in Berry and Wernick, *Shadow of Spirit,* 117.

19. Molly Myerovitz Levine, "The Gendered Grammar of Ancient Mediterranean Hair," in *Off with Her Head! The Denial of Women's Identity in Myth, Religion, and Culture,* ed. Howard Eilberg-Schwartz and Wendy Doniger (Berkeley: University of California Press, 1995), 76–130. Thanks are due to Fr. Michael Slusser for bringing this book to my attention.

20. Levine, "Gendered Grammar," 85.

21. Ibid., 102.

22. Amy Richlm, "Making Up a Woman: The Face of Roman Gender," in Eilberg-Schwartz and Doniger, *Off with Her Head!* 185–213. Quoted text is on 185.

23. Ibid., 186.

24. Howard Eilberg-Schwartz, "The Nakedness of a Woman's Voice, the Pleasure in a Man's Mouth: An Oral History of Ancient Judaism," in Eilberg-Schwartz and Doniger, *Off with Her Head!* 166.

25. Ibid., 173.

26. See Elisabeth Schüssler Fiorenza, "Feminist Spirituality, Christian Identity, and Catholic Vision," in *Womanspirit Rising: A Feminist Reader in Religion,* ed. Carol P. Christ and Judith Plaskow (San Francisco: Harper, 1979), 136–48.

27. Ibid., 142.

28. Mary Rose D'Angelo, "Veils, Virgins, and the Tongues of Men and Angels: Women's Heads in Early Christianity," in Eilberg-Schwartz and Doniger, *Off with Her Head!* 133.

29. Maria Clara Bingemer, "Women in the Future of the Theology of Liberation," in King, *Feminist Theology,* 314.

30. Patricia Klindienst Joplin, "Intolerable Language: Jesus and the Woman Taken in Adultery," in Berry and Wernick, *Shadow of Spirit,* 235.

31. Rebecca S. Chopp and Mark Lewis Taylor, "Introduction: Crisis, Hope, and Contemporary Theology," in *Reconstructing Christian Theology,* ed. Rebecca S. Chopp and Mark Lewis Taylor (Minneapolis: Fortress, 1994), 1.

32. Susan Brooks Thistlethwaite, "Every Two Minutes: Battered Women and Feminist

Interpretation," in *Weaving the Visions: New Patterns in Feminist Spirituality*, ed. Judith Plaskow and Carol P. Christ (San Francisco: Harper, 1989), 305.

33. These Hebrew texts have also been used by Christian theologians to justify their traditional theological anthropological position on women's "inferiority."

34. Fiorenza, *Discipleship*, 204.

35. Ranjini Rebera, "Challenging Patriarchy," in King, *Feminist Theology*, 106–7.

36. Rebera also writes, "When society closes the door to economic survival in the workforce, then a woman's body and her sexuality become the only tools of trade left." "Challenging Patriarchy," 107.

37. Shamara Shantu Riley, "*Ecology* is a Sistah's Issue Too: The Politics of Emergent Afrocentric Ecowomanism," in MacKinnon and Mcintyre, *Readings*, 221.

38. Ursula King, "A Newly Emerging Spirituality," in King, *Feminist Theology*, 301.

39. Ivone Gebara, "Cosmic Theology: Ecofeminism and Panentheism," in MacKinnon and Mcintyre, *Readings*, 210.

40. Ibid.

41. Naomi P. F. Southard, "Recovery and Rediscovered Images: Spiritual Resources for Asian American Women," in King, *Feminist Theology*, 384–85.

42. Marjorie Hewitt Suchocki, "God, Sexism, and Transformation," in Chopp and Taylor, *Reconstructing Christian Theology*, 35–36.

43. The distinctions among "patriarchal systems," "androcentric discourses," and "sexist practices" is made by Elisabeth Schüssler Fiorenza in *Discipleship*, 258.

44. Rosemary Radford Ruether writes: "An ecological-feminist theology of nature must rethink the whole Western theological tradition of the hierarchical chain of being and chain of command. This theology must question the hierarchy of human over nonhuman nature as a relationship of ontological and moral value." "Toward an Ecological-Feminist Theology of Nature," in MacKinnon and Mcintyre, *Readings*, 89.

45. Ortner, "Is Female to Male?" 54.

46. Elisabeth Schüssler Fiorenza, "The Bible, the Global Context, and the Discipleship of Equals," in Chopp and Taylore, *Reconstructing Christian Theology*, 94.

47. Joann Wolski Conn, "Women's Spirituality: Restriction and Reconstruction," in Conn, *Women's Spirituality*, 11–12.

48. Berry, introduction, 4–5. Sandra Schneiders writes,

> It is only in our own day, as more and more spiritual seekers have turned to the spiritualities of the East, that we have come to look critically at our bodydenying, overly methodical, highly verbal and intellectual, muscular, vertical, conquering model of the spiritual life. Suddenly interior silence, passivity, body-centered prayer, patience with oneself, compassion for others, and intuition, all stereotypically feminine elements, are emerging as desirable aspects of the spirituality of everyone, men and women alike.

"The Effects of Women's Experience on Their Spirituality," in Conn, *Women's Spirituality*, 40.

49. Grace Jantzen, "Healing Our Brokenness: The Spirit and Creation," in MacKinnon and Mcintyre, *Readings*, 294.

50. Ibid., 295.

51. Finn, "Politics of Spirituality," 112.

52. Berry, introduction.

53. Finn, "Politics of Spirituality," 113.

54. Many patriarchal religious traditions, theistic and nontheistic alike, recognize that the world always exceeds the conceptual categories we apply to it. In theistic traditions that acknowledge this to be true, divinity by definition cannot be contained within such categories.

The mystical strands of both theistic and nontheistic traditions may be properly said to begin where such conceptual categories leave off, although such traditions insist that their authentically mystical subtraditions will remain rooted in scripture, liturgy, and sacrament—hence remaining within the boundaries of doctrinal acceptability.

55. Sharon Welch, "Ideology and Social Change," in Plaskow and Christ, *Weaving the Visions,* 337.

56. Ibid., 341. Here Welch quotes Sandra Harding. Yet, I must insist on the crucial importance of women's freedom to name their experience without patriarchal mediation.

57. Carol P. Christ, "Why Women Need the Goddess: Phenomenological, Psychological, and Political Reflections," in Fiorenza, *Womanspirit Rising,* 281. She notes that many Goddess rituals perform such celebratory acts.

58. Sandra M. Schneiders, *Beyond Patching: Faith and Feminism in the Catholic Church* (New York: Paulist, 1991), 87.

59. Sallie McFague, "Human Beings, Embodiment, and Our Home the Earth," in Chopp and Taylor, *Reconstructing Christian Theology,* 142. See Sallie McFague, *The Body of God: An Ecological Theology* (Minneapolis: Fortress, 1993).

60. McFague, "Human Beings," 143–46.

61. Ibid., 146.

62. Bingemer, "Women in the Future," 314–15.

63. Fiorenza, "The Bible," 89.

64. See Fiorenza's model of feminist biblical interpretation. "The Bible," 90–91.

65. Joplin, "Intolerable Language," 235.

66. Aruna Gnanadason, "Women and Spirituality in Asia," in King, *Feminist Theology,* 355. She defines Shakti as "power, force, the feminine energy, for she represents the primal creative principle underlying the cosmos. She is the energizing force of all divinity, of every being and every thing. The whole universe is the manifestation of Shakti, a Shakta or follower of Shakti-worship, regards her as the Supreme Reality" (351).

67. Bingemer, "Women in the Future," *Feminist Theology,* 316, 317.

68. See Catherine Keller, "Eschatology, Ecology, and a Green Ecumenacy," in Chopp and Lewis, *Reconstructing Christian Theology,* 326–45. She writes, "My guess is that as the 1990's count down to the millennium, the rhetoric of 'the end of the world' stimulates anxious ecological associations for most white, middle-class North Americans, male or female. Apocalypse is being colored green" (326).

69. Keller, "Eschatology," 327.

70. Ibid., 327–28.

71. Gebara, "Cosmic Theology," 211.

72. Ibid.

73. Southard, "Recovery and Rediscovered Images," 383. See also Berry, introduction, 5.

Part II

Apocalyptic Violence

Chapter Eight

Apocalyptic Violence and the Politics of Waco

Charles B. Strozier

The April 19, 1993, fire that destroyed the Mount Carmel compound of the Branch Davidians near Waco, Texas, has left vivid images in the minds of all Americans. Seventy-four people died in the flames, including twenty-one children under fourteen years of age. Two viable fetuses, one full term, the other at seven months, were born spontaneously to their dying mothers. The fire was so hot, said the coroner, Rodney Crow, that bodies melted together. Helicopters hovered over the flames as battle tanks surrounded the flimsy wooden structure. It was the quintessential realization of the Branch Davidian notion of end time destruction, as well as the dangers they faced from what they colorfully called "Babylon." After it was over, the FBI recovered as many of the bodies and body parts as they could. These incomplete remains were turned over to relatives, and most were buried, including Koresh in his childhood home of Tyler, Texas. The FBI also carted off some debris from the site as part of its investigation, touching off charges of cover-up that have persisted to this day. Much less noticed but far more important psychologically, however, the FBI barely two weeks after the fire bulldozed the remaining ashes of the compound and its victims into an anonymous mass grave that lends Mount Carmel echos of Auschwitz and Hiroshima. David Koresh, no doubt, was a religious fanatic, stockpiled guns, and took an expansive view of his rights to the females of all ages in his charge. The authorities had legitimate grounds for a search warrant that could easily have been served by walking up to the front door of the compound or handing it to Koresh's Harvard Law School–trained follower, Douglas Wayne Martin, who had a practice in Waco and knew and was respected by the legal authorities. Koresh himself, after all, had responded peacefully in 1987 to charges of attempted murder against George Roden. He turned himself in, went through a trial, and returned to Mount Carmel when he was acquitted. Instead, the BATF raided the compound on February 28 in a great splash of violence that they euphemistically called a "dynamic entry." Fifty-one days later, on April 19, the FBI and the BATF jointly mounted a final military assault against the compound, using a form of tear gas banned as genocidal in warfare earlier that same year by the Geneva Convention. It was all a very sad tale that raises serious ethical, legal, and political questions.[1]

Waco also touched personal issues of loss for me, and my research trip there in August of 1995 opened me to experience the death-immersed aspects of the site in

unexpectedly powerful ways. The idea of visiting Waco actually evolved in idiosyncratic ways. It began with a plan to take my seven-year-old daughter to visit the
grave of my wife's beloved brother in Oklahoma City. We then added to our travels
a north Florida cottage on the Gulf of Mexico, where I had scattered my father's
ashes thirty-five years before. It was a trip after the ghosts. Then came the April 19
bombing of the federal building in Oklahoma City, along with the March 22 Aum
Shinrikyo poison gas attack in the Japanese subways. As many others were, I was
shaken by these events. Given my interests,[2] I began reading widely about both and
soon found myself commenting on them often in the media and elsewhere.[3] In all the
stories of Oklahoma City, of course, and in the biography of Timothy McVeigh,
Waco kept popping up. The date of the bombing was clearly chosen to mark the
anniversary of the fire at Waco. And so, with an accommodating sigh, my wife
agreed to add the federal building in Oklahoma City and the Mount Carmel compound outside of Waco to the itinerary of our trip. There was no way I could avoid
visiting the sites of these larger tragedies in a trip in which I so manifestly sought personal transformation through touching the sacred ground that held the remains of
loved ones.

I came into Waco on a scorching day in mid-August during a spell that was hot
even for Texas. Waco is situated due south of Dallas and halfway to Houston,
somewhat off the main interstate but still a midsized town at the juncture of several important Texas roads. Waco has a number of small-scale industrial enter-
prises, but much of it has the feel of a town in economic decline. The poor,
heavily black and Hispanic western side stretched much farther into the heart of
the city than I would have expected. "For sale" signs were everywhere on houses of the rich, the middling, and the poor. The few local people I talked with in
Waco about Mount Carmel felt embarrassed by it and went out of their way to
stress that the community had been quite far out of town and was not of their
world and that furthermore they had not even heard about it before the standoff. I sensed that they were disassociating themselves because they felt deeply
wounded by all the sly talk of wackos in Waco during the standoff. The people
I spoke with may have been dissimulating a bit, however, about their separate-
ness from the intense millennial fervor of the Davidians. Waco in this century
was perhaps the perfect site for an apocalyptic community. It is, as one scholar
has put it, a town with a "peculiar religious atmosphere" and more than one
hundred denominations represented among its population of about one
hundred thousand.[4]

   Mount Carmel itself is about ten miles to the east of town in a decidedly rural setting, far from the usual round of fast-food restaurants and malls that seek to wipe out
the remaining regional differences in America. I actually got lost trying to find the
compound, which meant I drove twenty miles getting there rather than the actual ten.
I bought gas and got directions at the Alpha Omega Food Store, which had a mar-
quee announcing, "Jesus Is Coming Back" and asking pointedly, "Are You Ready?"
I felt the air changing. In other respects as well the culture of Texas imposed itself.
Men at the Alpha Omega drove up in pickups and swaggered about in cowboy hats,

along with boots and tight jeans, while young women pointedly fiddled with tousles of hair on top of their heads.

After circling back to Loop 340, I found FM 2491, which is how they label local roads in Texas, and took it east through the dusty, hot countryside. Fields were mostly brown, and the few trees that survive in this barren land don't grow very high. I followed the road to a split, where I turned left until I came to two large metal gates. Just beyond that blocked entrance to a property is the gravel Double EE Ranch Road, where I turned left again for a short distance. The haunting remains of Mount Carmel quickly appeared on the right, though it was all so empty and abandoned that at first I hesitated.

Then I spotted a middle-aged blond woman in a long blue denim dress touching up with paint what looked like a seal of some kind on the side of a small and very dilapidated old wooden building. I parked the car in a makeshift circular driveway and walked over to talk with her. She explained that she had to repaint the seal that marked her sect because vandals were forever effacing it. She worked with a small brush and carefully painted over the abusing scratches and marks. There was something faraway about her general appearance. Perhaps it was the monotone of her voice. She was clearly not southern (it turned out she was originally from Maine). Her leathery skin had become quite tanned from all her time in the sun, which bore down on us as it does most days in Texas. When she finished she stepped off her ladder and introduced herself as Amo Bishop Roden, the wife (actually common-law wife, I learned later) of George Roden. She met my wife and daughter and welcomed us to "the site of the most persecuted church in the world."[5]

Roden offered to show us around the compound, which I soon figured out from a discrete sign cost five dollars and seemed to be her only source of support. But first she suggested we visit the "muscum," a grand name for the few sad photographs and exhibits hung inside a small, dilapidated wooden building. Mixed in with the relics from the compound were various Seventh Day Adventist tracts and short exhortations about end time matters. Two sets of photocopies of randomly selected documents relating to the standoff, the fire, and the trial were hung on string stretched across two beams. I found it all evocative but enormously depressing. These people did not need to die. Labeled a cult and ostracized for their bizarre beliefs, the Branch Davidians had been victimized in significant ways.

During our extended walk through the site, I was continually struck with how raw it still was. Burned out toys lay on the ground. Two buses destroyed in the fire sat next to where the compound had been, weeds growing up around the wheels. The remaining concrete slab that was the foundation for the buildings allowed one to conjure up images of the life it had supported. It was a rough place. The men slept separately from the women and children. The only running water inside was in the kitchen. There was no basement and no air conditioning. The men had rigged up a privy and a shower outside underneath a tree, but the women and children used chamber pots and took sponge baths. Waste water was carried to an old septic tank. Koresh had begun construction of a swimming pool before the raid, and at the time of our visit it was demolished and partly filled with rancid water. It was cold in the winter and unbearably hot in the summer. It was like camping indoors, as one member put it.[6]

Koresh and his followers were the direct descendants of William Miller from the 1840s. Part of the revivalist and evangelical upsurge after 1820, Miller had some fifty thousand devoted followers in the "burned out" region of upstate New York and hundreds of thousands of others more loosely associated with him in his mission of Adventism, or "the soon coming of Christ." Miller's apocalyptic movement became increasingly intense after he foolishly put a date on the return of Jesus. When the first date came and went, the movement remained together because Miller was able to convince himself and his followers that his end-time arithmetic had been flawed. Against his better judgment, Miller then endorsed a second date of October 22, 1844. As the (perhaps apocryphal) story goes, thousands clambered to the mountain tops of upstate New York in white "ascension robes" awaiting what came to be called the "Great Disappointment," which punctured an irreversible hole in the hot-air balloon of Millerism.[7]

And yet, Millerism hardly disappeared from the American religious scene. After the Great Disappointment William Miller himself went into a deep depression and died in 1849, and most of his followers drifted off to other sects and messages. A small coterie of devoted followers, however, remained true to the cause. One tiny group of Millerites in New Hampshire, led by Ellen G. White, was especially determined to figure out the biblical mistakes that had been made in the Great Disappointment. They returned to the text of Revelation, pondering over their calculations throughout the next two decades. Essentially, they worked out a new theology for Adventism, and in one of the more remarkable offshoots of the apocalyptic Civil War, they founded the new religion of Seventh Day Adventism in 1863. It was based on several tenets from the Old Testament (including the Saturday sabbath) and many dietary restrictions, including vegetarianism and a ban on alcohol and caffeine. But its heart lay in a revised millennialism. White and her group argued that in 1844 Christ had entered the inner room of the heavenly Temple in preparation for a return (as opposed to the actual Parousia, as Miller had argued). This interpretation put the church in a state of continual anticipation without having to name a date. It did mean, however, that in their view the hour of judgment was at hand. They also argued that the SDA had special knowledge of Christ's return, which was communicated in an unfolding revelation to the prophets of the church. It was their obligation to keep entirely separate from the false religious system of the evil world of Babylon. To them and them alone came the "Spirit of prophecy" or the "present truth" or "new light," which is progressively revealed.[8]

Seventh Day Adventism in the twentieth century, after Ellen White's death in 1915, has often fragmented into apocalyptic groups around charismatic figures claiming prophetic powers. In this regard, Koresh was the direct heir of Victor Houteff, who first emerged in California in the late 1920s. After persecution by the local SDA churches, he traveled to Texas with his devoted followers. In 1934 he set up the Mount Carmel compound outside of Waco (not the later site) and in 1942 named it the Davidian Seventh Day Adventist Association. The community lived a spartan religious life, entirely focused on their faith. None of the faithful expected Houteff to die, and when his health began to fail, a crisis gripped the community. At his death in 1955, his wife, Florence, claimed to be his rightful successor. Another group clustered around Ben Roden, who named his newly reconstituted community The Branch and moved to a new and now-familiar site in 1957. Florence Houteff heightened the apocalyptic intensity of her followers by proclaiming that God would return on April 22, 1959. Hundreds gathered in Waco for what became another great SDA disappointment. After that she fled to California with twenty thousand dollars of church funds. Ben Roden and his wife, Lois, then expanded their movement from Texas to include followers in Israel and Australia. When Ben Roden died in 1977, Lois, then a wiry woman in her 60s, continued his ministry. It was to the Waco base in 1981 that Vernon Howell arrived, "just a bonehead coming to see what was going on," he said later.[9]

Howell, who later became known as David Koresh, was born the illegitimate child of fourteen-year-old Bonnie Clark in 1959. The next year Bonnie married but soon divorced a man who beat young Vernon. By the time he was two, Vernon Howell was so hyperactive that Bonnie was forced to leave him with her parents in Houston for three years. Her father was apparently an alcoholic. Meanwhile, Bonnie got her life back on track in Dallas, started a small business doing construction cleanup in Dallas and Tyler, and remarried. When Howell was five he came to live with his mother and new stepfather, Roy Halderman. It was a sour working-class family who knew little but hard labor. Vernon's half brother, the only son of Bonnie and Roy, ended up in prison for burglary and drug abuse. Halderman was cold and unfeeling and spanked Vernon so hard that "he made me fly like a kite." Howell detested Halderman and always spoke of him disparagingly (including making up ugly stories about his past). He also said his mother had been a prostitute (which she vigorously denies), though his feelings for her were complex and nuanced, full of deep affection and longing, besides the seething resentments.[10]

Out of this turmoil and violence during his early years, Howell emerged deeply scarred. He spoke with something of a stutter. He failed so many early grades that he was dubbed "Mr. Retardo." He only learned to read and write at all when placed in a special education class; he never could spell well. But he had a passion for the poetic, the visual, and the musical. Religion brought it all together and became Howell's main form of self-expression. Bonnie had been raised a Seventh Day Adventist but was uncertain of her faith and only fitfully attended church. Still, she, and especially Vernon's grandmother, took him occasionally to services. That encounter with the SDA church, however limited, opened him up to the Bible with all its poetic flights and rich stories. Vernon also became fascinated with TV and radio evangelists and seems to have taken in the rock and roll preaching style of the evangelical South. He especially warmed to the image of flamboyant ministers spouting passages from the Bible. Like them, Howell took to memorizing large sections of text. By the time he was twelve, he had greatly impressed his family and friends with his religious precocity.[11] Such a display of learning was, of course, consistent with his culture but surprising for a boy with an apparent learning disability.

Besides God, Vernon Howell was drawn to guns. Guns defined an important part of Howell's life, and he had a deep knowledge of them.[12] He lived off weapons psychologically. Guns seemed to protect the deeply vulnerable core of Koresh's self that was based in his childhood traumas. In his early years he had five different principal caretakers, none of whom was reliable, three homes, and a mother who abandoned him at two, only to reappear magically again when he was five years old. A gun at least was a predictable source of power. The world was uncertain and dangerous. Without constant vigilance, he risked shaking the ground of his being. Later, at Mount Carmel, he needed to prepare for that imminent assault before it arrived. One cannot say he wanted to be attacked, though he was ready to fight back when attacked on February 28, killing four BATF special agents and wounding six more. In general, he eagerly sought to cooperate (within reason) with the authorities. But he was wary of the outside and all that lay beyond his completely controllable world of the compound. He needed to protect himself against all those dangers, which were both real and imagined. It was the stance of a brittle self that anticipates enemies. His arsenal of weapons, it seems, shored him up. Furthermore, those guns, especially his modified AR-15s, themselves fed his deep suspiciousness about the world. Their visual and concrete presence objectified the dangers. They embodied the violence that he prepared to fend off.

David Koresh's grandiose ideas about his own role in the end time process were an extension of the false security Vernon Howell gained from guns against a crumbling self. There was no question that he saw himself as a prophet in the SDA tradition of William Miller and Ellen White that became, in the twentieth-century hands of Victor Houteff and Lois Roden, Branch Davidian notions of the unfolding revelation of God. The question is how far Koresh went beyond that in radicalizing the millennialism of the Davidians into an apocalyptic theology of the seven seals, as he called it.[13] He was by no means consistent. James D. Tabor and Eugene V. Gallagher argue for the reasonableness of Koresh's claims. They point out he clearly saw himself "annointed" as a prophet, which is the literal meaning of the Greek *christos* or the Hebrew *messiah*. The Hebrew prophets, however, told of a specific or ideal prophet, a true "Messiah," who was to come and rule over earth and fulfill a number of specific prophesies. There is no question about Koresh's beliefs that that was Jesus Christ and that he was something quite different. On the other hand, Tabor and Gallagher allow that Koresh undoubtedly saw himself as the Lamb who opens the mysterious book sealed with the seven seals (Rev. 5:5–9), as well as the rider on the white horse.[14] That's already a bit much. And there's more. Vernon Howell, of course, changed his name to reflect his identification with the Persian king Cyrus ("Koresh" in Hebrew) and with David, whose kingdom he said he was recreating. As J. Phillip Arnold has pointed out, besides being the Lamb of Revelation 5, he also identified with the angel who holds the seven seals and then later fills a vessel with fire and throws it on the earth (8:3–5). He signed two of his last letters "Yahweh Koresh." And in one radio interview he identified with Jesus talking with the woman at the well (John 4:5–38).[15]

There was, in other words, a good deal of psychological looseness in the way Koresh played with biblical images that somehow reflected himself. In the process he became exalted and cosmic in his apocalyptic role, while stopping just short of actual madness. But he pushed up against the line. During the standoff Koresh launched into one of his endless monologues with an FBI agent about the Merkabah and how he "went up" with "these people" from Mount Zion. It was a typically Koreshan blend of SDA and Branch Davidian tradition shaped in the crucible of his own apocalyptic. Koresh blended images from Ellen White of innumerable worlds and from Lois Roden of heavenly flying saucers with an event he believed had occurred in his personal life. He thus felt he had ascended into heaven on a chariot, or Merkabah, in 1985 from Mount Zion during his visit to Israel. That story was, in turn, part of his general belief in UFOs and his conviction that what abductees report seeing is in fact concrete heavenly beings. God for Koresh was flesh. You can touch him. In fact, he had seen and touched him on that trip on the Merkabah in 1985.[16]

Koresh's theology, it might be said, allowed for a special orientation to the Divine. The SDA thus expects prophets to emerge continually. He differed from other prophets, however, in adding to that status an apocalyptic dimension. He knew where to draw the line; that is, he stopped short of claiming to be Jesus. As a real historical figure whom Christians also believe was *the* Messiah, Jesus was clearly a figure from another time and place. A claim to be a returned Jesus would have likely stretched the credibility of even gullible followers and certainly would have led to easy dismissal by any outside observers. But his claims to some kind of divinity, especially during the standoff, expressed his extraordinary grandiosity. Koresh seemed to find a comfortable mystical place for himself in the end time universe. As the Lamb who opens the seals and the rider on the horse, for example, he located himself in the appropriately dense texts in Revelation, which is dear to all end timers. Tradition has always made the rider on the horse to be Jesus, though that is not clear in the text, which leaves it open to interpretation. And that rider, freed when the first seal is opened, marches across the end time with a special mission, to reappear at the climax of the marriage of the Lamb, his eyes aflame, wearing a crown of thorns and clothed in a vesture "dipped in blood," with a suggestive sword sticking out of his mouth, with which he will "smite the nations" and rule with a "rod of iron," and on his thigh his name is written in bold letters, "King of Kings, and Lord of Lords" (Rev. 19:11–16).

The furthest reach of Koresh's dreams of omniscience, however, was with the females in the compound. By his "New Light doctrine," which he declared in 1989, Koresh claimed that in his role as a messiah he was the perfect mate for all female adherents. He would create a new lineage of God's children from his seed. His "spiritual wives" were to join him directly in his millennial project. The other Davidian men would find their spiritual mates in heaven, when they would also become purified and carry on God's annointed task of redeeming humanity. In the meanwhile, the other men were to be celibate. This grand experiment, which uniquely combined polygamy, even profligacy, with celibacy,[17] was all carried out with great thoroughness and the willing consent of adult participants; the consent of the underage girls who became Koresh's spiritual wives, though readily given, remains legally and ethically problematic. Koresh took most of the young teenage girls in his charge as his wives and appropriated as well many of the adult married females in the compound. By the time of the siege four years later he had twelve children by these females in a process that was still incomplete but moving toward totalistic resolution. The "New Light doctrine" was a major turning point in the radicalization of Koresh's apocalyptic project. It transformed the emotional fabric of life at Mount Carmel, vastly enhancing his powers over all members of the community, as well as deepening their dependence on him. At the same time, the new sexual arrangements began an inexorable process that led to the fall of David Koresh. It was the last straw for many members and turned some, especially Marc Brealt, into noisy opponents. Brealt made it a personal mission to arouse the outside world to the dangers of "cult" life inside Mount Carmel. He largely succeeded in his efforts. After 1989 and the New Light, a major confrontation of some kind with the authorities was almost inevitable.[18]

Koresh's extraordinary experiments with sex surely reflected his own need to ward off a fragmenting self after the traumas of his childhood.[19] But two other aspects of the sexual life of the Branch Davidians (or "Koreshans" as they preferred to be called) are worth noting. One is the general truth that radical religious experiments seem to require as well experiments with food and sex. The creation of monotheism among the Jews went along with strict dietary guidelines. Christians imposed celibacy on the priesthood. In such renunciation can lie transformative power. No one, for example, struggled more than Gandhi with *bramcharya* and vegetarianism. As an adolescent he once ate some lamb and heard the bleating in his stomach all night long. For years he refused to drink milk as part of a vow he had made to his mother before going to England, but then he had to admit to his wife, Putali Ba, in 1919 when he was dying of dysentery that his mother had meant cow's milk, not goat's milk. His flexibility with definitions saved his life.[20] Similarly, in his struggles with celibacy Gandhi kept failing but never gave up the idea of renouncing his sexuality. Only at age thirty-five, after having four children, did he finally succeed. For whatever psychological and spiritual reasons, that *bramcharya* vow gave him the strength to focus his tremendous energies and become the leader he was meant to be. This is not to say a search for one's truth legitimates a violation of another's body, as with Koresh and his young teenage wives. There are countless other such examples of abusive situations in communal and cult groups. There was good reason for the authorities to believe Koresh had gotten out of control by the early 1990s and was breaking the law with impunity.[21] At the same time and from a different perspective, it may have been that the intensity of Koresh's endism required radical experimentation with sexuality to keep it alive.

Second, the changes that New Light brought to the community vastly enhanced the charismatic power of Koresh and his hold over his followers. He held them in a kind of psychological bondage (which some resisted and left the compound). From the expansion of his sexual control, Koresh gained enormous power, which fed his own claims to grasp the ways of God. For his followers, in turn, identification with a charismatic leader brought its own kind of exaltation. After Koresh took over the 940-odd acres of barren East Texas land as sole leader in 1987, he and his followers felt the end was at hand and that God had annointed the Mount Carmel community with the responsibility of bringing on the Kingdom of God with Koresh as its appointed messiah. This was the remnant, the purified church, made lean and mean through persecution, ready to welcome the end. Koresh felt no need to evangelize vast audiences. All he wanted was his devoted community of followers to take on Babylon. Indeed, he was so isolated that few in Waco had knowledge of the religious community until a series of exposé articles about Koresh's sexual appetites appeared in the local paper the day before the February 28 raid.

The Mount Carmel world, in other words, became increasingly totalistic after 1989.[22] This desolate piece of Texas turned into an apocalyptic hothouse. Koresh, in turn, adapted his theology to meet these new millennial demands. Besides expanding the realm of his own divinity, he began arguing that perhaps the end would come in America rather than Israel as he had been preaching, and that tribulation would begin with an attack on Mount Carmel. His stockpiling of guns has been widely noted, but he also gathered in large amounts of dried food, MREs, and propane gas. He was preparing for an attack that he didn't exactly welcome but that he did not entirely resist. In 1992 Koresh renamed Mount Carmel "Ranch Apocalypse."[23]

Koresh and his followers believed that society had become corrupt and violent as they moved toward holiness, which in turn prompted (in their eyes) the continual harassment and persecution they suffered. But they also believed such suffering through persecution focuses the selves of those predisposed to encounter the world with a high degree of suspicion, confirming their sense of absolute purity. Koresh was an intense end timer and the community was highly agitated with an increasingly paranoid bent that found its tragically complicit partners in first local and then national police authorities. In other words, the Branch Davidians armed themselves to the teeth and prepared for what they felt was to be an armed attack, based as much on biblical text as political currents, while officials spied on them and planned raids and eventually set the place ablaze. Koresh's politics were not much to speak of, though he was personally a generous man and certainly the community was ethnically and racially mixed: a third were black, and an Israeli Jew joined after 1985. Culturally, Koresh was southern and of Texas, forever talking about how he was "fixin'" to do this or that. But he carried no fervent right-wing ideas in his head about evil government, or black helicopters, or conniving Jews, all key images from the Bible of the right-wing *Turner Diaries*.[24] In this he was not at all like the Christian Identity groups in the West; he was completely opposed to their theology (which argues, among other things, that Jews are the children of Satan). In fact, it is fair to say David Koresh had no personal or ideological connection with the right wing. It was his intense apocalypticism, his persecution, and his religious martyrdom in the fire that made him so potent an image for others.

Two symbols in this regard stand out. One is the makeshift "loud cry" museum at the site, funded by and dedicated to Lyndon Laroche, a wily right winger if there ever was one. But perhaps the most potent symbol is the stone marker laid on the second anniversary of the fire at the edge of the ruins by the Northeast Texas Regional Militia of Texarkana. Engraved in the stone are the names of the victims, along with the legend: "On February 18, 1993 a church and its members known as Branch Davidians came under attack by ATF and FBI agents. For 51 days the Davidians and their leader, David Koresh, stood proudly. On April 19, 1993 the

Davidians and their church were burned to the ground. 82 people perished during the siege. 18 were children 10 years old or younger."[25] The monument itself is next to a grove of trees that were planted to honor the victims in the general area where the ashes of the compound and its charred remains of believers were bulldozed. It was at this second annual ceremony of the fire, held on April 19, 1995, that the full transformation of Waco occurred. For at the very hour of the ceremony, as the Texas militia groups were giving speeches and others were bemoaning the tragedy of Waco, Timothy McVeigh allegedly parked his truck loaded with a huge bomb in front of the Murrah Federal Building and blew it up in direct retaliation for the government's assault on Waco two years earlier.[26]

The biography of Timothy McVeigh—the alleged Oklahoma City bomber—epitomizes this otherwise baffling overlap of right-wing violence and apocalyptic Christianity. The most remarkable thing about Timothy McVeigh's childhood is how unremarkable it was.[27] His mostly white community in upstate New York was a small-town haven from the tensions of urban America. People raised families, went to church, ate at local fast-food restaurants, and lived out their lives. Timothy's father, Bill, worked for thirty years as a night watchman and bowled in his free time. The children did well in school and seemed adjusted. There was nothing apparent about Timothy's life that suggested later violence. He was noticeably shy but did okay in school, where he also ran track. He was close to his sisters and even somewhat social. To attract friends, he once built a skateboarding ramp in the driveway and invited people over. Another time he created a haunted house in his basement and charged an admission price for all comers. He impressed at least one friend as a budding entrepreneur.

And yet, the divorce of his parents seemed to sow the seeds of trauma in ten-year-old Timothy. The divorce came without warning. Bill McVeigh was a stunningly boring man, who worked hard but had no real interests beyond bowling and bingo at the local Catholic church he attended. His wife, Mickey, had begun to roam for some years, going out at night on her own to bars and restaurants. It was the 1970s, an era of free sexuality and open marriage. Finally, it seems, she just got fed up with Bill. One day in 1978, without apparent warning or explanation to her husband or children, Mickey gathered up her four-year-old child, Jennifer, and just left (though a year or so later Jennifer joined the other children). Once Mickey showed up in a suit to visit for a few minutes, but otherwise she simply disappeared, as she chose, into the Florida landscape.

On the surface, things remained the same, as if nothing had happened. That may well have been how everyone in the family coped with the trauma of Mickey's departure. The father kept at his job and the routine of his life. Patty, two years older than Tim, assumed responsibility for discipline and organizing the household. And Tim always smiled and was polite. Even next-door neighbors commented on his apparent calm. He never showed anyone what was inside. And, most remarkably, he never, ever, talked about his mother. No one from the small world of Pendleton, New York, can remember his ever saying one word about his mother. It was completely shut up inside, where it festered.

By the time Timothy was in high school, the trauma within had begun to find expression in dark alternative visions. He developed his famous fascination with guns and became an avowed survivalist. He stockpiled food and camping equipment. He feared two things: nuclear attack and the Communists taking over the world. Those in whom he confided these thoughts connected them immediately to the pain of his absent mother and wondered whether he hadn't gone "over the deep end." Timothy was exceedingly bright, scoring high enough on the Regent's standardized tests to win a scholarship to college, but he was in general lackadaisical about his studies and got bad grades. He focused only on what interested him.

After school McVeigh drifted through several jobs. Once he worked as a guard on an armored car but was reprimanded when he showed up one day with cartridge belts strung across his chest like Pancho Villa. He owned and proudly displayed an AR-15 semiautomatic rifle, various handguns, and a semiautomatic Desert Eagle so large it took both his hands to hold it. At one point he even bought, with a friend, ten acres of remote woodland near Buffalo that he intended to turn into a survivalist bunker. The land also served as a shooting ground, where he could fire off his weapons for hours without fear of intrusion, literally shaking the ground with some of the explosions.

The army seemed the logical institution for directing all this violence. And when McVeigh joined in 1989, he took to it at first like a duck to water. He loved the order and the discipline, the external structure that kept his inner turmoil from bubbling over. His pants were always the best pressed, his bed the neatest. He excelled at the physical demands of training. When others finished their fifty push-ups, McVeigh kept at them for hours. In no time he made sergeant and seemed destined for a modestly successful career in the army (though his blatant racism was to haunt him in what is after all the most progressive institution in American society in this regard). There were, however, signs of the lurking dangers. He rented a nearby locker, which he kept stocked with MREs and fresh water and weapons as a kind of backup bunker. While his peers went off to bars and brothels, he stayed in the barracks and read his survivalist literature all alone. He never dated, before, during, or after his time in the army. He was not gay, just so painfully shy and cut off that the world of people terrified him. His only human contact was with his sister, Jennifer, whom he adored, wrote often, called, and was overheard telling how much he loved her. She was his emotional lifeline.

McVeigh's dream was to serve in the Special Forces, though just before he was to take the grueling exam, the Gulf War came along and he was sent to the Middle East. This peculiar war, which was so fast and bloody and violent but virtually without American casualties, directly involved McVeigh as it did few other soldiers. He was at the front with the tanks and fighting vehicles that led the assault of the VII Corps against Iraq. Countless thousands of enemy soldiers had been killed in the six weeks of bombing. But many more remained in desert trenches, hoping to stave off the Allied attack. It proved to be futile. Huge snow plows were attached to the front of the M1A1 tanks. Their task was to bury the Iraqis alive. Following close behind were the Bradley fighting vehicles to shoot at any soldiers who fled on foot from the trenches to avoid the sarcophagus of their trenches. McVeigh was the prime gunner in one of those Bradleys. McVeigh, in other words, directly touched death in the war. He took a bead on running soldiers, pulled his trigger, and watched blood run. McVeigh once boasted of blowing off an Iraqi's head with his cannon at eleven hundred meters.[28] His practice on his own firing range near Buffalo clearly stood him in good stead for the war, but nothing could prepare him for the emotional cost of actually killing any number of other human beings. It seemed to leave him numb, even further cut off from empathy for others.

Some specifics of the fighting are also relevant in the deadening of McVeigh's feelings. The battle was so hopelessly one-sided that it lent to the fighting the character of a massacre. The Iraqis were completely outgunned. Lying in wait in their trenches, they had only light arms and relatively small explosives. The few T-55 tanks they owned were old Russian castoffs that spewed smoke and lumbered across the desert at literally half the speed of the M1A1 tanks. In the second night of the war, Americans driving their huge tanks realized the battle was just a target range and often shot at each other with their lighter guns to see who could get to kill the Iraqi T-55s frantically trying to escape. The soldiers on the front lines called it fright night.[29] There was nothing noble in the killings of McVeigh. By the time the Iraqi soldiers were flushed from their trenches, they posed absolutely no threat to gunners like McVeigh firing from their Bradleys. It was, in fact, murder. When it was cut short after one hundred hours, McVeigh was enraged. He wanted the battle to last, the massacre to continue. He took out his camera and stalked the desert, taking photographs of dead Iraqis.

He was never the same. McVeigh returned shattered to his base at Fort Riley, Kansas. He tried for the Special Forces and washed out for psychological reasons, probably because of his intense racism. He then left the army but kept with him its trappings. He continued to wear fatigues, for example, and tote weapons as though preparing for battle. He also wrote some letters, especially one in February of 1992 to a local paper in upstate New York, in a uniquely disjointed style, full of halting phrases that reflect the trauma that makes him practically schizoid. That letter is cold, aloof, remote, flat. McVeigh's world is one of enemies and conspiracies, where "crime is out of control" and "criminals have no fear of punishment." Everything is becoming "cataclysmic." Politicians are a joke and only making things worse. Racism is destroying us. The lives of the poor have no value. Just because you don't wear a tie to work, he asks rhetorically, does that mean you are a lesser human being and don't deserve to live? What is going to wake people up? Do we need a civil war? And in a grand climax, he ends: "Do we have to shed blood to reform the current system? I hope it doesn't come to that! But it might."[30]

The ideological fragments seen in this letter are the inchoate ideas of much of right-wing politics in America: The system isn't working. Government is the enemy and politicians its appointed guardians of tyranny. The signs of decay are evident in rising crime and racism and the loss of dignity for working people. No one sees how it all works together, the "big picture," as McVeigh puts it in the letter. Only those with such vision can make the necessary connections. Things are so rotten that it may take civil war and bloodshed to change things. At this point of calling for outright rebellion, McVeigh stops short. He evokes such violence as possibly necessary, without actually embracing it. He has clearly pushed up against a line and is flirting both psychologically and politically with the idea of mass violence as the only means of redemption. But something was still missing from McVeigh's ideological system that could unite his political paranoia and personal trauma into a coherent set of ideas to guide his effective action.

That came with Waco. As with many others on the Right,[31] McVeigh was transfixed immediately by the image of BATF SWAT teams ("jack booted government thugs," as they are often called in the right-wing press) descending on the compound, killing some Branch Davidians *and* themselves taking casualties. That was one of the more appealing aspects of the standoff for people like McVeigh. When attacked, Koresh fought back with his own AR-15s. No one could have attempted more diligently to escape government tyranny than the Branch Davidians, nor could have been more vigorously persecuted by out-of-control officials. Sometime during the standoff, McVeigh even made his own pilgrimage to Waco to take in on his own the extraordinary sight of the compound surrounded by barbed wire, tanks, hundreds of reporters and armed troops, and the absurd noise of intentionally offensive music blaring out of speakers directed at the buildings. It was a scene of colossal apocalyptic chic that soon became genuine tragedy. No one was more transfixed by those events than Timothy McVeigh.

April 19 soon haunted his imagination.[32] After that, McVeigh's life was one of intense focus that ended with the bombing of the federal building in Oklahoma City. He hooked up with at least one old army buddy who was equally at odds with the system. It seems as though he carried out a number of robberies to support himself over the next two years. He was now completely outside the system, planning its actual destruction. He was a warrior on the move, alone, braving the vast odds. He traveled through the West in dingy motels, stockpiled materials for the bomb, and then drove everywhere from Michigan to Florida to Arizona and back again, possibly in pursuit of additional sites to destroy. The clear suggestion from what we know of McVeigh is of a man who had become a revolutionary. There were no longer any doubts or confusions. He had to take charge. He had to kill and destroy in order to redeem. To an extraordinary degree, it would seem that he saw himself as the lonely hero of *The Turner Diaries*, who plots revolution and plays a key role in ushering in the "new age" at the year 2000 by blowing up the FBI building with a manure bomb just like that used in Oklahoma City.

The key point to note in this transformation of Timothy McVeigh, however, is how grand and ultimate his objectives became after Waco. We have become familiar and perhaps a little numb now with terrorists who demand money, or the release of their leaders, or the return of their land. The level of violence associated with such objectives is usually relatively minimal and proportional. This is not to defend terrorism, which I deplore, but merely to note its contained quality. McVeigh, on the other hand, clearly sought to begin a process that would end in taking out the federal government. The April 19 bombing was the beginning assault. It was punishment for Waco (and perhaps Ruby Ridge) and evoked the founders, but it was only the beginning. There would be innocent death and suffering in the violence, but the end result would be rebirth, redemption, hope, freedom, indeed a New Age (capitalized as it is in *The Turner Diaries*). The apocalyptic had completely imposed itself on the mind of Timothy McVeigh.

NOTES

1. The best account of Waco is Dick J. Reavis, *The Ashes of Waco: An Investigation* (New York: Simon and Schuster, 1995), 167–69, 277. Note also James D. Tabor and Eugene V. Gallagher, *Why Waco: Cults and the Battle for Religious Freedom in America* (Berkeley: University of California Press, 1995); Stuart A. Wright, ed., *Armageddon in Waco: Critical Perspectives on the Branch Davidian Conflict* (Chicago: University of Chicago Press, 1995). A more diverse (and chaotic) collection is James R. Lewis, ed., *From the Ashes: Making Sense of Waco* (Lanham, Md.: Rowman and Littlefield, 1994). I also benefited from a personal conversation with Stuart Wright, October 2, 1995.

2. Charles B. Strozier, *Apocalypse: On the Psychology of Fundamentalism in America* (Boston: Beacon Press, 1994).

3. Charles B. Strozier, "The New Violence," *Journal of Psychohistory* 23 (1995): 191–201. Note also two edited books: Charles B. Strozier and Michael Flynn, eds., *Genocide, War, and Human Survival* (Lanham, Md.: Rowman and Littlefield, 1996); Charles B. Strozier and Michael Flynn, eds., *Trauma, Broken Connections, and the Self* (Lanham, Md.: Rowman and Littlefield, 1996).

4. Robert S. Fogerty, "An Age of Wisdom, An Age of Foolishness: The Davidians, Some Forerunners, and Our Age," in *Armageddon in Waco*, ed. Stuart A. Wright (Chicago: University of Chicago Press, 1995), 17.

5. Peter J. Boyer, in his account of the compound, "Children of Waco," *New Yorker*, May 15, 1995, 38, was also struck by the haunting presence of Amo Roden.

6. Reavis, *The Ashes of Waco*, 48–49.

7. Ronald L. Numbers and Jonathan M. Butler, eds., *The Disappointed: Millerism and Millenarianism in the Nineteenth Century* (Bloomington: Indiana University Press, 1987). Note also Malcolm Bull and Keith Lockhard, *Seeking a Sanctuary: Seventh-Day Adventism and the American Dream* (New York: Harper and Row, 1989); and Paul Boyer, *When Time Shall Be No More: Prophetic Belief in Modern American Culture* (Cambridge, Mass.: Belknap Press of Harvard University Press, 1992), 80–86.

8. Tabor and Gallagher, *Why Waco*, 47–49.

9. Reavis, *The Ashes of Waco*, 58–65; David G. Bromley and Edward D. Silver, "The Davidian Tradition," in Wright, *Armageddon in Waco*, 49–50.

10. Reavis, *The Ashes of Waco*, 22–25.

11. Ibid., 26–27.

12. Once he detected a spy sent to Mount Carmel who feigned to be a novice about guns but (in Koresh's words) "brought over [to the compound] this Eagle series, you know, .38, actually .45, you know, .38 upper on a basically a .45 caliber lower. . . . It had a special slide on it, it had a special compensator and everything. Anyway, you know, the guy's, the guy's telling me . . . that he really doesn't know that much about guns, and, and the very first thing he does is he brings over this weapon that, you know, no novice has." See Reavis, *The Ashes of Waco*, 68.

13. This useful distinction between millennialism and apocalypticism is made by Bill Pitts, "The Davidian Tradition," in Lewis, *From the Ashes*, 36–37.

14. Tabor and Gallagher, *Why Waco*, 205.

15. J. Phillip Arnold, "The Davidian Dilemma," in Lewis, *From the Ashes,* 29.

16. Reavis, *The Ashes of Waco,* 94–96; James Tabor, personal communication, September 30, 1995.

17. This rather unique combination of polygamy and celibacy evokes three great nineteenth-century counterparts: the Shakers, the Mormons, and the Oneida Community. Michael Barkun, personal communication, November 15, 1995.

18. Tabor and Gallagher, *Why Waco,* 68–74; Bromley and Silver, "The Davidian Tradition," in Wright, *Armageddon in Waco,* 59–60; Reavis, *The Ashes of Waco,* 11–119.

19. For a fuller explanation of this relationship between fragmentation and sexualization, see Heinz Kohut, *The Analysis of the Self: A Systematic Approach to the Psychoanalytic Treatment of Narcissistic Personality Disorders* (New York: International Universities Press, 1971).

20. Erik Erikson, *Gandhi's Truth: On the Origins of Nonviolence* (New York: Norton, 1969).

21. Still, child abuse was not within the jurisdiction of either the FBI or the BATF, Janet Reno's crocodile tears notwithstanding.

22. Erik Erikson, *Young Man Luther: A Study in Psychoanalysis and History* (New York: Norton, 1958), introduced the concept of totalism into psychohistory. Note also Robert Jay Lifton, *Thought Reform and the Psychology of Totalism: A Study of "Brainwashing" in China* (1961; reprint, Chapel Hill: University of North Carolina Press, 1989).

23. Bromley and Silver, "The Davidian Tradition," 61.

24. Andrew Macdonald, *The Turner Diaries* (Hilsboro, W.V.: National Vanguard Books, 1978).

25. They are counting all the deaths of the Davidians during the encounter with the FBI and the BATF: six during the initial raid and the standoff, seventy-four in the fire, and the two fetuses.

26. *New York Times,* May 17, 1995. Note also Tom Reiss, "Home on the Range," *New York Times,* May 26, 1995, op-ed.

27. I am indebted to Eric Nadler for sharing with me his vast file of newspaper and magazine articles about McVeigh, which I was able to add to my more limited collection. In all of it, there are significant redundancies, but two pieces stand out for the quality of the research and the thoughtfulness of the writing and reporting. They are Robert D. McFadden, "A Life of Solitude and Obsessions," *New York Times,* May 4, 1995, and Dale Russakoff and Serge F. Kovaleski, "Two Angry Men," *Washington Post National Weekly Edition,* July 24–30, 1995. Most of my factual information, unless otherwise noted, is from these two sources. My interpretation of the material is, of course, my own.

28. Jonathan Franklin, "Timothy McVeigh, Soldier," *Playboy,* October 1995, 78ff.

29. My son, Michael Strozier, was on those front lines and has shared his experiences with me.

30. *Lockport (New York) Union-Sun and Journal* (Lockport, NY), February 11, 1992.

31. There was quite a bit of right-wing agitation during the fifty-one-day standoff at militia meetings around the country, gun shows, parades, on the internet, and in all the forums where the Right meets. No one has yet studied systematically this early response to Waco. Stuart Wright, personal communication, September 23, 1995.

32. As McVeigh and others were to note, April 19 is also when the fighting occurred at Lexington and Concord, that is, when citizens' militias defended freedoms that present-day militia groups now see as long since extinguished.

Chapter Nine

Reflections on Aum Shinrikyo

Robert Jay Lifton

In my own explorations of Aum Shinrikyo, I'm increasingly impressed with the mystery that surrounds dangerous transformations—and with the whole phenomenon of impulses to destroy the world, or much of it. In the past year or so, my work has been devoted to the study of some varied forms of apocalyptic violence. I find myself at an early stage of trying to make certain connections among these forms. I try to move along a certain kind of psychohistorical path with that idea of mystery present. This is an early statement of certain themes that I encountered in Aum Shinrikyo. It cannot be more than that, because of the short period of time I've spent on this. But my sense is that we have to start such an exploration with a bit of attention to what Kurt Vonnegut called "plain old death."

In my work I have a model or paradigm of issues of death and death equivalents, on the one hand, and a larger human connectedness, or the symbolization of immortality, on the other. The latter principle is necessary to a scientific psychology and should not be a concern of only theologians and philosophers. I think that one really needs some such death-centered and life-continuity-centered model or paradigm to even touch these apocalyptic issues and, particularly, the issue of apocalyptic violence. One has to take into account the worldwide reverberations of any significant event, so that collective acts of killing have ramifications throughout the world system within which we all live. Such was the case of Timothy McVeigh's alleged bombing of the federal building in Oklahoma City. It was true, certainly and chillingly, of the murder of Yitzak Rabin in Israel. It is also true of Aum Shinrikyo and its attempt to kill very large numbers of people with sarin gas. So our own perceptions of collective death—and indeed of our individual death—are becoming more and more related to the world system.

Aum Shinrikyo connects with my most morbid preoccupations, starting with Chinese thought reform and ideological totalism, with the psychology of genocide, and also with a certain kind of proteanism. It embraces proteanism both in a perverse way—proteanism gone berserk, so to speak—and in its fundamentalist and

This paper is an edited composite version of two presentations at the Center on Violence and Human Survival, John Jay College, City University of New York, December 12, 1995, and June 6, 1996. It retains the spoken form.

violent antagonism to constructive forms of protean exploration. Aum also relates to my work with Nazi doctors and the whole principle of killing to heal. One cannot understand large-scale killing of any kind, or the attempt at large-scale killing, without positing the killers' claim to virtue, and in this case, spiritual elevation by means of killing.

Let me mention a few details about what Aum members did. They released their sarin gas on five different Tokyo subway trains—the trains all converging on the most populated downtown area and the seat of the national Japanese government. Twelve people were killed and five thousand injured. Before that there had been trial runs: in 1993 in Australia (where gas was apparently released in an isolated area) and in 1994 in Matsumoto, a Japanese city, where a sarin gas release killed seven people and injured two hundred.

More followed after the March 20, 1995, incident. On May 5 Aum members deposited plastic bags containing cyanide gas in Shinjuku Station (also in Tokyo), at a shopping mall, where only the alertness of a few station attendants prevented a very large number of deaths. There were then a series of "copycat" releases of gas in different subway stations and department stores, some of which are believed to have been done by Aum members. In addition, Aum members were definitely responsible for an attempt at assassinating the head of the National Police Agency on March 30 and for sending a parcel bomb to Tokyo City Hall on May 16.

But Aum had ambitions of much greater violence, associated with a vision of the end of the world. Their extensive stockpiles of sarin gas were such that, had the March 20 operation been conducted more efficiently, they could have killed thousands or even hundreds of thousands of people. They were also developing deadly biological weapons, notably anthrax and botulinus bacilli. And they were making active inquiries, especially in Russia, about uranium technology and possibilities for purchasing or building nuclear weapons. Aum engaged in a number of individual murders, mostly by strangulation, of recalcitrant members or people in one way or another opposing the cult. All this was preliminary to a plan, fortunately never realized, for a November release of enormous amounts of sarin gas from helicopters as a means of bringing about World War III, which in turn would be a path to Armageddon. To accomplish all this, Aum had branches not only throughout Japan but in such cities as Moscow (there were reported to be thirty thousand Russian members, as opposed to only ten thousand Japanese), Bonn, Sri Lanka, and New York.

The question that haunts this work, even in its early stages, is this: What factors brought about the crossing of a terrible threshold from merely *anticipating* the end of the world to engaging in large-scale violence aimed at *bringing about* that world ending? Aum is not just some arcane or distant cult from an alien society, but rather a manifestation of precisely the kind of issues that haunt us in our everyday life in America. Indeed, all that we are discussing today hinges on this end-of-the-world expectation and its relationship to the end, or death, or envisioned rebirth, of the individual self.

Aum Shinrikyo follows a profile of extreme religious and political cults in this country, a profile that has to do with issues of ideological totalism. I've tried to lay out such issues in earlier work. I will not go into them now in any detail, except to mention two of the basic characteristics of ideological totalism. The first is that of total *milieu control*—control of all information exchange and imagery in an environment, which seeks to extend itself to internal controls of every kind. The second is the ultimate and most significant dimension of ideological totalism, the *dispensing of existence,* the presumption of the right to decide who has the right to exist and who does not. Sometimes this last dimension is symbolic in terms of recognition or nonrecognition, and sometimes it is literal in terms of individual or mass murder, as we saw with Aum.

The extremity of guru worship was crucial in developing Aum's particular expressions of milieu control and the dispensing of existence. Asahara carried the idea of guru worship to a new degree. That guruism is a more complex and puzzling phenomenon than meets the eye. It is true that guruism is more culturally accepted in East Asian societies—especially in the esoteric Buddhism Asahara drew upon—than in the United States. But there is something very extreme and bizarre and unlimited in Aum's guruism. For example, guru worship reached such heights that it extended to creating, or claiming to create, actual connections to the brain waves of Asahara through technological attachments. It was Asahara's person and presence that had held the young people, former Aum members, whom I interviewed. He offered his disciples, as must always be the case, immortality, transcendence. Now he was not exactly a beautiful-looking man by most standards, as many Japanese pointed out to me. But somehow in the way he conducted religious practices, especially through his yoga and his version of Buddhism, he could inspire a sense of immortality and transcendence in what they considered to be genuinely mystical experiences. So we can't just dismiss Asahara or Aum as psychopathic, although indeed he and it did become psychopathic.

In terms of the guru's relation to violence, I would like to say a word about the way Asahara understood *poa,* or killing to elevate the status of the victim. Poa is a practice of tantric Buddhism, enabling the dying to enhance their journey to Buddhahood, that is, into the land of Buddha or the "true land." It is really a version of what you find in all premodern cultures—the individual soul merging with the collective soul, transforming death into a relationship with immortality. But in Asahara's and Aum's hands, poa became killing enemies; murder was justified in the name of poa. They killed people they considered their enemies, for example, a lawyer and his family; and sometimes they "poa-ed" recalcitrant members. The person who is killed by spiritually advanced beings is elevated into immortality, and the person who does the killing is further enhanced spiritually through enhancing the immortality of the victim. So you never actually kill anybody; you offer your victim poa, or killing in the name of healing.

Such a theory of killing reminds me of my work with Nazi doctors, who also killed in the name of healing. The difference is that the Nazis were trying to heal the Nordic race by killing Jews, who were an "infection"—and Gypsies, too, and some other groups, but mainly Jews—which had to be extirpated. But with poa, you are not really killing. You are rather elevating the victims. You are not healing your own group, as the Nazis were doing—but healing the victims themselves. The Nazis did not claim they were healing Jews by killing them. They were healing the Nordic race, because the Jews were evil and subversive to Nordic power and Nordic existence or survival. In poa you de-victimize the victim.

One person's cult is another's religion. There is no clear scientific distinction between them. In my work I consider the behavior of a "new religion" to be cultlike when it displays three particular characteristics. One is the shift from the worship of spiritual ideals to the worship of the guru figure, as in Aum with the headsets that ostensibly connected the listener to the brain waves of Asahara. Second, there is the combination of genuine spiritual search from below—on the part of ordinary disciples—and extreme exploitation, economic and sexual, from above, mostly on the part of the guru himself. Third, there are thought-reform—or brainwashing-like—methods actively employed. In Aum these methods included total immersion in the guru's words and images, along with intense exercises combining extreme isolation and a variety of pressures and threats that manipulate guilt, shame, and fear having to do with the threat of inner death as opposed to the promise of immortality.

Aum Shinrikyo is not just a new religion in Japan, but what is sometimes called a "new-new religion," a term meaning that it has been around not for a hundred or two hundred years, but rather only since 1970. Significantly, these new-new religions tend to stress techniques directed less toward responsible social behavior than toward the disciplines of personal salvation. In the case of Aum the focus was on what was called *gedatsu,* or emancipation, and *satori,* or illumination, to the exclusion of concerns about the well-being of the tainted masses outside the cult. These practices were bound up not only with primal issues of life and death but also with the pervasive end-of-the-world theme that so dominated Aum's existence.

Shoko Asahara came early to his apocalyptic preoccupations. The son of a poor tatami mat maker, resentful at being sent as a child to a school for the blind (although his vision was considerably impaired, he has always had a certain amount of sight), he was always aggressive and ambitious in his failures. As a young man he was arrested on two occasions, once for causing physical injury and once for selling fake Chinese medicines.

His apocalyptic plunge took many forms. His focus on yoga in creating Aum in the mid-1980s, when he was about thirty years old, involved what he called the "awakening of mystical *kundalini,*" or divine energy, thereby carrying yoga to a transcendent level. More specific to his world-ending vision was his particular image of Shambala, derived from Hinduism and early Buddhism and influenced by Islam. Shambala was seen as a mysterious valley somewhere in northeastern Asia and as a symbol of apocalyptic struggle, with some resemblance to Armageddon. Asahara reported a vision he had in 1985 in which he was called upon by Shiva, the Hindu god, to become "the God of light who leads the armies of the gods" in a struggle of light against darkness. Shambala stood for an ideal utopian community of perfect virtue that would emerge from the apocalyptic struggle. Asahara also embraced a pre–World War II Japanese visionary who plumbed "ultra-ancient history" for a version of Armageddon, followed by the emergence of a Japanese spiritual leader.

In addition to all these Eastern influences, Asahara went on to encompass Western Christian traditions of the end of the world. He fiercely embraced the book of Revelation, which he connected with his earlier vision of Shiva, and came to see himself as the Christ. He also immersed himself in the writings of Nostradamus, the early sixteenth-century French physician-mystic who predicted that the world would end in the year 2000 and added something that could be interpreted as a suggestion that the post-Armageddon spiritual leader would come from the East. So Armageddon for Asahara and Aum became something of a generic term that included all these religious images of the end of the world as well as the imagery of ultimate weaponry in a large-scale war. They all became blended.

When I discussed these issues with an articulate, strongly anti-Aum lawyer, he told me that he too believed in Armageddon "just like Asahara." Given his antipathy to Aum, I was surprised by the remark and said, "Well, doesn't Asahara have a whole religious structure?" He answered, "Oh yes, but those are just words. Look, these missiles could explode on all of us." What he was saying that was so important was that the nuclear culture in which we all grow up creates an Armageddon-like expectation or set of images in all of us that can be seized upon by a person with the right "words." Asahara thus, on behalf of world-ending, became an avatar of Shiva, a Jesus figure from the book of Revelation, a Nostradamus-imagined savior, and a Japanese-imagined savior as well. I believe that he carried an impulse toward ending the world further than anyone else has, creating a kind of calendar of Armageddon, which seemed to have a combination of Herman Kahn (remember Herman Kahn's scenarios of how many people would be killed in a nuclear Armageddon) and the atomic scientist's clock (ticking away toward Armageddon). So, at a certain point he would say, "If we mobilize enough true believers, we will hold off Armageddon." Then later he would say, "No, things are much worse in the world. There is no possibility of holding off Armageddon. It is already impossible to limit the victims to less than one fourth of the population of the world." He said the latter in 1989. Later on he shifted to the idea that everyone in the world would be killed except a tiny remnant of Aum Shinrikyo people, who would respiritualize the world.

He was obsessed with nuclear annihilation. One of the places (in the Tokyo subway) where the gas was planted was a place in a very deep subterranean area, which he had described as the best nuclear shelter available in Japan. He also spoke of building the perfect nuclear shelter for his group. And he insisted that Armageddon could be survived only by carrying out Aum's spiritual practices—though he also urged his disciples to be prepared for death at any time.

What we need to realize, psychologically, is that what happens in a man like Asahara is that self and the world become combined. But instead of the self becoming, so to speak, a part of the world, the world becomes an aspect of the self. The projection of Armageddon, buttressed by various forms of ideology, becomes, in a psychological sense, a reading of the self, a projection of the self and an assertion of the self, which contains the world. One cannot understand the ebbs and flows and violent explosions of Aum behavior, or the decisions made, without recognizing the state of the guru's self. A totalistic group process develops, but it is the guru who takes the group into the Armageddon-like series of events.

Another unique feature of Aum Shinrikyo was its involvement of professionals, which reminded me very much of my work with Nazi doctors. Aum had a kind of shadow government that included a ministry of health, a ministry of science, and a ministry of construction. All this had a certain absurdity, of course, but the group took it seriously; they had trained scientists, physicians, builders, architects, all of whom were involved in these so-called ministries. There is a mystery among many Japanese about how they could attract well-educated people, and there is no simple answer. People said to me, when I looked into it initially, "Oh, these people didn't believe. They're just given a lot of money and also opportunities to practice their craft. They could do medical research, or certain things in science and be paid for it better than they could otherwise." But it wasn't that simple. In some cases people left promising positions in the society—although it was also true that many of the professionals were floundering and confused before joining Aum. But as in the case of Nazi doctors, these people were drawn to the Aum message.

They were, like all Aum members, critical of existing Japanese society. Aum mounted a powerful critique of Japanese materialism, of the corrupt consumer society, of the authoritarian educational system and the lockstep requirements for moving up the ladder—and above all, of the absence of a sense of meaning. I would say that Aum tapped an immortality hunger, or a hunger for meaning and for larger human connectedness. Aum could provide for some a believable sense of immortality, and that could be decisive. We find similar patterns in our own society, and in relation to cult behavior. But the hunger may be particularly great in contemporary Japan, a society that is undergoing enormous tensions. All of our four trips to Japan, which my wife and I made within less than a year's time, had to do with these extraordinary tensions: the earthquake in Kobe, the Hiroshima and World War II commemoration, mass media confusions, and Aum Shinrikyo itself—all of these in the context of significant economic recession.

I want to briefly say something about my encounter with a former Aum member—a few themes from a three-and-a-half-hour interview—just to give a sense of Aum's inner psychological climate. He is a university-educated young man in his early thirties, a practitioner of several of the arts, but he had received some setbacks in his career and was floundering. He had always been spiritually inclined, was unsure about his future, and was very critical of the existing Japanese society. He encountered Aum at a public ceremony, was deeply drawn to it, and underwent a total immersion. He describes intense exercises to overcome the "the polluted data" of the outside world (computer language is frequently used in this way by Aum). He and others would repeat endlessly words written or spoken by Asahara, sometimes having them at the same time flashed visually before them even as they were being spoken into their earphones. These and related exercises, some of them drawn from esoteric Buddhism, had to be repeated in accordance with one's age: if under twenty, three hundred times; if between twenty and thirty, five hundred times; if between thirty and forty, seven hundred times; if over forty, a thousand times—the idea being that the older one is, the more severe the pollution. In the process this member had a number of mystical experiences, in which he saw magnificent images and bright lights, these in turn resonating with an earlier pre-Aum mystical experience that had occurred while he was acting in a play. So one can speak of a thought-reform–like process, but there were also, for him and many others, opportunities for experiences of transcendence, of high states and a sense that one was part of something in the way of cosmic meaning. He was told by Aum that one does not choose the means of salvation: it is given to you.

He said that he had some doubts about Aum, especially concerning the insistence that the conspiratorial manipulations of the Freemasons would endanger the whole world and threaten to bring about Armageddon. But he remained intensely bound to the group because "I needed Aum." It gave him the kind of spiritual anchor he had sought. He was admitted into an "Armageddon seminar," as it was called. Intensely and for many hours a day, they would see the effects of all sorts of weapons. They had videotapes from all over the world. (It reminded me of what had been done at Waco at one time.) These videotapes consisted of wars everywhere, and they were told the next war and the next set of weapons would be much worse. That, of course, would be Armageddon. That Armageddon seminar intensified this disciple's desire—indeed, hunger—for Armageddon. "I wanted to destroy this world," he said, "to make a new world." He came to believe more in Asahara through the Armageddon seminar, because only Asahara could help save him and the other followers. You could be best saved by Asahara by renouncing the world and becoming an Aum monk (or *shukke*), which he did. If that was not possible, the next best thing was to acquire the brain-wave headgear, which was extremely expensive if you were not a monk (Aum charged exorbitantly for its offerings) and which was said to give you the most desired kind of contact with Asahara from the outside, so to speak.

They were told to train themselves to become supermen. That was part of the message from the Armageddon seminar, and from Aum more generally. With the release of the gas, there was some confusion in this disciple's mind and in many disciples' minds, because most Aum Shinrikyo members knew nothing about what was going on (only small group of trusted top disciples had full knowledge of weapons stockpiling and Aum violence). As to who released the gas, they did not know. The Aum Shinrikyo story, which was vague, but put forward, was that it was released by the United States—or the Japanese government—in any case through the machinations of the Freemasons. He did not know whether to believe that. But what he felt was only excitement: "I didn't ask who did it. . . . I didn't care who did it. . . . This was Armageddon. . . . We're going to be the savior of the world!" In retrospect he compared it to "the feeling of being a star." He was telling me that the only thing that mattered was that the much-yearned-for world ending was occurring.

But after that he began to have doubts. Media reports, especially those including confessions of high-ranking Aum members, eventually convinced him that it was Aum Shinrikyo that had release the gas. It took him a few months to make his way out of Aum, with the help of media people he had met. But for those interim months after the sarin incident, he had a double mind-set. He served as a spokesman to the media, putting forth the official Aum explanation that others had done it, while at the same time thinking that there was "something fake" about this explanation and Aum Shinrikyo in general. Although he now has no doubt about Aum's responsibility for that event and other violence, he still struggles with his own earlier attraction to Asahara and his plunge into Aum mysticism.

At the end of our talk, I asked him why he thought Aum Shinrikyo had released the gas and why Asahara particularly had initiated the order. He said they made the gas because "they wanted to make their own world." He was suggesting a key aspect of a beginning explanation for how Aum came to cross the threshold I mentioned at the beginning of this talk. You must create your own Armageddon (that was part of Asahara's sense of self, and by extension, the same was true of the others in the cult) in order to control, and believe in, your claim to be a savior of others. Otherwise, you are an object of someone else's Armageddon. In that sense, crossing the line meant reestablishing a claim to meaning and to immortality, as opposed to being vulnerable to death, meaninglessness, and fragmentation.

The dynamic of the actual release of the gas emerges from a prior habit of violence—and a pervasive evil—which had evolved quite quickly over the relatively few years of the cult's existence. As is typical when a cult breaks out in some form of violence, it does so when under duress. There was threat from the authorities (the police were about to close in), and there were threats from within, the loss of cult members and Asahara's becoming ill. So the gas event was initiated, ironically and paradoxically, in order to reassert the integrity, the vitality, or the immortality of the cult itself, all of which were enormously threatened by these processes. There was also an attempt to cast Aum in the role of victims of a gas attack from the outside and thereby undermine the police investigation. The Gulf War played a part here, too, because during the Gulf War there was much talk of poison gas. And Asahara identified with Saddam Hussein as a victim of Western high-tech transgression. But all this occurred in connection with a long-standing preoccupation with the end of the world and with weapons capable of bringing about that end.

Once you embrace end time, there is a preoccupation with survival. And the myth always is that everything will be destroyed in order for the world to be renewed. Every single myth about end time, or about death and rebirth, involves renewal. The very idea of renewal is dangerous, I would say, when you connect it with ultimate weapons—which now exist in the world, which is our new situation. The weapons had a tremendous psychological attraction for Asahara. So the weapons are dynamic elements in the psychological process. Asahara was obsessed with nuclear weapons. He said Japan would be atom bombed again and would be destroyed. He also wanted to create a war with America. The weapons were thus a very psychological organizing force for him. We don't know how to talk about this; we talk about weapons as destroying everything. The weapons can encourage megalomania. Or encourage the individual tendency to imagine being alone able to destroy the world as one person. That's another reason why their very existence is doubly dangerous.

There are certain Japanese elements here. I will just suggest them, without diminishing the universal importance of this cult. The degree of Japanese dislocation and confusion may be greater than that of any other country, given the rapidity with which the culture has moved from a feudal culture (from the time of the Meiji Restoration in the late nineteenth century) to a modern and postmodern one; and then it experienced the extraordinary defeat and humiliation and the millions of deaths in World War II. The millions of dead could not be mourned in any significant way because of the dishonoring of the whole system for which all of those people died. There is also another Japanese dimension—the Japanese embrace of the impossible heroic task. It is sometimes referred to as "jumping off Kiyomizu," referring to a temple on a high hill outside of Kyoto. The image suggests a plunge into an extreme action, even if the effort will almost certainly fail. Admiral Tojo is said to have used the phrase when ordering the attack on Pearl Harbor. There is a relationship here to the samurai spirit and the kamikaze principle.

Finally, I would say that Aum Shinrikyo has enormous significance, not just for the Japanese, but for all of us. It is like a kind of intense, almost exaggerated and caricatured statement on the pathology of our time, as well as on the danger of destroying ourselves in the name of renewal, an impulse that end-of-the-world imagery creates. My contention is that by looking into the abyss we express a modicum of hope, because we see alternatives and we are capable of articulating those alternatives, but only if we explore and confront the danger.

Chapter Ten

Shifting Millennial Visions in New Religious Movements
The Case of the Holy Order of MANS

Phillip Charles Lucas

Scholars of millenarianism have tended to view millenarian visions as stable, fixed conceptions that somehow stand outside of time and history, inspiring their adherents to prodigious feats of self-sacrifice, social reform, and (sometimes) revolutionary violence. Such views correspond with the assumptions of believers, who often regard millenarian scenarios as irrefutable divine revelations vouchsafed to a group's spiritual leadership as both warning and consolation before the events of the last days. The history of Christian millenarianism, in particular, is thoroughly imbued with the notion of fixed, unchanging visions of the "new heaven and new earth," since these visions are often grounded in sacred Scripture, which itself is viewed by many believers as an immutable, infallible revelation of ultimate truth. Thus, the coded visions and symbols of the book of Revelation, although subject to varied interpretations, are themselves assumed to be "fixed in stone" by their inclusion in the Christian canon of Scripture.

From a psychological viewpoint, of course, believers derive a deep sense of security and consolation in their assumption that the millennial scenario they embrace transcends the venality and uncertainty of secular history. Because the vision is inviolable and eternally true in their minds, it is worth the considerable sacrifices a movement's leadership often calls for, including withdrawal from family ties, poverty, armed struggle, the risk of torture, and even death.

This "assumption of permanence" with regard to millennial visions on the part of scholars begins to unravel, however, when one examines the articulation, elaboration, and modifications of millennial visions in specific movements over time. In this essay I argue that, far from having a stable and immutable character, millennial visions are fluid and adaptable configurations of mythic, symbolic, and ideological elements and that nowhere is this more evident than in the millenarian scenarios of new religious movements (NRMs)—that is, both cult and sect movements during their first two generations of existence. In order to ground this contention in the lived experience of particular movements, I will examine the shifting millennial visions of a New Age religious community of the 1960s and 1970s, the Holy Order of MANS, as it slowly transformed itself into Christ the Savior Brotherhood, a sectarian offshoot of the Greek Orthodox Church, during the 1980s. This specific case will demonstrate the mutable and ephemeral quality of millennial visions and the way these visions adapt to change both in a group's self-identity and goals and in its larger cultural environment.[1]

The Holy Order of MANS emerged in the counterculture milieu of mid-1960s San Francisco. The group's founder and charismatic prophet was Earl W. Blighton, a retired electrical engineer and social worker who had studied in such esoteric subcultures as the fraternal order of Freemasons, Spiritualist churches, the Christian Yoga Church of Subramuniya (a Saivite Hindu community), the Ancient and Mystical Order of Rosae Crucis (a Rosicrucian group), and the Theosophical Society. After opening a meditation chapel on Market Street in 1966 to minister to vagrants and derelicts in San Francisco's notorious Tenderloin district, Blighton began to attract a small following of young people who were disillusioned by the excesses of the hippie lifestyle and intrigued by his nontraditional system of "esoteric Christianity." Out of this small coterie of followers developed a monastic-style service and teaching order modeled after such Catholic orders as the Jesuits and the Franciscans. The new community was officially incorporated in the state of California in July 1968.

Between 1969 and 1974 the order grew quickly, enrolling more than two thousand renunciate and lay members (lay members lived independently of renunciate centers) and establishing seventy-one training centers and mission stations in more than sixty cities throughout the United States. By 1973 the order's communal lifestyle and demanding work ethic was garnering annual earnings for the group of $1.2 million. The distinguishing features of the order's monasticism were its largely urban settings, its openness to both men and women as members, its ordination of women priests, its commitment to social service (the order was a pioneer in the establishment of shelters for victims of domestic violence), and its eclectic assortment of spiritual beliefs and practices.[2]

Following Blighton's sudden death in 1974, the order underwent four years of turbulent interim leadership during which it fragmented into competing factions and began to lose sight of its animating purpose and vision. The doubt, disillusionment, and disunity of this period ended with the elevation of Vincent Rossi, one of Blighton's earliest followers, to the office of director general in July 1978. In the wake of the anticult hysteria that gripped the United States following the Jonestown mass suicide in November 1978, the order struggled to reconfigure its public self-representation to deflect the increasing criticism it was receiving from the mass media and the anticult movement. As was the case in a number of new religious movements during the late 1970s, recruitment rates began to fall quickly, and the order contracted into ten large centers in the United States and Europe. The group revised its mission and encouraged members to marry and raise families. It also created exemplary spiritual communities wherein its children could be indoctrinated into the movement's increasingly traditionalist worldview and members could be protected from the alleged depredations of postmodern American society.

As part of an urgent attempt to ground the order in the Christian apostolic tradition, Director General Rossi began to study the teachings of the Eastern Orthodox Church. He experienced a conversion to Orthodoxy in the early 1980s and began orchestrating a radical reconfiguration of the order's teachings, purpose, and identity. Gradually, elements of Blighton's esoteric, New Age religious system were replaced by the doctrines and practices of Orthodox Christianity. This transmogrification was completed in 1988, when the movement's remaining 750 members were rebaptized by Metropolitan Pangratios Vrionis, an independent Orthodox bishop headquartered in Queens, New York. It was at this time that the Holy Order of MANS was officially renamed the Christ the Savior Brotherhood.

During the order's gradual transformation from a New Age cult movement into a traditionalist Eastern Orthodox sect, the tenor of its animating millenarian vision underwent a parallel series of changes. In its founding era (1967–74), the movement joined other NRMs of the period—the International Society for Krishna Consciousness (ISKCON), Transcendental Meditation (TM), the Sufi Order of the West, and the Subramuniya Yoga Order, for example—in embracing a hopeful vision of impending planetary transformation, a golden age of spiritual awakening that would raise the consciousness of the entire human race. Blighton began receiving a series of "revelations" in 1967 that members came to believe were messages from the "Master Jesus" himself. These messages suggested that the spiritual elite of humanity was being gathered together in order to prepare humankind for an intense period of planetary spiritual enlightenment. The debris of the counterculture—Blighton's early students—were, according to these messages, reincarnations of the early followers of Jesus who had returned to earth to prepare the way for the coming of Christ.

Blighton was fairly specific concerning the nature of the dawning New Age. In "fulfillment of the New Covenant," the earth's psychospiritual atmosphere was being supercharged with both the physical (solar) and the spiritual light of Christ. This intensification of Christic power was producing an alchemical regeneration of both the earth and the human body at the molecular level. For those who had undergone the requisite spiritual training and preparation, this planetary "illumination" would be experienced as a time of unspeakable joy, love, healing, power, and communion with God. For those who were unprepared, it would be a time of confusion, disintegration, and possible removal to another, less evolved sphere of life. This removal was in no way to be understood as eternal damnation in hell, however. In Blighton's mentalist vision of reality, the only hell a person would ever experience was that of their own making. All souls were embarked on a long-term journey of spiritual unfoldment, he insisted, and, however painful certain lessons proved to be, they were only temporary setbacks on an eternal spiral of growth and self-realization.[3]

In the coming millennium, Blighton foresaw the end of exclusivistic, tribal-based religions and the emergence of a unified global culture. A universal religion based on the brotherhood of man would be the religion of the future. In addition, women would be restored to their ancient oracular and psychic functions, and female hierophants would preside over women's own special mysteries. Drawing on theosophical traditions that spoke of a coming world teacher, Blighton predicted the coming of an avatar who would "be born free from relationships with any organization, sect, religion, dogma or movement." This great teacher would promote the "Ancient Wisdom" traditions in a way that transcended parochial political and religious divisions and engendered global peace.[4]

According to Blighton's revelations, the Holy Order of MANS had been divinely ordained to prepare the earth and its peoples for its spiritual apotheosis. It would do so through the esoteric training of large numbers of people and the administration of powerful "solar initiations" by order priests. The conventional Christian churches had lost their ability to perform this training, in Blighton's view, and the order had been commissioned to speed up the process of preparation so that humanity's psychospiritual circuits would be rewired in time for the tremendous surge of power that would accompany the arrival of the millennium.

The specific purpose of Blighton's initiatory rites was to help the student function consciously in higher dimensions of reality—one of the commonplaces of life in the millennial era—and to inaugurate the process of alchemical regeneration of the physical body. Put another way, the initiations moved the soul "up the ladder of vibration" and helped it gain the purity and wisdom necessary to become an effective servant of humanity. In the initiatory rite itself, a "seed of higher life" was believed to be planted in the student's physical body so that in time the person would be transformed into a "new creature" with a "Body of Light." Although these rites had long been available to selected initiates in the temples and mystery schools of antiquity, they were now being offered to all of humanity as the culmination of the redemption set in motion by the crucifixion and resurrection of Christ.[5]

Early order members were prepared to administer these initiatory rites through ordination into the group's New Age priesthood, which was open to women as well as men. The order's priestly hierarchy, according to Blighton, had been reconstituted to restore the ancient Christian mystery teachings to the Christian churches. There was an urgent need to train ministers of all denominations so that they were prepared to respond to the pressing spiritual needs of humanity in the imminent millennial dispensation. Order priests were ordained into "universal servanthood" under the auspices of what Blighton called the "Divine Order of Melchizedek." This hieratic priestly order appeared in human history by divine fiat whenever conditions warranted. Given the nearness of the millennial kingdom and humanity's relative state of unpreparedness, God had once again called his elite initiates into action. Following four years of service to the Holy Order of MANS, priests were free to work within established denominations or to start their own centers. Like leaven in the loaf, it was hoped they would raise the other priesthoods of earth to a level from which they could function productively as the new heaven and new earth were being born.[6]

The first of the order's three main initiations, baptism, was believed to trigger the infusion of the Christ light into the disciple's body. This infusion constituted a purging of the effects of past error and a beginning of the assimilation of the higher vibrations of the Christ force. Illumination and self-realization, the final two initiations, constituted the essential preparatory steps for advanced functioning in the New Age. In the rite of illumination, the new body of light was believed to be implanted in the disciple's physical body. When properly performed, this light body was sealed permanently in the physical body's molecular matrix, greatly accelerating the process of alchemical regeneration. In the initiation of self-realization, the psychic sheaths or "veils" surrounding the "God-Self" were rent, and the disciple was granted open access to the divine image at his core. A self-realized initiate had taken a giant step on the road to functioning as a Christed being—in a sense, the Second Coming had already occurred for that person.

In late 1969 Blighton received a message directing him to send forth the "Sons of Light" into the world, for "the New Heaven and the New Earth" were near. Within five years order centers had been planted in forty-eight states. The millenarian and elitist tone of Blighton's revelations during this period created in order missionaries a vision of themselves as spiritual crusaders whose planetary mission was to create a grid of light around the earth. In nightly visualization exercises, members saw themselves linked with the entire brotherhood over an invisible network of light. They also saw light radiating from their center throughout the city and around the earth. These visualizations were understood as a psychic rewiring of the planet's circuits as a preparation for the tremendous upsurge of energy that would take place when earth was raised to its illumined state.[7]

The order's sense of millennial urgency during this period was intensified by the radical cultural and political upheavals that were occurring around the world between 1967 and 1974. These upheavals were interpreted by Blighton as evidence of the momentous changes that were beginning to occur on spiritual and psychic levels throughout the planet. Until 1973 the tenor of the order's millennial expectation reflected the generally positive and optimistic visions of the future that were being articulated in such popular books as Charles Reich's *The Greening of America* and George Leonard's *The Transformation*. For Leonard, the 1970s would bring about the most comprehensive change in the quality of human life since the dawn of civilized states. For both authors, the changes would be gradual, benign, and occurring on the level of human consciousness—allowing for some resistance from entrenched interests.

In 1973, as the Vietnam tragedy slouched toward its grim denouement, as the Watergate scandal began to unravel, and as the Mideast oil embargo plunged the world into economic recession, the order's millennial vision began its first major shift. These larger political and economic occurrences were intensified by a series of negative events within the order itself, which included the firebombing of a large order center (Blighton's residence) in San Francisco, death threats against Blighton, and a series of unflattering articles about the director general in the *San Francisco Chronicle*. The momentum of these events fueled an increasingly apocalyptic tone to Blighton's revelations during the last year of his life. He warned that the dark forces of the anti-Christ were becoming active in the world and that days of sorrow and confusion loomed ahead for many. As the death throes of the old age commenced, economic breakdown would disrupt transportation and bring about food shortages. To make matters worse, the conventional churches were failing to minister to humanity's pressing spiritual needs. In response to these conditions, the order began stockpiling foodstuffs and stepped up efforts to transmit its initiatory rites through the commission of "Free Lance Missionaries" who would rove freely throughout the country over the next three years. Although the New Age was still imminent in the order's vision of the future, more emphasis was now placed on the darkness before the dawn.

Part of the reason that the movement's millennial vision was amenable to change at this time was that it did not have a canonized scriptural basis. Rather, the vision was transmitted in sermons, occasional letters or articles, teaching lessons, and revelations received by Blighton. None of these articulations of the vision was fully elaborated or definitively cast in stone. As is often the case in movements headed by charismatic leaders, the exact details of the vision were rarely stated openly. Instead, followers were given snippets here and there with the understanding that these were part of a more comprehensive picture that would be unfolded as they grew in spiritual awareness. In addition, the movement had the strong conviction that it was being guided on a daily basis by the Master Jesus and that outer conditions were highly fluid and subject to sudden shifts depending upon the response of the world to the order's activities. If Blighton should receive a new revelation that somewhat altered earlier messages, few were likely to question the contradiction.

Following Blighton's death, the movement struggled to maintain its identity as a new order of the Aquarian Age founded on "living revelation" and not bound by past scriptures, traditions, and institutions. Although the group began to adapt its public self-representation to the resurgence of evangelicalism that was taking place in America in the latter half of the 1970s, it retained its optimistic view of a dawning millennial age of universal reconciliation and spiritual enlightenment. The new director general, Vincent Rossi, argued that Jesus had commissioned the order to present his teachings in a new way during the dispensational transition era. In place of the particularity and exclusivity that had characterized much of Christian history, Rossi claimed that Christians were being called to follow Christ "beyond Christianity, beyond religion . . . beyond even Jesus himself, there to meet, soul to soul, soul to spirit" where all would find their true being in the "Father-Mother God." The universalist goal of the order's millennial mission was the destruction of all barriers separating humanity, and especially the barriers that had been erected in Christ's name. To this end the order stepped up its participation in the Christian ecumenical movement and cultivated contacts with prominent religious and social thinkers through its service projects and its new journal, *Epiphany*.[8]

Yet, even as Rossi sought to sustain Blighton's hopeful millennial vision for the movement, he himself began to doubt the validity of the order's mission and of Blighton's Rosicrucian-theosophical teachings. Some of these doubts had been catalyzed by the disunity and the power struggles in the group following Blighton's unexpected passing. But the decisive factor in his change of heart was likely the wave of religious intolerance that engulfed the United States following the Jonestown mass suicide in late 1978. As the order (and many other NRMs) became the focus of anticult organizations, Rossi realized that Blighton's eclectic religious system would not stand the close scrutiny of the zealous Christian conservatives who were moving front and center in the national debate concerning "cults." He began to search the Christian tradition for a place where the order could "fit," and in interviews with journalists and writers he proclaimed that the order was Christian in its essence, form, and practice. Along the way, Rossi experienced a personal conversion to Eastern Orthodox Christianity, which he regarded as the most authentic branch of mystical Christianity in the modern world.

Thus, at the same time as the Moral Majority and the New Christian Right were emerging as the outspoken champions of traditional patriotism, monogamy, heterosexuality, biblicism, and morality, and the nation as a whole turned in a conservative direction, Rossi recast the order's mission and identity. The movement would now promote itself as the upholder of an integral Christian worldview based on Scripture and patristic doctrine. It would create a subculture that preserved the authentic cultural traditions of ancient Christianity (including folk arts and crafts and seasonal religious festivals), revalorized traditional gender roles (including the proscription of women in priestly roles), fostered a work ethic in appropriate-scale businesses and trades, and established private, religious-based schools for its children. The movement's exemplary communities would constitute an "ark of safety" in a fallen world that was heading rapidly toward apocalypse.

The first evidence of this shift in identity and millennial vision appeared in a 1982 circular letter in which Rossi addressed the crisis of nuclear weapons. In making his moral and theological arguments, the director general painted a darkly apocalyptic picture of a world shuddering on the brink of global suicide, "rushing headlong toward an abomination of desolation" in which the "billion-year heritage of the planetary biosphere" was in danger of wholesale despoliation. The "noonday devil" had issued a naked challenge to humanity, and, if the "prince of darkness" gained the upper hand, Christians would have "consented to the crucifixion of the Son of God on a planetary scale." In Rossi's view only a new Pentecost could save the world from the mushroom fires of nuclear war. The traditional Christian apocalyptic language of this letter was a radical departure from the more hopeful, optimistic tenor of Blighton's millennial rhetoric.[9]

In winter 1983 this shift in millennial focus was reflected in an issue of the journal *Epiphany*, which suggested that the bright promises of computer technology masked a reckless descent into pure abstraction and the eradication of human imagination and creativity. Behind their playful and beneficent facade, computers were turning people to banal and meaningless pursuits and creating a technological centralization that could result in an unimaginable tyranny. The editors of the special issue, in the "spirit of prophetic witness," were attempting to alert humanity to the subtle "subrogation of the Absolute God by the cult of the meta-machine."[10]

As the order accelerated its wholesale substitution of Orthodox Christian beliefs and practices for Blighton's esoteric religious system, Rossi, in letters, sermons, and articles, hammered home the point that the postmodern world was really an anti-Christian world. This anti-Christian bias was the fruit of modernity, which had come into being by thoroughly rebelling against the traditional Christian worldview. Rossi distanced the order from its past by characterizing New Age philosophy, with its championing of pluralism, individualism, evolutionism, relativism, rationalism, and humanism, as a metaphysical Tower of Babel perfectly aligned with the malevolent spirit of the age. In the place of a deluded universalism, Rossi posited the need for a particular and historically grounded tradition that had developed the safeguards needed to discern spiritual authenticity in the face of prolific deception and falsehood. For those formed in the culture of the West, Rossi contended, this tradition was Eastern Orthodoxy. It was for this reason that the order was now called to teach the patristic writings and the lives of Orthodox saints, since these teachings alone could give believers an experience of the Mind of the Christ beyond historical conditions.

The new millennial vision embraced by the order was articulated most clearly in the writings of Seraphim Rose, a Russian Orthodox monk whose devastating critique of the modern world had convinced the director general of the dangerous deceptiveness of Blighton's religious worldview. In contradistinction to Blighton's optimistic vision of a progressive transformation of the earth and its peoples, Rose taught that modernity's rejection of traditional Christian Orthodoxy had led to a drastic degeneration of the human condition; modern life was characterized by confusion, disorder, fragmentation, and, most horrifyingly, apostasy—the willful rejection of orthodox truth for crude materialistic values.

As science and pseudospiritualities such as the New Age movement became authoritative religion, conditions would be ripe for the appearance of the "ape of God," the Antichrist. This figure, as portrayed in Rose's writings, would appear as the supreme problem solver of the age. He would promise to give in the material realm what Christ brought inwardly in the spiritual realm. Whereas Christ promised his followers the perfect kingdom of heaven, the Antichrist—whose master, Satan, had been exiled from heaven and given lordship of earth—would promise humanity a perfect millennial kingdom in the material world. A material paradise would appeal to the masses of humanity as far more realistic and desirable than a vague heaven in the afterlife. This promise of earthly paradise, in Rose's view, was simply another version of the ancient heresy of chiliasm—the belief that Christ would soon return to earth to reign with his saints in a thousand-year kingdom of peace and prosperity, after which the world would end. Rose saw the modern democratic preoccupation with charity, equality, brotherhood, and the ideal society as perversions of Christian doctrine designed to win over the masses with promises of earthly comfort and well-being. From the traditional Orthodox perspective, the coming kingdom was not of this world, and man's deification would take place only after the purifying destruction of the material dimension.

In contrast to Blighton's vision of a unified global culture, ecumenical harmony, and an avatar figure unfettered by denominational or sectarian loyalties, Rose posited a coming age of apostasy during which leaders would seek the false unity of a world-state. This one-world government, which would be closely tied to the United Nations, would espouse earthly brotherhood and a new religion of humanity. Indeed, the Antichrist himself would be hailed as a great humanitarian. Because of Rose's close association with the Russian Orthodox Church in Exile, the trial run for this satanic religion was believed to be the collectivist order of the Communist state. But whereas state socialism took care of humanity's economic and social needs, the new world-state would also address humankind's personal and spiritual needs with a pseudoreligion. This magical-occult substitute for true Orthodoxy would promise material abundance and spiritual empowerment and provide miracles and signs that would validate the Antichrist's claims.

Rose viewed the charismatic and New Age movements, the creation-centered spirituality of eco-feminists, and the Christian ecumenical movement as forerunner movements for the new world religion that would ensnare the human race in the Antichrist's clutches. Rose pointed to New Age discourse concerning "the Plan" for a "New World Order," the need for humanity to undergo planetary initiations to realize this plan, and the utility of a universal credit card system, a universal tax, and a central authority for controlling international trade as evidence of the New Age movement's satanic design. Clearly, the belief by Rossi and the order that they had been in the vanguard of the Antichrist's deception made the group all the more zealous to repudiate its past beliefs and practices.

The most controversial element of Rose's apocalyptic vision was his contention that Christians of all denominations, by preaching humanistic ideas of social and economic justice and by seeking ecumenical harmony and accommodating their traditional doctrines to those of other denominations, were unconsciously collaborating with the Antichrist. Toward the end of his life in 1982, Rose even made the claim that all ecclesiastical organizations would eventually submit to Antichrist. Sadly, even Eastern Orthodox bishops and priests were engaged in these apostate trends through their eager support for ecumenical dialogue and progress.[11]

Echoing Orthodox monastic prophecies dating back to patristic times, Rose contended that Jerusalem would be the world capital of the Antichrist. Following his coronation by Christian clergy in a grand cathedral there, the temple of Solomon would be rebuilt, and the Antichrist would be worshipped as God. At the same time, however, many Jews would come to accept Christ, in accordance with scriptural prophecies. The restoration of Israel would be a sign that the final judgment was near.

The independent jurisdiction under which the order was finally accepted into Orthodoxy, the Archdiocese of Vasiloupolis (Queens, New York), provided the order with a vision of its own destiny during the dark reign of Antichrist. By joining a "Church of the Faithful" that was completely devoid of earthly prominence and that upheld the dogma and tradition of the early church fathers, brotherhood members would be persecuted by both Orthodox and other Christians groups for Christ's sake. In spite of this persecution, they would become a "catacomb church" that would flourish in secret and welcome Christ when he returned in glory. The brotherhood's new mission would be to save people from an all-pervasive iniquity and apostasy that was propelling the human race down the fast track to eternal damnation.[12]

The end itself, as portrayed in order publications such as *Epiphany*, was envisioned as a time of great destruction and tribulation during which the earth would be purged by fire. This fiery purification, however, would not occur through thermonuclear destruction, nor through ecological suicide. Rather, it would be a fire sent "down from God out of heaven," which would bring to an end the present heaven and the present earth. Following this purgation, the entire creation would be renewed and spiritualized. It would become a habitation that was immaterial, eternal, and incorruptible. Both the new heaven and the new earth would be incomparably brighter than now and would be filled with ineffable beauty and joy. The new earth would be united with the noetic world and become a mental paradise inherited by the righteous and the meek.[13]

As the order's changing millennial scenarios demonstrate, visions of the end in new religious movements are highly fluid and ephemeral phenomena. Like other elements of a group's religious system, they are cultural constructions that are elaborated and refined in response to shifts in the larger culture, changes of leadership, and contact with new and more attractive teachings and visions. This ongoing elaboration and refinement poses two quandaries for new religious movements.

First, member commitment and willingness to sacrifice personal desires for the good of the group are often founded on a clear sense of divinely sanctioned mission and destiny. Thus, the millennial visions articulated by an NRM's charismatic leader must have a quality of ultimacy and veracity that inspires zealous commitment in followers to movement goals. When, as is often the case, the millenarian scenario begins to change, group members may experience a crisis of confidence both in their charismatic leader and in their group's millennial vision. As it becomes clear that this vision of the future is not carved in heavenly stone, the leader may find that the personal sacrifices members have made in the past out of a sense of millennial urgency are much harder to evoke.

For the members themselves, the crisis of confidence brought about by shifting millennial visions is usually resolved in one of four ways: defection and complete abandonment of the group's mission and religious system; defection and the establishment of a splinter group that upholds the original vision and mission; an attempt to seize power within the group and to restore its original vision and mission; or psychological readjustment through rationalization of the change as "God's will" or as a more comprehensive revelation of the divine design. In charismatically led NRMs, the credibility and prestige of the leader is usually powerful enough to head off wholesale defections or coups and to encourage rationalization and acceptance of the revised vision by members. When, however, it is new leadership that brings about changes in a millenarian scenario, widespread defections or attempts to restore the original vision are a likely outcome. In the case of the Holy Order of MANS, the movement experienced severe attrition when it began to alter Blighton's original religious system and vision. Even members who remained loyal to the brotherhood during its transition to Orthodoxy have recently begun to repudiate the more extreme apocalyptic scenarios of Seraphim Rose and the Russian Synodal Church.

A second quandary posed by shifting millennial visions in NRMs has to do with a group's identity and self-image. In millennial movements identity is intimately connected with a larger understanding of sacred history and of the group's special place within an unfolding cycle of eschatological events. Typically, the group understands itself as an elite remnant chosen by God for a crucial role in the end times. The reward for present persecution, hardships, and sacrifices is a privileged place in the millennial kingdom. When a millennial vision undergoes radical change within an NRM's first two generations, members not only have to adjust to a new sense of their future, but they also have to revise their understanding of sacred history and of their group's present role in the divine plan.

Such adjustments and revisions do not come about easily or without cost. Many members make their deep investment in a group precisely because of its authoritative answer to the questions, Where did I come from? Who am I? and Where am I going? When the group's answer to these questions begins to undergo radical change, its members are challenged to discard the deepest underpinnings of their collective identity and security. There inevitably ensues a period of collective resistance, disorientation, and fragmentation that can threaten the movement's very survival. In the case of Christ the Savior Brotherhood, even after its initial acceptance of the darkly apocalyptic visions of Seraphim Rose, some of its local churches have decided to join more established Orthodox jurisdictions and to de-emphasize millennial and apocalyptic speculations. In the eyes of many other members, the brotherhood exists only on paper and has no real future as a movement.

Although the Holy Order of MANS/Christ the Savior Brotherhood stands out as an example of the fluidity and instability of millennial visions in NRMs, it is but one of many examples that history provides of the phenomenon. The continual refinements in the end-time scenarios of the Jehovah's Witnesses, the Church Universal and Triumphant, and the Divine Light Mission, not to mention the early Christian movement, all provide parallel examples of gradual distortions of millenarian expectations. In these groups such changes were often the result of failed prophecies and the need to rationalize such failures and rescue the group from dissolution.

In the end, only a careful historical examination of a movement's literature, art, teachings, and pronouncements can uncover the continually shifting nature of its millenarian visions. Scholars must avoid the temptation to take for granted the seeming immutability and timeless quality of these visions—for this is certainly the way the group will present them at any particular moment in its history—and must regard this important constellation of symbols, rhetoric, and myth as being as fluid and amenable to alteration and refinement as an NRM's doctrines, rituals, and institutions.

NOTES

1. I am here accepting the distinction made by sociologist Rodney Stark between sect movements, which are offshoots from established religious denominations or communities, and cult movements, which are independent, original religious communities with no doctrinal or institutional links to a parent denomination or body.

2. Phillip C. Lucas, *The Odyssey of a New Religion* (Bloomington: Indiana University Press, 1995), 1–2, 13.

3. "Priest's Book of Revelations," messages received Mar. 22, 14, 1967, in Archives of the Institute for the Study of American Religion, Santa Barbara, California; John McCaffery, interview with author, Syracuse, New York, Oct. 13, 1991.

4. Earl Blighton, sermon transcript, Nov. 2, 1969, and Holy Order of MANS promotional booklet, 1969, in Archives of the Institute for the Study of American Religion, Santa Barbara, California; *History of the White Brotherhood on Earth and Its Teachings* (San Francisco: Holy Order of MANS, 1974), 106–21; Lucas, *The Odyssey of a Religion*, 41.

5. Holy Order of MANS, "Philosophy of the Sacraments," unpublished, undated manuscript, 2, 6–12.

6. Holy Order of MANS, *The Book of Activity* (San Francisco: Holy Order of MANS, n.d.), 34; idem, *The Cosmic Orders and Their Purposes* (San Francisco: Holy Order of MANS, n.d.), 2, 9; idem, *The Book of Alchemy* (San Francisco: Holy Order of MANS, 1974), 82.

7. Holy Order of MANS, "Priest's Book of Revelations," messages received Nov. 10, 1969, Jan. 22, 1970, in Archives of the Institute for the Study of American Religion, Santa Barbara, California.

8. Andrew Rossi, "Uniting All Faiths," *HOOM,* Sept. 1977, 5–9.

9. Vincent Rossi, circular letter, May, 1982, in Archives of the Institute for the Study of American Religion, Santa Barbara, California.

10. *Epiphany* (winter 1983): 1.

11. Monk Damascene Christensen, *Not of This World: The Life and Teaching of Fr. Seraphim Rose* (Forestville, Calif.: Fr. Seraphim Rose Foundation, 1993), 922.

12. Parish Directory of the Greek Orthodox Archdiocese of Vasiloupolis, 1990.

13. Stephen Muratore, "The Earth's End: Eschatology and the Perception of Nature," *Epiphany* (summer 1986): 46–47.

Chapter Eleven

On the Image of 2000 in Contemporary Cults

Margaret Thaler Singer

The terms *cult* and *cultic,* as well as *cult movement,* are used to refer to a vast array of groups that have sprung up in the past forty years. These groups were begun by self-appointed leaders who claimed to have special knowledge, a special mission, and secrets either old or new that they would share if a person became an adherent.

Scholars estimate that there are three thousand to five thousand such groups in the United States today. Debate about what to call these groups continues. *Cult, cultic, charismatic groups, sect, New Age, New Movement,* and even *New Religious Movements* are all terms that have been variously used over the years. The latter term, New Religious Movements, is limiting and often incorrect because not all cultic groups are religious in nature. Cultic groups come together around personalities and can form around any theme: psychological, philosophical, lifestyle, ecological, political, extraterrestrial, and so forth.

Robert Lifton elucidated,

> We can speak of cults as groups with certain characteristics: first, a charismatic leader, who tends increasingly to become the object of worship in place of more general spiritual principles that are advocated; second, patterns of "thought reform" [permeate the environment], and third, a tendency toward manipulation from above with considerable exploitation (economic, sexual, or other) of ordinary supplicants or recruits who bring their idealism from below."[1]

Lifton finds that such conditions produce totalistic environments, which in turn make possible ideological totalism. "The totalist environment seeks to re-educate participants into submission and conformity, not creative individual participation in society."[2]

As the year 2000 approaches, countless cult leaders and self-appointed prophets are convincing an untold number of persons that the world as we know it may end or change drastically before the start of the third millennium. Some portray their prophecies and predictions in images of Armageddon or the war between good and evil, whereas others say these are end times and the final holocaust, doomsday, and earthly oblivion is near. Boyer chose the poetic phrase, "when time shall be no more," to describe prophecy beliefs.[3] Strozier used Lifton's formulations about totalist environments in his writings on "endism." Endism is "the shadow side of our firm belief in renewal and second chances," as noted in the apocalyptic stances of the end-of-the-world prophecies abounding as the third millennium nears.[4]

Still others predict that despite the forthcoming occurrence of a cataclysm, a select group will survive and start a new world order. Those espousing this latter vantage point make quite specific predictions that only their group will survive and somehow become the leader of the new world order. Note also that certain leaders use current social, environmental, and political unrest as a theme for why and how end times may come. One example is the murderous cultic group Charles Manson gathered about himself in the late 1960s. Aware of certain racial tensions in the society, he predicted the nearness of what he called Helter Skelter, a war of destruction between the races, which he used to justify leading his youthful followers to the desert before directing them into murderous sorties.

In formulating their end-time prophecies, in general, these leaders reflect some universal human concerns about death and humankind's ever-present question, Why is death the inevitable end of life? The prophecies made down through time, as well as current ones, respond to this eternal awareness of death. As nuclear weapons and chemical and biological agents have been created as part of the world's ever-expanding scientific development, all of us have become aware that we, humankind, can obliterate ourselves from the world.

Periodically these end-time myths circulate widely in the media, at times receiving considerable attention. One researcher is following more than 1,100 groups and individuals that are proclaiming that the end of the world will come at the millennium through "global transformation" caused by warfare, floods, and earthquakes.[5] Here attention will be given to a subset of cultic groups whose leaders are prophesying in general about what the third millennium will bring.

End-Time Philosophy as a Recruiting Strategy

Certain enterprising cult leaders are capitalizing on some rather basic human concerns about the end of the world that have been present through the ages and which seem to be rekindled at the end of each century, and especially at the end of a millennium. They use these shared concerns to motivate their adherents to increase membership. By opportunistically crafting their recruitment strategies around end-of-the-world themes, leaders can urge people to join up quickly. They say that only through affiliation with the leader and his or her group can one attain heaven, a future in the hereafter, a healthy planet in another galaxy, or survival in some form or another.

An example of such a leader is Ching Hai, female head of one of the fastest growing groups worldwide. Reportedly since 1986 she has gathered around her one hundred thousand members in thirty-one countries, with thousands of followers in the United States. Ching Hai, whose group includes many Asians, plays upon the end-of-the-world theme in a variety of ways.[6] According to several who have researched the group, Ching Hai "has told followers that unless they redouble their efforts to convert followers, humanity faces world destruction as early as 1997, which is significant as the year when mainland China finally takes over Hong Kong, and many Asians jitterly await the possibility of violence breaking out."[7] In her speeches to throngs of followers, Ching Hai asks what will happen if the Earth does not exist anymore. Blame for bad outcomes in 1997 rests on her followers if they fail to recruit enough new members. Humanity faces destruction, she states, as she promises to take her faithful devotees, as well as their five previous generations of ancestors, to heaven with her when end times come.

In contrast to the more traditional end-times position of Ching Hai's group, a newly formed California cultic group is capitalizing on themes popular in current extraterrestrial literature: that is, some believers are portraying ETs as kindly explorers, while others see them as coming to Earth with advanced weaponry and the potential to wipe us out. The man who started this group claims to be in daily contact with beings from another galaxy. He tells his followers he is training them to be "peaceful welcomers" because the space people will be landing on the northern California coast "just after New Year's Day, 2000."[8] He says the space people will arrive hoping for a peaceful reception on planet Earth, but they will have powerful weapons beyond any we have. To avoid a clash between earthlings and space aliens, the forty or so adherents are learning to submit, obey, and control their aggressions. The group is especially seeking mechanics and carpenters so they can offer to repair spaceships that may be damaged on landing. Only by offering themselves as helpers to the extraterrestrials will these devotees be able to keep the space people from wiping out most of this planet. The leader teaches that most earthlings think space people are warriors, but he knows they are not, and he fears that ordinary citizens will try to shoot down the spaceships. Members are told they are responsible for preventing the "final war" that the millennium can usher in.

Not only have there been cultic groups using the coming millennium as a dire date, but also there has been a remarkable rise of other closed systems of thought in which we observe irrational, unscientific reasoning and acceptance without question of various New Age philosophies that promise life after death via transformations, or protection from the apocalypse by extraterrestrial aliens and angels.[9] The conspiracy theories dominating self-styled militia and patriot groups add another dimension of irrationality to the rampant swirl of poor reasoning.

Jim Jones and His Changing Predictions

Even though the Peoples Temple ended and Jim Jones perished in 1978 in a steamy Guyanese jungle, it is useful to see how Jones capitalized on end-time predictions from the start of his California days and how he tailored the predictions to fit the nearby environment as it changed. The original home base of the Peoples Temple was in the Ukiah Valley in California because Jones had read in an *Esquire* magazine article that if there were to be a nuclear war, the Ukiah Valley would be a naturally protected area. Supposedly, streams of jet air would carry the nuclear material over the area, and a constant updraft would bear the radioactive material away.[10]

As circumstances changed over the years, so did Jones's predictions of what would cause their demise. During those first ten years when the temple was situated in the Ukiah Valley, Jones labeled the neighbors as "local redneck racists."[11] He had some of his followers secretly shoot weapons outside the compound to prove to the members that danger lurked on the other side, outside the group. Yet, the real end he prophesied would be nuclear war.

Then Jones decided to move his group into the "anonymity of the city of San Francisco." He soon evolved from prophesying that the end of the world would come from a nuclear blast to saying that the end was coming through fascist despotism and that he and his followers would have to commit revolutionary suicide and meet "on the other side."[12] When his activities in San Francisco caused frequent negative comment in the press, he moved the group to Guyana in South America. With these changes in surroundings, Jones revised his predictions about the forces that would threaten him and his followers. Now he forecast that the nearby Guyanese Defense Forces were going to attack them. But he also resurrected his idea of nuclear tragedy.

The congregation hiked, built rafts, and prepared for survival. I spoke with many who had not been full-time Temple members, but nevertheless during their visits to the temple they had been persuaded to leave postcards with their addresses and phone numbers. Jones declared that, by his divination, he would know some days ahead when the nuclear blast was coming, and everyone on the mailing and phone lists would be notified so that they could get to the Peoples Temple before the end.

A number of Jones's followers survived the tragedy (in which 912 died) because they were in the United States when the Jonestown deaths occurred in Guyana. Those survivors have reported that Jones conducted nearly nonstop preaching about the coming nuclear holocaust. Tim Stoen, a young attorney who had joined the Temple in its early stages, said: "When I first joined the Temple, [Jones] talked about nuclear war. He saw it as inevitable. He taught us that there would have to be some sort of remnant that was very disciplined. He was determined to teach us survival skills so that we could recreate the utopian society out of the nuclear wreckage." Another man reported that "Peoples Temple was going to be a family that survived. We stored food in five-gallon cans. Rice, grain, even water was sealed in old Clorox bottles."[13]

Jones also carried out a long-standing fantasy of his about suicide. Many times over the years he ordered his followers to practice what he called "White Night," whereby he would trick them by telling them that they had already sipped poisoned wine or drinks when they had not. In the gruesome Final White Night, Jones in his delusion attempted to make it seem as though 912 people joined him in a suicide. But by listening to the tapes of the last hours at Jonestown, and hearing the tales of the few survivors who escaped the forced drinking of cyanide-laced fruit drinks, it becomes apparent that there was no choice for his followers.

And it was the ending of another utopian dream. One writer noted: "The majority of those who came to Jones were the needy ones; the poor, the discriminated against, the unloved; while the minority of his followers were middle-class, privileged, and joined Jones not out of need but out of need to help the needy. . . . And Jones led them all to the land of promise, and from the land of promise—into death."[14]

Who Joins Cults?

Some typical questions that come up repeatedly in my work are, Who are the people who get involved in cults? Are they defective-disordered-deviant persons? Whatever causes them to join these groups? Evidence to date suggests that most people who become involved with cults are relatively average individuals who were recruited at a period in their lives when they were in transition and somewhat depressed.[15] Individuals most at risk are those who are mildly to moderately depressed because of a recent personal loss (a death, a divorce, a broken romance) or those depressed over a situational problem (failure to get a particular job, failure in examinations), who at the same time are not embedded in a meaningful relationship with a partner, a group, or a job. Once approached by a cult recruiter, the person must also be interested in the content of what the recruiter offers and feel available (i.e., have the time) to explore what is being offered.

Most modern cults have been found to be very active, persistent, and skilled at recruiting. It is widely reported that there is much deception involved at the point of joining, for cultic groups withhold what life in the group is really going to be like. After someone joins the group and is cut off from family and friends, quickly the new member becomes totally dependent on the group socially, emotionally, spiritually, and often financially.

Cults in the United States in the late 1950s and early 1960s were primarily youth cults; but since then, cults have recruited among a wide age range. Recently they have been focusing on the elderly as well as the young, and on working adults, including professionals. Education is no vaccine against being led to join a cult.

Thus, cult followers come from a vast spectrum of ordinary people who, at a time when they are especially vulnerable, find that the offer of friendship and easy acceptance into a group are very appealing. Critical thinking is overcome by a trusting response to persuasive representations from the group.

Prophecies of Modern Cults

From what I have been able to glean from persons exiting cults recently, some of the more sophisticated cult leaders are not setting specific dates or predicting exact ways the end may come or a new order will begin. Rather they play on the fear engendered by vague threats of end times to keep followers worried that if they leave the group and the leader they will not be kept abreast of the inevitable progress toward the "end." Nevertheless, some cult leaders who sound less sophisticated continue to make concrete, specific prophecies about when the end times will come through floods, fires, nuclear bombs, poison gas, and so on. A few examples will illustrate the range of predictions and prophecies being made.

A man and a woman formed a UFO cult in the mid-1970s that still exists. They told their followers that a fleet of flying saucers would come and take them from earth to "the next evolutionary kingdom," thus saving them from the extinction that was sure to come. A number of young people left schools, jobs, and homes to follow these two. Interviews with members who left the group revealed a pattern. The leaders would send members to a certain city to work at jobs that are easy to find, such as busboy or waitress jobs. The goal was to get any job that was quick to locate but allowed a sense of freedom to be available whenever the spaceships announced their arrival. The leaders were in almost daily phone contact and would excitedly assign members to be on "alert" to depart quickly and go to another pickup point where the flying saucers would get them for the journey to the idyllic planet promised by the leaders. The leaders assigned four to eight members to one city. These members worked and sent money back to the leaders, but also they were always to have enough money to travel to the next "assignment" or supposed pickup point. The leaders told them how much the space people knew about the members' thoughts, as space people could read minds at any distance.

Over and over, either by phone or by an emissary sent by the leaders, the followers were told that their spirits, their minds, their dedication to "the plan" had been rated by the space people to be too low to enter the new galaxy where they kept being told they would go "if only they could clear their minds to perfection." Then the interplanetary craft would zoom in and pick them up. I have rarely met as depressed ex-cult members as some who have come out of this group. They suffered numerous and severe disappointments after becoming very excited and hopeful that a pickup was going to occur. Eventually these letdowns evolved into marked depression in some, and then when they could no long function and drifted out of the group, they felt that since their "mind" had failed, there was no hope here or anywhere for them.[16]

After Susan Alamo died, her husband, cult leader Tony Alamo, prophesied to their followers that Susan would arise and return. Vigils were held to witness the return. Her body was kept for nearly ten years in a sarcophagus in the group's Arkansas headquarters. Finally, Tony Alamo, who was a fugitive from the government at the time, phoned a Fort Smith, Arkansas, newspaper to announce that he had taken the body elsewhere. No further prophecies were made.[17]

Former members of a moderate-sized, midwestern-based Bible group reported that the leader was having marital troubles. He announced that he had received a vision that predicted his wife would die. He had followers pray for her death. He died first, however, and she is still alive.[18]

In the Northeast, a cult leader convinced a wealthy young female follower that among many pressing troubles the leader was having, the one that troubled him most was that his wife was dying of cancer. He implied that he needed money for her. He led the follower to donate several million dollars to his group. His wife, it was later learned, had always been healthy. He had bought a condominium in Florida with mirrors on the ceiling, and he and his wife were said to travel there frequently.[19]

Branch Davidian survivors have reported that David Koresh frequently told the group that he saw them going through fire to get to heaven, prophesying that they all would leave this world much in the manner that the group did at the end in Waco. Some reported that flammable materials were to be used if a shootout occurred with authorities, which eventually occurred. Koresh also told followers that his unique biblical knowledge gave him the capabilities to unleash earth-shaking catastrophes and guarantee all cult members entrance to Heaven.[20]

In the fall of 1989 Elizabeth Clare Prophet, head of the Church Universal and Triumphant, told about a thousand followers at the group's ranch in Montana that the nuclear war with the Soviet Union was not going to begin in October as she had prophesied. Instead, she moved the date into December. Late in December church officials modified the prophecy, saying that beginning on New Year's Eve a twelve-year period "will unfold during which the dreaded events could come at any time."[21]

A large international cult claims to have installed thermonuclear explosion–resistant doors on tunnels that hold the writings of their leader, who incidentally also claimed to have created a cure for the effects on the human body of a nuclear blast.[22]

Luc Jouret, a Belgian-trained physician who moved into politics, then homeopathy and occult lore, was among the top leaders in the Order of the Solar Temple, with members in Canada, France, and Switzerland. Jouret recruited about seventy-five members in Canada and another two hundred in Switzerland and France. These devotees were successful, middle-class, and educated; some were quite wealthy. They followed Jouret's views on ecofatalism and seemingly accepted his prophecy that doomsday was close at hand because of man's destruction of nature. Jouret said the ozone layer was damaged, the waters polluted, and the soil used up and that it would be best to die now while there was air to breathe and water to drink. Fifty-eight followers died in Canada and Europe, many from bullet wounds, others with plastic bags over their heads. According to the authorities, examination of the bodies indicated that some powerful drug had been administered by injection or intravenous drip.[23] Lying dead among empty champagne bottles, many were clad in colorful robes. The chalets where they were found had been booby-trapped to explode into flame at the time of the deaths. Jouret had predicted that they would all pass through a fiery death here and be reborn on a planet they called Sirius in another solar system.[24]

A Ukrainian woman cult leader in 1990 declared herself the Messiah, "the living God." Claiming to have tens of thousands of followers worldwide, she was a former Communist youth leader and her husband was a former cybernetics engineer. She proclaimed that the world would end on November 14, 1993. On that day she would commit suicide, she declared, and then ascend into Heaven in a huge ball of flame and the world would end. On the appointed day she and some of her followers seized the Saint Sophia cathedral in Kiev and awaited the gathering of the chosen 144,000 true believers for the end of the world. The prophecy failed. Only sixty followers showed up in Kiev on the day of the predicted end.[25] The police arrested the leader on a number of charges. On February 9, 1996, she was sentenced to four years in prison.[26]

In 1987 in Seoul, South Korea, another female cult leader, Park Soon Ja, who was called "Benevolent Mother," claimed God had told her to seek followers because the end of the world was coming. She demanded extreme spiritual discipline and blind obedience. One day in August, thirty-three bodies, bound and gagged, strangled and poisoned, were found stacked in the attic of a factory owned by Benevolent Mother. Three days earlier police began investigating accusations that she had swindled $8.7 million from about 220 people, many in the cult. Authorities could not confirm whether Park and her three children were among the dead in the factory, who apparently had been victims of a murder-suicide pact.[27]

What Do Cult Leaders Achieve by Making Prophecies?

The prophecies made by cult leaders appear to have at least four purposes:

> 1. They show that the leader is unique, powerful, and a supreme gatekeeper who knows what the future holds.

Forecasting the future appears to demonstrate that the cult leader has special omnipotent powers and knowledge. This prescient quality makes the leader appear to be omnipresent and omniscient. The leader is seen as controlling the pipeline to God, Heaven, the future, good health and life, enlightenment, or whatever the group espouses as its core theme.

It is also a form of image enhancement for the leader. By the time a relatively successful leader makes various predictions about the future, the leader will have already laid the groundwork of getting followers to believe he or she has special knowledge, special powers, a special mission in life. The leader will have established some credibility in the eyes of her or his followers, and especially will have led them to become dependent on him or her in many areas of their lives. End-time and other prophecies, then, provide the leader with a unique opportunity to try to convince followers that he or she has the ultimate capacity. The leader can read the future and is therefore a superior being.

The very fact that the leader self-proclaims superhuman powers is seen by followers as indication that the leader is not an ordinary mortal, humble, self-doubting, unsure, like they, the followers, are. The very hubris that it takes to self-proclaim magical powers, superhuman talents, or contact with God or space people is in itself powerfully convincing to many persons. Followers have said they believed the leader because the claims were beyond any they had ever heard a person make. It caused them to think that the person was not an ordinary being, because the ordinary person would be concerned with seeming too proud or too arrogant.

Only after time away from the leader and much time to think, read, learn, and talk with rational others, do many former followers begin to ask themselves and others, Were those proclamations made by a character-disordered, a delusional person, or what? All admit that they had become so trusting, dependent, and fearful in the group that the leader's words gave them a sense of sanctuary and security and engendered childlike faith. They "knew" that the leader was going to keep making prophecies and know what to do. Some have said to me, "The leader knew, I did not have to worry about another decision ever again, I thought."

> 2. They keep the leader in power and keep the followers in line.

Leaders are adept at using their so-called prophecies and their purported ability to secure messages from beyond Earth in ways that serve to maintain their control over the group. This happens even when a seeming board of directors or group of overseers is put into place to make the group appear more like an ordinary and democratic organization. If the board makes decisions the leader does not like, then the leader, who is the only one in the group with the claimed connection to higher beings and superhuman sources, simply "gets messages" from the beyond that corroborate the way the leader wants things to go.

3. They make the idea of leaving the group fraught with danger and fear.

Prophecies and predictions are designed to make followers fearful about leaving the leader and the group. Hundreds of former cult members from a variety of cults have told me that their respective leaders predicted that anyone who left the group would encounter lifelong bad luck, get hit by a car, develop cancer, be in fatal accidents, be murdered, and so on. Some cult leaders sense that predictions that elicit fear, guilt, and attachments to family members and loved ones can be manipulated to retain members. For that reason numerous predictions are about dire things that will befall the relatives of members who leave the group. Often cult leaders cite as proof various illnesses, accidents, and deaths that might have occurred in families of former members; some leaders even use their knowledge of such events in families of current members, saying that these are warning signs. To forecast that if a person leaves "our group," family members and loved ones will be at imminent risk of cancer, death, and unspeakable miseries has proven to be an effective method of keeping members from leaving the group.

4. They bind the group members close to one another and to the leader.

In observing the current groups whose leaders are making prophecies about the impending end of the world, I have noted that often these leaders waited until they had some solid and loyal followers who they felt sure would stick by them no matter what happened. Impetuous would-be leaders who make great prophecies before they have established a cadre of "true believers" may be abandoned early on by their followers.

As I have written elsewhere, the personality of the cult leader is all-important because that person wields unlimited and unmonitored power in the group.[28] That power is based on self-proclaimed gifts, missions, and allegedly secret knowledge, which, says the leader, will be shared with those followers who are sufficiently faithful and obedient. A good part of the power held by these leaders is based on their engendering fear and manipulating dependency and guilt in their followers. Failure to please the cult leader here on Earth means risking the future since the leader is believed to control all his or her followers' future. Followers are led, a step at a time, to submit, obey, and believe. The leader presents herself or himself as *the one* who controls the lives of the followers for the rest of all time here and in the great beyond. If followers do not do as they are told, they must face not only their own fears but also the one who is said to be the gatekeeper to Heaven, or any future whatsoever.

The Third Millennium Is Approaching

Centuries-old beliefs that the world as we know it will end have been promulgated for so long and so frequently that it is difficult to imagine that such prophecies and predictions will decrease. To that end, however, researchers, journalists, writers, and speakers of many persuasions are calling for rationality as we come nearer to the third millennium. Theologians, too, have cautioned that even though "all three major Western religions do expect a dramatic end to history: Judaism through the coming of the messiah, Islam through a day of judgment, and Christianity through Christ's return, . . . setting a date is discouraged."[29] Yet, after interviewing members of the clerical hierarchy of the three large faiths, and learning that each basically prohibited predicting dates for the end times, one reporter concluded, "Such prohibitions have done little to block the current flood of end-of-time speculations, which threaten to surpass even the doomsday eruptions of the last century."[30]

With the current flight from rationality rampant in our society, our responsibility to bring about awareness of this societal dilemma is perhaps even greater.[31] Should not all rational beings view the coming of the third millennium as a time to vigorously support rational, scientific, and humanitarian thinking? We need to combat primitive reasoning in all its forms and guises and support those among us who convey rational, positive, hopeful, and future-oriented outlooks. Having countless citizens waiting for the end of the world is not an invigorating atmosphere, but one that aids cult leaders to seek followers as they have done at the ends of countless centuries, emboldened by the shared mythologies about the end of the world.

In a sense, nuclear threat has made us all "end timers," as the means of destruction are now scientific and real.[32] So not only are the means of producing world destruction through governments' decisions known to us all, but also we now live with the knowledge that some cult leaders, zealots, and terrorists worldwide can use scientific knowledge and skills for destructive ends. The leader and many members of the Aum Shinrikyo cult in Japan are currently on trial for spreading deadly sarin gas in the Tokyo subway in March 1995, killing twelve and wounding fifty-five hundred other persons.

Let us work toward encouraging positive outlooks and truly empowering ourselves and all others philosophically, psychologically, and economically within a context of cooperation and peace.

NOTES

1. Robert Jay Lifton, *Thought Reform and the Psychology of Totalism: A Study of "Brainwashing" in China* (1961; reprint, Chapel Hill: University of North Carolina Press, 1989). Note also Robert Jay Lifton, "Totalism and Civil Liberties," in idem, *The Future of Immortality and Other Essays for a Nuclear Age* (New York: Basic Books, 1987), vii; Robert Jay Lifton, "Cult Formation," *Harvard Mental Health Letter* (1991): vii.

2. Cited in Margaret T. Singer, "Thought Reform Today," in *Trauma, Broken Connections, and the Self,* ed. Charles B. Strozier and Michael Flynn (Lanham, Md.: Rowman and Littlefield, 1996).

3. Paul Boyer, *When Time Shall Be No More: Prophetic Belief in Modern American Culture* (Cambridge, Mass.: Belknap Press of Harvard University Press, 1992).

4. Charles B. Strozier, *Apocalypse: On the Psychology of Fundamentalism in America* (Boston: Beacon Press, 1994), 155.

5. Phone interview with Ted Daniels, editor of *Millennial Prophesy Report,* August 13, 1996.

6. Eric Lai, "Supreme Master Ching Hai," master's thesis, University of California, Berkeley, 1995; Rafer Guzman, "Suma in the City: Immaterial Girl," *San Jose (California) Metro,* March 28, 1996, 20–25.

7. Lai, "Supreme Master Ching Hai," 10.

8. Margaret Thaler Singer, interview with former members, March 26, 1996.

9. Wendy Kaminer, "The Latest Fashion in Irrationality," *Atlantic Monthly,* July 1996, 103–6.

10. Mel White, *Deceived: The Jonestown Tragedy* (Old Tappan, N.J.: Revell, 1979), 69.

11. Margaret Thaler Singer, interview with former members, June 15, 1979.

12. Ibid.

13. White, *Deceived,* 26–27.

14. Ibid., 26–27, 69.

15. Margaret Thaler Singer, with Janja Lalich, *Cults in Our Midst: The Hidden Menace in Our Everyday Lives* (San Francisco: Jossey-Bass, 1995), 105–24.

16. From interviews by author with former members.

17. "Fugitive Evangelist Steals Body, Claims He's Keeping It from Feds," *Washington Times,* February 28, 1991, A4 (as cited in the *Cult Observer,* 1991, 8[3], 4).

18. "CUT Modifies Holocaust Prophecy," *Cult Observer* (January–February 1990): 11 (citing *Livingston [Montana] Enterprise,* October 3, 1989, and *Norfolk Virginian-Pilot and Ledger Star,* January 1, 1990).

19. From interviews by author with former members.

20. Richard Lacayo, "In the Reign of Fire," *Time,* October 17, 1994, 59–60.

21. "CUT Modifies Holocaust Prophecy," *Norfolk Virginian-Pilot and Ledger Star,* Knight Ridder News Service, January 1, 1990, cited in *Cult Observer* (January–February 1990): 11.

22. From interviews by the author with former members.

23. Paul Naughton, "Drug Found in Bodies of Swiss Religious Sect," *Chicago Sun-Times,* October 7, 1994, 9.

24. "Cult Feared Slain Infant Was the Antichrist," *San Francisco Chronicle,* November 21, 1994, A12.

25. "Doomsday Passes with the World Intact," *San Francisco Chronicle,* November 15, 1993, A11.

26. "Kiev Goddess Draws Prison Sentence," *Watchman Expositor* 13 (1996): 31.

27. "33 Bodies Found in Factory Attic," *Boston Globe,* August 30, 1987, 2.

28. Singer, *Cults in Our Midst,* chap. 4.

29. Gus Niebuhr, "On the Horizon: Apocalypse," *Washington Post,* March 4, 1993, 1.

30. Ibid.

31. Margaret Thaler Singer and Janja Lalich, *"Crazy" Therapies: What Are They? Do They Work?* (San Francisco: Jossey-Bass, 1996).

32. Lifton, *Thought Reform;* idem, *The Future of Immortality;* Strozier, *Apocalypse.*

Chapter Twelve

Phallic Millennialism and Radical Environmentalism

The Apocalyptic Vision of Earth First!

Lois Ann Lorentzen

An upraised clenched fist and the battle cry "No Compromise in Defense of Mother Earth!" mark the presence of the militant environmentalist movement Earth First! Although contemporary apocalyptic movements are often associated with the radical Right, non–right-wing movements exist and are often tied to environmental concerns. As Catherine Keller notes, "Apocalypse is being colored green."[1] Earth First! represents a radical version of such an ecological apocalyptic movement.

In this chapter I explore the apocalyptic vision of Earth First!, implications for ethics and practice emerging from Earth First!'s apocalyptic framework, splits within the movement, and ways in which the movement is gendered. Theologian Bernard McGinn remains ultimately hopeful concerning the potential for "apocalyptic spirituality" to serve as a prophetic voice with the power to "galvanize protest against demonic forces in history." Yet he also expresses an ambivalence, which I share, over its tendency to serve as a "projection of the least noble aspects of human hopes and fears onto history."[2] Earth First!'s apocalyptic vision of ecological collapse and strategies in defense of the earth have stirred the imagination of the U.S. public and have provided models of ecological protest. As a prophetic voice Earth First! has galvanized parts of the environmentalist movement and has called us to more responsible ways of living on the earth. Although I am in deep sympathy with Earth First! and glad to hear its prophetic voice, I also am uncomfortable with certain less than "noble" aspects of Earth First! thinking and practice.

Ecological Apocalypse

The beginnings of Earth First! have been mythologized in song, story, and even in scholarly writings. Environmental lobbyists frustrated with what they saw as the slow, reformist approach by such groups as the Sierra Club, the Wilderness Society, and the Friends of the Earth in the face of what they perceived to be severe environmental crises, founded Earth First! in 1980. As Earth First! cofounder Dave Foreman tells it, several disillusioned environmental lobbyists camping together in

Mexico's Pinacate Desert "began talking about sparking a fundamentalist revival within the environmental movement."[3] Unfurling a three-hundred-foot sheet of black plastic down the Glen Canyon Dam (simulating a giant crack in the dam), with seventy-five people gathered for the 1981 spring equinox, was one of Earth First!'s first actions. Foreman's book *Ecodefense: A Field Guide to Monkeywrenching* soon became a handbook for many radical environmentalists. Earth First! now boasts more than fifty largely autonomous groups and activities in most of the fifty states. Earth First!, especially during the 1980s, captured the imagination of the U.S. public in a way nearly unparalleled by grassroots movements.

Foreman writes, "We set out to be radical in style, positions, philosophy and organization in order to be effective and to avoid the pitfalls of co-optation and moderation which we had already experienced."[4] Earth First! is radical both philosophically and in tactics and actions. What makes radical environmentalism *radical,* according to Peter List, is (a) a wilderness fundamentalism that relies on deep ecology and biocentrism for its philosophical underpinnings, (b) a strong activist orientation that favors unconventional direct tactics such as monkeywrenching and ecotage, (c) a social and political philosophy that emphasizes anarchism and bioregionalism, and (d) ecofeminism.[5]

Earth First! shares the characteristics of, and is perhaps the prototype for, the radical environmentalism described by List. Yet the radicalism of Earth First! is fueled by its apocalyptic vision, which holds a particular eschatological vision of ecological collapse. Charles B. Strozier writes of the widespread forms of endism in contemporary culture in which the self is located in "some future, ultimate narrative."[6] Earth First!'s particular form of endism claims that humans have created an ecological crisis that will result in the end of history. We have "connived in the murder of our own origins," writes Edward Abbey.[7] Earth Firster Christopher Manes explains, "The understanding of radical environmentalism begins at the end of the world as we know it, the meltdown of biological diversity that our industrialized culture has set in motion."[8] The world or human world history will end, according to Earth First! endism, because of an anthropogenic ecological collapse. Although great suffering will occur, Earth First! moves past a mere endism in which society creates an "ecological catastrophe containing the seeds of its own destruction" to an apocalyptic eschatology. Earth Firsters are not left without hope. The end of the human world may not be an entirely bad thing. Earth First!'s eschatology allows for a utopian vision of an ecologically balanced future. As Bron Raymond Taylor notes, Earth Firsters believe that "after great suffering, if enough of the genetic stock of the planet survives, evolution will resume its natural course. If human beings also survive, they will have the opportunity to re-establish tribal ways of living, such as bioregionalism[,] that are compatible with an evolutionary future."[9] Abbey believed that this utopian future would be characterized by scattered human populations, modest in number, that live by "fishing, hunting, food-gathering, small-scale farming and ranching, that assemble once a year in the ruins of abandoned cities for great festivals of moral, spiritual, artistic and intellectual renewal—a people for whom the wilderness is not a playground but their natural and native home."[10] Earth First! is pessimistic that humans can avoid the coming ecological collapse. This is the negative vision of Earth First! endism. Yet, in the positive eschatology of Earth First!, this end is followed by a new beginning of ecological renewal.

Apocalyptic movements, believing as they do that the world will end, generally identify reasons or causes for the predicted impending doom. According to Strozier, in a Christian fundamentalist apocalyptic framework, the world is "an evil place to be resisted, and it is in any event on a sure path toward imminent destruction."[11] Although for different reasons, the pagan fundamentalists of Earth First! would agree. The ecocollapse predicted by Earth Firsters also stems from human wrongdoing. Taylor, arguably the best scholar of Earth First! thinking and activism, writes that "Earth Firsters perceive many forms of human-caused defilement, including commercial developments (and the accompanying pavement); most forms of tourism . . . human efforts to "manage" nature. . . . Indeed for most Earth First!ers, few corners of modern society have not profaned Sacred Earth."[12] But of all these evils, "the human enclosure and privatization of land escalating with the emergence of industrial societies is often thought of as the central, arrogant, desecrating crime."[13]

Human evil has created land privatization, water pollution, deforestation, species endangerment, and numerous environmental crises. These human evils emerge from patriarchy, hierarchy, and anthropocentrism, "related forms of domination that destroy the natural world."[14] Given Earth First!'s philosophical grounding in deep ecology, anthropocentrism—the extreme hubris of a human-centered perspective—holds central place as the primary domination that must be overcome. Biocentrism is for Earth First! a moral imperative. As Taylor notes, Earth First!'s moral claim is that "non human life is valuable even apart from its usefulness to humans" and "every species has intrinsic worth and each should be allowed to fulfill its evolutionary destiny." Humans then, are "not more valuable than other species."[15]

Locating evil generally presumes that there are enemies who embody evil and against whom one must battle. Abbey writes: "We have created an iron monster with which we wage war, not only on small peasant nations over the sea, but even on ourselves—a war against all forms of life, against life itself. In the name of Power and Growth. But the war is only beginning."[16] This "iron monster," or technology, embodies domination in its multiple forms—anthropocentrism, hierarchy, and patriarchy. In our times, according to Earth First!, the most powerful form this domination takes is industrial society. An early member of Earth First! states, "We further believe that the enemy is not capitalism, communism, or socialism. It is corporate industrialism whether it is in the United States, the Soviet Union, China or Mexico."[17]

Locating evil also presumes the possibility of salvation, or an escape from evil. How does one get "saved" from industrialized society? Lee notes that the salvation offered by Earth First! is similar to that of other millennial ideologies and movements in that it is "anticipated as imminent, ultimate, collective, and this-worldly."[18] Conversion, both personally and collectively, to biocentrism is needed. Given our deep internalization of anthropocentric ways of thinking and being, the change of consciousness that is imperative for Earth First! salvation may need to come through ritual and affective practices. Deep ecology philosopher Arne Naess claims that the strong identification with nature that is necessary for ecological conversion is the "spontaneous, non rational process by which the interests of another being are reacted to as our own."[19] Examples of affective practices include the Council of All Beings workshops, in which other life forms speak through council participants; singing; dancing; howling like wolves; "road shows"; and even monkeywrenching.

Earth Firsters are often involved in "ecoevangelism," as road show balladeer "Dakota" Sid Clifford refers to attempts at securing ecological conversion. Yet, given the magnitude of the change needed for salvation, few Earth Firsters hold the optimistic belief that salvation will appear through massive individual and collective transformation. As Lee notes:

> The end of civilization could only be prevented by a complete change in government, industry and cultural values--at the minimum there would need to be an immediate halt to industry, a ban on the use of automobiles, elimination of range cattle, and the restoration of major wilderness areas. . . . the sooner the system collapses the better because each day its destruction continues, more irreplaceable wilderness is lost."[20]

The earth can be saved only through massive systemic societal changes. Lee chronicles divisions between Earth Firsters who differ as to their belief in the possibility that these changes will occur. Those who believe in human perfectibility believe that humans are capable of the social change needed for ecological conversion. Others, who are essentially pessimistic about human nature, despair of social transformation. Yet, whether one holds a notion of human perfectibility or not, few within the movement predict that the radical transformation needed for an Earth First! style of salvation will occur soon, if at all.

Earth First!'s apocalyptic eschatology is used to justify ecodefense, ecotage, and monkeywrenching. "They remember that they are engaged in the most moral of all actions: Protecting life, defending the earth," says Dave Foreman of those who practice strategic monkeywrenching. Direct action, or ecodefense, is action taken in defense of a forest, a river, or an endangered species and may include acts of civil disobedience such as blockading a logging road, staging a protest, or chaining oneself to a tree. Strategic monkeywrenching involves halting wilderness destruction through actions such as pouring sand into gas tanks of large vehicles; in paper monkeywrenching, flurries of legal documents are generated in order to end destructive practices. Ecotage might consist of spiking trees in an area to be clear-cut or pulling up survey stakes—in short, any attempt to sabotage an operation that would destroy one's place. In this sense the militant actions of Earth First! are seen as self defense, or as the earth defending itself. As self-defense, the actions are morally justifiable.

Ecotage, direct action, and monkeywrenching are viewed as not only morally justifiable, but even at times as obligatory. Taylor points to three pillars of Earth First! thought that yield the moral justification for militant action. First, the biocentric ethic makes individual human life no more intrinsically valuable than a grizzly bear's. Second, the fact that we are "in the midst of an unprecedented, anthropogenic extinction crisis, and consequently many ecosystems are presently collapsing provides the essential underpinning and rationale for militancy—without this claim there is no basis for urgency."[21] Finally, to the moral and environmental claims is added a political claim. Democracy in the United States, they believe, either does not work in light of the urgency of the current environmental crisis, or it works too slowly. Those who make major political decisions are the very people who destroy the wilderness, "wealthy corporations and large government agencies such as the United States Forest Service and the Bureau of Land Management."[22]

Actions that support wilderness are therefore morally good and justifiable because of apocalyptic urgency, a biocentric moral philosophy grounded in deep ecology, and flawed democratic processes. Compromises are evil. The apocalyptic urgency of Earth First!, when coupled with moral claims emerging from deep ecology and political claims concerning democracy, makes radical tactics morally obligatory.

Besides monkeywrenching the current system, Earth Firsters offer proposals for the future—a vision of the new order that must be built after this one collapses as a result of our anthropocentric, self-destructive, world-destroying history. The most common vision in the Earth First! future is that of primitive societies of hunter-gatherers. According to Lee, the movement has never advocated the overthrow of the capitalist economic system per se but "instead argued that the return to small scale economic ventures and agriculture would yield the good society."[23] Bioregionalism, the idea that humans should live sustainably with other creatures within distinct ecosystems, is promoted by many Earth First! members. Earth First! has been trying, as Foreman puts it, "in various ways to help industrialized civilization find its own dharma nature, and become an egalitarian, tribal society that respects people and respects the earth once again."[24]

Green Warriors

A great schism occurred in Earth First! at the beginning of the decade. Its end result was the mass resignations of the *Earth First! Journal* editorial staff and the departure of Dave Foreman on September 22, 1990. For some time the conflict had been developing between Judi Bari and Dave Foreman. Judi Bari is an Earth First! organizer and one of the chief promoters of Redwood Summer, the nonviolent campaign to save California's old growth forest. Prior to leaving Earth First!, Foreman denounced Bari and her compatriots for injecting "class struggle" and "humanism" into the wilderness movement. Bari, in organizing Redwood Summer in 1990, had mustered a broader based coalition of Central American groups, peace and antinuclear movement activists, labor, and women's groups than is generally the case for an Earth First! action. Bari claimed that the environmental movement had become too separatist. Deep ecology, according to Bari, claims that all is related. How then can the activist movement separate wilderness off and say it is not related to society? Society is built on the exploitation of lower classes and the earth. Thus, it is consistent for a radical biocentric movement to include a class analysis.[25]

Foreman denounced the organizing strategies of Redwood Summer, claiming that "west coast yippies and hippies had taken over," who were "more interested in pursuing the wildness within than the wildness out in the forest."[26] Foreman left and soon founded a new journal *Wild Earth*, which focuses strictly on wilderness. However, the schism between those who are purely biocentric and those who believe that social issues need not be divorced from biocentrism does not call into question the apoca-

lyptic visions sketched thus far. Ongoing tensions have occurred over the use of monkeywrenching, feminism, political strategies and tactics, and the role of spirituality.
Although Lee claims that the essential split is over views of human nature (whether it
is perfectible or not) and Taylor contends, more accurately, that the schism is over
strategy and tactics, both agree that the sides remain biocentric and hold wilderness as
a moral norm or ideal. Both sides agree that ecological collapse (endism) is imminent
and have similar eschatological visions of a new order of ecological harmony.

In spite of these schisms, Earth First! members bear some remarkable similarities,
similarities that set them apart from what many come to expect from apocalyptic
groups. Strozier notes that in apocalyptic thought, hope is deferred; thus it is "often
associated with the poor and oppressed."[27] Lee claims that millenarian ideologies
and movements appeal to marginalized groups who have "little to lose from the
apocalyptic destruction of the present."[28] Given this general tendency, the profile of
Earth First! members discovered in a study by Kamieniecki, Coleman, and Vos is
intriguing. According to their data, Earth First! members tend to be "post-material-
ist," white, middle-class, educated; possess a biocentric identification with nature;
hold global and long range concerns; and accept a level of self-deprivation in terms
of material gain.[29] Earth First! members, unlike what one might expect from an
apocalyptic movement, are not the "poor and oppressed" of society. Many have voluntarily given up privilege to defend the earth.

Members of apocalyptic movements often see themselves as God's chosen people,
regardless of their social standing. In the case of Earth First!, members often describe
themselves as warriors. List notes that adherents of Earth First! depicted themselves
as "warriors in the racial land army while activists in the Sea Shepherd Society under
Watson were called its 'navy.'"[30] Industrialized civilization wages war against nature
in Earth First! mythology; thus, ecowarriors are morally justified in their battling
since they are merely acting in self-defense. Abbey writes, "A bulldozer ripping up a
hillside to strip mine for coal is committing terrorism; the damnation of a flowing
river followed by the drowning of Cherokee graves, of forest and farmland, is an act
of terrorism."[31] The war in which Earth First! is engaged is therefore a justifiable
defense of homeland. And in this battle there must be no compromise: "For Earth
First! it is all or nothing. Win or lose. No truce or cease fire. No surrender. No par-
titioning of the territory."[32] The Earth Firsters, rather than being an elect chosen by
God, are the self-chosen warriors who fight those waging war against nature.

The battle metaphors of Earth First! might lead one to assume that the movement
promotes violence. The question whether Earth First! in particular and radical environmentalism in general are violent and even "terrorist" rose most dramatically
with claims made about links between the infamous unabomber and Earth First![33]
The first principle of "strategic monkeywrenching" in Foreman's *Ecodefense: A
Field Guide to Monkeywrenching* is that of nonviolence—the action must not harm
human or other life.[34] Militant actions, monkeywrenching, and civil disobedience
are all nonviolent; this remains an important tenet of Earth First! activism. To my
knowledge, no one has ever been harmed as a result of an Earth First! action.[35]

Violence that occurs comes rather as reaction against Earth First! Journalist Susan
Zakin quotes a mailing to Earth First! women:

> It has come to our attention that you are an Earth First! lesbian. . . . Not only have we been watching you . . . but we also know and have distributed your phone number to every organized hate group that could possibly have hostile tendancies [sic] toward ilk of your kind. . . . We know who you are, where you live, and continue to hone [sic] in on you. . . . we will specifically hunt down each and every member. . . . Signed by the Committee for the Death to Earth First brought to you by Fed Up Americans for Common Sense.[36]

Earth Firsters have become accustomed, in an uneasy way, to such hostility and backlash. Yet, the 1990 car bombing of Judi Bari and Darryl Cherney proved that at least one of the writers of hate mail was serious. Bari had been receiving regular warnings from a writer who called him/herself "The Lord's Avenger." In a letter to Bari, the Lord's Avenger wrote, "I felt the Power of the Lord in my heart and I knew I had been chosen to strike down this demon."[37] In spite of their battle metaphors, Earth First! is denying accusations of its "terrorist" tendencies. Its members have been *victims* of such activities, rather than perpetrators.

Phallic Millennialism

Few of the scholars who write about Earth First! (with the exception of Taylor) explore the gendered nature of the Earth First! movement. List, Taylor, and others accurately note that ecofeminism has been an important influence within radical environmentalism in general and Earth First! in particular. Many current Earth Firsters consider themselves ecofeminists. Yet, women within the movement at times express concern about the "male" flavor of Earth First!, especially in the early years. For example, women within the movement may be alarmed over Earth First!'s stances on overpopulation. The *Earth First! Journal,* often through the writings of Christopher Manes, has called starvation and disease Gaian solutions to overpopulation. Since the human species as a whole is innately destructive to the environment, Gaia herself is purging the species. Women within the movement may agree with the seriousness of overpopulation but feel that the fears of women and people of color who have been victimized by population control programs in the past are ignored. Women, they feel, should control their own reproduction. Analyses that ignore social institutions, consumption patterns, and the impact of education and increased economic status on women and childbearing while focusing on population control are suspect.

Many of the preceding debates have appeared in the *Earth First! Journal* over the years. Sharon Doubiago claims that male failure is nowhere more apparent than in the exclusion of feminism from the radical ecology movement.[38] Reminiscent of the civil rights movement, early in the movement women claimed that language, organizing styles, leadership, policy formation, and so forth, were male-dominated. Bari claimed that women were simply seen as "more expendable"[39] and that Redwood Summer represented a "feminization" of Earth First! organizing strategy. Foreman and other male leaders, according to Bari, were uncomfortable with feminist organizing styles, preferring either acts of individual bravado or mass organizing. According to Bari, the Redwood Summer model was a result of nonhierarchical organizing; it was an attempt to learn new ways to relate and engage in collective nonviolence. She says environmental problems are inextricably linked to gender: "If we want to save the planet we must address root causes like patriarchy and the destructive exploitative society. . . . we can't separate it."[40] Part of the rift between Bari and Foreman was that Bari remained firm in her conviction that Earth First! should embrace feminism.

A danger exists when Gaia and Mother Earth language are used in ways that uncritically associate women with nature. Earth First! uses female imagery for the earth. The earth is Gaia or Mother Earth, as is clearly evident in the slogan, "No Compromise in Defense of Mother Earth." Quite frankly, this gender-typing of the planet is extremely problematic for me. Patrick Murphy asks, "Does this re-person-ification of the planet as a female nurturer truly oppose the patriarchal ideology of domination that destroys the very environment that sustains human life, or does it through its metaphoric implications inadvertently reinforce elements of that ideolo-gy and thereby limit its own effectiveness in subverting the system it opposes?"[41] I suspect, as does Murphy, that a gender-typing that happens within a society full of particular gender biases cannot expect to avoid reinforcing those prejudices. The his-torical impact of this model is not adequately addressed by Earth First!, in spite of the ecofeminist presence. And the language of Mother Earth does little to increase our understanding of the planet in a way that is not anthropomorphic.

The gendered nature of Earth First! language relates also to its frequent images of war and battle. Dave Foreman once remarked that "if you come home and find a bunch of Hells Angels, raping your wife, old mother, and eleven year old daughter, you don't sit down and talk balance with them or suggest compromise. You get your twelve gauge shotgun and blow them to hell. . . . people out there are trying to save their mother from rape."[42] The message is clear. The earth is female and men are the ideal protectors of the earth, yet the historical impact of this model is not addressed.

Bari is right. As a concerned environmentalist and feminist, I have been drawn to Earth First! With their moral fervor, their understanding of the severity of environ-mental crises, and their clear view of human culpability in destroying the planet, they provide a needed prophetic voice. Yet the language at the beginning of this chapter frightens me. An ecowarrior crying "No Compromise in Defense of Mother Earth" makes me uneasy. The protector defending female earth is merely a step away con-ceptually from the same warrior (male) raping and pillaging the earth. The language isn't right; it reflects a deep-seated approach both to who I am and to what the Earth is. I am heartened by the ways many members of Earth First! are attempting to main-tain the passionate commitment of Earth First! while moving in an ecofeminist direc-tion. If we continue to associate the earth with woman and hate both, neither the earth nor women will be safe, no matter how many ecowarriors howl like wolves.

NOTES

1. Catherine Keller, "Eschatology, Ecology, and a Green Ecumenacy," in Rebecca S. Chopp and Mark Lewis Taylor, eds., *Reconstructing Christian Theology* (Minneapolis: Fortress Press, 1994), 326.

2. Bernard McGinn, "Apocalyptic Spirituality Approaching the Third Millennium," paper presented at the Power of the Millennium Conference, October 19–20, 1995, Graduate Theological Union of Berkeley, Calif.: 5, 11.

3. Dave Foreman, "Defending the Earth and Burying the Hatchet," *Whole Earth Review* 69 (1990): 110.

4. Dave Foreman, "Earth First!" in Peter C. List, ed., *Radical Environmentalism: Philosophy and Tactics* (Belmont, Calif.: Wadsworth, 1993), 17.

5. List, *Radical Environmentalism,* 17.

6. Charles B. Strozier, *Apocalypse: On the Psychology of Fundamentalism in America* (Boston: Beacon Press, 1994), 1.

7. Edward Abbey, "Earth First! and the Monkey Wrench Gang," in List, *Radical Environmentalism,* 151.

8. Christopher Manes, cited in Martha F. Lee, *Earth First: Environmental Apocalypse* (Syracuse, N.Y.: Syracuse University Press, 1995), 1.

9. Bron Raymond Taylor, "The Religion and Politics of Earth First!" *Ecologist* 21 (1991): 261.

10. Edward Abbey, cited in Taylor, "The Religion and Politics of Earth First!" 261.

11. Strozier, *Apocalypse,* 164.

12. Bron Raymond Taylor, "Resacralizing Earth: Pagan Environmentalism and the Restoration of Turtle Island," in David Chidester and Edward T. Linenthal, eds., *American Sacred Space* (Bloomington: Indiana University Press, 1995), 116.

13. Ibid.

14. Bron Raymond Taylor, "Earth First! and Global Narratives of Popular Ecological Resistance," in Bron Raymond Taylor, ed., *Ecological Resistance Movements: The Global Emergence of Radical and Popular Environmentalism* (Albany: State University of New York Press, 1995), 17.

15. Ibid., 15.

16. Abbey, "Earth First!" 152.

17. Quoted in Lee, *Earth First,* 32.

18. Lee, *Earth First,* 17.

19. Arne Naess, "Self Realization: An Ecological Approach to Being in the Woods," in Joanna Macy and John Seed, eds., *Thinking like a Mountain: Towards a Council of All Beings* (Philadelphia: New Society, 1988), 14.

20. Lee, *Earth First,* 40–41

21. Taylor, "Earth First!" 16.

22. Lee, *Earth First,* 15.

23. Ibid., 36.

24. Foreman, "Defending the Earth," 114.

25. Judi Bari, "Judi's World: The Life and Thoughts of Earth First! Organizer and Bomb Victim, Judi Bari," interview by Christina Keyser, *Express: The East Bay's Free Weekly* 13, no. 17 (1991): 21.

26. Lee, *Earth First,* 139.

27. Strozier, *Apocalypse,* 2.

28. Lee, *Earth First,* 5.

29. Sheldon Kamieniecki, Duane Coleman, and Robert O. Vos, "The Effectiveness of Radical Environmentalists," in Taylor, *Ecological Resistance Movements.*

30. List, *Radical Environmentalism,* 6.

31. Abbey, "Earth First!" 252.

32. Foreman, "Earth First!" 190.

33. Claims that links existed between the unabomber and Earth First! are unfounded. See

Bron Raymond Taylor, "Radical Environmentalists and the Unabomber—A Terrorist Connection?" *Los Angeles Times,* May 17, 1996.

34. Dave Foreman, *Ecodefense: A Field Guide to Monkeywrenching* (Tucson: Ned Ludd Books, 1985).

35. A logger in Oregon was injured by a spike placed in a tree, but Earth First! was not implicated in the spiking.

36. Susan Zakin, *Coyotes and Town Dogs* (New York: Viking, 1993), 370.

37. Taylor, "The Religion and Politics of Earth First!" 258.

38. Sharon Doubiago, "Mama Coyote Talks to the Boys," in Judith Plant, ed., *Healing the Wounds: The Promise of Ecofeminism* (Philadelphia: New Society, 1989).

39. Bari, "Judi's World," 21.

40. Ibid.

41. Patrick D. Murphy, "Sex-Typing the Planet: Gaia Imagery and the Problem of Subverting Patriarchy," *Environmental Ethics* 10 (1988): 155.

42. Cited in Lee, *Earth First,* 65.

Chapter Thirteen

Coercive Purity
The Dangerous Promise of Apocalyptic Masculinity

Lee Quinby

In this final decade of the final century of the second millennium of the Christian era, a new form of apocalyptic masculinity has emerged, one that combines Christian fundamentalism, New Age fervor, and sports rally fever. This marvel is the rapidly growing evangelical Christian men's movement called Promise Keepers, whose slogan is "A man's man is a godly man" and whose stated agenda is to help men regain the leadership of their families.[1] What should we make of this new configuration of apocalypticism in which fifty thousand to seventy thousand men huddle in football stadiums across the country, chanting, singing, hugging, praying, and weeping in order to commit themselves to God and family? As an organization, Promise Keepers has exhibited exceptional skill for shepherding fellow worshipers into rallies lasting fourteen hours over the course of two days. In 1996 more than twenty cities around the country hosted rallies bringing almost a million men together and producing a robust yearly budget of $120 million.[2] Official publications include three books, *Seven Promises of a Promise Keeper, The Power of a Promise Kept,* and *Go the Distance,* a magazine called *New Man,* and numerous tapes and CDs of religious songs, not to mention a host of kitsch items, ranging from T-shirts to coffee mugs. Clearly, a new brand of evangelicalism is on the rise—but this contemporary Great Awakening comes with a "men only" sign on the door.[3]

At the outset I want to indicate that I am ambivalent about Promise Keepers. On one hand, it is undeniable that a large number of men today experience personal pain, frustration, and discontent about what it means to live *as a man.* As a feminist and a mother of two adult sons, I sympathize with this view, especially since Promise Keepers accentuates men's self-transformation. On the other hand, it is equally indisputable that Promise Keepers promotes social inequality by insisting on hierarchical gender roles and compulsory heterosexuality. It could emphasize self-transformation in the name of gender and sexual equality, but it has chosen not to. The organization has chosen instead to lead men down a path of enmity, deceivingly in the name of love. Furthermore, its goal of forging a Christian nation is one more crack in the wall of separation of church and state.[4] My overall assessment is that the promises made by Promise Keepers threaten democratic freedom.[5]

The remarkable success of Promise Keepers is sufficient to warrant its examination as a cultural phenomenon. Its rapid rise and national sweep prompt certain questions. Psychological questions readily spring to mind: What perceived needs are being tapped or met through this new men's movement? Structural questions follow: What are the organizational and economic arrangements that have enabled Promise Keepers to emerge now and grow exponentially? And, crucially, What social-political consequences have ensued, and might ensue, from its efforts? But to my mind the most important question—and one that helps illuminate the others—is, Why, at this particular time, has a *fundamentalist religious* organization fired the imagination of so many men from across this nation?[6]

Apocalypticism is a sense of an impending end—to time and the world as we know it—and an expectation that with the end will come a new era of perfection. Apocalypticism often traffics in violence as a feature of the end time, especially in the fundamentalist Christian version, in which an Antichrist wreaks terrible destruction on human beings in the final struggles between forces of good and evil. Marked by twin features of redemption and demonization, apocalyptic logic polarizes camps between a victimized elect and an odious enemy. I have found it useful to analyze expressions of apocalypticism through three primary modes: the divine, a metaphysical belief system that ranges from fundamentalist religion to New Age thought; the technological, which sees technology as bringing either catastrophe or salvation to humanity; and the postapocalyptic, which operates through postmodern apathy or ironic self-interest.[7] As a discourse, contemporary apocalypticism is often a mix of these modes, which makes it internally contradictory yet insistently absolutistic.

Promise Keepers combines the first two of these modes with a slight tint of the third. Briefly put, its blend of premillennialist and New Age thought functions squarely within the divine mode. Its Internet dissemination of information across the globe and its video savvy draw on the technological mode. In regard to the postapocalyptic mode, although Promise Keepers tends to be more earnest and sincere than most postapocalypticians, its emphasis on personal transformation steers it away from involvement with certain forms of political activism and links it to a generalized apathy over issues of poverty and racism. At the same time, the organization exhibits a kind of duplicity characteristic of postapocalypticism's ironic self-interest: certain political affiliations are concealed and denied through an insistence that "Promise Keepers does not have a political agenda."[8]

In regard to the group's political effects, I want to clarify the ways in which Promise Keepers fuels antifeminist and homophobic attitudes and behavior. This is particularly egregious because Promise Keepers has incorporated the criticism of absent fathers and emotionally diminished manhood developed by feminism and the gay movement, yet it has turned these appropriations into denunciations of each movement. Ultimately, what I want to show is how Promise Keepers, in the name of leading men to manly Christianity, produces what I call "coercive purity." Promise Keepers's pursuit of purity of body and soul creates a fault line in members' masculine identity that divides between scapegoating nonpure others and fearing that impurity within themselves. This dynamic may be likened to the way the concept of purity was deployed by eugenic-minded scientists and legislators in the early part of this century to denounce Eastern European immigrants as genetically impure.

Current efforts to limit immigration focus on purity of the English language. In the Promise Keepers formulation, operating through a Christian model of internal temptation, purity is used to demonize homosexuals and feminists; though much of the emphasis is on self-coercion, the concept also functions to coerce others toward a fundamentalist mandated concept of purity. In each instance those deemed impure are scapegoated as a threat to the pure community. Whether this scapegoating erupts in violence, which is a potential threat within apocalyptic groups, or fuels legislative oppression, which has already occurred and is on the organization's agenda, the foundational beliefs of Promise Keepers breed injustice.[9]

The Life and Times of the Apocalyptic Male Subject

The double-edged point I want to stress is that the dominant narrative of order in this country has been, since colonization, an apocalyptic one, and that apocalypticism has been one, if not *the,* predominant mode of antidemocratic belief and behavior. Phillip Greven's work is especially significant in this regard because he has shown correlations between apocalyptic belief systems and corporal punishment, indicating a spiral of biblically sanctioned abuse that gives rise to an adult willingness to inflict pain on children in the name of discipline and see punishment as a proper means of upholding order and obedience.[10] This is relevant to Promise Keepers in a number of ways. Even though a great deal of Promise Keepers rhetoric emphasizes love over wrath, it maintains the fundamentalist orientation toward the justified punishment of hell. The men who gather at the rallies are of the generations that Greven shows to be very likely to have received physical punishment from their parents. As he indicates, fundamentalist ministers from Billy Graham to James Dobson have argued for corporal punishment as a necessary means to stave off the eternal punishment of hell. Greven demonstrates persuasively that such beliefs give rise to adult psyches that suffer the scars of this abuse.

I am arguing, further, that apocalypticism constitutes a regime of truth that blurs religious and secular lines, informing a range of beliefs and practices that include popular culture, fashion, science, social science, technology, and so on. Consider this popular culture example of apocalypticism, which, though innocuous enough, from a genealogical perspective shows the intricate connections between disciplinary power, truth, and (in this case male) subjectivity: Marvel Entertainment Group's "Archangel II, an action toy figure based on a comic book character."[11] Here's what the back of the box has to say about him:

> As the high-flying Angel, Warren Worthington III was one of the original members of the X-Men. Years later, Worthington's real wings were dissected, replaced with razor-sharp wings of steel, and he was transformed into Archangel, one of the four Horsemen of the Apocalypse. Now, having fought against the conditioning that tainted and turned him into a living weapon, Archangel has embraced his humanity and strives to regain the purity that once surrounded him.[12]

With just a touch of qualification over the literal or metaphorical status of Worthington's wings, this could be a description of a Promise Keeper. It is a description that should be read in light of what is referred to these days as the crisis in masculinity, a confusion and a precariousness in men's gender identity that corresponds to the postmodern acceleration of many cultural uncertainties, including declining economic power under late capitalism and a drop in the status of the United States as supreme imperialist power. Both the crisis in and the attempt to "rehabilitate" masculinity seem to be occurring most intensely for the generation of men who grew up in the X-Men era, men who probably read these top-selling comics of the past few decades and who, as fathers, are likely to have children who play with these figures and watch them on television.[13] These men, like their comic counterparts, have been deeply affected not only by growing economic and military insecurity but also by feminism and other civil rights movements of the past four decades.[14] The promises of restored order in apocalypticism offer a ready-made way not only to assuage their anxiety and uncertainty but also to rectify perceived losses.[15]

A toy like Archangel is both symptomatic and productive of current confusions about masculinity. Attempts to quell these confusions can take many forms, ranging from feminist transformation to aggressive masculinist backlash. Given the conditions of today's society, the latter is a significant threat. As Robert Jay Lifton and Charles Strozier have documented, the violent imagery and fixed-self framework of apocalypticism damages the psychological well-being of those who live within its grip.[16] I am going to be even more blunt by saying that the book of Revelation and the secular forms that incorporate its imagery provide both a paradigm of masculinist fantasy and a contemporary training manual in apocalyptic justification of violence. Recurrently, this psychological disposition has been systematically aimed against women and a variety of cultural others, including homosexuals, blacks, Arabs, and Jews.

I am not exonerating women or these groups—they can be and have been apocalyptic. But I am stating the feminist point so starkly because it is too often ignored.[17] The gender and sexual dynamic of the book of Revelation celebrates violence between men and against women.[18] We see this celebration through the 144,000 men who "follow the Lamb" and who *because* they are "not defiled with women," are ushered into the New Jerusalem (14:3–4). We see violence against women enacted in the punishment of Jezebel, who has dared to be a teacher and has challenged men's sexual prerogative: "Behold I will cast her into a bed, and them that commit adultery with her into great tribulation, except they repent of their deeds. And I will kill her children with death" (2:22–23). We see it with the Whore of Babylon, the feminized trope through which evil and corruption are depicted. Her punishment is to be made "desolate and naked," to have her flesh eaten and then burned (17:16). And we see continuities of such violence throughout history in the systematic rape and slaughter of women and their children as part of apocalyptically inspired warfare.

Such reminders may well sound hyperbolic given Promise Keepers's saccharine-sounding rhetoric. But it is important to see the spectrum of apocalyptic masculinity, which, whether moderate or extreme, defines itself as pure by designating and demonizing categories of impurity. As Robert Jay Lifton argues in regard to ideological totalism, "by defining and manipulating the criteria of purity, and then by conducting an all-out war upon impurity, the ideological totalists create a narrow world of guilt and shame."[19] A genealogy of the apocalyptic male subject makes visible these otherwise hidden branches of connection between biblical Truth, demonization of women's sexuality and homosexuality, and obsession with punishment exacted in this world or in hell. Promise Keepers masculinity, through its insistence on purity, sets men up to pursue an impossible eradication of desire, fueling that desire through evocation of its treachery while condemning its expression.

Looking for Mr. Apocalypse

By far the most distinguishing feature of Promise Keepers is its innovative twist on evangelical revivalism. In this respect it bears comparison to earlier revival movements in the United States. In fact, it bills itself as part of this lineage by referring to its endeavor as the next Great Awakening or the Grand Awakening.[20] Yet, both its ambitions and its successes far exceed the capacity of the old-time revival tent. More on the order of the urban evangelical gatherings of the late nineteenth century organized by Dwight L. Moody and brought to an art form in the twentieth century by Billy Graham, and in keeping with the televangelism of our own time, Promise Keepers gatherings are staged in large football stadiums equipped with giant video screens.[21]

So what is a Promise Keepers rally like? Reports from participants and video footage from the Promise Keepers organization are in accord on certain features. Rallies open with high-spirited cheers. From one side of the bleachers, a shout goes out: "I love Jesus, yes I do! I love Jesus, how 'bout you?" A moment later, the response marches back: "We love Jesus, yes we do! We love Jesus, how 'bout you?"[22] Music and clapping join with call and response to excite and unite the men; prayer and preaching bring them to tears and embraces. Hour upon hour, the men are urged to confront their deep emotional wounds and to grasp how their personal suffering has led them to be absent or uncaring fathers, sons, and brothers. Some of the messages are expressly political, as was the 1994 speech of the Reverend E. V. Hill, who called the ACLU satanic, declared abortion an epidemic, and decried the teaching of evolution.[23] And some of the chants take on a decidedly aggressive face. Shouts of "Hit him! Hit him! Hit him!" accompanied by fist clenching no doubt raise collective energies to a militant pitch, acceptable here because the "him" in question is the Devil.[24] The finale of each rally is usually an appearance by Bill McCartney, former coach of the University of Colorado football team and the man credited with founding Promise Keepers. McCartney's final words return to the call and response device that opened the rally and emphasize the triumph of the believer: "There's nothing I want more in life than to serve Jesus Christ, because I want Almighty God's favor on me. How about you?"[25]

McCartney, a former Roman Catholic who is now a member of Denver's charismatic Vineyard Church, exemplifies the paradoxes of fundamentalist Christian brotherhood. He calls for men to be more loving and caring, yet his rhetoric turns on warrior metaphors and an evocation of violence, as when he proclaims, "We have been *in* a war but not *at* war! If we are to make a difference, it will require much more than we've been doing until now."[26] He beseeches men to become more loving toward each other but in a 1992 news conference condemned "homosexuality [as] an abomination against Almighty God."[27] He urges men to reclaim their manhood but espouses surrender as part of God's divine plan: "It could be that God has brought us to Boulder to oversee our death. Become dead and open yourself up to him."[28]

McCartney's often-repeated use of his own life story to represent this theme of becoming dead to one's unchristian values is selectively candid and slightly self-aggrandizing in the spirit of Nietzsche's insight about the contradictory pride of self-renunciation. He confesses that he had himself failed to be a leader in his own home and that his marriage had faltered. Even more devastating to his role as leader, he reveals that his unmarried teenage daughter had become pregnant by one of his football players. The story takes an especially dramatic turn in the telling because the father of this grandchild died from stomach cancer, but not before McCartney had aided his conversion to Christ.[29] The story as told thus activates a struggle for male purity in which a woman's body becomes the battlefield, the territory for the victor to claim. Actually, Kristy McCartney had two children by two different members of her father's football team, one in 1988 when she was nineteen years old by Sal Aunese, who died, and another in 1993 by Shannon Clavelle when she was twenty-four.[30] Of course, this version lacks the emotional drama of the conversion narrative. McCartney's story also takes something of a contradictory turn at the next point with his resignation of his highly successful coaching position (at a salary of $350,000 per year). Most Promise Keepers would not be in a financial position to follow suit; hence he is distinguished as Promise Keeper *par excellence*. He capitalizes on his action by saying he did so in order to devote more time to his family while also expanding Promise Keepers, but given the number of speaking engagements required of him at the rallies, one has to wonder how much time he does devote to home and family.[31]

Bill McCartney has clearly been an inspiration to and a driving force behind Promise Keepers, but the organization is by no means dependent on him. Its financial and organizational structure can easily maintain itself without him. *New Man,* the magazine put out by Promise Keepers, is one of the devices through which the movement continues to grow and spread the word. Like McCartney's rhetoric and the rallies' rituals, the magazine's message oscillates between love and hatred—in the name of purity. An article in the September/October 1995 issue is a case in point. Entitled "The Silent Struggle," it profiles several Christian men struggling against homosexuality. As with many of the articles throughout, readers are assured of the manliness of the men in question. In this case we are introduced first to John, who at 240 pounds is "built like a starting linebacker." Although we are not given the outcome of John's struggle, several others are cited who are triumphant in their defeat of this biblical sin. The testimony of Jeff Konrad, a former homosexual who had lived with another man for eleven years but who is "now married with two children," reveals a link between rigid gender roles, the proclaimed sinfulness of homosexuality, and the theater of self-loathing: "I used to hate myself. I felt ugly and feminine. Today I can look in the mirror and like what I see. God has made me into a man." The rest of the article encourages prayer as a means of struggle and male mentoring as an acceptable way to gain "same-sex intimacy" and provides a list of organizations and books that can help provide "freedom from homosexuality."[32]

Just as Promise Keepers associates heterosexuality with purity and homosexuality with impurity, so too does this binary reinforce strict gender roles. In the first Promise Keepers book, Dr. Tony Evans, a pastor and also the chaplain of the Dallas Mavericks basketball team, argues that the national crisis in families has occurred because of "the feminization of the American male," by which he means "a misunderstanding of manhood that has produced a nation of 'sissified' men who abdicate their role as spiritually pure leaders, thus forcing women to fill the vacuum."[33] Clearly, from Evans's perspective, when women have filled this vacuum, they have gone seriously awry—in ways that look a lot like feminism. For Promise Keepers, feminist insistence on equality in the family challenges the divinely mandated plan of male leadership and female submission.

At least as worrisome as this enforced gender hierarchy is the Promise Keepers disregard of the issue of domestic violence (at least during the first five years of the organization's history). Nothing in the three books or the group's study series guide even mentions this sizable problem within U.S. family life, despite the fact that the life stories in the second book include such chapters as "A Promise Keeper Strengthens His Marriage" and "A Promise Keeper Loves and Disciplines His Children." This lack of focus on domestic abuse serves to exacerbate the urgent concern that feminists have repeatedly raised in correlating male violence in the home with the combined factors of assumed male supremacy and declining male cultural status. Instead, readers are offered a questionable transformation through the life story of Warren Risniak, touted as a father who learns about loving and disciplining his children. The "real changes" that are recited include the fact that the "entire family sits down together for breakfast and supper almost every day" and that his children "feel involved with their dad." The nexus of their involvement? "They all get a kick out of stuffing envelopes and helping send out his business mailings. To recognize their help, Warren got all of them their own business cards."[34]

A dubious race understanding intersects with Promise Keepers's clouded vision of family life. Women-led homes within the African American community are blamed for undermining national (read male) security. Or, as Tony Evans, himself an African American, puts it, "in the black community, . . . women run the show to an alarming degree."[35] Again, for Promise Keepers the danger lies in the way that women feminize men, a stance that leads away from recognizing that poverty for African American women and women in general does indeed threaten the well-being of the nation as a whole. As June Jordan has indicated, "the welfare of the majority [women] will determine the welfare of the state."[36] There is particular irony in the racial stance of Promise Keepers literature, since the group explicitly seeks "racial reconciliation," has appointed minority men to the board, and includes African Americans as speakers, like Evans, and singers at the rallies. Despite these efforts and the multicultural impression that their publicity videos give, minority attendance remains at a low 7 percent.[37] This inconsistency between goal and success derives, I believe, from whitist assumptions that fail to grasp minority issues, especially the social and economic sources of the feminization of poverty. In this light, Promise Keepers's appropriation of the name P.U.S.H. (Jesse Jackson's organization,

People United to Serve Humanity) as their acronym for "Pray Until Something Happens" comes off as more of a ploy co-optation than an effort for reconciliation; the shift from service to prayer is a telling reminder that, when it comes to social justice, Promise Keepers has its eyes on the deferred prize.

Such an appropriation is even clearer in regard to the language of gender. Witness this striking usurpation of female reproduction: "Promise Keepers have become impregnated with personal revival. Our changed lives are obvious. Like a woman who is pregnant and nearing the end of her term, we Christian men are about to burst forth with the coming of the Lord in ways we have never experienced."[38] Lest the men confuse such a bursting forth with being (god forbid) feminine, Promise Keepers reinforces "real men" masculinity by organizing members into follow-up groups for the purpose of training them in "progressive sanctification."[39] Their grassroots organizational method is spelled out in *Seven Promises of a Promise Keeper*. Readers are urged "to work through the book for at least eight weeks in a small group of men—three to five is the ideal number."[40] At the end of each of the chapters written by "proven warriors," specific instructions are provided. A cross between a social science questionnaire and a catechism, these begin with a personal evaluation, in which a man ranks himself on a scale of 1 to 10, "with 1 being very weak and 10 being perfect." That is followed by an explicit instruction to pray together about the issue at hand, questions that the men in each group should discuss as well, and a biblical verse to memorize. Finally there is an assigned activity—writing a prayer, for example—to be practiced during the week until the next group meeting. Promise Keepers kits provide even more extensive guidance for small group disciples, with instructions for forty-five one-hour sessions geared to four to ten men in attendance.

Such small group meetings are the tried and true of many other mass movement efforts, from Marxist cells to feminist consciousness-raising. Combined with large rallies, they can be quite effective as a means of spreading whatever teachings a group wishes to promote. This disciplinary technique, which combines confessional elements with exercises for self-transformation, has its roots and its greatest successes in the dissemination of the apocalyptic within Christianity. This is in part because of the promise of perfectibility and the drama of seeing one's group as persecuted. It is hardly surprising, as we near the end of the millennium and as media-fed contemporary life continues to have a dizzying effect, that these groups create a sense of stability and bonding. It is even less surprising, given the dulling effect of late capitalist work life, that the rallies' generation of emotion and cathartic outlet should be so compelling.

What is troubling—whether Marxist, feminist, or fundamentalist—is the feverish dogmatism of the apocalyptic approach. The thread between purity and self-righteousness stretches thin and snaps easily. When applied programmatically to teachings against "the feminization of the American male," to strategies for taking back leadership of the family, or to ways to eradicate abortion and homosexuality, coercive purity contaminates the democratic principle and practice of equality. From this angle of vision, Promise Keepers looks more like power keepers.

But what if the transformation of men were to take a different turn? What would happen if large numbers of men began replacing the canned sentiments of Promise Keepers morality with ethical activities that minister to others' physical, emotional, and spiritual well-being? This would require, of course, a change in the totalizing limits of apocalyptic imagination, a shift that would make us more mindful, as Toni Morrison has put it in regard to the white-supremacist imagination that produces racism, "of the places where imagination sabotages itself, locks its own gates, pollutes its vision."[41] The other day I imagined a Promise Keepers rally in which a performance of Tony Kushner's *Angels in America* comprised the two-day event. Kushner's work came to mind because it appeared in the same years as Promise Keepers's founding and growth. It too has reached large audiences through its Broadway production and national tour. Like the Promise Keepers rallies, *Angels in America* provides a spectacle prompting reflection on the pain of men's lives, set against a backdrop of apocalyptic urgency. But unlike Promise Keepers, *Angels* submits not only the mandates of hetero-normative masculinity but also apocalypticism itself to reexamination.[42]

Begun facetiously, my reverie took a serious and then somber turn. I found myself wondering just what it would take for these self-proclaimed godly men to ask themselves new ethical questions. In place of apocalyptic oratory, music, chants, and prayer, I tried to envision a stadium full of men bearing witness to the final lines of the play when Prior Walter says to the audience, "You are fabulous creatures, each and every one. / And I bless you: *More life.* / The Great Work Begins." Momentarily, I imagined a vast sea of men who suddenly realized what it means to have granted *less* life to gay men and lesbians; men who had undergone a transformation more vital and loving than anything yet envisioned by Bill McCartney. As new men, might they not grasp, perhaps for the first time in their own lives, what it means to create more life?

To be truthful, on that day my imagination could not take me as far as I wanted it to, which was to see this transformation carried forth as an ongoing and everyday challenge to apocalyptic fundamentalism. I just could not get my mind to envision a multitude of Promise Keepers promising to embrace women's equality, support minority self-determination, and advocate homosexual freedom. But I am going to work on it—or at least toward that transformation. Not because I am given to fits of wild fancy but because I believe that acts of shared imagination can help unsettle the apocalyptic mind-set. The importance of a work like *Angels in America* is that it unfixes absolutes by presenting forms of knowledge that disrupt certainty, a citizenry that dismembers the heterosexist body politic, and love as a force against moral tyranny. Through these breaches in the apocalyptic social standard, hope can emerge.

NOTES

1. I would like to thank student assistants Laurel Allen and Juliet Evans for their help in gathering information on Promise Keepers. I also thank Adrienne Leban for adding to my collection of Promise Keepers materials and offering suggestions on an earlier draft. Discussion of this essay at the Twentieth Century Seminar at the City University of New York Graduate

Center helped sharpen the critique; I am particularly grateful to Frances Bartkowski, who gave the response, and to Nancy K. Miller and Louis Menand for inviting me.

2. David Van Biema, "Full of Promise," *Time,* November 6, 1995, 62–63; Nancy Novosad, "God Squad," *The Progressive,* August 1996, 27.

3. This is not the first time that a men-only religious movement has been organized, however. In 1911 and 1912, the Men and Religion Forward Movement had over a million people attend its events, which were organized to bring men into Protestant churches. Whereas they sought to combat the feminization of religion, Promise Keepers is fighting the feministization of values. See Gail Bederman, "'The Women Have Had Charge of the Church Work Long Enough': The Men and Religion Forward Movement of 1911–1912 and the Masculinization of Middle-Class Protestantism," *American Quarterly* 41 (September 1989): 432–65.

4. Scott Raab's *GQ* piece points this out humorously but makes it clear that religious tolerance of non-Christian values is not a Promise Keepers principle. See Raab, "Triumph of His Will," *GQ,* January 1996, 110–17, 127–30.

5. Since the founding of Promise Keepers, there has been controversy over whether the organization has a political agenda. Official statements insist that the group is politically neutral. In terms of its overt effort toward ideological transformation, this is obviously inaccurate. The most significant connection in this respect is with psychologist Dr. James C. Dobson and his Colorado-based organization known as Focus on the Family, founded in 1977 and now with an annual budget of $90 million. Dobson is one of the contributors to the first Promise Keepers book, and his organization is the publisher for all of them. Through his nationally syndicated daily radio program and several magazines, Dobson provides a forum for virulent antiabortion leaders like Randall Terry and antigay activists like Gene Antonio, author of *The AIDS Cover-Up.* Dobson's group also provides resources for affiliates that work actively in legislative efforts to promote Religious Right sex education for public schools and to repeal gay and lesbian civil rights protection. There are additional links between Promise Keepers and overtly political right-wing organizations and individuals; several board members also belong to the Council for National Policy, and Promise Keepers has sponsored Jerry Falwell for speaking events.

6. Donna Minkowitz's assessment of Promise Keepers is shortsighted in this regard. Although I agree with her argument that feminists need "to understand the contradictory impulses that have brought [Promise Keepers] swarming to the stadiums," I find her analysis of the group too forbearing. She seems torn between a positive response to the experience of love she witnessed among the men and that she herself felt while attending one of the rallies (in drag) and the male supremacist and homophobic aspects of the Promise Keepers program. This particular paradox of love and hatred is endemic to apocalypticism, and contradictoriness has rarely been an obstacle to oppressive power relations. Her view that the group's contradictoriness may mean that they "may have themselves caught in a quasi-feminist whirlwind" is unfoundedly optimistic. See Donna Minkowitz, "In the Name of the Father," *Ms.,* November/December 1995, 64–71.

7. Lee Quinby, *Anti-Apocalypse: Exercises in Genealogical Criticism* (Minneapolis: University of Minnesota Press, 1994). At the time of writing *Anti-Apocalypse,* I used "ironic apocalypse" as the third mode, seeing postapocalypse as a version of it, but I have since been persuaded by James Berger that postapocalypse is a more apt term. See his *After the End: Representations of Post-Apocalypse,* forthcoming from the University of Minnesota Press.

8. Brian Peterson, "God Will Do His Part," *New Man,* September/October, 1995, 8.

9. Also see Frederick Clarkson, *Eternal Hostility: The Struggle between Theocracy and Democracy* (Monroe, Maine: Common Courage Press, 1996), chapter 9 in particular.

10. Phillip Greven, *Spare the Child: The Religious Roots of Punishment and the*

Psychological Impact of Physical Abuse (New York: Alfred A. Knopf, 1991).

11. Special thanks go to Betty Bayer and Susan Henking, who, by giving this toy to me as a birthday present, introduced me to the world of X-Men.

12. TM and Toy Biz, Inc., Marvel Entertainment Group, 1995.

13. I would like to thank Kent Worcester for providing me with a brief history of the X-Men. His work demonstrates some of the links between "outsider media," popular culture, and the formation of masculinity. The term "rehabilitation of masculinity" is drawn from his presentation at the New York State Political Science Association Conference, April 15, 1995.

14. See Elayne Rapping's valuable discussion of the secular men's movement in regard to their assimilation of certain feminist values alongside their failure to reflect on the socioeconomic power relations that most affect men's lives. *The Culture of Recovery: Making Sense of the Self-Help Movement in Women's Lives* (Boston: Beacon, 1996), 167–74.

15. See David F. Aberle, "A Note on Relative Deprivation Theory as Applied to Millenarian and Other Cult Movements," in *Millennial Dreams in Action: Studies in Revolutionary Religious Movements,* ed. Sylvia L. Thrupp (New York: Schocken Books, 1970), 208–14.

16. For a full discussion of the shortcomings of the fundamentalist self as a totalistic view, see Robert Jay Lifton, *The Protean Self: Human Resilience in an Age of Fragmentation* (New York: Basic Books, 1993), chap. 9; Charles Strozier, *Apocalypse: On the Psychology of Fundamentalism in America* (New York: Beacon Press, 1994).

17. For a discussion of the inherent sexism of the book of Revelation, see Tina Pippin, *Death and Desire: The Rhetoric of Gender in the Apocalypse of John* (Louisville: Westminster/John Knox Press, 1992). For a discussion of the homophobic features of apocalypticism, see Richard Dellamora, *Apocalyptic Overtures: Sexual Politics and the Sense of an Ending* (New Brunswick, N.J.: Rutgers University Press, 1994).

18. See Mary Wilson Carpenter's insightful analysis, "Representing Apocalypse: Sexual Politics and the Violence of Revelation," in *Postmodern Apocalypse: Theory and Cultural Practice at the End,* ed. Richard Dellamora (Philadelphia: University of Pennsylvania Press, 1955), 110.

19. Robert Jay Lifton, *Thought Reform and the Psychology of Totalism: A Study of "Brainwashing" in China* (1961; reprint, Chapel Hill: University of North Carolina Press, 1989), 425.

20. Wellington Boone, "Why Men Must Pray," in *Seven Promises of a Promise Keeper* (Colorado Springs: Focus on the Family Publishing, 1994), 31.

21. For discussions of American revivalism, see Charles Boyer, *When Time Shall Be No More: Prophetic Belief in Modern American Culture* (Cambridge, Mass.: Belknap Press of Harvard University Press, 1992), chap. 3; Strozier, *Apocalypse,* chap. 8; Robert C. Fuller, *Naming the Antichrist: The History of an American Obsession* (New York: Oxford University Press, 1995), 120–25.

22. Larry B. Stammer, "Teaching Patriarchs to Lead," *Los Angeles Times,* June 19, 1994.

23. Ibid.

24. "Winning the Races," *Christianity Today,* February 6, 1995, 23.

25. Bill McCartney, "Seeking God's Favor," in *Seven Promises of a Promise Keeper,* 207.

26. McCartney, quoted by Randy Phillips in "Seize the Moment," in *Seven Promises of a Promise Keeper,* 9.

27. "Christian Men's Movement Taps into Identity Crisis," *Los Angeles Times,* July 6, 1994, A10. McCartney's remarks in public have gotten him into some trouble. The ACLU pointed out that he had used the university podium to denounce homosexuality as ungodly and threatened to sue. See Stammer, "Teaching Patriarchs to Lead."

28. "Movement Seeks to Revive Traditional Role for Men," *Washington Post,* August 1, 1994, A11.

29. "Manhood's Great Awakening," *Christianity Today,* February 6, 1995, 21–28.

30. Raab, *GQ,* 114.

31. "New Men for Jesus," *Economist,* June 3, 1995, 21–22.

32. Bob Davies, "The Silent Struggle," *New Man,* September/October 1995, 44–47. Exasperation from reading an article like this prompts me to ponder the kind of question and comment that Adrienne Leban has pointedly posed: "Why *exactly* is the Religious Right against homosexuality? It cannot be that the Christian coalitions have risen up just to defend their interpretation that the Bible says homosexuality is sinful. The Bible also forbids greed and hate and killing; but there is no Christian Coalition for National Income Redistribution, or Eagle Forum for Racial Harmony, or Moral Majority for Gun Control." See Adrienne Leban, "Sexual Beggars," *Global City Review,* Sexual Politics Issue, vol. 1 (spring 1993), 23–28 (quotation from 24). At the same time, I shudder to think about the political groups that might arise if the Religious Right really did follow to the letter all of the biblical mandates of punishment!

33. Dr. Tony Evans, "Spiritual Purity," in *Seven Promises of a Promise Keeper,* 73.

34. Gregg Lewis, *The Power of a Promise Kept: Life Stories* (Colorado Springs, Co.: Focus on the Family, 1995), 108.

35. Evans, "Spiritual Purity," 73.

36. June Jordan, "The Case for the Real Majority," *On Call* (Boston: South End Press, 1985), 38.

37. "Winning the Races," 23.

38. Boone, "Why Men Must Pray," 31. For an excellent discussion of the apocalyptic implications of actual projects of male pregnancy, see Peter Stokes, "Literature and Apocalypse: Writing, Gender, and the Discourse of Catastrophe," Ph.D. diss., State University of New York, Stony Brook, 1996, chap. 5.

39. *The Power of a Promise Kept,* 2.

40. *Seven Promises of a Promise Keeper,* 9.

41. Toni Morrison, *Playing in the Dark* (Cambridge, Mass.: Harvard University Press, 1990), ix.

42. I discuss *Angels in America*'s challenges to the absolutism of the Promise Keepers in a longer version of this essay, in my book in progress, *Apocalyptic Gusta.*

Part III

Politics

Chapter Fourteen

The Paucity of the Millennial Moment
The Case of Nuclearism

Richard Falk

The Millennial Moment: The 1990s

With the advent of a new millennium, there exists a strong cultural presumption that the search for terrestrial answers will grow bolder, veering as it did in the 1890s toward radical visions of an imminent apocalypse or else the start of an extraordinary reign on earth of the divine spirit. Yet instead, in the 1990s there exists a pervasive sense of complacency, a turning toward immediate satisfactions, and an imaginative fatigue that is seemingly content with muddling through, barely taking more than ritualistic notice of the millennial shift that awaits us. William Gibson, already in 1984, captured the distinctive mood of our era in the revelatory opening sentence of his classic *Neuromancer*: "The sky above the port was the color of television, tuned to a dead channel."[1] Perhaps this dullness of outlook is highly provisional and will soon be superseded by a more dramatic and visionary set of expectations; but there are currently few indications that this might happen, by some sort of retuning process in the next several years, a last-hour recovery of imaginative vividness before crossing the threshold of a new millennium.

Accounting for this lack of millennial enthusiasm is a highly conjectural matter, which if undertaken seriously would involve a detailed inquiry into the current state of cultural consciousness. Such an inquiry extends far beyond the scope of this essay, but a summary assessment provides a necessary background for a more specific concern with the future of nuclear weaponry. Several complex developments, which can be briefly identified, have converged to undermine the millennial impulse: the settlement of the cold war has removed from active political consciousness all serious concerns about the apocalyptic dangers of a war fought with nuclear weapons or the prospect of a war in which nuclear weapons would be exploded over the territory of major states; the related disappearance of serious ideological and geopolitical conflict from the global setting left the way open for the ascendancy of consumerist preoccupations with economic growth and the expansion of world trade, an essentially materialist calculus; the imposing discipline of global capital has induced even strong states to transfer significant amounts of sovereignty over economic policy to international institutions and arrangements (NAFTA, Maastricht, World Trade Organization); in these circumstances, the role of states is changing, with its welfare function declining while its military function is being highlighted, especially in relation to the protection of the world economy; television also plays its part in dulling cultural sensibilities, as do the libertarian proclivities of the Internet, encouraging an apolitical embrace of virtual reality. It is this admixture of underlying developments that works against the heightening of political and social consciousness and helps explain why the advent of a new millennium appears to be striking so few responsive chords.

When it comes to a political project such as ridding the world of nuclear weapons, there is a more obvious line of explanation for why the wellsprings of initiative appear so dry. The collapse of the Soviet Union as a rival provided an apt occasion for discrediting both socialism and large-scale projects for societal reform. The basic learning experience of the cold war, as taught by the victors, was that market economics proved their superiority, that the military strength of the West contained the Communist enemy without causing a mutually destructive war, and that nuclear weapons, along with the credible willingness to use them, played a decisive part in this achievement. Further in the background is the historical failure associated with the disarmament efforts launched after World War I, which are widely blamed for facilitating the appeasement policies that emboldened Hitler to embark upon his grandiose scheme for German expansion.

Given these synergistic tendencies and historical memory, it is probably not surprising that the millennial mood seems so tepid. Any explicit millennial emphasis would be an implicit challenge to the secular, materialist consensus that governs debate in the public domain, and it would be generally interpreted as an exaggeration of danger in the existing order, or worse, as a covert expression of religious fundamentalist modes of thought. Even the advocacy of any drastic modifications in world order arrangements would seem to have failed to grasp the dysutopian outcomes that result from "successful" utopian projects, as well as revive the kind of doomsday thinking, expressive of fears about either a nuclear or an ecological cataclysm, that was periodically prominent in the cold war era. Despite the persistence of high risks, these concerns with fundamental sustainability have been effectively banished from public consciousness, and any effort to perceive reality through the prism of millennial end and beginning would inevitably refocus attention on these types of basic vulnerability and the sort of radical restructuring that would be needed if adjustments were to be made.[2]

The Persistence of Nuclearism

Against this background, it seems important to acknowledge this temporary flattening of expectations about the future and to comprehend, to the extent possible, the paucity of the millennial moment and its relevance for specific projects of reform. In this chapter my concern is with secular possibilities, and most particularly with achieving a decisive turn away from a reliance by governments upon nuclear weapons as a foundation for their "security," whether conceived as "national security" or "global security." Without scrutinizing the historical unfolding of the present, one might have expected the emergence of a strong disposition toward denuclearization at this time. Such an adjustment would have confirmed the insistence that these weapons of ultimate destruction were indeed intended only for deterrence and that thus, with the collapse of the bipolar structure at the end of the cold war, the rationale for retaining the weapons essentially disappeared. Why, under such circumstances, would not a political leader seize the millennial moment to counter the persisting apocalyptic dangers and threats embedded in nuclear weaponry and the disturbing omnicidal pretensions that unavoidably accompany any willingness to threaten credibly to unleash a nuclear war under certain unspoken conditions?

Taken at face value, the nuclearist mind-set represents, as Robert Lifton has so persuasively demonstrated, one type of "genocidal mentality."[3] This mind-set continues to control the outlook of policymakers in the nuclear weapons states, and public opinion remains mainly indifferent, presently regarding the issue as effectively closed by the collapse of the Soviet Union and the end of a strategic rivalry between two superpowers, each long poised to deliver a knockout nuclear punch of catastrophic proportions if sufficiently provoked or frightened.

In fact, the apocalyptic potentialities of nuclear weaponry were effectively ignored in policymaking circles as soon as a managerial mentality gained control of government soon after the end of World War II. The role of the weaponry was specified by reliance on the power and authority of secular reason, with feelings of revulsion and fear, as well as ethical concerns, banished to the margins. Part of the managerial effort was to reassure the public and political leaders that the weaponry could be prudently managed and that, if so, its contributions to security were valuable and even indispensable. This managerial orientation has retained its influence in the post–cold war era but has needed to shift its emphasis somewhat in light of the disappearance of a strategic enemy.

The new managerial priority pertaining to nuclear weapons is directed mainly toward the issue of proliferation, especially a concern about such weaponry falling into the hands of so-called rogue states, that is, those secondary states that are perceived as inherently irresponsible and hostile to the prevailing hierarchies of privilege and power embedded in the established structures of world order. The managerial undertaking is global, but the proliferation issues are matters of regional concern for geopolitical leaders and their advisors and are not treated as of globally apocalyptic dimensions. Even if states with radical agendas should acquire nuclear weapons, it is implausible to assume any serious danger of planetary scope of the sort that existed during the cold war. What is true is that more powerful countries themselves, if faced by a nuclear adversary in the Third World, might be deterred from opposing aggressive moves by lesser states in the settling of regional conflict if confronted by the prospect of even a single nuclear warhead falling on their own military forces or on the capital city of a closely allied country. We do not know, for instance, to what extent the Arab governments have turned away from confrontation with Israel in the past twenty years or so partly because of their realization that Israel possessed nuclear weapons that it was likely to use if its security was endangered beyond a certain point.[4] Under such circumstances, confrontation as a continuing policy for these Arab governments was literally a dead end.

The Gulf War provides another text for such speculation. If Iraq had possessed a few nuclear weapons, the response to Saddam Hussein's conquest and annexation of Kuwait might well have been more muted in 1990–91, but whatever form the encounter assumed, it would not have threatened humanity with an immediate apocalypse in the manner associated with the main crises during the cold war, especially the Cuban missile crisis of 1962. Of course, any use of nuclear weaponry against a populated area would prefigure wider possibilities, and its intrinsic horrors would reawaken human consciousness anew to apocalyptic possibilities, as was certainly the case with respect to the use of atomic bombs against Hiroshima and Nagasaki. It is likely, then, that an actual use of nuclear weaponry, even in the limited settling of a regional conflict, would arouse severe anxieties associated with human survival and would undoubtedly give an impetus to those social forces throughout the world that insist upon the unconditional renunciation of the nuclear weapons option. It might also lend decisive support to those advocating the negotiation of a disarmament process that would reliably eliminate this weaponry by stages from the face of the earth. This dynamic of nonproliferation and regional conflict has been managed in the years since 1989 without so far agitating public consciousness about the possible outbreak of a war fought with nuclear weaponry. By keeping the public calm in relation to nuclear weaponry, the managerial approach has been able to survive the end of the cold war with only a modest "downsizing" of the nuclearist establishment.

A similar process of managerial adjustment has emerged in relation to nuclear testing, which had been the occasion in recent years, especially in the Pacific area, of intense antinuclear activity. But with the Comprehensive Test Ban Treaty finally agreed upon in 1996, endorsed by the United Nations General Assembly and signed by virtually all major countries, this irritant, also, has been in all probability successfully removed from the scene in a manner that is likely to insulate the nuclearist status quo from further public pressures without challenging in any way the reliance on the weaponry, or even its further development and refinement; new "tests" of warheads by reliance on computer simulation ensure that old weapons can be kept operational and that new innovations will continue to be proposed and adopted, but, even more so than in the past, that only the most advanced nuclear weapons states will have this capability to "test" without testing.

India's refusal to decouple that regime of constraint associated with live testing, which amounts to a ban on most types of further development, from its insistence on a simultaneous commitment by the nuclear weapons states to achieve nuclear disarmament by a certain date appears to challenge the arrogance and complacency of nuclearism in its current phase. The unfortunate consequence of India's position, however, is to imperil the prohibitions imposed on further testing, a development that is important to the public, enjoys an unprecedented degree of support from both the declared and threshold nuclear states, and represents an arrangement that has been fashioned after decades of difficult negotiations. To discard this denuclearizing step, then, does not seem helpful as a tactic to achieve a nuclear-free world. What is worse, there is no prospect that India's refusal to go along with a comprehensive test ban as negotiated will have any impact on the current reluctance of the nuclear powers to put nuclear disarmament on their agenda as a serious security option. Furthermore, if India withholds its assent, nuclearists in other nuclear weapons states may yet prevail even with respect to traditional modes of testing, or at least slow down the process of assent, with the danger that the whole arrangement on testing could collapse if any state decided that its vital security interests could be upheld only through further test explosions of nuclear weapons in its possession.[5] In this regard, as long as the managerial approach is in command, it makes sense to take those steps that diminish risks even if the underlying retention of nuclear weaponry is not subject to challenge. Of course, it is possible to say that such an exclusion explains India's frustration with the existing approach and makes more understandable their assault on conventional ideas of risk reduction and prudence.

It is evident that two features of nuclearism persist: the managerial outlook controls policies relating to nuclear weaponry, and despite the end of the cold war it has not altered its disposition to avoid nuclear disarmament. The managerial approach is also diametrically opposed to the sort of visionary thinking associated with an active millennial consciousness.

Challenging Nuclearism at the End of the Millennium

What is extraordinary, and somewhat mystifying, is that notwithstanding this disappointing mood dominating political culture and the contrary specific priorities of the managers of nuclearism, there are several encouraging developments that disclose the vitality of an antinuclear movement conceived along abolitionist lines. How can this be?

One context of intensifying activity is associated with grassroots efforts mounted over the years to challenge the legality of the threat or use of nuclear weapons. Those efforts recently culminated in a historic decision by the World Court in The Hague that went a long way, although not the entire way, and not unanimously, toward an acceptance of the antinuclearist argument. But the entire court, composed on this occasion of fourteen judges, did agree without exception that all states have a solemn legal obligation to pursue in good faith general and complete disarmament, including nuclear disarmament.[6] The fact that this advisory opinion exists at all is something of a marvel, because the main nuclear weapons states, especially the United States, had used their diplomatic muscle to dissuade the General Assembly from seeking a response from the World Court as to the legality of the threat or use of nuclear weapons; they then argued vigorously at the court against responding to the question at all even after it was formally posed.[7] Undoubtedly, the most controversial and significant conclusion reached in this advisory opinion was that the "threat or use of nuclear weapons would generally be contrary to the rules of international law applicable to armed conflict," but that the court could not "in view of the current state of international law" rule out the possibility of legality of the threat or use in "an extreme circumstance of self-defense where the very survival of a State would be at stake."[8] Note that the court does not validate the claim to use nuclear weapons in conditions of extreme self-defense, but it finds itself unable, on the basis of the law as it finds it, to say that such a claim is assuredly illegal. Given the unwillingness of the declared nuclear weapons states either to pursue nuclear disarmament or to conform their deployment patterns and doctrines as to use with these highly restrictive norms of international law, as set forth by the judicial arm of the United Nations, there is now a problem of profound illegitimacy that pertains to the basic security arrangements relied upon by leading states. In a genuine sense, then, there is a growing tension between the policies and the managerial approach of the nuclear weapons states and the antinuclear consensus of governments and grassroots sentiment, with the latter claims now substantially affirmed by an authoritative reading of the relevance of international law. Whether such a normative gap will give rise at some point to a climate of opinion that effectively challenges the persistence of nuclearism is difficult to say, especially when the waters of strategic conflict among states seem so remarkably unruffled. Except for a hard core of antinuclear crusaders, effective pressures on nuclearism have always depended on a more active agitation of public fears than results from the mere existence of the weaponry, however big the arsenals.

Another set of hopeful developments arises from a reemergent concern about the dangers of nuclearism that is reaching a fragment of those who have been associated directly or indirectly with the managerial approach. Perhaps the combination of a possibly momentary historical opening to a nuclear-free world and the increased uncertainties of managing nuclear weapons successfully in the future account for this unprecedented interrogation of nuclearism by representatives of the political establishment. Such a disposition is evident among some of the most prominent and respected elite public servants, including former high-ranking military officials and defense professionals. Often the focus of their concern is not the weapons, as such, but the managerial dangers attributed to proliferation and terrorism so long as nuclear weapons are retained by the nuclear weapons states. The breakup of the Soviet Union contributed to these fears both by suddenly adding inexperienced government in unstable societies to the ranks of existing nuclear weapons states (e.g., Ukraine, Belarus) and undermining confidence in the Russian command and control over huge stockpiles of fissionable materials, raising the possibility that something could go wrong in the event of a major civil war within a nuclear weapons state.[9]

In this atmosphere the Australian government in November 1995 established an independent commission of seventeen members with the mandate "to propose practical steps towards a nuclear free world including the related problem of maintaining stability and security during the transitional period and after this goal is achieved."[10] The report complements the advisory opinion of the World Court by explaining how a denuclearizing process can be prudently carried forward to achieve the goal of what is called a "Nuclear Weapon Free World." The commission was chaired by Richard Butler, currently Australia's ambassador to the United Nations, and included among its membership Field Marshal Lord Carver from the United Kingdom; Robert McNamara; the Swedish disarmament specialist, Rolf Ekeus; the British military expert, Robert O'Neill; and the 1995 Nobel Peace Prize winner, the nuclear physicist and moderate antinuclear activist, Joseph Rotblat. It is a heartening sign that such a range of prominent individuals, many with close ties to the governments of the nuclear weapons states, should so definitively associate themselves with the advocacy of total nuclear disarmament at this time. It may be a preliminary disclosure that a favorable political climate for a shift in attitude at the highest levels of government exists after all. A commission like this is a barometer of sorts that assesses what kind of global reforms are feasible at a given historical moment. The membership of such a body is intent above all on projecting an image of credibility with respect to its policy recommendations, and credibility is generally understood by how a given set of ideas would be viewed by political leaders and their expert advisors in the most powerful governments, especially that of the United States in this instance.[11] The listing of experts consulted by the commission confirms this impression of reliance on the managerial sensibility to reach a set of conclusions that challenges the basic commitment to nuclearism. Of course, it needs to be appreciated that the initiative for the Canberra Commission was taken by a government of a nonnuclear country that has been sensitized to some of the dangers of nuclearism by the testing issue that arose in the Pacific region, and further, that all through the cold war there were occasional defections from the nuclearist consensus by high-ranking members of managerial elites. Even with these qualifications, this commission and its report represent a step forward because they have given an alternative outlook on nuclear weaponry a degree of formalization that it never possessed before.

The Canberra Commission is scheduled to submit its report to the United Nations General Assembly during its session in 1997. It is doubtful that there will be much immediate impact, but what does seem likely is that the combination of the World Court decision and the Canberra report will encourage antinuclear grassroots groups throughout the world to insist more vigorously upon the illegality of this weaponry and upon the obligation of governments to move rapidly and genuinely in the direction of nuclear disarmament. Such a momentum could be further accelerated in the years ahead by any nuclear mishap, whether military or not, such as the Chernobyl meltdown.

This combination of developments suggests that the end-time occasion of a new millennium is providing a somewhat more propitious opening, at least subconsciously, for the promotion of a radically different conception of global security. The elimination of nuclear weapons, as commitment and process, would be radical even though it would not challenge, in all probability, the basic assumptions of war as a social institution. If the path to nuclear disarmament roughly followed the route proposed by the Canberra Commission, it would be accompanied by elaborate assurances that other weaponry could accomplish the military missions previously assigned to nuclear weapons, including especially the deterrence of expansionist states and the possession of the military capabilities required to address any kind of aggression that challenged the basic structures of political economy now underpinning world order. In other words, nuclear weapons would be removed from the instrumentalities of power available, but the role of force and military capabilities would be adjusted to compensate for this removal.

After World War II there was an attempt to confine legitimate warfare to defensive operations in response to prior aggression, restricting in various ways the discretion of a state to use force or to claim to be acting in self-defense. The United Nations Charter was drafted with these goals primarily in mind, driven by the belief that international society might not survive a third world war and that, in any event, it was the primary mission of the United Nations to avoid the recurrence of major warfare. There were five basic ideas embodied in its approach:

- To prohibit all uses of force in international life that were not justifiable claims of self-defense
- To restrict valid claims of self-defense to proportionate responses taken in reaction to an armed attack across an international boundary
- To require claims of self-defense to be reported to the Security Council where the ultimate responsibility for judging the validity of the allegedly defensive action taken would be determined
- To have available the mechanisms and the capabilities for protecting any state that was the victim of aggressive uses of force
- To commit members to the peaceful settlement of all international disputes

These conditions were never satisfied, partly because the framework of the United Nations was constructed to depend on the continuing cooperation of the five permanent members of the Security Council, but more fundamentally, because none of these leading states was prepared to live within the normative constraints of the charter system and because all of them operationally retained discretion to determine under what conditions force would be used in relation to the pursuit of security interests. In other words, the charter failed in its central enterprise of imposing narrow legal limits on recourse to war, and to the extent that contemporary international law regulates the use of force at all, it has arguably now incorporated several large exceptions to the central restrictive notion embedded in the charter that force is legal only in situations of self-defense, and then only if it is preceded by a prior armed attack.[12] Whether the context is protection of nationals overseas, antiterrorism, the drug war, humanitarian intervention, control of proliferation (e.g., North Korea, Iraq, Libya), reprisal, or anticipatory self-defense, leading states act as if their own uses of force along these lines are in accord with international law and uphold the best interests of international society.[13] In these respects, the moderate ambitions after World War II to contain war as a social institution have been thwarted, at least for now, and the basic security postulates of sovereignty and self-help at the level of the state seem operationally descriptive. Analyzing international relations from such an angle would seem to vindicate acquisition and possession of nuclear weapons as one expression of self-help, but the situation is far from clear. The leading nuclear powers seem to deny *some* nonnuclear powers a self-help option in relation to nuclear weaponry (e.g., North Korea, Iraq), while retaining the weaponry for themselves, but these are matters of geopolitics, not law.

Can nuclear weaponry be disentangled from this wider failure to restrict the role of force in international life, given the pressures that exist to create a regime of unconditional prohibition by way of legal proscription, and more significantly, through a reliable process of phased nuclear disarmament? Nuclear weapons are, of course, the most awesome category of weapons of mass destruction; biological and chemical weapons are proscribed unconditionally by way of widely accepted norms, embodied to varying degrees in international treaties.[14] Unlike other weapons of mass destruction, world order arguments have been made in favor of the contributions of nuclear weaponry to the avoidance of war and the deterrence of aggression, and these arguments would have to be cast aside in any movement toward an unconditional repudiation of a nuclear weapons option and the elimination of the weaponry itself. There are two broad paths toward repudiation that bear on our inquiry into the relevance of the millennial moment.

The most plausible path to repudiation involves the acknowledgment that although nuclear weapons have in the past played important security roles, in the altered atmosphere of current international relations these roles are either unnecessary or can be more safely fulfilled by other means. This argument is based on a mixture of prudence and responsiveness to "the nuclear allergy." It does not draw directly on the wider historical consciousness of the end time except to the extent that the pressures to eliminate nuclear weapons would become more formidable if a more robust millennial sense of foreboding and opportunity had been forthcoming. The other path to repudiation is much more directly associated with the apocalyptic properties of the weaponry and the intrinsic conviction that such destructive capabilities should not be wielded for *any* human purpose, no matter how compelling the security-oriented rationale. Of course, it seems clear that the World Court and the Canberra Commission articulated their support for repudiation on the basis of the path of prudence.[15] It is equally clear that grassroots antinuclear forces, although occasionally venturing onto the path of prudence, have always been primarily motivated by an insistence that nuclear weaponry, as well as the strategy surrounding its use, involves an unacceptable embrace of genocidal policies in the name of security.[16] This antinuclear path has never clearly or consensually adopted a view that the reliable elimination of nuclear weaponry entails the repudiation of war as a social institution and the reconfiguration of world order to achieve such an outcome, although these latter goals often have an independent appeal for antinuclear activists.

Achieving a Nuclear-Free World: An End-Time Project?

Returning to our overall theme, the cause of antinuclearism seems to be advancing despite the paucity of the millennial moment, but if a more intense millennial consciousness were to take shape in the years ahead, then the prospects for achieving total nuclear disarmament would be quite favorable now. Yet, this prospect is not likely, at least not without some further unexpected jolt that regenerates a degree of apocalyptic nervousness among elites and wide segments of public opinion.

Short of this, the strength of the nuclear establishment is such that nuclearism in its present forms seems likely to persist, partly on the basis of bureaucratic inertia, partly on the basis of what is treated as a successful record of constraint and deterrence since 1945, partly because any denuclearizing process creates anxieties about trust and cheating, and partly because leading states resist any significant reduction in their options to use force.[17] National security policy is generally resistant to public pressures so long as nothing dramatic goes wrong, and thus it seems unlikely that the nuclearist consensus in government can be seriously challenged by the present play of forces.

But what if a sudden mood swing occurs: What if a major leader seizes the millennial moment instead of evading it? What if a serious nuclear accident occurs or there is a terrorist incident involving nuclear facilities or weapons? Or nuclear weapons are used in a regional conflict? Or "the Hiroshima temptation" resurfaces in an armed conflict to encourage a nuclear weapons state to use or even to threaten nuclear weapons as a way "to save lives" or "shorten the war." It is evident that the alternative to a millennial breakthrough based on bringing a higher consciousness to bear is some sort of managerial collapse. In this regard the success of the movement against nuclearism is as catastrophe-driven as ever, still depressingly dependent on a traumatic intervention in the domain of thought and action as a result of some kind of apocalyptic push that it is impossible to foresee and fearful to imagine.

It is impossible, of course, to pronounce definitively on this paucity of the millennial moment, but its consequence is to deprive humanity of much prospect of starting the twenty-first century by moving freely toward a nuclear-free world. Assuredly, this paucity is one of the shadow sides of economic globalization's taking hold in circumstances of geopolitical moderation and intercivilizational tension and disparity. Such a combination of conditions reinforces the perception that the future of world order will continue to depend on the capacities and willingness of the strong to control the weak and dissatisfied, by persuasion if possible, by force if necessary. So conceived, policymakers in nuclear states will all too readily find an array of pretexts for the retention of nuclear weapons in the hundreds, if not the thousands.

NOTES

1. William Gibson, *Neuromancer* (New York: Berkeley Publishing, 1984), 1.

2. This evasion of fundamental risk as a project of strong cultural forces is discussed from another angle in Paul R. Ehrlich and Anne H. Ehrlich, *Betrayal of Science and Reason: How Anti-Environmental Rhetoric Threatens Our Future* (Washington, D.C.: Island Press, 1996); see also Ulrich Beck, Anthony Giddens, and Scott Lash, *Reflexive Modernization: Politics, Tradition, and Aesthetics in the Modern Social Order* (Cambridge, Eng.: Polity, 1994), esp. Beck's contribution, 1–55.

3. Robert Jay Lifton and Eric Markusen, *The Genocidal Mentality: Nazi Holocaust and Nuclear Threat* (New York: Basic Books, 1990).

4. There were reliable reports that at the time of the 1973 Middle East War, in the early days when Israel was on the defensive and concerned about the outcome, nuclear weapons were assembled and readied for use.

5. There is already some opposition to the comprehensive nuclear test ban forming in the nuclear weapons states, including the United States. Opponents insist that testing is needed for the development of defensive systems and to ensure operational readiness of stockpiled warheads.

6. The World Court cites and relies upon Article 6 of the 1969 Nonproliferation Treaty but also relies on a broader argument that appears to rest on customary international law.

7. The U.S. government succeeded in persuading the court to refuse to respond to a parallel question put to it on the legality of nuclear weapons use by the World Health Organization.

The decision explaining the refusal, "Legality of the Use by a State of Nuclear Weapons in an Armed Conflict," was issued on the same day, General List No. 93, 8 July 1996.

8. This crucial language is to be found in paragraph 2E of the *dispositif* of the advisory opinion entitled "Legality of the Threat or Use of Nuclear Weapons," ICJ Advisory Opinion, 8 July 1996, General List No. 95. The overall legal conclusion reached generated intense controversy, with seven judges dissenting for contradictory reasons, three believing that the court cast too dark a shadow of illegality over the weaponry, three insisting that the shadow was not as dark as it should be, and one feeling that it was a mistake for the court to address the issue at all. For one attempt at legal commentary, see Richard Falk, "Nuclear Weapons, International Law, and the World Court: An Historic Encounter," to be published in the *American Journal of International Law* 91 (1997): 64–75.

9. See Graham T. Allison, Owen R. Cote, Jr., Richard A. Falkenrath, and Steven E. Miller, *Avoiding Nuclear Anarchy: Containing the Threat of Loose Nuclear Weapons and Fissile Material* (Cambridge, Mass.: MIT Press, 1996).

10. For the text see the report of "The Canberra Commission on the Elimination of Nuclear Weapons," issued by the Australian government as an official document, 14 August 1996, and obtainable overseas from Australian embassies and consulates.

11. For a critical discussion of this issue of credibility for international commissions, see Richard Falk, "Liberalism at the Global Level: The Last of the Independent Commissions?" *Millennium* 24 (1995): 563–76.

12. For extensive analysis along these lines, see Anthony Clark Arend and Robert Beck, *International Law and the Use of Force* (London: Routledge, 1993); compare the World Court adherence to the charter framework in the important decision in the case of *Nicaragua v. United States,* ICJ Reports, 27 June 1986.

13. States are far more circumspect about departing from the charter conceptions of legality when it comes to adversary uses of force. In this regard propaganda wars and patterns of state practice that have departed from the charter have definitely undermined the authority of international law with respect to the use of force.

14. The Chemical Weapons Treaty is an elaborate treaty that is not yet in force but is expected to be so by the end of 1997. Even without the treaty, which calls for the destruction of stockpiled chemical weapons, a legal regime of unconditional prohibition exists.

15. The dissenting opinions of Judges Christopher G. Weeramantry, Abdul G. Koroma, and Mohammed Shahabuddeen in the advisory opinion of the World Court, note 4, straddle the two paths of, but are mainly an expression of, the view that international law repudiates apocalyptic weaponry on principle.

16. For classic statements of this second perspective, see Jonathon Schell, *The Fate of the Earth* (New York: Knopf, 1982), which expresses a view somewhat moderated in a sequel, Jonathan Schell, *The Abolition* (New York: Knopf, 1984); Schell's preoccupation was with whether abolition could proceed within the confines of a world of sovereign states; he shifted in the second book to the more optimistic view that no fundamental world order adjustments were needed to achieve total nuclear disarmament of a reliable variety; see also Robert Jay Lifton and Richard Falk, *Indefensible Weapons: The Political and Psychological Case against Nuclearism,* rev. ed. (New York: Basic, 1991).

17. Most of the arguments for retaining a nuclear weapons option and against abolitionist postures are set forth in influential form by Joseph Nye in his book *Nuclear Ethics* (New York: Free Press, 1986).

Chapter Fifteen

Is the Apocalypse Coming?
Paramilitary Culture after the Cold War

J. William Gibson

The April 1995 bombing of the federal building in Oklahoma City brought massive attention to America's paramilitary culture and militia movement. Both print and broadcast news media told of thousands of angry men, dressed in camouflage and armed with military-style combat weapons, all prepared to do battle on American soil, with the enemy none other than the U.S. government. It was a frightening spectacle of impending civil war and social collapse: apocalypse appeared on the horizon.

But armed men in camouflage are not a new phenomenon. Modern paramilitary culture dates back twenty years to the mid-1970s. During that era a series of social changes shook the foundations of American culture and society. First, the United States lost the Vietnam War. This defeat created a crisis in the ability of the United States to threaten and conduct military intervention in Third World countries—what came to be known as "the Vietnam Syndrome." Defeat also created a cultural crisis, in that much of American national identity, and masculine identity in particular, had been shaped by the country's long history of victory in warfare. Men's identity was further challenged by the feminist movement, which grew phenomenally in the 1970s and the early 1980s. The middle and late 1970s also marked the beginning of de-industrialization and declining opportunities for most workers. Finally, during the 1970s both racial and ethnic minorities articulated their criticisms of white racism and, through their demands for programs such as affirmative action, were able to make some progress in upward mobility.

In response to these changes, many white men began to dream, to fantasize of remaking the world and returning to an imaginary golden age, a time before Vietnam, before feminism, before civil rights. A new cultural mythology emerged in a wide variety of forms. The *Rambo* movies and their ilk are but the best-known examples. Other forms included pulp novels such as *The Executioner* series, magazines such as *Soldier of Fortune*, games such as paintball, the growing popularity of military-style semiautomatic rifles and pistols, and the establishment of privately run combat training schools and shooting ranges. The fantasy always involved fighting a *new war;* only by fighting new battles against America's enemies abroad and at home could the world be made right again.

Unlike America's traditional image of the hero in post–World War II movies, the hero of this new war mythology was not a member of a conventional military or police unit. The makers of America's popular culture instead reworked the old myths in line with the conservative analysis of why the United States lost the Vietnam War, namely that liberal political elites had imposed what the Joint Chiefs of Staff called "self-imposed restraints" upon the U.S. military. These restraints, rather than the tenacity of the Vietnamese opposition and structural contradictions in the U.S. war effort, were the cause of defeat. The domestic equivalent of this reasoning claimed that the police were similarly handicapped in fighting crime by restraints imposed upon them by politicians and the news media. Consequently, the hero of the new war was an independent warrior—he fought alone or with a handful of comrades. The mythological fighting powers of the American man were released by fighting outside the system.

Given the hero's antagonistic relationship to the establishment and autonomy as a warrior, the new culture that was created can best be called paramilitary rather than military. And any man could participate in the paramilitary culture—it did not require a full-time occupational commitment such as joining the police or the military.

For most of the millions of men who became involved in the paramilitary culture, the warrior identity was only a partial identity. These men retained their "normal" lives of work and family. Fantasizing about their warrior alter ego through movies and novels, and buying weapons and practicing with them, were leisure activities. That does not mean that the paramilitary culture was not serious. To the contrary, it was a new symbolic universe that gave men an important understanding of who they were, what the world was about, what was wrong with it, and what needed to be done to make the world right again.

In this perilous cosmos, warriors made a fundamental distinction between primary and secondary enemies. Communists were the principal enemy—a small elite of military officers, KGB commanders, and party bureaucrats who subjugated and sacrificed everyone else to meet their infinite desires for power, lust, and the expansion of their totalitarian system. Terrorists were another kind of primary enemy, men who were simultaneously tools of the communist elite and perverts who loved to kill and rape for pleasure. Drug dealers and mafiosi shared characteristics of both the communist elite and the terrorists in that these criminals controlled people through their organizations and enjoyed perverse pleasures.

Paramilitary heroes in the 1970s and 1980s fought these villains again and again. However, in addition to fighting these gross forms of evil, the heroes also fought on a second, more subtle front. In virtually all of the new war films and novels, the heroes also struggle against America's political and military leaders. For the most part it's not a violent struggle—the warriors don't often make war against the U.S. government or local authorities, but rather the establishment treats the warriors with contempt and hinders their ability to fight the enemy. In the mythology of the New War, the U.S. government and, more generally, the political power structure across the country are seen as liberal, weak, and corrupt: the system no longer has legitimate moral authority.

The paramilitary culture reached its peak in the middle to late 1980s. During that period Hollywood produced scores of action-adventure films; some twenty to forty pulp novel series showed up each year on the nation's newsstands, each series appearing four times a year with print runs from 100,000 to 300,000 per issue. *Soldier of Fortune* sold up to 185,000 copies per issue and had several clones competing for market niches. SOF's annual conventions also became highly successful, drawing more than one thousand men each year for several days in Las Vegas. And the Reagan administration launched its own paramilitary adventures in Afghanistan, Latin America, and Iran.

But as the decade came to a close, the world changed in ways that made the paramilitary mythology of the New War begin to appear dated. The dissolution of the Soviet Union's control over Eastern Europe and then the collapse of the Soviet Union in 1989 cannot be overestimated as a crucial change in world history. All of a sudden, what Ronald Reagan had called "the Evil Empire," vanished. Even the inner sanctums of communist power, the KGB and the party apparatus, dissolved. The face of the devil during the long cold war from 1947 to 1989 was gone.

Second, in the spring of 1991 the United States and its allies fought a highly successful military campaign against Iraq. It was no secret that one crucial reason for fighting the war was overcoming the legacy of defeat in Vietnam. President George Bush explicitly said, "By God, we've kicked the Vietnam Syndrome once and for all." The United States inflicted high casualties upon Iraq, with little loss of American lives. Unlike Vietnam, our high-technology, capital-intensive mode of warfare overwhelmed the opposition. And the enemy, the Iraqi dictator Saddam Hussein, clearly embodied evil. Just as in the last unequivocally good war, World War II, American might and right united in triumph. Victory made both technological and moral sense to Americans; the mystery and shame of defeat that accompanied Vietnam were banished.

As might have been expected, these political developments did indeed lead to a decline of the paramilitary culture. The market for action-adventure pulp novels and movies dropped significantly; even *Soldier of Fortune* just barely limped as most of its competitor clones vanished. But still, the paramilitary culture did not completely disappear—the warrior identity for men retained much appeal.

And given the appeal of war and the warrior identity as a way of life, the end of the cold war represented a tremendous threat. Mobilization for war had been a constant part of American life since the beginning of World War II in 1941. The long cold war against communism had for decades been presented not as a manageable conflict with a socioeconomic system that differed from Western democracy and capitalism, but rather as a holy war against the presence of the devil in the modern world. The cold war consumed vast economic resources, helped consolidate political power in the executive branch of government, and created a huge standing military and covert intelligence apparatus. At a cultural level, war mobilization against the enemy created much of American identity—both in terms of how much war dominated the mass media, and in a more pervasive and elusive sense that at any moment the world could be destroyed through nuclear war. Moreover, for males, becoming a soldier constituted the one clearly certified path in American society for the ritual transition from boyhood to adulthood.

Thus, war as a way of life was too deeply embedded in American society and culture to readily give way to peace. Instead, during the early 1990s different parts of American society began to frantically search for new faces of the devil against whom they could struggle and so make their lives meaningful.

Ironically, even though the war against Iraq was itself a kind of ritual continuation of the cold war against communism, victory over Hussein was perceived as a dangerous omen by the far Right. President Bush had explained that the allied coalition had as its objective not just the mission of liberating Kuwait from the Iraqi army, but the larger task of helping to establish what he called a "New World Order." As Bush used the term, New World Order was not well defined, but instead referred to a system of international relations among states that would be different and less antagonistic than the cold war bifurcation of the world.

To the extreme right wing, though, the phrase New World Order indicated a Freudian slip, a confession by Bush that he favored the establishment of a powerful world government in which U.S. sovereignty and freedom would be surrendered to the United Nations. The United Nations in turn would do exactly what the former Soviet Union had tried to do and failed, namely create world socialism, redistribute wealth, and make everyone equal—slaves to a bureaucratic party elite dominated by Jews. To enforce this new international system, United Nations troops—including troops from former communist bloc countries—would be brought in to conquer and subdue the American people. The forerunners of these invasion forces were thought to be black helicopters with no identifying insignia that patrolled the skies of western states and secret teams of pathfinders who traveled on the interstate highway system, marking highway signs with directions to be decoded by the invading main-force units of United Nations soldiers.

To be sure, these were still extremist ideas in the early 1990s, ideas that did not have widespread credibility. However, during this same period other issues and events emerged that also helped to frame the U.S. government as the new enemy. The escalating national debate on gun control triggered a strong, visceral response in the mainstream of conservative America.

Passing new federal legislation to increase regulation of firearms ownership had been an item on the liberal agenda all during the 1980s. Ironically, it was John Hinckley's assassination attempt upon President Reagan on March 30, 1981, that rekindled interest. Although Reagan recovered from the wound to his lung, his assistant, James Brady, suffered injuries that left him with severe disabilities and chronic pain. His wife, Sarah Brady, subsequently became a spokesperson for Handgun Control, Inc. After Reagan left office in January 1989, Jim Brady joined his wife to push for federal legislation requiring a five-day waiting period for those who wanted to purchase handguns.

In April 1989 a man named Patrick Purdy armed himself with a semiautomatic version of the AK47 assault rifle and attacked a school yard full of Asian immigrant schoolchildren in Stockton, California. Purdy killed five and wounded twenty-nine people before he killed himself. Immediately thereafter the gun control movement put forward the idea of banning various models of military-style semiautomatic rifles. The California legislature passed its own ban list late that summer. At the national level, the Bush administration instructed the Bureau of Alcohol, Tobacco, and Firearms to review its procedures determining which guns may be imported. Within weeks, the BATF devised criteria declaring that guns with "non-sporting" features such as pistol grips, folding stocks, high-capacity magazines, bayonet lugs, and flash hiders were placed on a temporary ban list. A subsequent agency review some months later made this temporary ban permanent.

By mid-1990 most foreign manufacturers of military-style weapons had devised ways to accommodate the new rules. For example, the Chinese and the former communist bloc countries of Eastern Europe followed the same two-track policy. First, they reached back into their warehouses to dust off the old ten-shot SKS carbine, predecessor of the AK47. Firing the same 7.62mm x 39mm cartridge as the AK, millions of SKS carbines were shipped to the United States in the early 1990s—prices in some parts of the country fell as low as one hundred dollars. Second, manufacturers simply made a few changes to their supplies of AK47s: the bayonet lugs, flash hiders, and pistol-grip stocks were removed. The gun was then renamed the MAC90, given a new "thumb-hole" style stock, and shipped to the United States with a five-shot magazine. By 1991, then, purchasers could buy a legal rifle and then turn to the weapon "after-market" for larger, thirty-round magazines—although the resulting combination would be illegal.

When President Clinton came to office in 1993, Democrats renewed their campaign for more stringent firearms regulation. That fall the Brady Bill was passed, legislating a mandatory five-day waiting period for handgun purchases in states not already meeting this minimum requirement. Another piece of legislation, commonly known as the assault rifle ban, listed nineteen types of semiautomatic weapons that could no longer be imported or manufactured inside the United States. This legislation took a somewhat broader, more generic approach to defining which weapons were banned. The AK47 or MAC90 series could not be further modified to become legal; the entire weapons family was banned.

Still, the term "assault rifle ban" that was used on both sides of the controversy and in the mass media, is extremely misleading. By no means were all types of military-style semiautomatic rifles banned. The popular .30 M-1 Carbine and the Ruger Mini-14 .223 rifle—both semiautomatic models that have sold millions—were not on the list. Colt Firearms was required to modify the action of its AR-15 to make it much more difficult to convert it to full-automatic, and remove the bayonet lug and flash hider, but the post-ban model is readily available. Equally important, the new law did not apply to guns already in the gun stores and warehouses. Since the entire gun industry knew a ban was possibly forthcoming, by the time the law took effect in 1994 there were millions of military semiautomatics stockpiled. The 1993 assault rifle ban was more about political symbolism—a way of saying that combat weapons symbolized evil—than it was about stopping crime. After all, FBI crime statistics during the 1980s and 1990s showed that rifles of all types were used in only 2–3 percent of homicides. Removing a handful of rifles, even though they are combat weapons, would not significantly affect crime rates.

The symbolism of the so-called assault rifle ban frightened the right wing. The ban was seen as the complete negation of the Second Amendment. And to many conservatives, the Second Amendment was the most fundamental feature in the Bill of Rights. The right to bear arms was interpreted as the material basis for all the other rights. Moreover, many gun owners interpreted the Second Amendment in religious terms, as a sacred covenant between God and the American people. God intended the American people to keep and bear arms. With these weapons the colonists beat off the British at Lexington and Concord, so becoming anonymous members of the Founding Fathers, creators of the republic. Their descendants, also armed, began the journey west, defeating the Indians and building American civilization.

From this religious or mythological perspective, the semiautomatic combat rifle came to symbolize the entire American creation myth, and gun control in turn represented an abridgement of God's covenant by the forces of evil. With the covenant no longer in place, the collapse of American freedom, prosperity, and whole way of life could not be far away. Hence, as the countdown to the year 2000 proceeded, the political symbolism of gun control started to be partially framed in terms of impending apocalypse.

Two major confrontations in the early 1990s between federal agencies concerned with enforcing gun control laws and extremist groups reinforced this idea. In 1989, a white separatist named Randy Weaver had sold two sawed-off shotguns to an informant working for the Bureau of Alcohol, Tobacco, and Firearms in Idaho. Weaver had extensive contacts with right-wing paramilitary groups in the region. When federal marshals first tried to arrest Weaver, he ordered them off his property at gunpoint. He subsequently ignored court orders to appear in court for a hearing. Instead, his family became progressively convinced that, after the 1991 war against Iraq, United Nations forces were headed toward Idaho and Armageddon would begin at the foot of their home on Ruby Ridge.

In August 1992 federal marshals conducted a close surveillance mission near the Weaver home and were discovered; a gunfight took place that left both a deputy marshal and Weaver's son dead. The FBI's Hostage Rescue Team was then brought in for the siege; wartime rules of engagement were issued: any adult holding a gun was a legitimate target. A sniper fired at Weaver and missed, but the bullet killed Weaver's wife. Weaver gave up only after Bo Gritz, the former U.S. Army Special Forces officer (and inspiration for Rambo), helped Weaver negotiate terms of surrender.

In the winter and spring of 1993 a second, even larger confrontation took place. David Koresh, leader of a religious cult called the Branch Davidians, created a following by combining elements of paramilitary culture with apocalyptic religion; like many on the extreme religious Right, they saw themselves as warriors for God. Koresh's followers often wore camouflage clothing; they amassed an arsenal of weapons, including Barret semiautomatic sniper rifles with telescopic sights that accurately fired .50 machine gun shells capable of penetrating several inches of steel-plated armor at over a thousand meters. BATF agents planned to search the Branch Davidian compound near Waco, Texas, for hand grenades, explosives, and rifles illegally converted to full-automatic capability. The BATF raid did not achieve tactical surprise. Although who fired first is still a controversy, there is no doubt that four BATF agents were killed and sixteen wounded. Months later, on April 19, 1993, the Branch Davidian compound went up in flames—from a fire either deliberately set by

Koresh's followers or accidentally caused by the heat generated from tear gas canisters fired by the FBI Hostage Rescue Team—killing more than eighty members (including children) of the cult.

To many people the conflagration looked like something much more sinister than a tragedy caused by a bungled operation. During the late 1970s and the 1980s America's police forces—particularly federal agencies—had become militarized and turned into paramilitary forces for the war against drugs. Although conservatives generally applauded this escalation when it first took place, after the end of the cold war these forces became ready candidates for the new enemy. Unconstitutional paramilitary law enforcement agencies were now bent on destroying freedom of religion and the right to bear arms, God's covenant with the American people.

Thus, by the middle of 1993 several overlapping sectors of the American right wing saw the U.S. government as the embodiment of totalitarian evil, an enemy even more sinister than the Soviet Union at the height of the cold war. Despite the differences in the right wing's conceptions of the government as enemy, the solution to this horrible political development was the same: it was up to the ordinary man in the street to transform himself into a paramilitary warrior. When a man had his combat weapons, then he was the true descendant of the Minutemen at Lexington and Concord; he participated in the covenant and gained strength from its aura.

April 19, 1995, marked the second anniversary of the conflagration of the Branch Davidian compound near Waco. It was also the 220th anniversary of the beginning of the Revolutionary War: on April 19, 1775, militiamen rallied at Lexington, Massachusetts, to stop a force of British troops sent to disarm the colonists. It was an extraordinarily auspicious moment to launch a direct attack upon the U.S. government. The attacker would become one of the new Founding Fathers as he initiated a second revolutionary war. At the same time the Branch Davidians would be avenged. One hundred sixty-nine people were killed when a truck bomb exploded outside the federal building in Oklahoma City that day.

Timothy McVeigh was not a card-carrying member of a militia group. But for years he had lived his life as a paramilitary warrior with an extensive collection of combat weapons and a keen interest in pulp novels and *Soldier of Fortune* magazine. During the Persian Gulf War, he served as a 25mm cannon gunner on a Bradley Fighting Vehicle. Afterward McVeigh attempted to join the U.S. Army Special Forces. He quit the initial "Q" course—the Special Forces three-week test of stamina and leadership skills—after two days. When McVeigh returned to his home unit at Fort Riley, Kansas, his fellow soldiers found him depressed and disenchanted with army life.

He did not reenlist, but instead drifted, soon becoming a transient vendor on America's gun show circuit, living in his car, traveling from city to city. McVeigh sold military surplus duffel bags and other paramilitary accoutrements at the gun shows and annual *Soldier of Fortune* conventions. But most of all he hawked copies of William Pierce's futuristic novel of a successful white revolution, *The Turner Diaries*. That was his mission in life—he sold the books cheaply and is said to have slept with a copy under his pillow. The book and his Glock 17 9mm pistol were his constant companions.

In the fall of 1993, when the Brady Bill and the ban on assault rifles passed, McVeigh is accused of having begun to plot an attack on the federal government. He followed the example of Robert Matthews, leader of a white supremacist group called "The Order" in the early 1980s, in trying to ritually enact the creation myth narrated in *The Turner Diaries*. In the novel, disgruntled whites begin to go underground and start guerilla warfare after the federal government (called ZOG for Zionist Occupational Government) announces that private ownership of firearms is illegal. Later on the white guerrillas blow up the FBI's new computer center using a truck bomb filled with ammonium nitrate fertilizer laced with diesel fuel, a combination known as ANFO. The attack radically reduces the FBI's ability to function and inspires the oppressed white masses to join the revolutionary forces. In acting out the plot of the novel, McVeigh undoubtedly had similar hopes of inspiring a widespread white uprising.

In this respect, McVeigh's warrior dream did not come true. Most Americans were appalled and sickened by the sight of firemen holding dying toddlers in their arms and the pictures of crying men and women, mourning the deaths of their spouses, children, and friends. Killing social security clerks and children was not the same thing as manly face-to-face fire-fights with armed villains. The bombing did not appear as the triumph of good over evil. There was no white uprising after Oklahoma.

Instead, American society and politics became *destabilized* after the bombing attack. Destabilization means that the very contours of what the vast majority of people take as normal politics and normal life suddenly fall away and the future becomes uncertain: if truck bombs were killing hundreds in middle-America places like Oklahoma City, then potentially *anything* could happen.

The news media heightened this anxiety. Quite frequently militia leader claims to hundreds of thousands of organized followers who were ready for armed struggle were presented without sufficient skepticism. Congressional Republicans did their part, too, with official hearings on the confrontations at Ruby Ridge and Waco. Certainly those two failed sieges were worthy of careful investigation and censure of those responsible, but the timing and conduct of the congressional hearings left no doubt that the intent was to portray the federal government as evil, out of control, and a threat to ordinary Americans. Weaver's and Koresh's participation in paramilitary activities and their beliefs in approaching apocalypse were virtually ignored. Implicitly, these hearings sought to legitimize the bombing of Oklahoma City.

During this same period the National Rifle Association issued a fund-raising letter to its membership describing federal agents as "jack booted government thugs . . . wearing Nazi bucket helmets and black storm trooper uniforms." Not to be outdone, G. Gordon Liddy, the former Watergate burglar, *Miami Vice* guest star, and author of *Warrior* (his autobiography), told the audience of his syndicated radio show that when BATF agents came to confiscate their guns, citizens should shoot each federal agent twice in the head to avoid their armored vests. For his brave stand on head shots, Liddy received the National Association of Talk Show Hosts 1995 Freedom of Speech Award. Finally, in July 1995 one Republican congressman expressed his opposition to the Environmental Protection Agency by claiming that the agency was the new Gestapo.

This harsh right-wing rhetoric contributed both to the broad sense of destabilization and, more specifically, to the demoralization of political liberals and leftists. Already stung by the 1994 congressional elections, in which conservative Republicans took control of the House, the post-Oklahoma rhetoric frightened many progressives into mimicking the far Right's vision of the future. There was talk of "10,000 McVeighs" in the American hinterland, implying that a neofascist movement would soon destroy the country.

That image of apocalyptic destruction was more compelling than contrary indicators that pointed to a different outcome. For example, former president George Bush resigned his NRA membership after the jack-booted thug appeal, an indicator that Republicans were split over this new far-right vehemence. Secondly, prices for military-style semiautomatic rifles remained stable or declined in 1995 even though the supply of many models was fixed by the 1993 legislation; if war fever had been genuinely building, sales would have taken off and prices would have gone way up.

By the middle of 1996, two additional confrontations with paramilitary groups had taken place. The Montana Freemen, a bizarre mélange of swindlers who claimed the federal government was illegitimate and printed their own cashier's checks for money, were finally persuaded by the FBI to leave their ranch and face charges in court. It was a redeeming occasion for the FBI, who brought the conflict to a conclusion without a gunfight. The FBI's strategy was to allow the Freemen to meet with other members of the nation's far right wing, who were soon alienated by the group's financial frauds. Eventually, the Freemen in Montana realized that they had little outside support and gave up.

In June BATF agents announced the arrest of ten men and two women in a terrorist group called the Viper Militia on charges of plotting to blow up a complex of federal buildings in downtown Phoenix. But when the case went to court, the judge dropped charges of conspiracy against half the members, saying there was no evidence. It also emerged that the lead investigator for the BATF had never even warned federal agencies in Phoenix because no attack was pending. Instead, the Vipers played along the edges of violence: they made ammonium nitrate explosives, blew up things in the desert, practiced with their weapons, wore camouflage uniforms and a unit patch, and talked about the evils of government. The Vipers also allowed the undercover agent who infiltrated the group to make a videotape—a homemade war movie—of them talking tough and dirty and doing all these heroic deeds.

Although the Freemen and the Vipers are but two groups, they are telling examples. American society is not going to have a civil war, a race war, or systematic terrorism that totally transforms social life. The end is not near; the apocalypse is not coming. The U.S. government is simply not as compelling an image of evil incarnate as was the communist or terrorist from a foreign land.

That is the good news. But the Freemen and Viper stories have their sadder implications as well. These groups, with their apocalyptic claims of impending social collapse and their desire to remake the world, contribute to the sense of political and social destabilization. They succeed in destabilizing even though they do not carry out attacks or have any significant following; their mere existence and pronounced desire to transform society through warfare is sufficient. Moreover, although most members of the paramilitary culture or the militia movement are participating at a fantasy level of some kind, real terrorist assaults will probably continue in the next few years. It is unrealistic to expect law enforcement agencies to successfully disrupt all plots or end all standoffs without bloodshed: people will die, either in bombings or in gunfights. There will be no return to "normality" in the foreseeable future.

Late-twentieth-century America is thus only a partially secular society. The nearly continuous fifty years of war mobilization beginning in World War II and continuing through the long cold war left its influence on culture even after the political conflicts ended. The notion that life involves unending violent struggle against evil continues to have its appeal—especially to men. That the year 2000—the millennium—was only a few years away helped to partially revitalize the war culture during its crisis when the cold war ended. We can take heart that the revitalization had only partial success. Although we have not transcended this era of occasional political killings and more general destabilization, the paramilitary far right has reached its limits.

If we dwell too much on their presence, then the possibility of progressive political change will be lost. Already the post–Oklahoma City climate has led to legislation attenuating civil liberties. To become paralyzed with fear would simply hand the paramilitary right wing a political victory and encourage them to further action. But if we acknowledge both the dangers and the limitations posed by the paramilitary movement after the cold war, we can move on with our lives and try to create a more just society as we approach the twenty-first century.

Chapter Sixteen

Racist Apocalypse
Millennialism on the Far Right

Michael Barkun

For the last quarter-century, America has been saturated with apocalyptic themes. Indeed, not since the 1830s and 1840s have so many visions of the end been disseminated to so wide an audience.[1] Current apocalyptic scenarios range from secular forecasts of nuclear war and environmental collapse, articulated by Robert Heilbroner and others, to the biblically based premillennialism of Hal Lindsey and Jerry Falwell.[2] Although the former have spread widely among secular intellectuals and the latter among a large fundamentalist audience, they do not exhaust America's preoccupation with the end of history. There are other future visions, neither so respectable nor so widely held, at the fringes of American religious and political discourse.

These outer reaches of the American mind are filled with many complex growths, but my concern here is with one form the fringe apocalypticism has taken, as part of the ideology of the racist Right. These are the groups customarily referred to in the media as white supremacist and neo-Nazi. Though they are uniformly committed to doctrines of racial superiority and are often open admirers of the Third Reich, to categorize them merely as white supremacist or neo-Nazi is simplistic, for these organizations bear little resemblance to earlier American fringe-right manifestations.[3] The groups most representative of the new tendencies include Aryan Nations in Hayden Lake, Idaho; the now-defunct Covenant, Sword, and Arm of the Lord, whose fortified community was located near Pontiac, Missouri, until 1985; and most elements of the Ku Klux Klan and the Posse Comitatus. Their distinctiveness lies in their novel religious character. Whereas earlier groups on the radical Right occasionally maintained links with American fundamentalism, the rightist groups that have grown since about 1970 are more often connected to a religious position outside of and opposed to conservative Protestantism.

The religious roots of the contemporary radical Right give it an ideological complexity far beyond the slogan mongering of its predecessors and infuse its political agenda with millenarian fervor. This religious position is usually referred to as Christian Identity, the term that will be employed here. In view of its deviant and esoteric character, it seems advisable to begin by sketching the main points of its theology, and in particular to indicate why so-called white supremacists adopt so hostile a posture toward fundamentalists, with whom, on superficial examination, they might be presumed to have some commonality of interest. In fact, their mutual hostility results not only from such fundamentalist issue positions as support for the state of Israel but also from basic theological differences. Against this background I will then examine Christian Identity's apocalyptic scenario and, finally, assess the character of its millennialism.

Christian Identity is an American offshoot of British-Israelism, an eccentric but innocuous point of view that continues to enjoy very modest attention in England, where it originated, and in other parts of the English-speaking world.[4] The idea of a direct link between Anglo-Saxons and Israelites may be found as far back as the early-nineteenth-century English millenarian Richard Brothers, and in a still earlier and weaker form among the seventeenth-century Puritans.[5] Nonetheless, as a coherent movement British-Israelism owes its existence to the writings of John Wilson and the proselytizing of Edward Hine during the second half of the nineteenth century. By the 1870s an organizational framework was in place.[6]

The central argument of British-Israelism was both simple and arresting: that the "ten lost tribes of Israel," far from having vanished, were the progenitors of the British peoples as a result of migrations that had taken them from the Near East into Europe. By implication, then, the British were themselves Israelites, although as yet unenlightened concerning their true "identity." Through all the mutations British-Israelism was to undergo, this belief in hidden Israelite identity remained constant. Striking though the conclusion was, it rested on, to put it kindly, a frail evidentiary base, which ranged from tortured interpretations of linguistic and archaeological evidence, to crude folk etymologies (e.g., "Isaac's sons" became "Saxons," the tribe of Dan founded Denmark, and so forth). However, it was doubtless easy to lose sight of evidentiary matters in light of British-Israelism's sweeping religious corollaries, for if the British were indeed Israelites, then they were God's chosen people, the vehicle through whom biblical prophecies would be fulfilled. It also meant, not incidentally, that their imperial enterprise was ordained by God and protected by his favor.

From an early point, however, British-Israelism was beset by divisive tendencies, notably by disagreements about precisely which peoples possessed Israelite identity. Were the true Israelites merely the peoples of the British Isles, or did the tribes also populate the Continent? And if so, how much of it? Only western Europe, or central and southern Europe as well? The issue of geographic scope eventually encompassed the role of the United States, particularly as British power declined and American power increased. John Wilson could speak somewhat patronizingly of a common enterprise with "our American brethren," but it became clear that the American brethren would soon eclipse their British kinsmen, a development that eventually gave rise to an American-centered and genuinely sectarian form of British-Israelism, Herbert W. Armstrong's Worldwide Church of God.[7]

Mainstream British-Israelism, whether in England or elsewhere, was not conspicuously anti-Semitic, which is to say no more so than evangelical Protestants tended to be in the late nineteenth century. Jews were regarded as having been cursed by God for having rejected Jesus, and in the view of some they had been doubly cursed by having, in their exile, intermarried with "the worst of the Gentile—the Canaanites and Edomites, children emphatically of the curse."[8] Nonetheless, salvation lay open to them through conversion, and the expectation of British-Israelites was that in God's good time the Jews would convert, although some disagreement remained over whether in the meantime missionary efforts among them were of any use.

More might be said of historic British-Israelism, but that should suffice for present purposes. For Christian Identity significantly alters British-Israelism by grafting onto it an elaborate racialist and anti-Semitic apparatus that the original did not possess.

British-Israel writers originally were content to deal with the fate of the "lost tribes" alone, by implication conceding that modern Jews still descended from the remaining tribes. Christian Identity writers, however, insist that all of the tribes migrated northwestward into Europe; that there is no link, biblical or otherwise, between Jews and Israelites; and, further, that virtually all non-Slavic European peoples are Israelites, each nation having descended from a different tribal ancestor. Identity literature then explains the existence of Jews through two different but reinforcing theories. Jews, far from being Israelites, are in reality "Khazars," descendants of the Khazar people of the Black Sea, whose leadership stratum converted to Judaism in the eighth century.[9] The Khazar hypothesis neatly interlocks with the older anti-Semitic dictum that Jews, as "Asiatics," were unassimilable by Western societies. The other, and currently more influential, Identity explanation of the Jews flows directly out of Identity theology.

The dominant view of contemporary Identity rightists in America is that Jews are offspring of the Devil, not in some mere metaphorical sense but in a concrete, biological manner. For example, when Aryan Nations's religious arm, the Church of Jesus Christ Christian, asserts that "there are literal children of Satan in the world today," it means precisely that.[10] For in Identity theology, the creation of Jews is directly linked to the sin in the Garden. Original sin consisted in the copulation of Eve with Satan, from which came Cain, the ancestor of the Jews, transmitting the ancestral curse.[11] This cosmic anti-Semitism sits within a more comprehensive Identity view of racial origins, according to which only "Aryans" (i.e., whites) can trace their origin to Adam. Blacks, according to Wesley Swift, were part of Lucifer's rebellion against God, serving as troops transported to earth "from other planets in the Milky Way."[12] These inferior races had lived on earth for millions of years before "Aryans" were first planted by God in the Garden of Eden (located, Identity writers claim, on the Pamir Plateau in Central Asia) seventy-four hundred years ago in an effort to get the disordered earth back in shape.[13]

Even this sketchiest of summaries should suffice to indicate that Christian Identity owes little to the tendencies that have shaped modern Protestantism, but much not only to British-Israelism, but also to pseudoscience and the occult, including nineteenth-century racial theories, and the mystic, conspiratorial anti-Semitism of *The Protocols of the Elders of Zion*.[14] This bizarre mixture also suggests that, unlike the political anti-Semitism of turn-of-the-century Europe, Christian Identity returns to the folk religion of the Middle Ages, retheologizing anti-Semitism as the center of a dualist vision in which the powers of light and darkness confront one another in a battle whose implications will be both universal and everlasting.[15]

Apocalyptic visions traffic in the currency of transformation: the changes will be total, imminent, collective, this-worldly, and, in some sense at least, miraculous.[16] British Protestant millennialism, transported to America at the very beginning of the colonization process, placed the apocalypse within a set of religious conventions. The ultimate transformation itself would be signaled by upheavals of increasing frequency and severity, portents of the even more frightful calamities to come when the older order would be swept aside, Jesus would descend in glory, and the thousand-year reign of the saints would commence. The accelerating tempo of portentous events meant that life on earth would get worse before it got better, that catastrophe and chaos should be welcomed as harbingers of the millennial consummation. This provided psychological solace, since the most frequently noted portents were either natural disasters or major wars. Indeed, the millennialists' grammar of portents was a way of imposing moral order on an apparently anarchic world, since unsettling events in which both the good and the evil suffered could still be assimilated to a vision of God's providence by identifying them as inevitable signposts on the way to the millennium.

This understanding of portents, modified but not significantly altered over the years, continues to be shared by American fundamentalists. Although generally careful to avoid interpreting portents in ways that point toward specific dates for events such as the Second Coming, contemporary millennialists nonetheless continue to look for "signs of the times." This predilection, which provides a line of continuity from Puritan chiliasts to contemporary televangelists, is not, however, shared by Christian Identity. To understand why, we must first understand why it is that Christian Identity so vehemently rejects renascent fundamentalism.

Christian Identity believers do little to conceal their contempt for fundamentalism and its highly visible clergy. There is distaste for any interpretation of events that even implies a timetable for the apocalypse: "We now have a plethora of dates that have been published to predict this and that, and more often than not, none of these dates is productive."[17] Instead, "our victory will be won in Yahweh's good time."[18] But the quarrel goes beyond dates and methods of interpretation. The heart of the dispute lies in the form of premillennialism that has taken hold among the majority of American fundamentalists.

Since the turn of the century, American premillennialism has been dominated by the system of biblical interpretation commonly called dispensationalism, which arose in the early 1800s among the Plymouth Brethren in England. The view of the "latter days" offered by most TV evangelists is a version of dispensationalism. At its point of origin, dispensationalism sought to avoid the potential embarrassments of date-setting by arguing that most biblical prophecies still remained unfulfilled, a condition that placed the end of history in the indeterminate future. Dispensationalists reached this conclusion by a circuitous line of reasoning that may be summarized by saying that dispensationalism makes the history of the Jewish people central to the fulfillment of Christian eschato-logical hopes.

At an early point in the church's history, after the expectation of an imminent return by Jesus had passed, it became commonplace to read scriptural references to the Jewish people allegorically, as referring not to Jews themselves but to the church as the "new Israel," the position particularly associated with Augustine. The originality of dispensationalism lay in its insistence that passages referring to Israel be read literally rather than allegorically, and that only when these prophe-cies concerning the Jews were in the process of fulfillment would the "latter days" commence. As formulated in the nineteenth century by John Darby and others, such a view did not envision any rapid march to the millennium, since, among other things, Jews continued to be scattered through the Diaspora. This condition was radically altered, of course, by the founding of the state of Israel in 1948, which convinced many dispensationalists that the "prophetic clock" had now begun to run. This view, solidified by the Israeli reunification of Jerusalem in 1967, led many dispensationalists to predict the beginning of the "end time" within the generation of persons then living.[19] This remains the view of most American fundamentalists.[20]

It is not difficult to imagine the attitude of Christian Identity toward a chiliastic system in which Jews are central and in which the politics of the Middle East and the security of Israel play an essential role. As far as Identity believers are concerned, Jews and all their works are literal offspring of Satan; hence Protestant ministers and theologians who adopt dispensationalism are Satan's agents.

Like fundamentalism, Christian Identity is a millennial movement with an apoc-alyptic view of history, but its millennialism is in almost every significant respect dif-ferent from that held by the vast majority of Protestant millennialists. The system of portents by which the latter have traditionally marked the redemptive trajectory is irrelevant to Identity. Contemporary dispensational premillennialists hang on wars and rumors of war in the Middle East, both because war has been an accepted apoc-alyptic portent for centuries and because the fate of Israel is central to the dispensa-tionalist view of history. Christian Identity, having developed separately, is less influenced by traditional interpretive considerations and rejects utterly the orthodox identification of modern Jews with biblical Israelites.

It is worth noting in this connection that mainstream British-Israelism demonstrated no such tendency. Although British-Israelism never sought to pro-mulgate a single orthodox view of the millennium, many British-Israel writers have been dispensationalists who sought to modify the system in order to accommodate a special salvationist role for Great Britain. Given British interests in the Middle East, this was not particularly difficult. Thus, H. Aldersmith, writ-ing in the early 1930s, saw the British victory over Ottoman Turkey in the Great War as precisely the kind of fulfillment of prophecy that might be anticipated by both dispensationalists and British-Israelites: "We fully expected and fore-told this great European war-woe, the drying up of the Turkish power, the occupation of the promised land by Great Britain and the return of the Jews to Palestine."[21]

Christian Identity, by fusing British-Israelism with a racial and demonic anti-Semitism, pulled the Identity doctrine into paths alien to dispensationalism.

If Christian Identity has nothing but contempt for the millennialism that presently saturates American religious broadcasting, what millennialism does it offer in its place? It offers a vision of a racial apocalypse, in which both sacred and secular history are systematically read as an epic of racial treason and promised racial redemption. Its followers see white Americans as a "dispossessed majority." Their resentments against the civil rights movement, civil rights legislation and court decisions, and affirmative action programs have thus been channeled into religious myths.

Dispensational premillennialism has been dominated by the question of the timing of the Second Coming, particularly the search for the precise sequence of events that will predict its imminence. Christian Identity effectively abandons this search for the chiliastic timetable and instead emphasizes the rising tempo of racial struggle and conflict. Identity believers are certain that Jesus will eventually reign over a millennial kingdom, but they tend to minimize his role in bringing it about. Their preoccupation is with the earthly battle between forces of light and darkness. The victory, though understood to be inevitable, will not occur until a massive final struggle takes place against the Jewish conspiracy that Identity believes presently dominates America. The traditional battle of Armageddon is here transformed into a prolonged confrontation among Jews, nonwhites, and the "Adamic race of Aryans."

Like other apocalyptic visions, Christian Identity links the final cosmic victory with tumult and violence. But here, in place of the conventionalized portent analysis of premillennialism, there is a complex set of four forms of disaster specific to particular periods and contingencies. There are, first, ancient disasters, the calamities that befell "Aryans" in biblical times and that remain partly responsible for the unredeemed condition of the world. Second, there are portentous disasters, the present signs that the last days are near. Third, there are hypothesized disasters that will occur in the future if redemption is not achieved. Although all apocalyptic systems wrestle with the tension between the inevitability of divinely ordained events on the one hand and human choice and weakness on the other, Christian Identity has particular difficulty in resolving it. The world will be saved because God wills it—but then again it may not be, as if lurid visions of a final calamity are required to keep the faithful at their tasks. Finally, Identity lays out a series of cleansing disasters that will occur after the "Aryan" victory in order to purge the world of its corruption. Like other millenarians, Identity believers are a good deal more precise about what will happen before the millennium than during it. Identity is vague in specifying what the new order will be like, perhaps because so much of its energy goes into painting the picture of the struggle required to reach it.

In one respect, Christian Identity hews to a line set over many decades by the fringe Right, the presumption that the world is under the effective control of a conspiracy, whose secrecy, cunning, and power make it virtually invisible and all but invulnerable. Richard Masker, a self-proclaimed "conspiratologist" associated with Aryan Nations, sees "a supersecret shadow government controlling not only the United States but most of western society," enveloping America in an "alien, Asiatic mentality, so evil in its intent and debased in substance as to be almost incomprehensible to our western minds."[22] Like most in the movement, James K. Warner of the New Christian Crusade Church is fond of speaking of "ZOG"—the acronym for Zionist Occupation Government—that with "a hidden hand . . . secretly controls the flow of events in Mainstream America."[23] Earl Turner, the eponymous hero of the movement's underground novel *The Turner Diaries,* bemoans an America in which "We have allowed a diabolically clever, alien minority to put chains on our souls and our minds."[24]

In this literature there is never much question as to who this minority is: Jews in the demonic incarnation first given wide currency in *The Protocols,* a volume sold by most of the book services run by Identity organizations.[25] The metaphors are predictably crude: Jews are "the cancer invading the Aryan body politic," "an army of two-legged ants," "Satan's spawn."[26] In the mind of Christian Identity, the Jew as absolute evil confronts the absolute good of the "Aryan" racial adversary, which must inevitably lead to a final conflict in which the issue of racial dominance is settled once and for all. As Aryan Nations puts it, "We believe there is a battle being fought . . . between the children of darkness (today known as Jews) and the children of light (God), the Aryan race, the true Israel of the Bible."[27] No rhetoric is too extreme to characterize what is at stake. Defeat means that "*everything* will be lost—our history, our heritage, all the blood and sacrifices and upward striving of countless thousands of years. . . . If we fail, God's great Experiment will come to an end, and this planet will once again, as it did millions of years ago, move through the ether devoid of higher man."[28]

In any case, to read Identity literature is to assume that victory is assured, for like countless millennialists before them, Identity believers take it for granted that God is on their side: "When He moves in these last days against the armies of Communism and the Edomites, He will accomplish their destruction in a very short time."[29] Richard Girnt Butler, the leader of Aryan Nations and the pastor of the Church of Jesus Christ Christian, assures his followers that "all the laws, all the federal agents, all the informers in the world will not stop the coming, preordained Aryan Victory over the world order of Jewry."[30] The same determinism infuses the writings of one of Butler's mentors, Wesley Swift. As Swift saw it, "God . . . is not only with you, but is on your side, . . . and has ordained that His Kingdom shall triumph."[31] Earl Turner, after being permitted to read the secret writings of the revolutionary order into which he is about to be inducted, suddenly recognizes that "We are truly instruments of God in the fulfillment of His Grand Design."[32] As we shall see, beneath this sense of certitude lurks nagging doubt. For the moment, however, it is sufficient to note that in the movement's own terms, the future millennium is preordained.

Nonetheless, as in most apocalyptic visions, believers expect the culminating events to be accompanied by requisite forms of natural and manmade fury to defeat the evil cabal and uproot the old order. However, as already indicated, Christian Identity generally de-emphasizes the older apparatus of earthquake, flood, and warfare in favor of a more complex panoply of disasters. The changed role of disaster derives in part from the fact that Christian Identity is in many respects an extended revenge fantasy, built on the belief that the "Aryan" inheritance was lost through a combination of God's punishment for earlier sins and the theft of chosenness by Jews, impostors who now pose as Israelites, depriving the "true" Israelites of their birthright. Hence, as far as Identity believers are concerned, history itself is a prolonged crime for which only the most awful retribution will suffice.

Disasters even preceded the creation of the world. In Wesley Swift's cosmic mythology, the void referred to in the first verse of Genesis was the result of Lucifer's rebellion against God, when the world was torn apart.[33] Later, disaster destroyed the Garden of Eden. Adam's "Aryan" descendants lived on the Pamir Plateau where the Garden was located. There the "Adamic race" built the "forty ancient cities of Takla Makan"—famous, Swift assures us, for "their knowledge, their wisdom, and their science." But the Adamites sinned by "mongrelizing" with the older, nonwhite races, and in consequence God caused great cracks to open up, flooding the plateau from subterranean water sources, in Identity's quirky version of the biblical deluge. The mysterious cities were destroyed and the few surviving "Aryans" forced to firmer ground.[34] The nonwhites through whom sin had come were not created by God, having been brought by evil forces from the far reaches of the galaxy. In another twist on an already bizarre story, William Potter Gale, like Swift a major Identity figure in the 1960s, suggests that Satan had already "mixed his seed with the preAdamic races, thus producing Asiatic Jews and black Jews," before he got around to cohabiting with Eve.[35] Be that as it may, Identity views all of creation under the aspect of disaster, from primal catastrophes to those still in progress.

When Identity addresses the disasters of the present, it comes closest to a traditional apocalyptic view, for if the world experiences dislocations and stresses, that must surely indicate the closeness of the end. The "signs of the times" do in fact sometimes turn out to be remarkably traditional: a natural world out of joint where withheld rain threatens famine and imminent earthquakes place cities at risk and a social world out of kilter, polluted by immorality and vice.

An Aryan Nations publication says that the massive "killer earthquake . . . we are told of in the Bible" will wreak destruction on both California and the Pacific Northwest. But disaster is already present, the author goes on to note, in the form of drought with the consequent threat of famine, all part of "the divine cleansing this planet will undergo shortly."[36] Drought conditions also catch the attention of Pastor Dan Gayman of the Church of Israel in Schell, Missouri, who asks, "Are we on the brink of national famine?" Like the Aryan Nations author, Gayman is less concerned with disaster as a signal of the end—a genuine portent—than he is with disaster as punishment for sin: "Our nation is now suffering from the excesses of man's law and the abuses and judgments that are always incurred when men deny God's law and enthrone the edicts of men." On a practical level, he suggests that the prudent should store grain for the future and that city dwellers should establish links with rural settings to which they could flee if they need to escape the city.[37] Here one begins to sense the powerful link between Identity and the overlapping phenomenon of survivalism, since the faithful must prepare redoubts where they can cluster during the calamities ahead.

Just as nature is out of joint, with the clouds withholding rain and geological faults about to change the very landscape, so too does Identity perceive society to be

in the throes of calamitous change. The change is often described as the transformation of a once pure world into one corrupted by evil. Indeed, in a single paragraph
Gayman likens AIDS and other sexually transmitted diseases with acid rain, smog,
the destruction of the ozone layer, and the chemical contamination of groundwater.
All represent "the judgment of God," and before the errant population is appropriately humbled, millions will "probably . . . perish."[38] The litany of sins seems endless: infanticide, sodomy, miscegenation, adultery, materialism, substance
abuse—scarcely different than in more mainstream jeremiads, except that in this
case the desired end is less a return to a virtuous past than it is an advance to a racially purified future. In the meantime, the contaminated present generation can only be
regarded with contempt. Even the implacable Earl Turner concludes that "there is
no point in killing them all. This moral weakness will have to be bred out of the race
over hundreds of generations."[39]

There are the passing references to earthquakes and drought and the somewhat
more frequent invocations of AIDS and general moral rot, yet all have an empty, ritualistic sound compared to the main disaster that overhangs them, the continually
reiterated fear of racial extinction. The ultimate disaster for Identity believers is
demographic, a disappearance of the white race described in terms no less vivid than
those employed by such turn-of-the-century racists as Madison Grant.[40] Now, however, the fears are if anything more intense, for the white race is the true Israel, the
instrument of God's purposes on earth. The white population of America, characterized as a bare majority, is about to slide into the status of an embattled minority
on its way to extinction: "The imminence of the disaster is overwhelming."[41]

These chroniclers of racial catastrophe agree not only about the magnitude and
imminence of the threat but also about its cause. According to David Lane, an
imprisoned member of The Order: "The political entity known as the United States
of America has attempted with near single-minded determination, almost from its
inception, to destroy any White territorial imperative, of any size and on any continent where such a state could be found. Genocide of the White Race has been the
aim and result of the American political entity."[42] Since America is deemed to be
ruled by Jews, it is they, says Identity, who perpetrate this scheme of racial destruction. "Racial genocide is being perpetrated—by ZOG," writes James K. Warner. In
a telling comparison, he goes on to say that, "unlike the Hoax of World War II, *this*
holocaust has been confirmed by countless uncontested studies."[43] Just as the Jews
have tried to steal the claim to be God's chosen people, the argument goes, they try
to steal the rightful claim to be the sole victims of genocide. Just as the Jews are not
Israelites, so there was no Holocaust.

The specter of racial destruction allows Identity believers to attack multiple
issues: Jews in control of the government and media; "illegal fecund aliens" brought
in to dilute the white population; American policy in South Africa, which will
destroy yet another white sanctuary; and abortion, through which white children are
deliberately murdered. But they are less certain about how to respond.

The New Christian Crusade Church is not at all sure of the outcome. "[Our]
White race enters the twilight of its very existence. . . . Without your help, this truly
is—The End."[44] Dan Gayman agrees that "the handwriting is on the wall! America

is becoming a non-white nation." He suggests that whites "remove your children from the mixed multitude, and regroup with clusters of your own people."[45] This survivalist emphasis on commune-like enclaves reappears in more grandiose form in the proposal by David Lane and others for racial states: "Nothing less than a political state, with inviolate borders can secure our existence."[46] Since the prospect of such redrawn boundaries is remote in the extreme, it calls forth a virtual renunciation of all conventional political loyalties. "God [is] our only government," declares Robert Miles of the Mountain Church.[47] David Lane puts it more bluntly: "I do not recognize the existence of a government whose single principle [sic] aim is to exterminate my race."[48]

Identity writings convey a very different sense of doom than one finds in such dispensationalist authors as Hal Lindsey. Lindsey's millions die horrible deaths in the nuclear attacks during the Tribulation, but the Second Coming and the millennium are assured, and the saved, having been Raptured, will not endure the Tribulation in any case. Identity writers ride a sharper knifeblade between hope and despair. "Any really constructive ordering of human affairs now necessarily lies on the far side of a great disaster. . . . We are entering upon a gaudy, lurid, rotten and unworthy age which can only end in total disaster for the Jews as well as for everybody else."[49] In the meantime, there is the solace of bloody revenge fantasies, when the "New Order" cleanses the world of its impurities. In the denouement of *The Turner Diaries*, massacres in North America and Europe will cause blood to flow "ankle-deep in the streets," after which by "a combination of chemical, biological, and radiological means . . . 16 million square miles of the earth's surface, from the Ural Mountains to the Pacific and from the Arctic Ocean to the Indian Ocean, [will be] effectively sterilized."[50]

Identity writers assume in their more optimistic moments that they will eventually establish a new order, but they tend to be predictably vague about its details. Like most millenarians, they seem far more interested in describing the evil they oppose than in the salvation they desire. Some elements of the postdisaster utopia are clear, however. It will be designed by and for a racial elite. Wesley Swift tells his audience, "You are the elect of God from before the foundation of the world. . . . My friends, you are not little people; you are the children of the Most High, and you are still in a creative work."[51] Earl Turner describes the secret society he has joined as "the vanguard of the Coming New Era, the pioneers who will lead our race out of its present depths and toward the unexplored heights above."[52]

That "New Order" is usually identified with Jesus' millennial reign, although Jesus tends to play a rather passive role in these scenarios. Aryan Nations promises "a day of judgment and a day when Christ's Kingdom (Government) will be established on earth as it is in heaven," and Karl Schott, Wesley Swift, and others promise that Jesus will reign from Jerusalem and unite the twelve tribes of Israel.[53] "Aryans" will rule, for "God's intended purpose was that his racial kinsmen were to be in charge of this earth."[54] Dan Gayman adds that the Temple in Jerusalem will be rebuilt and its worship service restored, "and it will include the altar, the candlesticks, and all else that was central to the worship established by Yahweh in ancient Israel."[55] (It is worth noting that dispensationalists, for their part, expect Jews to rebuild the Jerusalem Temple prior to the Second Coming, and in fact some American premillennialists have given financial support to ultraorthodox groups in Israel that wish to see such a project advanced.)[56]

In short, Identity millennialists foresee a period of mounting violence in which the destruction of the white race will be narrowly averted, their racial adversaries either killed or subordinated, and a Jesus-led "Aryan" regime installed for earthly rule from Jerusalem. It is, to put it mildly, an eccentric mixture, simultaneously fundamentalist and antifundamentalist, optimistic and pessimistic, Christian and occult, where anti-Semitism is intent on demonstrating that the ostensible Israelites are in fact impostors, while the ostensible Gentiles are in fact Israelites.

The far Right is an organizationally fluid phenomenon, made up of countless small shifting groups whose memberships often overlap. Only such gatherings as the periodic "Aryan Nations Congress," organized by Richard Girnt Butler, supply some measure of cohesion. Neither all of the organizations nor all of their members are fully committed to Identity. Despite these signs of fragmentation, Christian Identity supplies the radical Right with a philosophical center of gravity, explicitly or implicitly acknowledged even by those not immediately identifiable as Identity believers.

Louis Beam, a former Grand Dragon of the Texas Knights of the Ku Klux Klan, predicts that increasingly "the New Right will be marked by a large scale acceptance of Identity doctrine. . . . Identity will be, for a major segment of the movement, a cornerstone upon which religious thought is based."[57] Even a casual perusal of right-wing publications demonstrates that Identity figures and organizations are closely linked with non-Identity groups through lectures, social visits, and joint meetings. Identity leaders, such as Richard Butler, are the subject of deferential, affectionate comments in the newsletters of the Mountain Church's Robert Miles and White Aryan Resistance's Tom Metzger. In fact, even among those whose roots lie in Klan groups or the American Nazi Party, one senses that Identity is accepted as a quasi-official movement worldview.

The reasons for Identity's rise over the last twenty years include the more general politicization of American religion; the weakening of religious and intellectual authority, which permits the broader circulation of previously stigmatized positions; and a cultural ambience supportive of apocalyptic views. As deviant as Christian Identity is in comparison with most forms of American political and religious expression, it nonetheless grows from and reflects a larger context, supportive of millennial views of history. Whereas earlier racists and anti-Semites rarely went beyond the articulation of fears and resentments, Identity purports to offer a framework that explains the past, provides guidance in the present, and predicts the future, giving to the American far Right an ideological coherence it never previously possessed. In considering Christian Identity as a millennial movement, three facets require further examination: attitudes toward Jews, the uneasy equilibrium of optimism and pessimism, and the highly syncretic character of the belief system.

It might appear at first glance as though nothing further need be said of Identity's view of Jews. Its anti-Semitic rhetoric varies only in the degree of its coarseness. The obsessive hatred of Jews and their alleged responsibility for every evil are constants.

Nonetheless, there is in fact an interesting quirk in the treatment of Jews by Identity, for Identity conceives its relationship to Jews to be one not merely of hostility but also of rivalry. For Christian Identity is one of a small class of millenarian movements that instead of merely asserting millenarian claims, seek to appropriate the millenarian claims of others. Millennialists customarily claim access to special knowledge and to a special saved status that assures them of information concerning the coming millennial order and their place in it. Occasionally, however, they go beyond these assertions to claim that their access to special knowledge has been deliberately kept from them by deceitful means and that those responsible for the deception have wrongfully appropriated the knowledge for themselves. The millennial task, therefore, becomes not only the conventional one of doing whatever must be done to prepare for and hasten the last days, but also the prior task of unmasking the deception. Thus, some of the Melanesian Cargo Cults claimed that Europeans were able to dominate the native population because missionaries had ripped from Bible copies the pages that proved Jesus had been a Papuan.[58]

Such instances of *appropriative millennialism*—claiming as one's own the special status claimed by another group—exaggerates the Manichaeanism present in all apocalyptic groups, their tendency to view the world as a battleground between pure good and pure evil. The adversary has a seemingly limitless capacity for misrepresentation and evil-doing. Indeed, the enemy is often described as a conspiracy, working its will in secret. In cases of appropriative millennialism, the evil conspiracy is deemed not simply to be committed to the destruction of the forces of good, but also to have literally stolen from those forces the knowledge of their own special destiny. The millennium has been taken from its rightful bearers by those who have no legitimate claim to it.

This exaggerated form of conspiratorialism has multiple attractions for Christian Identity. First, it confirms them in their sense of their own elite status, a status deemed so valuable the adversary will stop at nothing to seize it for itself. Second, the alleged theft of millennial knowledge appears to offer an explanation for Identity's failure to secure a mass following: other "Aryans" ignore or oppose them because they have been taken in by the deception and fail to recognize that they themselves are actually Israelites. That "explains" too why dispensationalists continue to give Jews a major role in the economy of salvation, for fundamentalist clerics have also been duped. Third, the myth of the stolen patrimony provides yet another seeming confirmation of the cunning of Jews. Finally, the tale of the stolen millennium also allows Identity believers to appropriate Jews' claims to being historic victims. In this version "Aryans" are the true victims, because their birthright has been stolen. Jews' claim to victim status is merely a manipulative device to enhance their own power. Hence the frequent references in Identity literature to "Holocaust revisionism": the Holocaust never occurred, confessions by Nazis were procured by torture, and so forth. Indeed, the post-Holocaust Right must find a way to, as it were, de-victimize Jews in order to confirm their own article of faith that Jews run America and will soon rule the world, a position on its face incompatible with the destruction of European Jewry.

The attitude toward Jews is also closely related to Identity's unstable balance between optimism and pessimism. At one level Identity believes that the new

"Aryan" order is inevitable, and that progress toward it is accelerating. But this conviction of an imminent millennium is in constant conflict with fear that the adversary will triumph. The demonization of the Jew, to whom is imputed virtually limitless power over the government, the media, and the mainstream churches, suggests that no power may be great enough to prevent Jewish domination of the world. This is, of course, an example of what Richard Hofstadter recognized as a running theme of American right-wing thought, the so-called paranoid political style, complete with an apparatus of spurious scholarship that "proves" the existence and breadth of the conspiracy.[59] Yet, Hofstadter erred, I think, in too readily identifying all such politically "paranoid" groups as millennialist, for one can view the world under the aspect of conspiracy while having reservations about whether the conspiracy can be defeated. Thus, Mrs. S. E. V. Emery dedicated her famous Populist tract, *Seven Financial Conspiracies,* to "the enslaved people of a dying republic," as though she was unsure that even her propagandistic efforts would be sufficient to rouse the citizenry for the final battle.[60] The same doubt creeps into the words of an Identity minister, Pastor Karl Schott, when he says that "today, Israel [read: Aryans] is in bondage to the Communists, and Edomites [read: Jews], and other anti-Christ powers and we seem powerless to break this bondage. It will take the Almighty God to break their power."[61] The same unease is reflected in the frequent contemptuous references to Americans as so soft and corrupt that they are scarcely worth saving. As *The Turner Diaries* puts it, "Americans have lost their right to be free."[62]

Identity teeters, therefore, on the edge of despair, committed to an inevitable new order but not always certain that it really is inevitable. This dialectic of hope and despair, of retreat and engagement, produces a fundamental ideological instability that can easily slip into armed confrontation. It did so in the spring of 1996, when the Montana Freemen faced off against federal law enforcement, and it will doubtless do so again. Identity has moved out of the political shadows at a time of general cultural uncertainty common to *fin de siècle* periods, and there is every reason to believe that the coming end not only of the century but of the millennium will induce even greater political volatility.

NOTES

1. On the millennialism of the pre–Civil War period, see my *Crucible of the Millennium: The Burned-Over District of New York 1840s* (Syracuse, N.Y.: Syracuse University Press, 1986); and, of course, Whitney Cross, *The Burned-Over District: The Social and Intellectual History of Enthusiastic Religion in Western New York, 1800–1850* (New York: Harper and Row, 1950).

2. I have discussed the similarities between secular and religious apocalypticism in "Divided Apocalypse: Thinking about the End in Contemporary America," *Soundings* 66 (1983): 257–80. The best study of contemporary religious apocalyptic thought remains Timothy P. Weber, *Living in the Shadow of the Second Coming: American Premillennialism (1875–1982)* (Grand Rapids: Zondervan, 1983).

3. I discuss the relationship between present-day and earlier right-wing movements in greater detail in "Millenarian Aspects of 'White Supremacist' Movements," *Terrorism and Political Violence* 1 (1989): 409–34.

4. Although there have been sectarian outgrowths of British-Israelism, in general the movement did not take sectarian form, its adherents feeling free to remain affiliated with other groups whose views they felt were compatible with the British-Israel position.

5. For a discussion of Brothers, see Clarke Garrett, *Respectable Folly: Millenarians and the French Revolution in France and England* (Baltimore: Johns Hopkins University Press, 1975).

6. For a brief but useful history of British-Israelism, see John Wilson, "British Israelism: The Ideological Restraints on Sect Organization," in Bryan Wilson, ed., *Patterns of Sectarianism: Organization and Ideology in Social and Religious Movements* (London: Heineman, 1967), 345–76. The author is, of course, not to be confused with the John Wilson who founded British-Israelism.

Ideas akin to those of British-Israelism received separate development in the theology of the Church of Jesus Christ of Latter-Day Saints. Janet F. Dolgin, "Latter-Day Sense and Substance," in Irving I. Zaretsky and Mark P. Leone, eds., *Religious Movements in Contemporary America* (Princeton, N.J.: Princeton University Press, 1974), 531.

7. Armstrong's position is succinctly expressed in Herbert W. Armstrong, *The United States and Britain in Prophecy,* 8th ed. (Pasadena, Calif.: Worldwide Church of God, 1980).

8. John Wilson, *Lectures on Our Israelitish Origin,* 5th ed. (London, 1876), 368.

9. Although there seems little doubt that the upper reaches of Khazar society converted, most scholars place little weight on the suggestion that any significant segment of contemporary Jewry is of Khazar descent. An exception is Arthur Koestler, who argues that European Jews are predominantly of Khazar ancestry. He would doubtless have been horrified to learn that his book on the subject is both admired and sold by Identity organizations. Arthur Koestler, *The Thirteenth Tribe: The Khazar Empire and Its Heritage* (New York: Random House, 1976).

10. *This Is Aryan Nations,* n.d., brochure.

11. William Potter Gale, *Identity* (Glendale, Calif.: Ministry of Christ Church, n.d.); reprint, Hollywood, Calif.: New Christian Crusade Church, n.d.), 11.

12. Wesley A. Swift, *Testimony of Tradition and the Origin of Races,* rev. ed. (Hollywood, Calif.: New Christian Crusade Church, n.d.), 39. Originally part of a sermon delivered to the Church of Jesus Christ, Christian, Hollywood, California, this passage is indicative of an occult influence that is common, but little remarked upon, in Identity publications.

13. Swift, *Testimony of Tradition,* 15; Gale, *Identity,* 14.

14. I discuss the occult element in Identity more fully in "'Christian Identity' Groups and the Cultic Milieu," paper presented at the annual meeting of the Association for the Sociology of Religion, San Francisco, August 6–9, 1989.

15. An extended discussion of the origins of political anti-Semitism appears in part 1 of Hannah Arendt, *The Origins of Totalitarianism* (reprint, New York: World, 1958). Political anti-Semitism was of course dependent upon attitudes transmitted through the much older folk traditions, but political anti-Semitism transmuted these archaic notions into new forms.

16. Norman Cohn, *The Pursuit of the Millennium: Revolutionary Millenarians and Mystical Anarchists of the Middle Ages,* rev. ed. (New York, Oxford University Press, 1970), 15.

17. *Watchman* 11 (winter 1989): 11. *The Watchman* is published by the Church of Israel, "Diocese of Manasseh," Schell, Missouri.

18. Parisfal [pseud.], "Our Sword for the Struggle," *Seditionist* 1 (winter 1988): 12–13.

19. The most widely circulated example of the genre is the best-selling nonfiction paperback of the 1970s: Hal Lindsey and L. L. Carlson, *The Late Great Planet Earth* (reprint, New York: Bantam, 1973).

20. For an example of the penetration of such views, see A. G. Mojtabai's description of religious views in Amarillo, Texas, in *Blessed Assurance: At Home with the Bomb in Amarillo, Texas* (Boston, Little, Brown, 1986).

21. H. Aldersmith, "Appendix E," in Denis Hanan and H. Aldersmith, eds., *British-Israel Truth,* 14th ed. (London: Covenant Publishing Co., 1932), 256. Subsequently, British-Israel writers did become notably hostile toward Zionism for helping push Britain out of Palestine.

22. *Calling Our Nation,* no. 59 (1989): 26 (published by Aryan Nations).

23. James K. Warner, "Land of the ZOG," *CDL Report,* no. 112, special ed., 1. This is a periodical published by the New Christian Crusade Church, Metairie, Louisiana.

24. William Pierce [Andrew Macdonald], *The Turner Diaries,* 2d ed. (Arlington, Va.: National Alliance/National Vanguard Books, 1980), 33. Although the National Alliance is not an Identity organization, *The Turner Diaries* has circulated very widely throughout the far Right, including among Identity believers.

25. For a detailed history of *The Protocols,* including its ties to the occult, see Norman Cohn, *Warrant for Genocide: The Myth of the Jewish World-Conspiracy and the Protocols of the Elders of Zion* (reprint, Chico, Calif.: Scholars Press, 1981).

26. *This Is Aryan Nations;* Fred Farrel, "Understanding Your Jewish Masters," *CDL Report,* no. 109 (August 1988): 5.

27. *This Is Aryan Nations.*

28. Pierce, *The Turner Diaries,* 34–35.

29. *Come My People Hide Thyself for a Little While* (Spokane, Wash.: Christian Gospel Fellowship Church, n.d.), brochure. In Identity literature "Edomites" is a frequent synonym for Jews.

30. Mimeographed letter from Richard G. Butler to Aryan Nations members, December 1, 1988. Anti-Defamation League archives, New York City.

31. Swift, *Testimony of Tradition,* 34.

32. Pierce, *The Turner Diaries,* 71–72. The actual organization known as "The Order" and later as "The Silent Brotherhood" or "Bruders Schweigen" was patterned after the group described in the *Diaries.* Kevin Flynn and Gary Gerhardt, *The Silent Brotherhood: Inside America's Racist Underground* (New York: Free Press, 1989), 140.

33. Wesley A. Swift, *You: Before the World Was Framed* (reprint, Hollywood, Calif.: New Christian Crusade Church, n.d.), 26. Probably this was a sermon delivered to the Church of Jesus Christ, Christian.

34. Swift, *Testimony of Tradition,* 10. Gale, *Identity,* 11.

35. Gale, *Identity,* 11.

36. "Last Days of ZOG," *Calling Our Nation,* no. 59 (1989): 25.

37. "Will There Be National Drought in 1989?" *Watchman* 11 (winter 1989): 14; "Watchman's Warning!" *Watchman* 11 (winter 1989): 40.

38. Dan Gayman, "Editorial: To the Remnant in Israel," *Watchman* 11 (fall 1988): 1–6.

39. Pierce, *The Turner Diaries,* 166.

40. Madison Grant, *The Passing of the Great Race, or the Racial Basis of European History* (1918; reprint, New York, 1970).

41. David Lane, "Migration," *Calling Our Nation,* no. 59 (1989): 8.

42. Ibid.

43. Warner, "Land of the ZOG," 15.

44. Ibid., 16.

45. Dan Gayman, "Life in the Country," *Watchman* 11 (winter 1989): 15.

46. Lane, "Migration," 8.

47. Robert Miles, *From the Mountain* (Cohoctah, Mich.: Mountain Church, March-April 1987), brochure. E. Miles, the church's pastor, espoused a form of dualism rather than Identity. Nonetheless, he regarded his beliefs as compatible with Identity, and his theology

included themes present in Identity writers, including belief in "Aryans" as descendants of God and the belief that "Aryans" had a spirit existence prior to embodiment on earth.

48. Quoted in *WAR '86* (Fallbrook, Calif.: White Aryan Resistance, 1986).

49. Farrel, "Understanding Your Jewish Masters," 5.

50. Pierce, *The Turner Diaries,* 209–10.

51. Swift, *Testimony of Tradition,* 6; Swift, *You,* 29–30.

52. Pierce, *The Turner Diaries,* 203–4.

53. *This Is Aryan Nations; What We Believe* (Spokane, Wash.: *The Pathfinder,* Christ's Gospel Fellowship Church, n.d.), brochure; Wesley A. Swift, *Standards of the Kingdom* (Hollywood, Calif.: New Christian Crusade Church, n.d.), 33 (originally a sermon delivered at the Church of Jesus Christ, Christian, Hollywood, California).

54. *This Is Aryan Nations.*

55. *Watchman* 11 (winter 1989): 27.

56. Barbara Ledeen and Michael Ledeen, "The Temple Mount Plot," *New Republic,* June 18, 1984, 20–23.

57. *Seditionist* 1 (winter 1988): 1.

58. Peter Worsley, *The Trumpet Shall Sound: A Study of "Cargo" Cults in Melanesia,* 2d ed. (New York: Schocken, 1986), 137.

59. Richard Hofstadter, *The Paranoid Political Style and Other Essays* (New York: Knopf, 1965).

60. Mrs. S. E. V. Emery, *Seven Financial Conspiracies Which Have Enslaved the American People* (reprint, Westport, Conn.: Hyperion Press, 1975).

61. *Come My People.*

62. Pierce, *The Turner Diaries,* 33.

Chapter Seventeen

Political Millennialism within the Evangelical Subculture

Sara Diamond

Amid the signs that a new millennium was near, Pat Robertson—the pioneer religious broadcaster, one-time presidential candidate, and founder of the politically powerful Christian Coalition—broke into the world of popular fiction with his first novel *The End of the Age* (1995). It begins in the year 2000 when a three-hundred-million-pound meteor hits the southern California coast, plunging the planet into a fit of tidal waves and nuclear meltdowns, killing five hundred million people and dooming the rest to subservience under a demonic dictator who assumes control of the U.S. government. From a base camp in New Mexico, a small group of Bible-believing Christians survive the natural disasters and economic chaos. They use satellite TV and radio transmissions to coordinate a Christian resistance to satanic government agents until finally the Rapture begins and they are transported into heaven to spend eternity with Christ.

Throughout, the plot is thickened with gems from the mind of Pat Robertson. After the president of the United States kills himself, while on national television, in remorse for not warning the country about the meteor, the Hillary Clinton–like wife of the drunk and degenerate vice president moves into action. A bisexual who has dabbled in New Age religion and feminism, she conspires with a foreign billionaire named Tarriq Haddad, who arranges the assassination of her husband and the ascent to the presidency of one Mark Beaulieu. He is the Antichrist, having first become possessed by the Hindu god Shiva while on a Peace Corps stint in India. Shiva, it turns out, is Satan, as are all non-Christian deities, which makes evangelization of the non-Western world all the more imperative before the year 2000.

That is the intended message of Robertson's book. In an interview with *Charisma* magazine to promote *The End of the Age,* Robertson said he wrote the novel not because he has any idea when the end will come but because the world is moving inevitably toward two major spiritual events: "worldwide evangelization and revival of epic proportions" and "world judgment," seen in "an increase of progressively severe warnings and judgments of God—things like the earthquakes, tornadoes, floods and heat waves we've recently experienced." The message of the book, said Robertson, is that Christians have just a short amount of time to "take the gospel to the world." He wanted "readers to be seized with the sense of absolute urgency."[1]

Indeed, many were. In 1996 Robertson's book was one of the best-selling fiction books sold in Christian bookstores.[2] It was heavily promoted on Robertson's own *700 Club* program, and though it was uninspiring as a work of fiction, it was right in step with late-1990s thinking within the evangelical subculture. On the eve of the new millennium, evangelical Christians talked of redoubling their global missionary efforts, fueled by hopes and fears that the end of the age was truly near.

Most had long since abandoned the possibility of setting a date through the widely discredited practice of reading current events as the fulfillment of metaphors found in the book of Revelation. There were still a few well-known preachers who practiced what I will call in this article *hard millennialism,* linking a timetable for Christ's return to current events in world politics. But most were committed to a soft millennialism. They heeded the New Testament warning that "no man can know the day or the hour" of Christ's return (Matt. 24:36). They instead looked generally at objectionable trends in society and saw in them signs of difficult times ahead.

There were political overtones to both hard and soft versions of late-1990s evangelical millennialism. The handful of date-setters were criticized for making the evangelical community look foolish when expected dates of Christ's return came and went. Moreover, the hard millennialism of expecting Christ to return within a few months or years had the effect of making believers uninterested in the rigors of long-term political activism. That is why the vast majority of evangelical leaders taught their flock to work as if Christ would not return in their own lifetimes but to be prepared at any moment for the final day. Hard millennialism tended to coincide with a conspiratorial reading of political events: the misdeeds of world leaders were read as signs that they were doing the bidding of the Antichrist. Soft millennialism was more consistent with on-the-ground evangelism, which requires a willingness to deal with people of foreign cultures, though always with the goal of making converts.

In the late 1990s, both hard and soft versions of millennialism intensified among evangelicals. Particularly noticeable was the increase in missionary interest directed toward Third World countries. The drive to win the world for Christ revealed the unwillingness of evangelicals to coexist gracefully with people of different, though no less authentic, cultures.

The Beginning of the End

Robertson's book was probably best appreciated by evangelical believers steeped in eschatology, the study of the "end times." One cornerstone of the Christian Gospel is belief that Christ will eventually return to earth. There has always been great controversy over when that event will take place. The dominant expectation among modern U.S. evangelicals has been based on a belief in "premillennial dispensationalism," which holds that God has divided human history into several ages or dispensations. We are in the final dispensation, which will end when Christ returns to rule and reign over the earth. But there is debate about the timing of events that will precede Christ's return. At some point there will be a Rapture, during which all born-again Christians will ascend into heaven with Jesus. Some premillennialists believe this will happen before a seven-year Tribulation period plagues the earth with wars, famines, and natural disasters. Some—apparently including novelist Pat Robertson—believe the Rapture will occur midway through the Tribulation period, whereas the most pessimistic believers expect they will have to endure the suffering of the entire Tribulation along with unbelievers. In any case the Rapture will be tied closely to a Battle of Armageddon between the forces of good and evil. The righteous will prevail, and their victory will herald the beginning of Christ's new millennial Kingdom.[3]

Among conservative Christians, a small proportion adhere to a postmillennial eschatology. These are advocates of Reconstructionism or "dominion theology," who believe they must establish a theocracy on earth before Christ will return.[4] Among the much larger camp of premillennialists—these are evangelicals, including Baptist and charismatic/pentecostal subgroups—there has been, in recent decades, fervent debate about when the end will begin. Many of the conflicting interpretations have revolved around political and military events in the Middle East. The establishment of the state of Israel in 1948 was seen by many as the beginning of the generation that would witness Christ's return. The 1967 Six Day War, during which Israel took control of Jerusalem, was another sign that the end was near.

Prophecy writer Hal Lindsey's best-seller *The Late Great Planet Earth,* which has sold fifteen million copies since it was first published in 1970, popularized premillennial eschatology for lay evangelical audiences. The book was a pastiche of Bible quotes and intimations that Armageddon would begin with a Soviet nuclear strike on Israel. Throughout the late 1970s and 1980s—the period of cold war retrenchment and heightened public fears about nuclear war—Lindsey was a frequent guest on Trinity Broadcasting Network TV talk shows. Using maps and claiming to be privy to inside tips from military experts, he would read current events as signs that the end was near. Though he never set a precise end-time date, Lindsey's millennialism was "hard" in that he used real world events as signs of an impending final battle. Only God's people would be raptured and thus spared from a fiery holocaust, but in the meantime Lindsey promoted the 1980s U.S. nuclear buildup and massive U.S. military aid to Israel.

Lindsey's popularity inspired a long lineup of prophecy writers to add to the popular genre of hard millennial books. Through the late 1990s, typical Christian bookstores continued to stock special "prophecy" sections with titles by Lindsey, Jack van Impe, David Webber, John Walvoord, and others. Walvoord's 1974 classic *Armageddon, Oil, and the Middle East Crisis* was reprinted in 1990 and sold over one million copies around the time of the U.S. war against Iraq.[5] Walvoord, a chancellor of the premillennialist Dallas Theological Seminary, was careful not to claim that the Persian Gulf War itself signaled the beginning of the end. His point was that because biblical prophecy predicts that the Middle East will be "the battleground for the road to Armageddon and the second coming of Christ," and "with world attention on the Middle East . . . the major components of the end time are in place."[6]

Walvoord, Lindsey, and most of their colleagues refrained from the kind of precise date-setting that would have damaged their credibility—and future sales of their next books. Not so with a couple of end-times date-setters who enjoyed brief notoriety on the evangelical media circuit. In 1987 Edgar Whisenant, a retired engineer and amateur Bible student, published *88 Reasons Why the Rapture Will Be in 1988*. Based on a bizarre set of calculations extrapolated from events mentioned in the New Testament, Whisenant predicted the Rapture would occur between September 11 and 13, 1988. By the time those dates had come and gone, he had sold 4.5 million copies of his booklets, and then audaciously sold thousands more of subsequent tracts.[7]

Similarly, Harold Camping, a once-respected broadcaster with the shortwave Family Radio ministry, in 1992 began predicting that the world would end in September of 1994. Using what other Bible scholars considered a tortured reading of dates and numerical clues in the Bible, Camping claimed that the Tribulation period had begun in 1988.[8] Because Camping had been a reputable figure among evangelicals, his critics were particularly concerned when his book *1994* became a best-seller. Throughout 1994 the southern California–based Christian Research Institute, which monitors "heretical" Christian groups and broadcasts the nationally syndicated weekday "Bible Answer Man" radio program, made Harold Camping a key focus. Radio host Hank Hanegraaff took particular issue with Camping's claim that after September 6, 1994, no new believers could be converted. Hanegraaff and other critics indicted the date-setters for encouraging fatalism and thereby abandoning the Christian mandate to go out and make new disciples.[9]

Most evangelicals held to a soft millennialism, to the effect that because the timing of Christ's return could not be known but was, nevertheless, imminent, proselytization of the "unsaved" was urgent. Especially within the milieu of charismatic Christians—who believe that the abilities to prophesy and heal and other "gifts of the Holy Spirit" or "charismata" are as real today as during Christ's lifetime—the most popular preachers emphasized the approaching year 2000 as an impetus to escalate evangelism. In a book summarizing the teachings of leading charismatic figures, including Oral Roberts, Kenneth Copeland, Kenneth Hagin, Lester Sumrall, Marilyn Hickey, Jack Hayford, Benny Hinn, and others, pastor James Horvath concludes that most see the year 2000 not as the definitive "end time" but rather as a "target date" for the goal of preaching the gospel to the whole world. "We must not retreat from society; we must advance," Horvath writes. "As the end of time draws closer, the body of Christ is to be actively involved in every arena—economically, socially and politically."[10]

Yet, the temptation among some premillennialists was, in fact, to begin to withdraw from society, if only by focusing rhetorically on divisions between the "saved" and the "unsaved." That division was a major theme in Pat Robertson's novel and in other popular books published shortly before the year 2000. One of these, *Left Behind*, by Peter and Patti Lalonde, was written putatively for readers who would witness "the disappearance of millions of people from the earth" during the Rapture.[11] The book purported to help these poor souls figure out what had happened to their saved loved ones and how they, too, could—better late than never—repent and still make it into heaven.

There were political overtones to both the hard and soft versions of premillennial eschatology. The harder theories tended to promote a sort of siege mentality. Lindsey and his cohorts read every Middle East peace negotiation, every shift in the balance of forces between the global superpowers, as a sign that Christians should hunker down and wait to be raptured. This brand of millennialism might have been a comfort to the sizable minority of the population that believed the end was near. A 1993 *Time* magazine/CNN poll found that 20 percent of a general U.S. sample responded "yes" to the question, "Will the second coming of Jesus Christ occur sometime around the year 2000?"[12] A 1994 poll by *U.S. News and World Report* found that 59 percent of a national sample believed the world would come to an end. Twelve percent thought the end would come in a few years; 21 percent, within a few decades. Forty-four percent of the same sample said they believed the Bible literally, that there would be a Battle of Armageddon and a Rapture of the church.[13]

Clearly, the prophecy writers enjoyed a large potential market for their theories and books. But their popularity was matched by the prominence of soft premillennial leaders, who urged a more involved, proactive response to the uncertainty over Christ's return. For the political activists of the Christian Right, it was far more expedient to promote the idea of Christians getting involved in all spheres of life than to suggest that they fatalistically sit tight, waiting for the Rapture. The heroes in Pat Robertson's *The End of the Age* are able to rally Christian resistance to the Antichrist only because they spent the last years of the twentieth century amassing the technological know-how to preach the gospel. Robertson's book is intended as a wake-up call to Bible believers: Know that secular political institutions are controlled by demonic conspirators, but take advantage of existing freedoms to harvest as many souls as possible before it is too late.

Windows of Opportunity

Toward that end, and spurred by the approaching celebration of Christ's two-thousandth birthday, the 1990s were for evangelicals a time of renewed commitment to global mission fields. In the 1980s U.S. evangelicals saw the world as a battleground on which the United States fought communism from Central America to the Philippines. With the fall of the communist menace, and with technology making the world increasingly smaller, all that remained was to convert the whole world to Christ. The major obstacles were the non-Christian religions indigenous to foreign cultures. Global evangelization, therefore, would require cooperation between U.S. evangelicals and their counterparts abroad.

In May of 1995 four thousand evangelists from nearly two hundred countries met in South Korea for a one-day Global Consultation on World Evangelism to strategize on how to bring the Christian Gospel to every corner of the earth before the year 2000. The event was billed as the broadest gathering of evangelicals in Christian history,[14] but it was one event in a larger effort called the A.D. 2000 and Beyond Movement. Founded in 1990 and with headquarters in Colorado Springs, Colorado, A.D. 2000 and Beyond was a clearinghouse for a series of projects geared toward massive worldwide evangelism in the year 2000—and beyond. There was an emphasis on continuing the work well after the dawn of the new millennium, and there was no suggestion that the world was about to end. Instead, the idea was to create international networks of evangelicals so as to establish a church for every ethnic and religious group by the year 2000 as a birthday gift for Christ. Among the A.D. 2000 and Beyond Projects were "Praying through the 10/40 Window" and "the Joshua Project." The "10/40 Window" project zeroed in on the overwhelming majority of thus far unevangelized "people groups" living in parts of the world between ten degrees north and forty degrees south of the equator. One can look on a map and see that this span of the planet includes much of Africa, the Middle East, all of India, and most of Asia—in other words, that part of the world where people practice Islam, Hinduism, Buddhism, and other indigenous religions.[15]

"Praying through the Window" was a project promoted throughout the late 1990s. It was organized by evangelical leaders, including Christian Broadcasting Network chairperson Michael Little, theology professor C. Peter Wagner, and others. Publicized through evangelical media outlets, "Praying through the Window" involved getting churches and individual Christians who were not otherwise active in missionary work to select one of the one hundred "gateway cities" in the 10/40 window region and then pray for a successful evangelical revival in that area. The "gateway cities" included Cairo, Istanbul, Baghdad, Tehran, Delhi, Bangkok, Beijing, and Tokyo.[16] In 1993 A.D. 2000 and Beyond reported that over twenty million Christians from 105 countries prayed for 62 nations in the 10/40 Window.[17] The subsequent campaign focused on directing prayer toward cities with populations in excess of one million; areas representing the "spiritual, political, and economic centers in their respective countries," and areas that were also "the centers of Islam, Buddhism, Hinduism, Shintoism, Sikhism, and Taoism—religions which dominate this unreached region and hinder the growth of Christianity."[18]

Along with "Praying through the Window" came the Joshua Project, launched in December 1995: Christians from seventy-seven countries met in Colorado Springs to start a five-year plan to establish churches among "1,700 peoples whom mission leaders have agreed are most in need of a church planting effort."[19] The idea was to search out ethnoreligious groups least touched already by the Christian Gospel and to match these "people groups" with local churches willing to pray for them and/or help financially to establish a church.[20] Critics of the A.D. 2000 and Beyond projects noted that the 10/40 window emphasis was trendy and had the potential to take attention and resources away from more accessible mission fields. One critic suggested that the emphasis on just praying for "unreached people groups" might lead to a de-emphasis on personal evangelism.[21]

There was no evidence that the popularity of the A.D. 2000 and Beyond prayer project was a detriment to more traditional, on-the-ground forms of evangelism. What was evident within the evangelical subculture was a surge in the focus on something called "spiritual mapping." This is a concept that involves researching the demographics and the history of a given geographic area, identifying particular social problems and "territorial spirits" associated with that area. One of the advocates of "spiritual mapping" was Pastor Bob Beckett of the Dwelling Place Family Church in Hemet, California. He had mapped significant sites in his community, including the location of intertribal Indian warfare and the location of a failed water company drilling effort th' had drained the water supply for native people in the area. He then used this information to encourage prayer and repentance by local Christians, and he later claimed effective evangelism of Native Americans and other people in the areas he had "mapped" as spiritually difficult.[22]

Beckett's approach to "spiritual mapping" was explicit and somewhat controversial because it suggested that evangelists focus on demonic spirits. Nevertheless, "spiritual mapping" had the support of a number of groups active within the A.D. 2000 and Beyond project,[23] and it was an approach that resonated with A.D. 2000 and Beyond's focus on particular "people groups" and "gateway cities" as centers of non-Christian belief, that is, centers still under the sway of Satan. Spiritual mapping was part of a broader charismatic practice called "spiritual warfare," which involved praying for God to "intercede" to tear down "satanic strongholds" ranging everywhere from a believer's personal life to the highest echelons of political decision making.[24] More than an esoteric practice, spiritual warfare was also a psychological mind-set through which believers focused their attention on specific outcomes: winning a loved one to Christ, electing candidates to office, seeing a foreign country become open to missionaries. Regardless of whether secular observers believe that prayer really works, there was something potent about large groups of people naming and committing themselves to tangible events in the material world. Within Christian Right political circles, people were usually asked first to pray about a problem, before specific activist tactics were suggested. After praying about a situation, believers had a stake in seeing their prayers answered and were more willing to actually do something toward that end.

Within the evangelical subculture of the 1990s, there was much media attention given to foreign missionary work. The popular magazine *Charisma,* for example, frequently published stories chronicling evangelistic efforts abroad. Coverage typically had a political angle. In 1995, for example, a *Charisma* issue focusing on "The Holy Spirit around the World" began with a story about Haiti, where U.S. troops had recently been deployed ostensibly to restore order. The reporter began her article on Christian challenges to Haitian voodoo by quoting a Haitian pastor who was skeptical about the return of President Jean-Bertrand Aristide, the progressive priest who had been ousted in a military coup. The article, titled "An Invasion of Mercy in the Caribbean," featured a full-page photo of a smiling U.S. soldier holding a smiling Haitian boy, waving as if to say to the reader: we were saved by the U.S. military.[25] The Haiti story was accompanied by one on the spread of Christianity in North Korea, titled "Penetrating Stalin's Last Stronghold," and another on Colombia titled "Revival behind Enemy Lines."[26] Consistently, *Charisma* covered evangelism in hot spots such as the Middle East, the Philippines, Brazil, and elsewhere, always with a subtle or not-so-subtle slant suggesting Christianity as the antidote to crime, disorder, and political dissent.

Apart from a renewed interest in praying for revival in these nations, the overseas mission field remained fairly static through the mid-1990s. Generally, missions-minded U.S. evangelicals hoped to support native-born converts who could more easily and inexpensively evangelize their compatriots. World Vision, one of the largest of the international mission agencies, had a southern California–based research division, the Mission Advanced Research and Communications Center (MARC), which compiled handbooks on worldwide evangelistic efforts and demographic facts about "unreached people groups," numbering five hundred in the mid-1990s. In terms of numbers of missionaries sent abroad, both short- and long-term, the top-ranking U.S. sending agencies were the Southern Baptist Convention, Wycliffe Bible Translators, New Tribes Mission, the Assemblies of God denomination, the Churches of Christ denomination, and Youth with a Mission.[27] Combined, a total of about a hundred sending agencies had about 50,500 fully supported missionaries in the field as of 1988.[28]

MARC's 1993–95 handbook noted that between 1988 and 1992, the total number of missionaries sent by U.S. and Canadian organizations actually decreased, reversing the steady growth over many previous years. MARC found increases, however, in U.S. missions' financial support and training for national workers evangelizing in their home countries, as well as an increase in short-term missionary projects led by nondenominational groups.[29] The MARC report lamented the fact that only about 1.2 percent of foreign missionary funding was devoted to reaching the 1.2 billion people living in the least evangelized parts of the world.[30] The most heavily evangelized areas remained those already most hospitable to intrusions by North Americans: Latin America, western Europe, a handful of countries in Africa, and the south Pacific.[31] Despite the rhetoric from groups affiliated with the A.D. 2000 and Beyond project about "praying through the window," there were few tangible resources directed to the least evangelized areas.

Winning the World

This gap between the rhetoric about reaching "unreached people groups" and the reality of a fairly static foreign mission field raised questions about the future politics of evangelical millennialism. The A.D. 2000 and Beyond project correctly identified a dearth of Christian missionizing in those parts of the world where people practice Islam, Hinduism, Buddhism, and other indigenous religions. But there was no sense on the part of the A.D. 2000 and Beyond missionaries that they ought to cede parts of the world as places where people had the right to their own culturally relevant forms of religious expression. On the contrary, as the year 2000 approached, evangelicals remained convinced of their prerogative to convert people of other religions. But the resistance and hostility to Christianity in much of the 10/40 window made actually going there a difficult prospect. Thus the focus on "spiritual warfare"—unless, around the time of the new millennium, U.S. Christians actually increased their physical outreach to "unreached people groups."

That raised the specter of Christians coming into conflict with authorities in "unreached" countries. Anticipating increased problems for missionaries abroad, in 1996 the National Association of Evangelicals adopted a "Statement of Conscience" on "worldwide religious persecution" of Christians. The NAE urged the Clinton administration to appoint a special adviser for religious liberty and to rescind foreign aid to countries that persecuted Christians.[32] Also in 1996, a congressional committee on human rights held a hearing on alleged abuse of Christians abroad with testimonies on incidents of harassment by governments in China, Cuba, North Korea, Vietnam, and the Islamic nations.[33] Neither the National Association of Evangelicals nor missionary agencies expressed concern about well-known and large-scale human rights abuses in countries where the greatest numbers of U.S. missionaries were sent: Indonesia, Brazil, and Colombia, for example. Instead, the possibility loomed that U.S. evangelicals might at some point challenge the prerogatives of U.S. foreign policymakers over countries deemed hostile to Christian missionaries. What if U.S. evangelicals began protesting U.S. support for governments in Kuwait, Saudi Arabia, and other oil-rich Islamic countries?

The soft millennial focus on converting people of other faiths kept the attention of evangelicals focused on international affairs, but in a very narrow way. They were not particularly concerned about the uneven distribution of wealth in most parts of the world, though some missionaries saw life-threatening poverty as an impediment to the spreading of the Gospel. Like the characters in Pat Robertson's novel, evangelical Christians viewed the rest of the world's religions as satanic strongholds—not as the cultures of people with the right to live and worship as they pleased, but rather as fields just waiting to be planted with the seeds of the one acceptable faith.

NOTES

1. "Are We Headed toward Doomsday? An Interview with Pat Robertson," *Charisma,* Nov. 1995, 76.

2. According to *Bookstore Journal,* the monthly trade journal of the Christian Booksellers Association, Robertson's novel was steadily among the five best-selling fiction books in early 1996, based on sales figures from Christian retail stores.

3. On the many versions of end-times theology, see esp. Paul Boyer, *When Time Shall Be No More: Prophetic Belief in Modern American Culture* (Cambridge, Mass.: Belknap Press of Harvard University Press, 1992).

4. Boyer, *When Time Shall Be No More,* 303–4; Sara Diamond, Roads to *Dominion: Right-Wing Movements and Political Power in the United States* (New York: Guilford Press, 1995), 246–48.

5. "Prophecy Books Become Big Sellers," *Christianity Today,* Mar. 11, 1991, 60.

6. John F. Walvoord, *Armageddon, Oil, and the Middle East Crisis* (Grand Rapids: Zondervan, 1990), 15.

7. See Paul Thigpen, "The Second Coming: How Many Views?" *Charisma,* Feb. 1989, 42; interview with Edgar Whisenant, *Charisma,* Feb. 1989, 58–89. For a critique of Whisenant and other date-setters, see also B. J. Oropeza, *99 Reasons Why No One Knows When Christ Will Return* (Downers Grove, Ill.: InterVarsity Press, 1994).

8. "End-Times Prediction Draws Strong Following," *Christianity Today,* June 20, 1994, 46–47; "Camping Misses End-Times Deadline," *Christianity Today,* Oct. 24, 1994, 84; "The Man Who Prophesied the End of the World," *San Francisco Chronicle,* Mar. 12, 1995.

9. I was a regular listener to Hank Hanegraaff's "Bible Answer Man" radio program in 1994 during the controversy over Harold Camping.

10. James Horvath, *He's Coming Soon!* (Orlando: Creation House, 1995), 121.

11. Peter Lalonde and Patti Lalonde, *Left Behind* (Eugene, Oreg.: Harvest House Publishers, 1995), 16.

12. The poll is found in a small box under the heading "Vox Pop," *Time,* May 17, 1993, 13.

13. "The Christmas Covenant," *U.S. News and World Report,* Dec. 19, 1994, 63.

14. "Mobilizing for the Millennium," *Christianity Today,* July 17, 1995, 53; "Christians from 20 Countries Gather to Reach the World by the Year 2000," *EP News Service,* May 19, 1995, 6.

15. A.D. 2000 and Beyond, literature packet provided to me, Apr. 1996.

16. "Millions to Pray in Worldwide Rally," *Christianity Today,* Oct. 2, 1995, 106–7.

17. Sept. 14, 1994, press release from A.D. 2000 and Beyond, author's collection.

18. Ibid.

19. A.D. 2000 and Beyond, *Joshua Project 2000,* brochure provided to me, Apr. 1996.

20. Ibid.

21. "Millions to Pray," 106.

22. "Spiritual Mapping: A Powerful New Tool or an Overhyped Spiritual Distraction?" *EP News Service,* Nov. 3, 1995, 5–8.

23. Ibid. These included Mission America 2000, DAWN Ministries, and the Sentinel Group.

24. Spiritual warfare was a prominent theme among charismatics during the 1980s and the 1990s. The supernatural novels of Frank Peretti, in which angels did invisible battle with Satan's emissaries in struggles to control churches and local governments, helped to popularize spiritual warfare. However, there were also numerous well-known charismatic leaders who promoted the idea, relying on a passage from the book of Ephesians that calls on believers to wrestle with dark forces. For a succinct overview of the practice of spiritual warfare, see, e.g., Steven Lawson, "Defeating Territorial Spirits," *Charisma,* Apr. 1990, 47–55. The same issue of the magazineincludes an excerpt from a major book on spiritual warfare, John Dawson's *Taking Our Cities for God.*

Among numerous *Charisma* articles on spiritual warfare, see esp. Dan O'Neill, "The Supernatural World of Frank Peretti," *Charisma,* May 1989, 48–52; John Archer, "The Devil, Demons, and Spiritual Warfare," *Charisma,* Feb. 1994, 52–57; and Angela Kiesling, "The Lady Is a General," *Charisma,* Mar. 1994, 20–28. The latter article profiled Cindy Jacobs, leader of a "prayer warrior" group called the Generals of Intercession. Jacobs was active with the A.D. 2000 and Beyond pray for God to tear down satanic strongholds and make nations open to the gospel. The Archer article was a question and answer panel with C. Peter Wagner, John Dawson, Cindy Jacobs, Jack Hayford, Larry Lea, Gwen Shaw, Dick Bernal, Tom White, Joy Dawson, and Dick Eastman. Together in 1990 they formed the Spiritual Warfare Network, which became part of the United Prayer Track of A.D. 2000 and Beyond.

25. Kim A. Lawton, "An Invasion of Mercy in the Caribbean," *Charisma,* Jan. 1995, 22–26.

26. *Charisma,* Jan. 1995.

27. John A. Siewert and John A. Kenyon, eds., *Mission Handbook: A Guide to USA/Canada Christian Ministries Overseas* (Monrovia, Calif.: MARC, 1993), 60.

28. Ibid., 59.

29. Ibid., 55–57.

30. Ibid., 55–56.

31. Ibid., 73–79. The countries to which more than seven hundred North American missionaries were sent were Brazil, Colombia, Ecuador, France, French Guiana, Germany, Indonesia, Japan, Kenya, Mexico, Papua New Guinea, and the Philippines.

32. "NAE Convention Charts a Course for Evangelicals in 21st Century," *EP News Service,* Mar. 8, 1996, 2.

33. "House Subcommittee Hears Testimony about Worldwide Christian Persecution," *EP News Service,* Mar. 1, 1996, 4–5.

Chapter Eighteen

The Millennial Concept and the Evolution of Leadership in Black Pentecostalism and the Nation of Islam

Clarence Taylor

The millennial notion, the discontinuation of the world as we know it and the estab-lishment of a harmonious universe that only a select group may inhabit, has always been an important theme in African American religion. In fact, a major attribute of some African American religious groups has been on the prophecy of an inevitable global holocaust and the restoration of a perfect world. In their early development conversionist groups such as black Pentecostalism and nationalist messianic groups such as the Nation of Islam have embraced the notion that the planet is facing impending annihilation because of its iniquitous practices. In fact, the apocalypse has been a core belief among black Pentecostals and the Nation of Islam for most of their existence.

However, in spite of the fact that the notion of the imminent end of the world and the creation of a paradise has been an important focus among many African Americans who have embraced the theology of black Pentecostalism and the Nation of Islam, as we draw near to the year 2000, some of the leaders of these groups have deemphasized the millennial notion. What accounts for the movement away from the theme of the imminent destruction of the world? Undoubtedly, the theologies of religious groups have been altered by socioeconomic conditions. To be sure, like all groups, conversionists and black nationalist messianic sects are not static, frozen in time with little change in their theology. No matter how dogmatic a group is about its tenets, the greater the organization's social, economic, and political achievements are, the more likely it is that the organization will move away from its more radical positions and adopt a more mainstream line. The purpose of this chapter is to deter-mine why black Pentecostal leaders and the Nation of Islam have moved away from the concept of the millennium.

Black Pentecostalism and the Millennium

Black Pentecostalism had is beginnings in the Azusa Movement of the early twenti-eth century. In 1906 William Seymour, an African American holiness minister, began a revival on Azusa Street in Los Angeles, declaring that the act of speaking in tongues was a sign of the baptism of the Holy Spirit. The movement attracted numerous people and helped establish Pentecostal denominations. The Pentecostal Assemblies of the World, a group Seymour was associated with, was organized either during or right after the Azusa Street Revival. Other Pentecostal groups were organized by ministers who were despondent over the inertia they experienced in the Methodist and Baptist churches.[1] For example, Charles Harrison Mason, an ordained minister who pastored a Baptist church in Arkansas, left the church because of the "strict Calvinistic teachings of the Baptist faith." Mason, along with another former Baptist minister, Charles Jones, formed the Church of God in Christ (COGIC). Jones later left the COGIC and formed the Church in Christ Holiness after Mason adopted the notion of speaking in tongues.[2]

Although there are a number of black Pentecostal groups, they all adhere to similar beliefs and practices. They accept the Protestant concepts of repentance and conversion. Once a person confesses his belief that Jesus is God, Pentecostals contend that the believer dies, letting go of his old sinful practices and adopting a new life "in Christ." Closely connected to conversion is the concept of sanctification. In order for the believer to live a life "in Christ," he or she must attempt to live free of sin, giving up the pleasures of the world. The baptism of the Holy Spirit, the third tenet of faith, is manifested by speaking in tongues.[3]

The notion of "otherworldliness" was an important concept among Pentecostals. They said the world was evil and thus in the camp of Satan. Believers should not have bothered "indulging" in worldly pursuits but should have devoted their life to God. In their early history, Pentecostals constantly stressed, "You are in the world but not of the world." Dedicating one's life to God and staying clear of the pleasures and concerns of the world, were the key to an eternal life. Hence, pursuing higher education, becoming involved in civic and political affairs, or taking part in amusement was proscribed. Because Pentecostals insist that the sole criterion for the ministry was a "divine calling," seminary training among the clergy was more the exception than the rule. St. Clair Drake and Horace Cayton note in their study on blacks in a northern city that "most lower-class churches required no formal training for pastors, and the alleged authenticity of the 'call' is deemed more important than any type of preparation." In his work on a "storefront church," Ira E. Harrison argues that "the value of education is questioned because 'it won't give remission of sins,' 'it won't give you the Holy Ghost.'" Harrison points out that although education has been considered a major avenue for social mobility by the dominant society, this has been rejected by black Pentecostal ministers. The "storefront church minister, rather than emphasizing values associated with social mobility, constantly preaches sin and doom in this wicked world."[4]

As noted, a major feature of early black Pentecostalism was its stress on the approaching destruction of the world by God. Some of these groups have even adopted a premillennial view. Premillennial doctrine holds that Christ will soon reign on earth for one thousand years. This is to occur after a complete destruction of the earth and the creation of a new one. But before these events, Jesus will return and rapture his church (take his followers to Heaven), and there will be a seven-year period called the Tribulation. Champions of premillennialism maintain that participation in civic society and seeking political office is futile because Christ's return for his church is just around the corner. In sermons, writings, and doctrinal statements, various holiness and Pentecostal sects have warned that the Tribulation will bring devastation. These tenets were a major focus of black Pentecostals.[5]

Relying on the Bible for justification of the claim of the approaching cessation of the earth and the beginning of God's millennial reign, Garfield T. Haywood, who served as the first presiding bishop of the Pentecostal Assembles of the World (PAW), predicted that judgement would take place at the end of seven thousand years after creation: "Not only will Israel be resurrected at the white throne of judgement and placed on the new Earth, but the wicked, also and all those who died without the baptism of the Holy Spirit, and yet walked in all the light that they had." "Satan shall be bound and death shall be restrained." The "new Israel," according to the Haywood, consisted of people who had obeyed God. Those who failed to convert were doomed to destruction.[6]

The leader of the PAW argued that global events were signs that the rapture was at hand. He charged that the "restoration of Israel" was proof positive that the Second Coming was approaching. Declaring that a restored Israel has never heard the gospel, missionaries were rushing to it because the "Gospel of the Kingdom must be preached in all the world before the end comes." These were the signs, Haywood asserted, that indicated "that the coming of the Lord is very, very near at hand." The near return of Christ was such an important aspect of the PAW that the group publicly noted its belief in divine healing and the "premillennial return of Christ" in its tenets of faith.[7]

Similarly, Charles Harrison Mason, founder of the largest black Pentecostal denomination in the United States, the Church of God in Christ (COGIC), declared that "the World giveth light and understanding that all may be baptized with this one baptism of the Holy Ghost. He will show us then Christ is coming soon again on earth. Prepare to meet your God in His glory." Mason's rhetoric was not unique. In fact, the millennium is included as an important part of the official doctrinal statement. Jesus, according to the doctrinal statement, will "reign on the earth in millennial power and glory."[8]

Besides PAW and COGIC, the Fire Baptized Holiness Church of God of the Americas noted in its doctrinal statement the "premillennial second coming of Christ," thereby expressing its strong belief in the nearness of a great spiritual transformation. Social Scientist Arthur Huff Fauset states that a minister associated with the Mount Sinai Holy Church declared in a sermon that the world was rapidly reaching the millennium, the darkest hours before the break of dawn. Drake and Cayton maintain that "lower-class ministers" accentuate the millennium. "Their choirs sing ominously that 'God's gonna move this wicked race, and raise up a nation that will obey.' . . . They teach that we are living in the 'last dispensation.' Jesus will return 'in clouds of glory,' destroy the wicked and set up the millennial kingdom."[9]

The early songs of black Pentecostals also demonstrate their belief that the apocalypse was predetermined and imminent. In one such song, "Coming As a Thief in the Night," written by Garfield T. Haywood in 1914, the lyrics contended that the signs of Christ's return were all around.

> The earthquakes are telling His Coming is nigh;
> He's coming as a thief in the night.
> The Storms and the lightning speak loud from the sky,
> He's Coming like a Thief in the night.

"Day of Redemption," written by Haywood in 1919, also predicted that Armageddon was around the corner:

> The Nations are breaking, And Israel's a waking, the signs in the Bible foretold; the Gentile days numbered, with horrors encumbered; E-ternity soon will unfold. The day of redemption is near. . . . Men's heart are failing for fear up!
>   Your redemption is near.

Playing on the fear that these events could take place at any moment, one song, entitled "The Judgement Day," warned the "nonsaved" to rethink their sinful ways before it was too late:

> O be ready for the morning of the coming of the Lord!
> He has warn'd you of your danger in His most holy word.
> The heav'ns melt and pass away; O be ready for the judgement day!

According to Charles Price Jones, his song "Where Shall I Be?" "was once used to warn and win souls." Indeed, Price could have made the same comment about a number of his songs. For instance, in "There's Coming a Time," he explicitly expressed the urgent need to get right with God before it was too late:

> There's coming a time when sinners shall hear Him saying in anger
>   "from me depart"
> And driven to doom, shall wail that they never gave to the Lord the love
>   of their heart.[10]

These songs were more than just hymns sung by a choir at a Sunday morning service. They expressed a belief among some black Pentecostals that God's return was near and that they must be prepared before the great apocalypse. Like other groups that were convinced of the pending desolation of the earth, Pentecostal members clearly believed that their role was to act as soldiers in God's army and to alert the world that it was in grave danger if it did not turn to God. For Pentecostals, national and international events were testimony that the apocalypse was "nigh." Thus, World War I, the Russian Revolution, the large immigration of Jews to Palestine, migration to cities, and race riots in urban centers all played roles in persuading them that the end of time was near.

Numerous scholars have noted that black Pentecostalism has attracted mostly working-class people. According to sociologist E. Franklin Frazier, "lower class" people were drawn to the "storefronts" because they wanted a religious environment that would help create warmth and sympathetic association, as well as status, in a urban center. Historian Dennis Dickerson contends that black migrants to western Pennsylvania in the early part of the twentieth century felt uncomfortable in the elitist churches and for that reason formed their own religious institutions, including Baptist, Methodist, and Pentecostal churches. Likewise, Allan Spear declares that as a result of the Baptist and African Methodist Episcopal churches' adoption of a "more decorous order of worship and a program of broad social concern," Chicago black working-class migrants joined holiness and Pentecostal churches. In Milwaukee, according to historian Joe William Trotter, holiness churches best depicted the changing class structure of that city because they attracted members of the growing black working population.[11]

A major reason for the black proletariat's affinity for Pentecostalism was that it helped forge a black identity by redefining their blackness. They saw themselves not as despised and dispossessed, but as a select group who were in constant communion with God. Some called themselves saints, but all black Pentecostals declared themselves saved from the corruption and vice of the modern world. Their historical memory extended back to Israel. They considered themselves to be God's chosen people, who would soon be liberated from this "wicked world." Their future was clearly bright, assured a spot in the new paradise. The concept of faith and deliverance was a major part of the black Pentecostal consciousness.

Just as important, Pentecostalism was an attempt to assert their humanity and achieve self-actualization. Working-class African Americans were at the helm in Pentecostal churches, able to express themselves, take leadership positions, and practice a style of worship that was not acceptable in the large black mainline churches. Black Pentecostalism was used as a means to adjust to a racist and class-stratified environment that consistently challenged black humanity. Black Pentecostals found themselves the victims of racial bias in the larger white society and class bias among middle-class blacks. The larger society denied working-class blacks access to resources and social status. Black Pentecostalism helped protect black working people's self-worth. Moreover, the strong eschatological belief among black Pentecostals was a form of resistance to the hostility and deprivation they faced in a racist and class-conscious society. It helped arm them with the belief that God will bring about justice by destroying the world of Satan.[12]

More recently there has been some evidence suggesting a greater indulgence in worldly concerns among black Pentecostals. Many of the clergy have become involved in civic and political affairs. A growing number have become active in various civic organizations. Rev. Henry Butts, pastor of a church in Daytona Beach, Florida, reflects the increasing community involvement. In 1989 Rev. Butts was a member of the Ecumenical Ministers Fellowship as well as of a business and professional association and the Daytona Beach Chamber of Commerce. Charles Edward Blake and Duane Adrian Darkins also exemplify the civic-minded Pentecostal minister. It was reported in 1989 that Rev. Charles Edward Blake, pastor of a COGIC church in California was President of the Interdenominational Ministers Alliance near Los Angeles and Commissioner of a fire department. Duane Adrian Darkins, a COGIC pastor in Pittsburgh, is chair of the Mayor's Commission on Human Relations. In Memphis COGIC ministers provided the headquarters for the sanitation workers who were on strike in 1968.[13]

One of the best examples of the activist black Pentecostal minister is Bishop Smallwood Williams, founder and leader of the Bible Way Church of Our Lord Jesus Christ World Wide. Williams argued that the "black minister, in particular, has an even greater role to be politically involved, than clergy of other races because of so many unsolved problems left over from 300 years of human slavery and degradation of his people." Clearly not relying on the Rapture, Williams wrote, "The social sins of racism found in segregation and economic exploitation can be solved through the political process." Furthermore, he felt that the politically active minister should be concerned not only with domestic affairs but also with the country's foreign policy. Williams joined Mary Church Terrell, a founder of the Black Women's Club Movement, and the radical grassroots leader Annie Stein in building a movement that successfully challenged segregated restaurants in the nation's capital in the early 1950s. Williams also led a campaign to help integrate the public school system of Washington, D.C.[14]

The political and civic activity among Pentecostal pastors points to their greater worldly consciousness and diminished emphasis on the millennial notion. It was not that they were pushing aside a sacred worldview for secular concerns. They had become more holistic, recognizing the social conditions of blacks and attempting to seek palpable solutions to those problems. Rev. Smallwood Williams expressed this changed consciousness when he asserted that "There is a valid call to preach the 'full' Gospel, spiritually, socially, and economically."[15]

Besides the increasing activity in the political and civic realm, black Pentecostals have been seeking higher education. Author Sherry Sherrod Dupree has provided the educational backgrounds of hundreds of black holiness-Pentecostal ministers in her *Biographical Dictionary of African-American Holiness-Pentecostals, 1880–1990*. Whereas very few of the first and second generations of black Pentecostal ministers had more than a high school education, some data indicate in more recent times that a growing number of such ministers are seeking undergraduate and graduate degrees. Of the eighty-seven ministers and pastors born after 1930, forty-three attended college and twenty-nine had master's degrees or better. Some groups have established their own colleges to train clergy. C. Eric Lincoln and Lawrence Mamiya note that the Church of God in Christ is affiliated with seventy Bible colleges and requires candidates for the ministry to attend one of those schools for at least two years. Many of the twenty-nine Pentecostal ministers holding graduate degrees attended prestigious institutions of higher learning, including Fuller Theological Seminary in California, Fordham University, the University of Virginia, the University of Pittsburgh, Wayne State, Morgan State, Temple, New York University, Rice, Indiana, Colgate-Rochester, and Harvard.[16]

The search for higher education among the black Pentecostal ministerial class strongly signifies that a growing number of churches are seeking a better trained clergy. It is not only important to have a person who preaches the word and has asserted that he or she has received the call; it is equally important that the person receive proper training. The fact that some have attended mainstream educational institutions suggests that more attention is being paid to reaching God through intellect and not just through experience. Moreover, the long preparation for college degrees means that there is less urgency put on the approaching millennium. Apparently, a growing number of black Pentecostal ministers feel they have time before the apocalypse and are willing to postpone or interrupt their ministry while they seek additional training.

The Nation of Islam and Millennium Doctrine

To be sure, one of the most ardent advocates of millennialism has been the Nation of Islam (NOI). Its leader from the early 1930s until his death in 1975, Elijah Muhammad, consistently predicted the imminent annihilation of the world as we know it. In his book *Message to the Black Man,* Muhammad declared, "Today, we live at the end of the World of People." Dividing the world into good and evil forces, the NOI leader claimed that personality and character were not developed or nurtured but determined by spiritual matters. Borrowing from Nobile Drew Ali and his Moorish Temple, founded early in the century, Muhammad declared that blacks were really "Asiatic" and that their natural religion was Islam. They were from the lost tribe of Shabazz and were God's chosen people. Whites were devils by nature, created six thousand years ago by Allah's enemy, Yacub. Whites were debased by nature and caused black suffering. Allah, proclaimed Muhammad, will soon destroy the devil race and restore the "Asiatic Blackman" to his rightful place as ruler of the earth.[17]

The periodization of history was an important concept in the Nation of Islam theology. The group asserted that the first period began trillions of years ago before the earth existed and that the "original man" lived on the moon. An explosion caused by a black scientist led to part of the moon's splitting off in space. This spliter (the earth) was inhabited by people of the moon, or "the original man," who resided not in Africa but in Mecca. During this period, whites did not exist and these first inhabitants of the earth lived in harmony.[18]

The second major period, beginning six thousand years ago, was the age of white rule. God allowed black earthly rule to end and allowed whites to take command. Because of the evil nature of whites, this second period was a time of great suffering of all people of color. The third period was the fall of the white race and the restoration of black rule. Thus, space and time were also important notions in black Muslim ideology. The evil nature of whites is not limited to a specific locality; it is global. "Today, they have filled the earth with their wickedness." Everywhere you find the white race, you will find evil. In terms of time, the NOI asserted that the destruction of the world began in 1914, the start of World War I. World War I, Muhammad claimed, was the beginning of the Antichrist. It was a war against the righteous. However, a sixty-year reprieve was granted by Allah in order to bring Islam to the "lost tribe of Shabazz." After the end of the reprieve, God was to continue destroying the world of the "white devil." The destruction was to be completed before the year 2000.[19]

Although Muhammad argued that whites in general were "naturally" evil, he contended that white Americans took the prize in wickedness. Because white Americans are "the most wicked" whites on the planet, God has targeted them first for destruction. Blacks in America, according to the NOI leader, must separate before God destroys White America.[20]

Like black Pentecostals, the NOI used global events as evidence to support their prognostication of the millennium. The growing tension between Japan and the West was a case in point. The historian Ernest Allen notes that in the 1930s the NOI and other black messianic organizations maintained an apocalyptic vision by embracing Japan as the champion of the darker races because it was destroying the "caucasian devil."[21]

Muhammad's message was clearly for a black audience. Although the prophet, as his followers called him, predicted that the end of the white race and the liberation of blacks was extremely close, it was not only whites who were facing certain death; the "so-called Negro" who refused to embrace the prophet's teaching also faced a violent end. After arguing that the destruction of white America was near, he noted that whites could actually save themselves. All they had to do was to give the "black man" freedom, justice, and equality and Allah would spare them a cruel end. Since this was highly unlikely and white racism would not be abated, whites were not part of the dialogue. It was a "black thing." They were simply used in order to convince nonbelievers and reinforce believers with regard to the correctness of Black Muslim theology. There was a passive quality to Muhammad's teachings: no one could physically prepare for the end. It was predetermined.[22]

The NOI attracted working-class blacks, as did black Pentecostalism, because the theology gave a clear explanation for the state of black America. The NOI gave a spiritual explication for the plight of blacks. It attempted to restore black humanity by noting that blacks were victims of the "wicked white race." But the NOI doctrine went beyond victimization. It stressed a black agency whereby black men and women who were naturally righteous could collectively come into communion with the Supreme Being and be restored to their rightful place as rulers of the earth. Unlike Pentecostals, the NOI saw the devil not as an abstraction but as a tangible being. Thus, racist theory that espoused the superiority of one group over another was turned on its head and used by an oppressed minority against the dominant society. The millennium was not merely a spiritual event but also a political opposition to an oppressive society. A millenarian vision is attractive to poor people because it empowers them. The future belongs to those who have been the victims of oppression.

Muhammad's failed predictions on the fall of the white race moved him away from apocalyptic ideas. During this period a great deal of emphasis was placed on entrepreneurial adventures: overseas trade, acquiring farm land, and operating restaurants, grocery stores, department stores, bakeries, barber shops, and clothing stores. By the 1960s the NOI paid more attention to self-help than prophecy. This shift may also have to do with the bourgeoisification of the NOI. Elijah Muhammad did not abandon his belief in eschatology, but no dates were given for the millennium. As Martha Lee notes, although the fall never disappeared from Muhammad's rhetoric, there was a "de-eschatologizing" of the millennium. In fact, near the end of his life, the NOI leader contended that not all whites were going to be destroyed; some could actually find salvation. However, unlike Muhammad's earlier assertion that salvation for whites was dependent on whether they granted blacks their freedom, this statement recognized that individuals could be saved by adopting Islam. Thus, salvation was no longer group based but based on individual actions.[23]

Notwithstanding the fact that Minister Louis Farrakhan, the current leader of the NOI, asserts that he still adheres to the teachings of Elijah Muhammad, it is quite apparent in his speeches and writings that he also has moved away from apocalyptic notions. Although it was reported that Farrakhan said, in his multination tour of Africa and the Middle East, that God was going to destroy America, there is little evidence that the NOI leader pushes this view. In fact, his message has become much more ecumenical. Without a doubt his central concern is the state of black America and the best way to improve conditions. He has gone so far as to declare himself a "Pan-Africanist," concerned about the plight of blacks in the Caribbean, America, and Africa. He continues to stress self-help and moral uplift. Because of his concern, he has turned to the political arena. He registered to vote and in 1984 supported Jesse Jackson's bid for the presidency. More recently, Farrakhan has joined with Benjamin Chavis, former executive secretary of the NAACP, to form the Black Leadership Conference, calling on blacks to work for black unity despite their religious and ideological differences. Farrakhan noted at the first such summit that he was a lifetime member of the NAACP, and he has given thousands of dollars to that organization. He declared that he has learned "through growth" the value of all black leaders and black organizations. The link that should unite black leaders, Farrakhan insisted, should be black suffering. He noted that the decay of the educational system and the fleeing of corporations from the inner city were the major problems facing black leadership and that it was up to the various black organizations to come up with viable solutions.[24]

The nonracialized message of self-help is repeated in Farrakhan's work *Torchlight for America*. Although his concern is the plight of black America, the leader of the NOI claims his objective is to help the entire country. Unlike Elijah Muhammad's *Message to the Black Man*, *Torchlight* does not demonize whites. Farrakhan contends that nature cannot explain white racism. It is based on ignorance and other environmental conditions. In fact, ignorance of truth has caused America to head down the path of annihilation. Racism is just one of many liabilities of the country. He notes that class exploitation and sexism are used to keep people divided and that these three evils threaten to obliterate the nation. "America must deal effectively with these lines of division or face anarchy and revolution." Although he declares America is near peril, he does not retreat to a mystical destruction of the country based on prophecy. It is social upheaval, not a predetermined apocalypse, that Americans must fear. The potential agency for America's fall is not God but the broad category of the oppressed. Consequently, Farrakhan's message is not limited to a black audience: it is for all Americans interested in social justice. The minister has gone so far as to argue that he does not consider America's destruction inevitable. If the country is willing to adopt his suggestions, revolution can be prevented. Thus, the major theme of his book is hope.[25]

Farrakhan specifically addresses some generic problems over which Americans across race and class express concern, including unemployment, crime, escalating drug use, and the threat of financial bankruptcy. He notes that the end of imperialism in Asia, Africa, and Latin America has caused an economic downturn in America, which is unable to exploit these regions as it did in the past by grabbing their resources.[26]

Although he has moved to more political themes, Farrakhan has not altogether given up a spiritual analysis. He contends that the "wickedly wise" are the culprits of black suffering and consistently use people of African origins as scapegoats. But the wicked behavior is not linked to a certain race. Farrakhan presents a class analysis of suffering in America. The greed of leaders and the very rich is the cause of the problem. The poor, says Farrakhan, have nowhere to go, implying that he is their voice.[27]

Farrakhan does not advocate class warfare or accentuate the spiritual destruction of America but returns to his positive theme by emphasizing self-help. Instead of anticipating destruction, he has taken an activist role, and with great enthusiasm he offers his services to America. This is not to say that he is not still defiant. Throughout his work he identifies with black revolutionaries, including Malcolm X, Martin Luther King, Jr., Sojourner Truth, and Denmark Vesey. This is also not to imply that he has argued that God is an inactive being in the human process. Farrakhan also contends that "God has set His hand against this economy as He set His hand against the riches of Egypt." Thus, at times he falls back into a religious explanation for the plight of America. But the message is devoid of an inevitable spiritual holocaust striking America.[28]

What accounts for this movement away from a spiritual emphasis on the inevitable desolation of white America? Clearly, the failure of Muhammad's prophecy of the fall contributes to the new emphasis on more direct social, economic, and political themes. Farrakhan cannot consistently predict the religious fall and not have it come to pass without his organization's suffering the consequences. The accent on and accomplishment of more attainable terrestrial resolutions is more attractive in the long run than unprovable predictions. Farrakhan realizes that if the NOI is to reach out to a larger audience and grow in black America, it must continue to address worldly interests.

Scholars have noted that the NOI message is attractive to the poor. But because the work ethic has been stressed by the NOI, many members have experienced success, being transformed from the wretched of the earth into productive working- and middle-class people. Farrakhan's audience consists not only of working class, however, but also members of the growing black middle class, including college students. Farrakhan and other high officials of the NOI often appear at major universities and colleges and draw large crowds. Predictions on the apocalypse of America are not going to satisfy this more sophisticated constituency. Instead, the focus on obtainable economic, political, and social objectives within a black nationalist rubric are used to appeal to a broader assembly. Thus, the success of the NOI has clearly moved it away from more radical dogma.

Farrakhan's de-emphasis of the millennium also has to do with his own objectives and ambition. He greatly desires to be accepted as a mainstream black leader. As noted, he has participated in the Black Leadership Summit, emphasizing the argument that blacks, no matter what their religious or political views are, should unite and work for unity. Moreover, his continual appearance on national television, pushing the theme of black self-help, undoubtedly is evidence of the move to the mainstream.

Farrakhan's migration to mainstream politics and orthodox Islam has not gone unchallenged within the NOI. The vitriolic public speeches by Khallid Abdul Muhammad, attacking Jews, Catholics, and gays, shows that not every NOI member is happy. The day before the historic Million Man March in October 1995, black activist Alton Maddox, a strong supporter of Khallid Abdul Muhammad, hinted at a split between Farrakhan and Muhammad when he asserted that Muhammad was Farrakhan's "moral compass" and that the litmus test for black unity would have to be Farrakhan's, along with other black national leaders', publicly embracing Muhammad on the day of the march.

With little doubt, Farrakhan is sensitive to this rift and wants to avoid a split within the organization. His consistent use of fiery rhetoric could probably be attributed to his attempt to hold onto the more militant members of the NOI who wish for a return to its old positions. Nevertheless, in spite of the apparent opposition within the organization, the leader of the NOI continues to move toward the mainstream.

The de-emphasis on an apocalypse by black Pentecostals and the Nation of Islam should be viewed as a positive transformation in black America. During a period marked by a mass exodus of the black middle class from urban areas, the growth of a black underclass, and a diminishing commitment of the federal government to social programs that assist the truly needy, greater effort on the part of black-led institutions is needed. The attempt by a growing segment of the leadership of each of these movements to place greater emphasis on political and civic activities and devote more time to the social concerns of a large portion of black America by providing political leadership and outreach services will benefit poor people in both a material and spiritual way.

The historian David Howard-Pitney has argued that an American jeremiad, a "rhetoric of indignation, expressing deep dissatisfaction and urgently challenging the nation to reform," is an important part of the history of African Americans. Although black Pentecostalism and the Nation of Islam have de-emphasized the millennium, to the benefit of Americans, they have become strong voices in the call for the nation to dedicate itself to racial justice.[29]

NOTES

1. Hans Bear and Merrell Singer, *African American Religion in the Twentieth Century: Varieties of Protest and Accommodation* (Knoxville: University of Tennessee, 1992), 150–51; E. Myron Noble, "Genesis of W. J. Seymour in Perspective," *MAR Gospel Ministries Newsletter* 10, no. 1 (spring–summer 1990); Harvey Cox, *Fire from Heaven: The Rise of Pentecostal Spirituality and the Reshaping of Religion in the Twenty-First Century* (Reading, Pa.: Addison-Wesley, 1995), 56–65.

2. Clarence Taylor, *Black Churches of Brooklyn* (New York: Columbia University Press, 1994), 40–42.

3. Ibid., 43

4. Ibid.; C. Eric Lincoln and Lawrence Mamiya, *The Black Church in the African American Experience* (Durham, N.C.: Duke University Press, 1990), 130–32; St. Clair Drake and Horace R. Cayton, *Black Metropolis: A Study of Negro Life in a Northern City* (Chicago: University of Chicago, 1993), 630; Ira E. Harrison, "The Storefront Church as a Revitalization Movement," in Hart M. Nelson, Raytha L. Yokley, and Anne K. Nelsen, eds., *The Black Church in America* (New York: Basic Books, 1971), 242.

5. Cox, *Fire from Heaven,* 288–89.

6. Garfield T. Haywood, *Before the Foundations of the World: Revelation of the Ages* (Garfield T. Haywood, 1923), 51.

7. Ibid., 44–47, 50, 54–58, 64; Bureau of the Census of the United States, *Religious Bodies: 1936,* Pentecostal Assemblies of the World (Washington, D.C.: Government Printing Office, 1941), 36; Garfield T. Haywood, *The Finest of the Wheat* (Indianapolis: Christ Temple Book Store, n.d.), 31–32.

8. Mother Elnora Lee, *C. H. Mason: A Man Greatly Used by God* (Memphis: Women's Department of COGIC), 83.

9. Arthur Huff Fauset, *Black Gods of the Metropolis* (New York: Octagon, 1970), 17; Drake and Cayton, *Black Metropolis,* 618–19.

10. *The Bridegroom Songs* (Indianapolis: Christ Temple Bookstore, n.d.), 9, 37, 51; Charles Price Jones, "The History of My Songs," *Journal of Black Sacred Music* 2, no. 2. (fall 1988): 71–78.

11. E. Franklin Frazier, *The Negro Church in America* (New York: Schocken, 1963), 71; Dennis Dickerson, *Out of the Crucible: Black Steelworkers in Western Pennsylvania, 1885–1980* (Albany: State University Press of New York, 1986), 67; Allan Spear, *Black Chicago: The Making of a Negro Ghetto, 1890–1920* (Chicago: University of Chicago Press, 1967), 174–75; Joe William Trotter, *Black Milwaukee: The Making of an Industrial Proletariat, 1915–1945* (Urbana: University of Illinois Press, 1985), 130.

12. Taylor, *Black Churches of Brooklyn,* 64–65; Haywood, *Before the Foundation of the World,* 44–47, 50, 54–58, 64; Martha F. Lee, *The Nation of Islam, An American Millenarian Movement* (Syracuse: Syracuse University Press, 1996), 4–5.

13. Sherry Sherrod Dupree, *Biographical Dictionary of African-American Holiness-Pentecostals, 1880–1990* (Washington, D.C.: Middle Atlantic Regional Press, 1989), 17–18, 70–71; Baer and Singer, *African American Religion,* 175.

14. Rev. Smallwood Williams, *This Is My Story: A Significant Life Struggle* (Washington, D.C.: Willoughby, n.d.), 88–128.

15. Ibid., 89.

16. Dupree, *Biographical Dictionary;* Lincoln and Mamiya, *The Black Church,* 89.

17. Elijah Muhammad, *Message to the Black Man in America* (Chicago: Final Call, n.d.), 20, 110–12.

18. E. U. Essien-Udom, *Black Nationalism: A Search for an Identity in America* (New York: Dell, 1962), 48–49.

19. Muhammad, *Message to the Black Man,* 267; Essien-Udom, *Black Nationalism,* 153–55, 267.

20. Muhammad, *Message to the Black Man,* 287–88.

21. Ernest Allen, "When Japan was 'Champion of the Darker Races': Satokata Takahashi and the Flowering of Black Nationalism," *Black Scholar* 24 (no. 1): 23–25; in her work on the Nation of Islam, Martha Lee also points out that the NOI contended that recent global and national events indicated that in 1965 the fall had already begun. Lee, *The Nation of Islam,* 45–46.

22. Muhammad, *Message to the Black Man,* 293–94.

23. Lee, *The Nation of Islam,* 48–52; C. Eric Lincoln, *The Black Muslims in America* (Boston: Beacon Press, 1973), 95–102.

24. Lee, *The Nation of Islam,* 79–80; "African-American Leadership Summit," aired on C-Span, June 12, 1994.

25. Louis Farrakhan, *Torchlight for America* (Chicago: FCN Publishing, 1993), 3.

26. Ibid., 17–22.

27. Ibid., 22–38.

28. Ibid., 152–54.

29. David Howard-Pitney, *The Afro-American Jeremiad* (Philadelphia: Temple University Press, 1990), 6.

Chapter Nineteen

The Flight from Finitude

Jean Bethke Elshtain

The year 2000, as with the approach of any millennium, inspires thoughts about the alpha and omega, the first and the last. American culture, always so optimistic, no longer bursts with energy and a sense (political rhetoric to the contrary notwithstanding) that our best times lie before us. Why? In part, because American culture has always had difficulty recognizing and dealing realistically with the question of limits—limits to growth, limits to expansion, limits to opportunity and wealth, limits to being the best possible country or person—up to and including (or so I shall argue) those limits embedded in our very natures as creatures who are born and who die. In other words, we appear to be in a flight from finitude, from limits of all sorts. Perhaps the world itself seems so dense and intractable that our attention has turned to our embodied selves—or to how we can escape embodiment or bring it to heel. How, then, do we think about bodies or even what counts as health or illness at century's end?

America's recent, desultory debate about health care was fought on the ground of either utility ("the greatest good for the greatest number"), often with a heavy dose of "cost effectiveness" thrown in for good measure, or abstract justice. In our own day this means on the ground of right or rights rather than a substantive notion of "the good." One way or the other health care either becomes a right or is desirable because it helps to make people more effective and efficient as workers. Because productivity is a major buzz word in contemporary discussions, the notion that we are somehow not adding to our gross national product as dazzlingly as we might because too many people are taking too many sick days comes to seem compelling. Whether we are reforming the system incrementally or seeking total overhaul along the lines of managerial social science, this debate, and others involving our bodies, seems curiously impoverished from an ethical and political perspective.

What do I have in mind? Let us consider the following. First, if one thinks of politics as a realm of practical reason, the arena within which an ethics of responsibility is animated, health as a form of care is necessarily configured along explicit ethical lines. To whom and for what am I responsible? What is, or should be, within the purview of the state, the churches, the associations of civil society, families, and so on? Second, politics is also an arena within which prudential judgments are called for. Hannah Arendt considered judgment the supreme political capacity, following Kant in this regard. Judgment involves discernment, weighing alternatives, considering the options in the midst of the fog of uncertainty that attends human affairs. It is not always clear that there is one single right thing to do. Certainly, those hewing to an ethics of responsibility and aware of the need for prudential judgments repudiate utopian arguments that translate into totalizing ideologies. One walks a line between hope and illusion. One walks a line between realism and pessimism. One understands that in the realm of politics complex tradeoffs must be made.

So I will focus on how to walk that line. For the purpose of this discussion, I want to suggest that we are called to realistic hope framed by a recognition of finitude. How do we think responsibly about limits, not just the limits to what public policy can or should do, but the finiteness, the frailty and mortality, of the human body itself? What sort of body does our health-care debate presuppose? It turns out upon examination that, all too often, ours is an abstract, almost fetishized notion of the human body—a picture of Total Wellness. We who have good health-care coverage find ourselves being sonogrammed and MRI'd at the drop of a hat. Why take chances? Any glitch in the body is cause for alarm. Where's the cure? There must be one. Nearly every ailment or condition can be overtaken, overcome, eliminated if we just have the political will, if we just put our shoulders to the wheel, if we just defeat and block those who stand in the way. We believe that we can control for every contingency, name every possible problem, and find a cure for everything. Buried in these assumptions is a view of the human body as an entity prey to all manner of affliction, dysfunctions abounding at least until we enter the regime of Total Wellness. I have the impression that our obsession with our bodies, especially our determination to control every aspect of embodiment, from who gets born to how and when we die, is deepening and expanding as we near the end of the millennium. This may be a contemporary version of those chiliastic and eschatological enthusiasms and forebodings that we know were occasioned by the last turn of a millennium. Perhaps, we seem to be musing, we can create a more perfect body, even something akin to an immortal body, to better cope with the perplexing new world the next millennium is bound to bring. This assault on embodied limits amounts to the moral equivalent of war against all afflictions that torment human minds and bodies.

What is wrong with wanting to end misery? Nothing, surely. But there is something wrong with describing the human condition in such a way that finitude itself is construed as an unacceptable barrier to having the best of all possible human bodies, something akin to a temporary disorder we can overcome if we just plan and manage and pay. Rather than approaching the matter with determined humility, knowing that we cannot cure the human condition itself, we seek cures. And our desperate seeking—just look at the unending cascade of diets and exercise regimens and New Age nostrums and all the rest—bespeaks a brittle conviction that our bodies, our very creatureliness, *is* the problem.

Cosmetic surgery, once reserved to the rich and famous, is now a common thing. Not just a few nips and tucks but entire body remaking, face redoing. When the controversy erupted over the safety of silicon breast implants, a group of implantees immediately took to the airwaves and the Internet proclaiming that breast implantation was a basic "women's right," essential to the health and self-esteem of many women. For the government to disallow such implants would be to turn women's lives to dust and ashes, we were told. Think of all the times "war" has been declared on cancer, later on AIDS, as if those were human foes that could be bested in a medicalized version of war without limits. When cures do not follow, politicization, which usually helps to spur medicalization in the first place, also follows fast upon it and fuels paranoid suspicion that the *only* reason there is not a cure yet is that some people profit from or take pleasure in the suffering of others for political reasons or benefits. The country is dotted with health-care resorts and spas that promise not a relaxing good time, but total rejuvenation, a virtual remaking of the human subject, for a hefty fee.

Consider, as well, much of the current language surrounding mental health. We proliferate literally hundreds of categories of mental unwellness—dysfunctions blooming like determined weeds—and then we declare a "mental health crisis." What does a crisis require? Mobilization, yet again, of resources and man- and womanpower—for many who are dysfunctional do not yet know it and must be tracked down and brought to wellness—and, of course, someone ought to pay. Something similar is going on in the area of disabilities, where dozens of freshly minted disorders are discovered with each passing year. Let me be clear that I am not one of those who thinks mental illness is just an arbitrary "construction." I believe it is real and leads to genuine suffering. But we are close to effacing the distinction between what Freud called "hysterical misery and ordinary unhappiness." This is especially true when it comes to children. In our quest to make our children perfect and successful, we often fall into moral panics about some new "dysfunction."

Case in point: two years ago the *New York Times* ran a piece on a disabilities program that "got out of hand." The story, highly condensed, went like this—and it involved the privileged, not the poor, for it is the relatively privileged who define what counts as well or ill, healthy or unhealthy. A wealthy socialite donates money in order to make provision for "bright youngsters with learning disabilities," and she chooses an elite Manhattan school for this purpose. The program starts out in a modest way, but things quickly get out of hand. A school of four hundred children suddenly finds itself with fourteen full- and part-time learning disability specialists. The "need" to prescreen all children is instituted. More money comes in for this new "need." The article notes, "The disabilities field has boomed," as all sorts of people, with training that is often more than a little suspect, bill themselves as experts on "language problems" or "reading problems" or "self-esteem problems" and the like.[1]

What happened at the Dalton school is that remedial specialists "suddenly began finding enormous numbers of bright little children with learning problems." In one three-year period fully 77 of Dalton's 215 five-year-olds were labeled "at risk." Parents panicked when told that a child tested at risk for "sequencing ability deficits" or "potential visual motor problems." A "learning disability industry grew at Dalton." Yet more specialists were brought in, at higher prices, to handle the growing caseload—a caseload determined by the specialists themselves. Finally, some of the teachers "battled back, refusing to let the specialists in their rooms."[2] The upshot was an out-of-control bureaucracy with a huge stake in keeping its clientele at high numbers. The more learning disabilities they found, the more their own jobs were justified. This is a sobering parable for our time. Normal kids are declared at risk and at-risk kids—really at-risk kids—are going to schools that are unsafe, studying from teachers that are stressed out, using textbooks that are outdated or an insult to everyone's intelligence; the lucky ones just keep their heads above water, but most fall through the cracks.

On yet another new, if not final, frontier, we now deem it possible to create perfect human "products" if we enhance and control genetic engineering. Those committed to major interventions in human reproduction in the name of "preventing useless suffering" and improving the species overall (think, here, of the Human Genome Project) construe biology itself as a foe. Nature is there to be overcome; where human beings find the will to indulge in acts of transcendence, they must find a way; only the fearful and the backward will cavil at these remarkable developments. In the words of two enthusiasts:

> If the creation of new forms seems a godlike power, what more noble goal can humanity have than to aspire to it? Like Prometheus, the mythical Greek hero who defied the gods and stole from them the secret of fire, should we not challenge the gods and make their powers our own? Or to put it in more scientific terms, should we allow ourselves to remain at the mercy of genetic accident and blind evolution when we have before us the prospect of acquiring supremacy over the very forces that have created us?[3]

We must use godlike powers to control what would otherwise be uncontrolled, subjected to the vagaries of "nature" itself.

Much of what this has yielded in practice is the attempt to screen out and to eliminate "imperfect" fetuses, on the grounds that early detection and selective elimination of the imperfect unborn is a compelling social good. And why not? Such beings are less likely to be productive in the way all human beings are enjoined to be and, as well, will surely suffer, and that is something bad we can stop, so stop it we must. Genetic screening and testing, intervention into reproduction, manipulating the stuff of life itself: on what grounds can we possibly resist or even raise questions if we think about the body's wellness or illness on utilitarian-econometric grounds or in and through a nearly exclusive language of rights? It is important to stress just how widely accepted and little debated much of this is. In a recent review of four new books on "the genetic revolution" that appeared in the *Times Literary Supplement*, the reviewer opined, matter of factly, that

> we must inevitably start to choose our descendants. We now do this by (at least in theory) informed and strictly individual choice in permitting or preventing the birth of our own children according to their medical prognosis, thus selecting "the lives to come." Kitcher's [Kitcher is the author of the book under review] is a full and thoughtful argument for a better future based not on certainties but on taking the best bets we can on the quality of our offspring . . . in a society which does not cramp the individual's freedom of action by economic and social deprivation; his genetic utopia is decent, practical and humane. Ideally, our choice over who is born and who is not should be exercised by the parents, with a regard for the potential of the foetus to develop into a person with a fulfilled life not marred by an excess of pain or disability."[4]

The search for the almost-perfect person, able to be productive on the standards of the dominant culture; choice over who lives and who dies. Prometheus unbound.

So the body we currently inhabit—the old body—is our foe and decried; the new body to come—the body embedded in health-care debates, extolled in New Age manifestos, promised by experts, sought by policy scientists, embraced by many ordinary citizens—is our gleaming fabrication. For the unstated problem seems to be this: The body weakens, but we must not, so the body must not be permitted to falter. The body grows older, but we should not, so we devise multiple strategies to fend off aging. These strategies and concerns and gnawing uncertainties speak to our repudiation of finitude. Ours has become a gnostic society for whom the body is a source of pollution, not itself good, the gift of life. Thus, we come to repudiate built-in limits, framed by natality and mortality.

Because we do not accept finitude, it is more difficult for us to distinguish that which is given from that which is fabricated by humans, hence subject to change. Because we do not accept finitude, in other words, we find it almost impossible these days to separate injustice, with its roots in politics, from the given, with its roots outside ourselves, for we are creatures as well as creators. For example, it would be odd—although it has been done frequently enough in some forms of feminist argument—to call inhabiting a female body itself an "injustice."[5] But if we speak of the injustice of a social order that systematically disregards or dishonors the contributions of women in contrast to those of men, then we are confronted with a political and ethical dilemma that we can and ought to do something about in the name of a more decent and fair human community and in order to honor our responsibility toward our neighbor.

Without framing by finitude, and in a quest for cure-alls and perfecting re-formation of bodies themselves, what counts as "good health" is distorted beyond recognition. We know—there is plenty of good social science data on this—that whenever a new ailment is "named," hundreds of people, then thousands, are discovered to be suffering from it. In societies without such categories, human beings appear not to be present with the symptoms. This is not to suggest that illness is merely a social construction. But it is to argue that much of what we take for "ill" or "well" depends on how we have defined those terms. If we are on a quest for perfect wellness, out of disdain for finitude, our projects take on a kind of limitlessness. Rather than concentrating on the sorts of preventable ailments and conditions that some—say, the poor—suffer from disproportionately, we up the ante on what counts as health.

If we accepted our bodies with better grace, meaning if we recognized and honored the human life cycle and the fact of aging, the creaks and wrinkles and moans and groans that are part of a lived life, we could more realistically think about what a complex, various, sprawling late-twentieth-century society can reasonably expect to accomplish in the realm of health-care provision. Framed by finitude, our debates and expectations would alter. We would refuse to discuss access to certain highly technical and extraordinarily expensive forms of treatment as a basic right, knowing, as we do, that this "right" in practice winds up being a prerogative of the already privileged. Thus, we have the irony of diseases that cannot be cured representing a huge drain on our medical expertise and gobbling up resources that might otherwise go, for example, to traveling doctors and clinics-on-wheels to reach rural

America and inner-city America and bring minimal baseline treatment and prevention to the out-of-reach and underprivileged. We would certainly not involve any public funding in what might be called "vanity health care" of the sort that has as much to do with aesthetics as it has with decent health. Because we accept no outer limit to wellness; indeed, because we seek wellness as a continuing condition in a wonderful new world from which bodily woes and ailments have been banished, we wind up concentrating as much in our public debates on such vaporous categories as "self-esteem" as we do on vaccination against childhood diseases. This leads us to the sober recognition that in late modernity the standards of ill and well are set by those who can take basic wellness pretty much for granted and who then go on to discover all sorts of new entitlements to wellness that go far beyond catastrophic care and routine screening for preventable or treatable conditions.

In addition, we would ask whether the presuppositions that lie behind current approaches invite us to think of unwellness and weakness as temporary conditions that a bevy of experts and technicians and fixers of all sorts can move in to control and overawe. If so, how would things change if we approached the question of health by asking, How are people well? How are they strong? What can they do for themselves? How can we help them? We would think of baseline care as a public good consistent with the dignity of human persons and with what it means to care for one's neighbor. We would set up clean, well-staffed clinics where people's dignity was honored when they entered, respected during their visit, and intact on their departure. We would radically alter current regimes of drastic and desperate intervention at the end of life that are designed not to ease the suffering of the dying, but to display our prowess at staving off death. True dying with dignity is not a "right" requiring the ministrations of physicians with death machines but a feature of our finitude, a way to take our leave of our loved ones and of this beautiful earth and to give thanks to our God for the gift of life and of death. At the beginning of life, we would welcome life in its many varieties and leave off playing god. We are already beginning to sow the whirlwind in this dangerous area of genetic manipulation, as if history had not already taught us the dangers and evils that flow when human beings take it upon themselves to decide to sever from the human community "life unworthy of life."

If finitude were respected, equality and fairness could rise as exigent concerns. By denying the real limits to what we can or should do to or for human bodies, we have turned health care into a kind of utopian projection. This means that the concrete steps that might make a real difference in our neighborhoods seem puny by comparison. If everything becomes a "public health issue," from day care to fitness spas to condoms in schools, we lose sight of children at risk because they have not had polio vaccine or because their diets lack certain basic nutrients without which brain damage may result. We lose sight of the hidden thousands who postpone trips to the doctor in spite of blood in the urine or a lump in the breast, because they cannot afford to pay for tests or subsequent treatment. We lose sight of the social ecology within which our understanding of health is embedded. Because ours is a society that does two things—refuses to acknowledge limits and celebrates the self—we wind up with a wholly unacceptable situation: too little care for too many; too much attention altogether paid to too few. At least, this is the direction waves of popular and expert opinion now tend.

Are there currents flowing through our culture at century's end that might help us to see ourselves as creatures as well as creators? that might help to chasten, at least somewhat, our aspirations to escape bodily limits? The answer, of course, is yes, for no late modern culture—especially not one as complex as that of the United States—is of a piece. Those who have not utterly closed the window to transcendence, who hold fast to a sense of awe and mystery, and who know that our minds cannot encompass the whole; those who honor God's sovereignty as a brake on human hubris; those who welcome into the human community humanity in all its many varieties, including children with handicaps who can never become perfect or even "normal" by the world's reckoning; those who tend to little things, who feed and warm our bodies and soothe our souls—all these and more embrace limits in the sure and certain knowledge that this acceptance helps them to truly see and to respond to the claims of their neighbors, near and far. In the 1850s Lincoln liked to quote Henry Clay's appeal that we not "blow out the moral lights around us." For too long too many have been blowing out the moral lights in our culture. But the flames still flicker. They need our tending more than ever.

NOTES

1. Michael Winerup, "A Disabilities Program That Got out of Hand," *New York Times,* April 8, 1994, 1, B6.

2. Ibid.

3. Peter Singer and Deane Wells, *Making Babies: The New Science and Ethics of Conception* (New York: Scribner, 1984), 157–58.

4. John R. G. Turner, "After Innocence," *Times Literary Supplement,* August 9, 1996, 3.

5. See, for example, texts by radical feminists that located women's oppression in biology itself, even before gender differences are constructed. The sex distinction—the division of human beings into males and females—constitutes a "biological tyranny, a fundamental inequality," according to Shulamith Firestone, one that extends even to nonhuman animals. Shulamith Firestone, *The Dialectic of Sex,* New York: Bantam, 1972. Others in this mode included Ti-Grace Atkinson and Susan Brownmiller in their texts from this era. Although this form of argument has fallen off among feminists, the presuppositions that undergird such conclusions continue to circulate in less polemically maladroit form.

Part IV

Culture

Chapter Twenty

Searching for Alternatives
Autobiography and Masculinity at the Bimillennium

Michael Flynn

I

Auden's scorn for autobiography spared neither writer nor reader. "Literary confessors are contemptible, like beggars who exhibit their sores for money, but not so contemptible as the public that buys their books." Not only were such endeavors founded on "the absolutely banal—'my own sense of my own uniqueness'" they inherently involved a great deal of distortion. "No man, however tough he appears to his friends, can help portraying himself as a sensitive plant." Never a champion of the practices and products ushered in by modernity (he listed his favorite "public entertainment[s]" as "religious processions, brass bands, opera, classical ballet. No movies, radio, or television"), he would be utterly repelled by the contemporary literary practice of "working through" one's traumas on the page; "a suffering, a weakness which cannot be expressed as an aphorism should not be mentioned."[1]

I must confess to belonging to the breed Auden finds so contemptible. And, given my deep respect for his critical assessment and poetic achievement, such an affiliation causes me both pain and shame. By way of excuse and explanation, although I am acutely aware that most literary purists have tolerance for neither, I must say that my appreciation of the genre is newfound, and the result of historical forces, namely the approaching bimillennium, that renders me powerless.

Prior to the fall of 1995 I had finished no more than twenty autobiographies. The emphasis on finishing is important because, at the urging of friends and mentors who knew of my obsessions with the predicaments of self and narration, I had started forty or fifty others, only to find completion an impossibility. To this date I have not completed Benjamin Franklin, Henry Adams, or William Dean Howells, and only the demands of an undergraduate project and the longing for sexual union with a beautiful Gertrude Stein devotee propelled me through the queen of expatriation's work. (I realize that such a confession renders me a philistine to some and a plain nincompoop to others.) My friends saw autobiography as literary "declarations of independence," acts that played a necessary and foundational role in the definition of an American style of being, but my reading had them as little more than exercises in chauvinism and false modesty.[2] If Robert Penn Warren's contention that Americans' self-understanding as "chosen People with a hotline to the Most High" required empirical backing, it could be found in these efforts.[3]

This aversion didn't extend to autobiographies or memoirs written by African Americans. In fact, well over one-half of my "completions" were from this subset. Although Franklin's and Howells's evocations left me bloodless and suspicious, the work of Douglass, Brown, Wright, and Malcolm deeply moved me. (That this appreciation coincided with my tenure in Idaho, then the whitest state in the nation and now the cradle of the right-wing apocalyptic movements, has always struck me as one of the delicious ironies populating late adolescence.) The writing in these works, writing that attempted to bear full and radical witness to a selfhood continually countermanded by legal, economic, religious, and scientific "realities," was performed in the service of transgression, not edification. The stakes seemed much higher; here the "I" was employed in order to establish ontological equivalence, not to singularize or establish the unmatched quality of one's existence or insights.[4]

In the midnineties I began finishing autobiographies written by whites. Not all, but well over 80 percent. At the time, I was teaching at York College of the City University of New York and became increasingly aware that my courses in human development and personality seemed to be lacking something. My students, though appreciative of the theorists' attempts to "enrich concrete experience," frequently complained that the theories, even the most recent ones, failed in both their descriptive and explanatory tasks.[5] At first I would use their complaints as a springboard for lectures on the perspectival nature of all theory and the limits of quantitative methodology, and although my students would keep time with my polemics by vigorous nods, they remained unsatisfied. They wanted access to subjectivity, to the beliefs, feelings, and attitudes animating late-twentieth-century life. For a semester or two I attempted to fill the absence with novels. I used Oscar Higuelos's *The Mambo Kings Play Songs of Love* for its evocation of immigrants' experience and the quest for fame; for their depiction of the consequences of trauma on family life, I used Marilynne Robinson's *Housekeeping,* Jane Smiley's *A Thousand Acres,* and Annie Prioulx's *The Shipping News;* I also used Russell Banks's *Affliction* and Tim O'Brien's *The Things They Carried* for their illumination of the connection between trauma and violence. Some students warmed to the texts, but many more wanted examples from "real life."

In the summer of ninety-two I fell under the spell of Doris Grumbach's *Coming into the Endzone* and decided to use it in an adult development course. At first I was a little nervous. Most of my students were embodiments of what many postmodern identity theorists have grown fond of labeling as "other," and here I was using a work written by a middle-class white woman. I half expected them to reject the book out of hand and demand a book written by "a woman of color."

I underestimated my students. They were enchanted with the book and greatly appreciated being allowed entry into the inner life of a "real person" struggling with the predicaments of aging. Many said the book gave them greater insight into their own parents' difficulties, and a few of my older students reported that it "gave them courage" for the "passage" awaiting them around the not-so-distant bend. After this success I used memoirs and autobiographies in all my courses, and although they were met with different levels of enthusiasm—the most successful have been Sister Souljah's *No Disrespect,* Nathan McCall's *Makes Me Wanna Holler,* Chris Offut's *The Same River Twice,* Maya Angelou's *I Know Why the Caged Bird Sings*—any "absence" my courses now have is solely of my making.

Using autobiography reacquainted me with my reasons for entering the field. Having taken up psychology believing in its ontological possibilities—if being "a science of what it means to be" was too grand a design, I would have settled for a discipline capable of accurately evoking the "politics of everyday life"—I had become increasingly disillusioned by its embrace of computational, physiological, and evolutionary models of the psyche. Because all three rendered the soul as epiphenomenal, they struck me as violently reductive. My interest had always been in the individual, not only as a meaning-seeking creature, but also as one capable of constructing meaning even in the most extreme situations, as a creature hosting and motivated by a swirling multitude of often contradictory desires and beliefs, as an intentional creature born into a certain cultural and historical situation yet capable of internalizing and enacting foreign "ways of being," as a biologically finite creature yearning for believable symbols assuring individual and collective immortality, as an ethical creature hungry for images of "the good" but in their absence or paucity capable of, and at times disposed to, demonic brutality. Because of this I much preferred the psychoanalysts, arrogant as they were, to the cognitivists, the sentimental humanists to the attentive behaviorists. At least in these schools inwardness wasn't said to be irrelevant or to adhere to computational principles.[6]

My belief in psychology's ontological possibilities was, of course, naive. But using autobiography allowed me and my students full entrance into the experiential field of life that contemporary psychology had rendered forbidden. Here were individuals, simultaneously girdled and enfranchised by past and present experiences, actively struggling against the nihilism and cultural flatness that characterizes much of our age. Here were individuals caught in the fragmentation of fin de millennium America engaged in the nonviolent pursuit of lives rich with meaning rather than wealth or power. Because all compelling stories, and lives, revolve around some tragedy or miscarriage, most of the authors had suffered greatly, yet their intent involved the augmentation of understanding and insight rather than the assignment of blame. What Auden would have lambasted as narcissistic pap I saw as narratives of engagement.

II

With more than one thousand memoirs and autobiographies published annually, the nineties have occasioned an explosion of the form. On the political front it seems that everyone is doing it, from the ex-president or ex–first lady to the retired general (and General Schwartzkopf is certainly on the mark: *It Doesn't Take a Hero* to orchestrate the slaughter of a Third World army in full retreat) to the retiring senator seeking to establish a bulkhead for a possible run at the presidency. For the bad boy athlete, the semiliterate television or radio talk-show host, the comedian turned sitcom star, and the actor in some form of recovery, their continued celebrity seems to depend on autobiography. It is only slightly cynical to suggest that a short run on the hardcover bestseller list (followed by a year or two of pulp life) has replaced Warhol's fifteen minutes as the culture's principal object of desire.

For the most part I see nothing laudable about this trend. In addition to saturating the market with books of no literary merit, it both circulates and promotes narratives of selfhood remarkable only for their fatuity and mendacity. Yet, contained within this fin de millennium flood floats a subspecies worthy of rescue and comment—the literary autobiography and memoir. Penned by writers rather than politicians or celebrities, the most noteworthy of this lot include Mary Karr's *The Lair's Club*, Carolyn See's *Dreaming*, Chris Offut's *The Same River Twice*, Elizabeth Wurtzel's *Prozac Nation*, Clark Blaise's *I Had a Father*, Henry Louis Gates's *Colored People*, and Mikal Gilmore's *Shot in the Heart* and constitute some of today's most compelling writing. The attribution of literary status to these works is my doing, not the authors'. I use the term both to elevate these efforts and as a rebuttal to the recent Post-Nietzschean efforts to devalue the term (witness Cioran's "everything literary looks to me like a chastisement"). The modifier, although no guarantor of the quality of the work (witness Michael Ryan's *A Secret Life*), signifies that the work aspires to artistic ends rather than being the project of celebrity or political power. Because it denotes subversive intent—here I draw from Sinyavsky's "by its nature literature is heterodoxy"—these works can also be read as efforts to weave alternative models of selfhood.[7]

How can the explosion be accounted for? One way, perhaps best represented by Alfred Kazin's "constantly explaining oneself and telling one's own story—is as traditional in the greatest American writing as it is in a barroom," is to invoke the hospitality of American literary soil to the form.[8] Although sound in many ways, such an explanation sheds little light on why so many writers are abandoning, at least temporarily, their traditional allegiances—Karr is primarily a poet, Gates a literary critic, Wurtzel and Gilmore are journalists, Stern and Offut practitioners of the short story, and Blaise, See, and Wideman novelists—for the autobiographical mode. Another route would be to argue that the explosion is simply a symptom of a culture pathologically fixated on matters of the self. In their evocation of Americans' obsession with "getting a life," Sidonie Smith and Julia Watson argue: "In postmodern America we are obsessed with getting a life—and not just getting it, but sharing it with and advertising it to others. We are, as well, obsessed with consuming the lives the other people have gotten."[9] Smith and Watson's assessment seems pretty accurate with regard to the explosion of the nonliterary species; yet, attributing equivalent motivation to the efforts of Karr or Clark Blaise (and their readers) with those of Colin Powell or Ellen Degeneris seems, to put it mildly, reductive.

A full appreciation of the phenomenon requires "factoring in" our proximity to 2000. Living in their simultaneous twilight, one has to be senseless not to feel the wisdom of Hillel Schwartz's contention that the ends of centuries and millennia possess a "force of their own that cannot be ignored." In the past few years end time prophecies have targeted not only the species but also those aspects of the species—work, the nation state, the city, secular history, the paperback—that render us modern. On one hand there is a sense that contemporary existence is being carried out "in an exhausted time"; yet we also feel that "events and inventions are spinning out of control, that everything is passing by much too quickly." Either way, we feel outflanked by the enormity of it all. We worry that humanity itself is on the verge of obsolescence and that any possibility of a "new age"—always an object of intense fin de millennium yearning—requires a return to the basilar. It is no wonder that "centuries' ends encourage the reduction of all things, including language to numbers: and of all numbers to common denominators, to points of origin and judgment."[10]

In such a climate the autobiographical act, with its insistence that individual existence, in all its banality and unseemliness, requires and deserves recitation rather than quantification, is a partial antidote to the period's reductionistic tendencies. Understood in this light, autobiography becomes a necessary act of resistance, an act that reaffirms the primacy of the alphabetical over digital and acronymistic language, rather than another manifestation of an age steeped in self-absorption. Indeed, in a period seemingly given over to fragmentation and extremity, an age pitched "at a millennial tenor," autobiography's commitment to the evocation of lived experience of ordinary individuals affirms the possibility of realizing the intellectual and emotional coherence (however fragile and ephemeral) necessary for the creation of meaning.

Camus's invective calling on the post-Hiroshima, post-Auschwitz subject to be neither a "victim" nor an "executioner" alone qualified him for some kind of Nobel acknowledgment. I invoke Camus because, although never an "autobiographer," he is an unparalleled literary witness to the vicissitudes of existence in an age in which "murder is legitimate and where human life is considered trifling." It isn't mawkish to characterize twentieth-century subjectivity as a subjectivity eviscerated by slaughter, a subjectivity awash in trauma. Not only has this "short century" (to steal a term from Eric Hobsbawm) been long on violence, but the civilian has become the principal and preferred victim. With this shift in targetry and the proliferation of nuclear and chemical weaponry, the physical and psychological realities of war no longer "come home" with the vanquished or victorious warriors; they occupy the basic fabric of everyday existence. And as evidenced by the fin de siècle genocides in Bosnia, Chechnya, and Rwanda, there is little reason to hope for bloodless closure to the millennium. Unfortunately, at least for those stubborn "liberals" still in the thrall of cosmopolitan ideals, these conditions render most seductive the Manichaeistic solutions, solutions that often employ violence as a means of enforcing obedience and bestowing meaning, proffered by fundamentalisms of religion and ethnicity.[11]

In such a world autobiography becomes a restorative act. Kazin, himself no stranger to the form, writes, "To write is in some ways to cut across the seemingly automatic pattern of violence, destructiveness, and death wish. To write is to put the seeming insignificance of human existence into a different perspective."[12] Levi and Delbo accomplished this, as did Baldwin and Canetti. In their hands the object of restoration becomes identity and meaning (and here I don't mean a sense of "self-sameness" over time but the experience of oneself engaged in the process of reflexive self-narration, a narration that intends the construction of meaning through addressing the questions, Who am I? What can and must I do? To what and whom must I be faithful? For whom must I speak? From where have I come? and What does the future hold?).[13] The century's atrocities assure that the identity effectuated will be fragmentary, the meaning disfigured, but if the attempt goes unmade, dissolution will be the consequence. Coherence and continuity may have always been a construction, a fiction offering a hope of unity and a center, a firewall against randomness. In the wake of Auschwitz and Hiroshima, many have lamented, and some have celebrated, their demise, but both camps agree that they are eternally gone. As a producer of "artifacts" rooted in experience, and usually an individual claustrophobic in any faction, the autobiographer simultaneously "knows" both the necessity and the "lie" of congruity.

III

The nineties have occasioned the explosion of another literary species—books on the state of manhood. Whether executed by leaders of the mythopoetic men's movement, the men's rights movement, or the religious Right, these books advance the claim that contemporary men are in crisis. Although differing on the cause of the current masculine malaise, all would agree that contemporary men are spiritually confounded, emotionally hobbled, and operating at a far diminished capacity. Most have enjoyed wide readership (Robert Bly's *Iron John* festooned the *New York Times Bestseller List* for over a year), and many of the authors have been granted the visionary status that often accompanies regular talk-show appearances and brisk sales.

Quite frankly, I would love to understand this concern with the souls of men in conspiratorial terms. Flood the marketplace with enough material detailing men's shortcomings, and a cultural agreement that there is something wrong, dangerously wrong, with the state of American masculinity will result. Yet, the concrete events of our era make it painfully clear that men are primarily responsible for the barbarism that diminishes our century. Not only are men the principal architects and perpetrators of the violence I mentioned previously, it is men who continue to argue for violence's necessity. It is also men who make up the membership of hate and paramilitary groups and constitute the leadership in most Christian fundamentalist churches.[14] And, if one can trust the polls, the primary responsibility for the most reactionary political climate this country has been hobbled with in over forty years lies with the voting habits of middle-class white men. (Given that these same men are the source of most of the "family values" flummery, it is interesting that the average white American father spends thirty minutes a week of unmediated time with his children.)

Of course, many American men collaborate in none of these derelictions. Many actively aspire to and succeed in embodying a masculinity punctuated by cooperation, compassion, and openness rather than detachment and control. Yet even these men, perhaps especially these men, feel "bewildered by the sea changes in our culture, besieged by the forces of reform, and bereft by the emotional impoverishment of our lives."[15] This combination of bewilderment, besiegement, and barrenness is terribly painful for most men and leaves them soft marks for the easy wisdom proffered by the "pop" masculinists (my main problem with the movement is its ahistoricism and its advocacy of an identity based on the repudiation of women).[16] If I

had my druthers, contemporary men would turn instead to male literary autobiographies—for example, Robert Olmstead's *Stay Here with Me,* William Kittredge's
Hole in the Sky, Clark Blaise's *I Had a Father,* John Edgar Wideman's *Fatheralong,*
Chris Offut's *The Same River Twice,* Richard Stern's *A Sistermony,* Blake Morrison's
When Did You Last See Your Father?—for insight and direction. Although not pur-
posefully prescriptive, these works, to steal from Susan Sontag's recent defense of literature, "enlarge" our "sense of human possibility of what human nature is, of what
happens in the world," and by doing so inform us "how one should live."[17]

Because all these works deserve a serious reading that is beyond the scope of this
essay, I will focus on Offut's book. As Offut's memoir is a coming of age tale in which
the protagonist actually "comes of age," it is an American anomaly. Although an infre-
quent event in the "real world," the achievement of psychological adulthood is almost
nonexistent in American literary history. Even in America's best literature most characters remain, to quote Leslie Fiedler, "stuck in a pre-adult-world." (In a brilliant critique of Hemingway's best work, Fiedler argues "his characters seem never really old
enough to vote, merely to blow up bridges: as they seem never old enough to repro-
duce, merely sufficiently mature to make the motions of the act of love.")[18]

Offut's is a hard-won maturity. With a pedigree notable mainly for its "crackpot-
tery" and "darkness" and as a beneficiary of neither means nor property, his beginnings would never be described as auspicious. Added to this is his propensity for
failure; until his luck is reversed by his wife-to-be, Offut is a chronic failure (more than
one of my students has affectionately referred to him as a "perennial fuck-up"). A high
school dropout judged unfit for admission into the armed services, the Peace Corps,
the fire and police departments, and the park rangers, he hitchhikes to New York in
quest of an actor's life—only to end up back in his native Appalachia, a semi-invalid.
Unable to sustain the basic codes of civility required for family life, he hits the road
again, drifting through a series of marginal jobs and errant relationships, succeeding
only in feeding an already well-formed reservoir of alienation and cynicism. His life
"on the road"—motivated in large part by an absence: "mountain culture expects its
males to undergo various rites of manhood, but genuine tribulation underfire no
longer exists. We've had to create our own"—can be considered a success only if one
considers "a sequence of half-hearted attempts at self-destruction" romantic.[19]

It is also pedestrian. America's mythological canon is replete with tales of transcendence over an impoverished or traumatized youth. These tales of self-making,
usually narrated with a muted righteousness, highlight the protagonist's resilience
and pragmatic canniness. Because the goal in these tales is always greatness, any set-
back is speedily overcome by an application of old-fashioned fortitude. In Offut's
memoir, perhaps because greatness is out of the question, there is, thankfully, none
of this. The memoir's end has Offut married and with a three-month-old child and
a couple of published short stories—hardly a Mailer or an Updike of the nineties.
His "victories"—being a writer, a father, a husband; reestablishing a civil relationship with his father—belong to the plane of the everyday, not the supernatural. With
none of the usual assurances of a bright literary future—no awards, grants, or even
four-figure advances—he could very well join the ranks of all the other one-book
memoirists. Yet, even if his next sixty stories are rejected, Offut won't go the way of

many failed writers. This isn't to say that such a calamity wouldn't result in onto-logical shakiness, and perhaps even a period of unsightly behavior, but I doubt that he would finish out most evenings with an alcohol-soaked whimper of despair.

Making predictions about an individual's future is a risky endeavor, but Offut's relationship with his wife emboldens me. It takes great courage for a man, especial-ly a man with lofty artistic aspirations, to admit that any success achieved is due to a committed and loving relationship with a woman. Although she may be immor-talized on the dedication page, canonized in the acknowledgments, or rhapsodized in the text (sensitive men might do all three), most authors will make it known, often in ways unknown to themselves, that every consequential achievement, both on the page and off, is self-made. It takes even greater courage to write that one's wife is "far more intelligent than I" (note the difference between this and "her special com-bination of love and understanding").[20] Offut does both, and these admissions are central to an identity realized through intimacy.

The radicality of Offut's maturity resides in his invocation of a masculinity achieved through mutuality. Although he engages in some "goddess language"—"she was Calliope making do with a mortal"—the power of the relationship clearly resides in its mutuality. "I showed her my poetry and she told me they weren't poems but only looked like them. We had our first fight, which ended when she suggested I write prose. I taught her to drive a car, play poker, and shoot pool. Rita returned me to the species with a careful formula of protection and guidance." Estranged from the species, Offut was condemned to a series of aborted half-efforts at identity, and although he may not have fulfilled his family's prophecy of ending up "dead or in jail," there is little doubt he would have continued to drift.[21] The relationship is salvational: without a sense of the "we," the "I" Offut writes from and of would be of little interest. And, although he may get the best end of the stick, Offut proves to be a good partner, capable of responding to Rita's needs and being a tender-hearted father.

The memoir has been well received—the reviewer from the *New Yorker* called it "the memoir of the decade." As the book works extremely well as an archetypal postmodern coming of age story—at least for a white, nomadic hillbilly with an "over-fondness" for drink and drug—such praise is well deserved. My students find the book compelling, and I would guess that over 80 percent read it cover to cover. In addition to being impressed by his embrace of mutuality, they appreciate Offut's idiosyncratic combination of gentleness and grit. They also agree that, despite recur-ring bouts of neurotic terror and crippling self-doubt, Offut has crafted a "good life." Most say that they admire him, that they could learn something from "hang-ing out" with him, and that they would be able to trust him.

I mention this because much of the conversation in my recent courses centers on the moral and ethical dimensions of selfhood. Given that my training in existential psychology included a heavy dosage of the early Heidegger and Levinas—and that early in each semester I introduce Freud's "I don't cudgel my brains much about good and evil, but I have not found much 'good' in the average human being. Most of them are in my experience riff-raff, whether they proclaim this or that ethical doc-trine" into the course equation—most of the blame rests with me. Yet, in contrast to the prevailing image of "nontraditional" students, my courses are stocked with students obsessed with questions about the ingredients of a good life. I'm sure that some of this is simply a manifestation of the stock-taking taking place throughout the society, but it also has an antiapocalyptic element: if the much-forecasted Rapture doesn't occur, they want to be in a position to reverse the dehumanizing political and economic trends aimed at deepening their disenfranchisement.

IV

My decision to focus on Offut's work was in no way accidental. Although I was raised in a far more urban setting, a setting exempt, at least in my family's corner of the grid, from the poverty of Offut's Appalachia, a setting considered by many if not idyllic then at least estimable, I too believed the creation of meaning within earshot of my family was an impossibility. So I too "took to the road," and although my affiliations were, for the most part, less marginal and more sustained than Offut's, I never experienced the sense of congruence that others seemed capable of establishing. In my quest to achieve "tortured genius status," I drank too much, suckerpunched my way to a few victories, involved myself in a number of sexual escapades I wish I could repress, and like Offut nursed a fairly deep reservoir of cynicism. And while no one, at least to my face, categorized me as a "failure," many lamented my proclivity for "doing things the hard way."

In my travels I met many other young men who shared my disquietude and talent for disaffection. It would be ridiculously self-righteous and inaccurate to describe us as some "lost generation," but we did share a belief that achieving manhood involved something other than renting one's body and soul for the paycheck that ensured both a comely mate and a manicured niche in some suburban "necropolis." We wanted work that amplified the self through revivifying the world and a species of love that sought engagement over contentment. We also, insipid though it might sound, longed for a cultural permission to relate to the world and others with the fullness of being; the levels of numbing and dissociation tolerated by our fathers and mentors seemed unbearable.[22] Our response to the culture's infatuation with pragmatism, which we read as a compulsive capitulation to the status quo, was to search. But, finding the alternative solutions offered by the "beats" too anarchic, those of the "punkers" ill suited to an extended life cycle, and those of the "New Agers" far too obsessed with self-salvation, we felt adrift and forestalled.[23] And, although most of us have patched together an approach to existence that bestows livable levels of meaning and passionately love the women we live with, we still do.

I mention this not to elicit sympathy for the "plight of the American male" but to suggest that the bimillennium's crepuscular stage is thick with men seeking more integrated forms of masculinity. Many young men are frightened by the ease with which they inhabit styles of masculinity antagonistic to the mutuality they desire, forms that operate on domination and indifference, forms that insure alienation and nihilism. They want the liberty to express gentleness, sadness, and confusion outside the confines of the barroom or the postconjugal embrace. They want it without having to adopt the affectations of either sensitivity or androgyny; there are certain aspects of a traditional masculine stance they don't seek to jettison. Neutralized by the requisites of corporate success or pinioned in mindless positions that serve only to keep them a paycheck away from homelessness (or their parents' home), they also seek the courage to follow a dream as senseless as it is vitalizing. For them Offut's memoir issues a thin but compelling light.

In the final poem of his autobiographical *The Glass Hammer: A Southern Childhood,* Andrew Hudgins writes, "All telling's a betrayal." Although he says that all this telling has left him "not as angry as I was, but tired. And guilty," I don't believe that his future poems will be barren of autobiographical material.[24] At least I hope not—Hudgins is always a pleasure, but when his poems "get autobiographical," they approach greatness. Besides, the type of betrayal Hudgins is describing is necessary if new forms of identity are to be possible. If we remain loyal to nine-tenths of the narratives currently animating humanity, I'm sure the violence and oppression we are now experiencing will seem picayune in a year or so. As we approach 2000, I'd rather get my clues about how to negotiate existence from the autobiographers than from the visionaries and the social scientists (and I'd rather that others do the same). At least the truths they offer emerge from the folds of experience.

NOTES

1. W. H. Auden, *The Dyer's Hand* (New York: Vintage, 1989), 95, 97, 99.

2. Ivan Illich and Barry Sanders, *ABC: The Alphabetization of the Popular Mind* (New York: Vintage, 1988).

3. Robert Penn Warren, *Democracy and Poetry* (Cambridge, Mass.: Harvard University Press, 1975), 55.

4. Henry Louis Gates, *Bearing Witness: Selections from African-American Autobiography in the Twentieth Century* (New York: Pantheon, 1991).

5. David Tracy, *Plurality and Ambiguity: Hermeneutics, Religion, Hope* (Chicago: University of Chicago Press, 1988), 31.

6. This paragraph is deeply indebted to the work of Robert Jay Lifton, Jerome Bruner, and Ernest Becker.

7. E. M. Cioran, "Some Blind Alleys: A Letter," in *The Art of the Personal Essay,* ed. Phillip Lopate (New York: Anchor, 1944), 407; Andrei Sinyavsky, "Dissent as a Personal Experience," in *Legacy of Dissent,* ed. Nicolaus Mills (New York: Touchstone, 1994), 417.

8. Alfred Kazin, "The Self as History: Reflections on Autobiography," in *Telling Lives: The Biographer's Art,* ed. Marc Pachter (Washington: Smithsonian, 1979), 76.

9. Sidonie Smith and Julia Watson, eds., *Getting a Life: Everyday Uses of Autobiography* (Minneapolis: University of Minnesota Press, 1996), 3.

10. Hillel Schwartz, *Century's End: An Orientation Manual toward the Year 2000* (New York: Doubleday, 1990), xvi–xvii.

11. Albert Camus, *Between Hell and Reason* (Hanover, N.H.: Wesleyan University Press, 1991), 119. See also Eric Hobsbawm, *The Age of Extremes: A History of the World, 1914–1991* (New York: Vintage, 1994), 6.

12. Kazin, "The Self as History," 88.

13. Philippe Lejeune, *On Autobiography* (Minneapolis: University of Minnesota Press, 1989).

14. See James William Gibson, *Warrior Dreams: Paramilitary Culture in Post-Vietnam America* (New York: Hill and Wang, 1994); and Charles B. Strozier, *Apocalypse: On the Psychology of Christian Fundamentalism in America* (Boston: Beacon, 1994). See also Lee Quinby's essay in this volume.

15. Michael Kimmel, *Manhood in America: A Cultural History* (New York: Free Press, 1996), 238.

16. E. Anthony Rotundo, *American Manhood: Transformations in Masculinity from the Revolution to the Modern Era* (New York: Basic Books, 1993).

17. Susan Sontag, "Interview," *Paris Review* (winter 1995): 97.

18. Leslie Fiedler, *An End to Innocence: Essays on Culture and Politics* (Boston: Beacon, 1952), 193.

19. Chris Offut, *The Same River Twice* (New York: Penguin, 1993).

20. Ibid.

21. Ibid.

22. For an interesting interpretation/indictment of the culture's "emptiness," see Philip Cushman's "Why the Self Is Empty: Toward a Historically Situated Psychology," *American Psychologist* 45 (May 1990); and his *Constructing the Self, Constructing America: A Cultural History of Psychotherapy* (Boston: Addison-Wesley, 1995).

23. See Robert Jay Lifton, *The Protean Self: Human Resilience in an Age of Fragmentation* (New York: Basic, 1993); and Wade Clark Roof, *A Generation of Seekers* (New York: Harper and Row, 1984).

24. Andrew Hudgins, *The Glass Hammer: A Southern Childhood* (Boston: Houghton Mifflin, 1994), 97.

Chapter Twenty-One

Hysteresis of the Millennium

Jean Baudrillard

Pataphysics of the Year 2000

> A tormenting thought: as of a certain point, history was
> no longer *real*. Without noticing it, all mankind sud-
> denly left reality; everything happening since then was
> supposedly not true; but we supposedly didn't notice.
> Our task would now be to find that point, and as long
> as we didn't have it, we would be forced to abide in our
> present destruction.
>
> —Elias Canetti

Various plausible hypotheses may be advanced to explain this vanishing of history. Canetti's expression "all mankind suddenly left reality" irresistibly evokes the idea of that escape velocity a body requires to free itself from the gravitational field of a star or a planet. Staying with this image, one might suppose that the acceleration of modernity; of technology, events and media; and of all exchanges—economic, political and sexual—has propelled us to "escape velocity," with the result that we have flown free of the referential sphere of the real and of history. We are "liberated" in every sense of the term, so liberated that we have taken leave of a certain space-time, passed beyond a certain horizon in which the real is possible because gravitation is still strong enough for things to be reflected and thus in some way to endure and have some consequence.

A degree of slowness (that is, a certain speed, but not too great), a degree of distance, but not too much, and a degree of liberation (an energy for rupture and change), but not too much, are needed to bring about the kind of condensation or significant crystallization of events we call history, the kind of coherent unfolding of causes and effects we call reality *(le réel)*.

Once beyond this gravitational effect, which keeps bodies in orbit, all the atoms of meaning get lost in space. Each atom pursues its own trajectory to infinity and is lost in space. This is precisely what we are seeing in our present-day societies, intent as they are on accelerating all bodies, messages and processes in all directions, and which, with modern media, have created for every event, story, and image a simulation of an infinite trajectory. Every political, historical, and cultural fact possesses a kinetic energy that wrenches it from its own space and propels it into a hyperspace where, since it will never return, it loses all meaning. No need for science fiction here: already, here and now—in the shape of our computers, circuits, and networks—we have the particle accelerator that has smashed the referential orbit of things once and for all.

So far as history is concerned, its telling has become impossible because that telling *(re-citatum)* is, by definition, the possible recurrence of a sequence of meanings. Now, through the impulse for total dissemination and circulation, every event is granted its own liberation; every fact becomes atomic, nuclear, and pursues its trajectory into the void. In order to be disseminated to infinity, it has to be fragmented like a particle. This is how it is able to achieve a velocity of no-return, which carries it out of history once and for all. Every set of phenomena, whether cultural totality or sequence of events, has to be fragmented, disjointed, so that it can be sent down the circuits; every kind of language has to be resolved into a binary formulation so that it can circulate not, any longer, in our memories, but in the luminous, electronic memory of the computers. No human language can withstand the speed of light. No event can withstand being beamed across the whole planet. No meaning can withstand acceleration. No history can withstand the centrifugation of facts or their being short-circuited in real time (to pursue the same train of thought: no sexuality can withstand being liberated, no culture can withstand being hyped, no truth can withstand being verified, etc.).

Nor is theory in a position to "reflect (on)" anything. It can only tear concepts from their critical zone of reference and force them beyond a point of no-return (it too is moving into the hyperspace of simulation), a process whereby it loses all "objective" validity but gains substantially in real affinity with the present system.

The second hypothesis regarding the vanishing of history is the opposite of the first. It has to do not with processes speeding up but slowing down. It too comes directly from physics.

Matter slows the passing of time. To put it more precisely, time at the surface of a very dense body seems to be going in slow motion. The phenomenon intensifies as the density increases. The effect of this slowing down will be to increase the length of the light wave emitted by this body as received by the observer. Beyond a certain limit, time stops and the wavelength becomes infinite. The wave no longer exists. The light goes out.

There is a clear analogy here with the slowing down of history when it rubs up against the astral body of the "silent majorities." Our societies are dominated by this mass process, not only in the demographic and sociological sense, but also in the sense of a "critical mass," of passing beyond a point of no-return. This is the most significant event within these societies: the emergence, in the very course of their mobilization and revolutionary process (they are all revolutionary by the standards of past centuries), of an equivalent force of inertia, of an immense indifference and the silent potency of that indifference. This inert matter of the social is not produced by a lack of exchanges, information or communication, but by the multiplication and saturation of exchanges. It is the product of the hyperdensity of cities, commodities, messages, and circuits. It is the cold star of the social, and, around that mass, history is also cooling. Events follow one upon another, canceling each other out in a state of indifference. The masses, neutralized, mithridatized by information, in turn neutralize history and act as an *écran d'absorption.*[1] They themselves have no history, meaning, consciousness, or desire. They are the potential residue of all history, meaning, and desire. As they have unfurled in our modernity, all these fine things have stirred up a mysterious counter-phenomenon, and all today's political and social strategies are thrown out of gear by the failure to understand it.

This time we have the opposite situation: history, meaning, and progress are no longer able to reach their escape velocity. They are no longer able to pull away from this overdense body that slows their trajectory, that slows time to the point where, right now, the perception and imagination of the future are beyond us. All social, historical, and temporal transcendence is absorbed by that mass in its silent immanence. Political events already lack sufficient energy of their own to move us: so they run on like a silent film for which we bear collective irresponsibility. History comes to an end here, not for want of actors, nor for want of violence (there will always be more violence), nor for want of events (there will always be more events, thanks be to the media and the news networks!), but by deceleration, indifference, and stupefaction. It is no longer able to transcend itself, to envisage its own finality, to dream of its own end; it is being buried beneath its own immediate effect, worn out in special effects, imploding into current events.

Deep down, one cannot even speak of the end of history here, since history will not have time to catch up with its own end. Its effects are accelerating, but its meaning is slowing inexorably. It will eventually come to a stop and be extinguished like light and time in the vicinity of an infinitely dense mass.

Humanity too had its big bang: a certain critical density, a certain concentration of people and exchanges, presides over this explosion we call history, which is merely the dispersal of the dense and hieratic nuclei of previous civilizations. Today we have the "reversive effect": crossing the threshold of the critical mass where populations, events, and information are concerned triggers the opposite process of historical and political inertia. In the cosmic order, we do not know whether we have reached the escape velocity, which would mean we are now in a definitive state of expansion (this will doubtless remain eternally uncertain). In the human order, where the perspectives are more limited, it may be that the very escape velocity of the species (the acceleration of births, technologies, and exchanges over the centuries) creates an excess of mass and resistance that defeats the initial energy and takes us down an inexorable path of contraction and inertia.

Whether the universe is expanding to infinity or retracting toward an infinitely dense, infinitely small nucleus depends on its critical mass (and speculation on this is itself infinite, by virtue of the possible invention of new particles). By analogy, whether our human history is evolutive or involutive perhaps depends on humanity's critical mass. Has the history, the movement, of the species reached the escape velocity required to triumph over the inertia of the mass? Are we set, like the galaxies, on a definitive course distancing us from one another at prodigious speed, or is this dispersal to infinity destined to come to an end and the human molecules to come back together by an opposite process of gravitation? Can the human mass, which increases every day, exert control over a pulsation of this kind?

There is a third hypothesis, a third analogy. We are still speaking of a point of disappearance, a vanishing point, but this time in music. I shall call this the stereophonic effect. We are all obsessed with high fidelity, with the quality of musical "reproduction." At the consoles of our stereos, armed with our tuners, amplifiers, and speakers, we mix, adjust settings, multiply tracks in pursuit of a flawless sound. Is this still music? Where is the high fidelity threshold beyond which music disappears as such? It does not disappear for lack of music, but because it has passed this limit point; it disappears into the perfection of its materiality, into its own special effect. Beyond this point there is neither judgment nor aesthetic pleasure. It is the ecstasy of musicality, and its end.

The disappearance of history is of the same order: here again, we have passed that limit where, by dint of the sophistication of events and information, history ceases to exist as such. Immediate high-powered broadcasting, special effects, secondary effects, fading, and that famous feedback effect that is produced in acoustics by a source and a receiver being too close together and in history by an event and its dissemination being too close together and thus interfering disastrously—a short-circuit between cause and effect like that between the object and the experimenting subject in microphysics (and in the human sciences!)—these are all things that cast a radical doubt on the event, just as excessively high fidelity casts radical doubt on music. Elias Canetti puts it well: beyond this point, nothing is true. It is for this reason that the *petite musique* of history also eludes our grasp today, that it vanishes into the microscopics or the stereophonics of news.

Right at the very heart of news, history threatens to disappear. At the heart of hi-fi, music threatens to disappear. At the heart of experimentation, the object of science threatens to disappear. At the heart of pornography, sexuality threatens to disappear. Everywhere we find the same stereophonic effect, the same effect of absolute proximity to the real, the same effect of simulation.

By definition, this vanishing point, this point short of which history *existed* and music *existed*, cannot be pinned down. Where must stereo perfection end? The boundaries are constantly being pushed back because it is technical obsession that redraws them. Where must news reporting end? One can only counter this fascination with "real time"—the equivalent of high fidelity—with a moral objection, and there is not much point in that.

The passing of this point is thus an irreversible act, contrary to what Canetti seems to hope. We shall never get back to pre-stereo music (except by an additional technical simulation effect); we shall never get back to pre-news and pre-media history. The original essence of music, the original concept of history, have disappeared because we shall never again be able to isolate them from their model of perfection, which is at the same time their model of simulation, the model of their enforced assumption into a hyper-reality that cancels them out. We shall never again know what the social or music were before being exacerbated into their present useless perfection. We shall never again know what history was before its exacerbation into the technical perfection of news: we shall never again know what anything was before disappearing into the fulfillment of its model.

So, with this, the situation becomes novel once again. The fact that we are leaving history to move into the realm of simulation is merely a consequence of the fact that history itself has always, deep down, been an immense simulation model. Not in the sense that it could be said only to have existed in the narrative made of it or the interpretation given, but with regard to the time in which it unfolds—that linear time that is at once the time of an ending and the time of the unlimited suspending of the end. The only kind of time in which a history can take place, if by history we understand a succession of nonmeaningless facts, each engendering the other by cause and effect, but doing so without any absolute necessity and all standing open to the future, unevenly poised. So different from time in ritual societies, where the end of everything is in its beginning and ceremony retraces the perfection of that original event. In contrast to this *fulfilled* order of time, the liberation of the "real" time of history, the production of a linear, deferred time may seem a purely artificial process. Where does this suspense come from? Where do we get the idea that what must be accomplished (Last Judgement, salvation, or catastrophe) must come at the end of time and match up with some incalculable appointed term or other? This model of linearity must have seemed entirely fictitious, wholly absurd and abstract to cultures that had no sense of a deferred day of reckoning, a successive concatenation of events, and a final goal. And it was indeed a scenario that had some difficulty establishing itself. There was fierce resistance in the early years of Christianity to the postponement of the coming of God's Kingdom. The acceptance of this "historical" perspective of salvation, that is, of its remaining unaccomplished in the immediate present, was not achieved without violence, and all the heresies would later take up this leitmotif of the immediate fulfillment of the promise in what was akin to a defiance of time. Entire communities even resorted to suicide to hasten the coming of the Kingdom. Since this latter was promised at the end of time, it seemed to them that they had only to put an end to time right away.

The whole of history has had a millennial (millenarian) challenge to its temporality running through it. In opposition to the historical perspective, which continually shifts the stakes on to a hypothetical end, there has always been a fatal exigency, a fatal strategy of time that wants to shoot straight ahead to a point beyond the end. It cannot be said that either of these tendencies has really won out, and the question, "to wait or not to wait?" has remained, throughout history, a burning issue. Since the messianic convulsion of the earliest Christians, reaching back beyond the heresies and the revolts, there has always been this desire to anticipate the end, possibly by death, by a kind of seductive suicide aiming to turn God from history and make him face up to his responsibilities, those that lie beyond the end, those of the final fulfillment. And what, indeed, is terrorism, if not this effort to conjure up, in its own way, the end of history? It attempts to entrap the powers that be by an immediate, total act. Without awaiting the final term of the process, it sets itself at the ecstatic endpoint, hoping to bring about the conditions for the Last Judgment. An illusory challenge, of course, but one that always fascinates, since, deep down, neither time nor history has ever been accepted. Everyone remains aware of the arbitrariness, the artificial character of time and history. And we are never fooled by those who call on us to hope.

And, terrorism apart, is there not also a hint of this Parousiac exigency in the global fantasy of catastrophe that hovers over today's world? A demand for a violent resolution of reality, when this latter eludes our grasp in an endless hyper-reality? For hyper-reality rules out the very occurrence of the Last Judgment or the Apocalypse or the Revolution. All the ends we have envisaged elude our grasp, and history has no chance of bringing them about, since it will, in the interim, have come to an end (it is always the story of Kafka's Messiah: he arrives too late, a day too late, and the time lag is unbearable). So one might as well short-circuit the Messiah, bring forward the end. This has always been the demonic temptation: to falsify ends and the calculation of ends, to falsify time and the occurrence of things, to hurry them along, impatient to see them accomplished or secretly sensing that the promise of accomplishment is itself also false and diabolical.

Even our obsession with "real time," with the instantaneity of news, has a secret millenarianism about it: canceling the flow of time, canceling delay, suppressing the sense that the event is happening elsewhere, anticipating its end by freeing ourselves from linear time, laying hold of things almost before they have taken place. In this sense "real time" is something even more artificial than a recording and is, at the same time, its denial—if we want immediate enjoyment of the event, if we want to experience it at the instant of its occurrence, as if we were there, this is because we no longer have any confidence in the meaning or purpose of the event. The same denial is found in apparently opposite behavior—recording, filing, and memorizing everything of our own past and the past of all cultures. Is this not a symptom of a collective presentiment of the end, a sign that events and the living time of history have had their day and that we have to arm ourselves with the whole battery of artificial memory, all the signs of the past, to face up to the absence of a future and the glacial times that await us? Are not mental and intellectual structures currently going underground, burying themselves in memories, in archives, in search of an improbable resurrection? All thoughts are going underground in cautious anticipation of the year 2000. They can already scent the terror of the year 2000. They are instinctively adopting the solution of those cryogenized individuals plunged into liquid nitrogen until the means can be found to enable them to survive.

These societies, these generations that no longer expect anything from some future "coming" and have less and less confidence in history, that dig in behind their futuristic technologies, behind their stores of information, and inside the beehive networks of communication where time is at last wiped out by pure circulation, will perhaps never reawaken. But they do not know that. The year 2000 will perhaps not take place. But they do not know that.

The Reversal of History

At some point in the 1980s, history took a turn in the opposite direction. Once the apogee of time, the summit of the curve of evolution, the solstice of history, had been passed, the downward slope of events began, and things began to run in reverse. It seems that, like cosmic space, historical space-time is also curved. By the same chaotic effect in time as in space, things go quicker and quicker as they approach their term, just as water mysteriously accelerates as it approaches a waterfall.

In the Euclidean space of history, the shortest path between two points is a straight line, the line of Progress and Democracy. But this is true only of the linear space of the Enlightenment. In our non-Euclidean fin de siècle space, a baleful curvature unfailingly deflects all trajectories. This is doubtless linked to the sphericity of time (visible on the horizon of the end of the century, just as the earth's sphericity is visible on the horizon at the end of the day) or the subtle distortion of the gravitational field.

Segalen says that once the earth has become a sphere, every movement distancing us from a point by the same token also begins to bring us closer to that point. This is true of time as well. Each apparent movement of history brings us imperceptibly closer to its antipodal point, if not indeed to its starting point. This is the end of linearity. In this perspective the future no longer exists. But if there is no longer a future, there is no longer an end either. So *this is not even the end of history*. We are faced with a paradoxical process of reversal, a reversive effect of modernity that, having reached its speculative limit and having extrapolated all its virtual developments, is disintegrating into its simple elements in a catastrophic process of recurrence and turbulence.

By this retroversion of history to infinity, this hyperbolic curvature, the century itself is escaping its end. By this retroaction of events, we are eluding our own deaths. Metaphorically, then, we shall not even reach the symbolic term of the end, the symbolic term of the year 2000.

Can one escape this curving back of history, which causes it to retrace its own steps and obliterate its own tracks, escape this fatal asymptote that causes us, as it were, to rewind modernity like a tape? We are so used to playing back every film—the fictional ones and the films of our lives—so contaminated by the technology of retrospection, that we are quite capable, in our present dizzy spin, of running history over again like a film played backward.

Are we condemned, in the vain hope of not abiding in our present destruction, as Canetti has it, to the retrospective melancholia of living everything through again in order to correct it all, in order to elucidate it all (it is almost as though psychoanalysis were spreading its shadow over the whole of our history: when the same events, the same conjunctures are reproduced in almost the same terms, when the same wars break out between the same peoples, and all that had passed and gone reemerges as though driven by an irrepressible phantasm, one might almost see this as the work of a form of primary process or unconscious), do we have to summon all past events to appear before us, to reinvestigate it all as though we were conducting a trial? A mania for trials has taken hold of us in recent times, together with a mania for responsibility, precisely at the point when this latter is becoming increasingly hard to pin down. We are looking to remake a clean history, to whitewash all the abominations: the obscure (resentful) feeling behind the proliferation of scandals is that history itself is a scandal. A retroprocess that may drag us into a mania for origins, going back even beyond history, back to the conviviality of animal existence, to the primitive biotope, as can already be seen in the ecologists' flirtation with an impossible origin.

The only way of escaping this, of breaking with this recession and obsession, would seem to be to set ourselves, from the outset, on a different temporal orbit, to leapfrog our shadows, to leapfrog the shadow of the century, to take an elliptical short-cut and pass beyond the end, not allowing it time to take place. The advantage is that we would at least preserve what remains of history, instead of subjecting it to an agonizing revision, and deliver it up to those who will carry out the post-mortem on its corpse, as one performs a post-mortem on one's childhood in an interminable analysis. This would at least mean conserving its memory and its glory, whereas currently, in the guise of revision and rehabilitation, we are canceling out one by one all the events that have preceded us by obliging them to repent.

If we could escape this end-of-century moratorium, with its deferred day of reckoning, which looks curiously like a work of mourning—a *failed* one—and which consists in reviewing everything, rewriting everything, restoring everything, face-lifting everything, to produce, as it seems, in a burst of paranoia a perfect set of accounts at the end of the century, a universally positive balance sheet (the reign of human rights over the whole planet, democracy everywhere, the definitive obliteration of all conflict, and, if possible, the obliteration of all "negative" events from our memories), if we could escape this international cleaning and polishing effort in which all the nations of the world can be seen vying today, if we could spare ourselves this democratic extreme unction by which the New World Order is heralded, we would at least allow the events that have preceded us to retain their glory, character, meaning, and singularity. However, we seem in such a hurry to cover up the worst before the bankruptcy proceedings start (everyone is secretly afraid of the terrifying balance sheet we are going to present in the year 2000) that there will be nothing left of our history at the end of the millennium, nothing of its illumination, of the violence of its events. If there is something distinctive about an event—about what constitutes an event and thus has historical value—it is the fact that it is irreversible, that there is always something in it that exceeds meaning and interpretation. But it is precisely the opposite we are seeing today: all that has happened this century in terms of progress, liberation, revolution, and violence is about to be revised for the better.

This is the problem: is the course of modernity reversible, and is that reversal itself irreversible? How far can this retrospective form go, this end-of-millennium dream? Is there not a "history barrier," analogous to the sound or speed barrier, beyond which, in its palinodial movement, it could not pass?

Hysteresis of the Millennium

We are, self-evidently, entering upon a retroactive form of history, and all our ideas, philosophies, and mental techniques are progressively adapting to that model. We may perhaps even see this as an adventure, since the disappearance of the end is in itself an original situation. It seems to be characteristic of our culture and our history, which cannot even manage to come to an end and are, as a result, assured of an indefinite recurrence, a backhanded immortality. Up to now immortality has been mainly that of the beyond, an immortality yet to come, but we are today inventing another kind in the here and now, an immortality of endings receding to infinity.

The situation is, perhaps, an original one, but clearly, so far as the final result is concerned, the game is already lost. We shall never experience the original chaos, the Big Bang: the file is closed on that; we were not there. But, where the final moment is concerned—the Big Crumb—we might have some hope of seeing that. Some hope of enjoying the end, to make up for not being able to enjoy the origin. These are the only two interesting moments, and since we have been denied the first, we might as well put all our energies into accelerating the end, into hastening things to their definitive doom, which we could at least consume as a spectacle. Just imagine the extraordinary good luck of the generation that would have the end of the world to itself. It is every bit as marvelous as being present at the beginning. But we came too late for the beginning. Only the end seemed to be within our means.

We had come close to this possibility with the atomic age. Alas, the balance of terror suspended the ultimate event, then postponed it forever(?), and now that deterrence has succeeded, we have to get used to the idea that *there is no end any longer, there will no longer be any end,* that history itself has become interminable. Thus, when we speak of the "end of history," the "end of the political," the "end of the social," the "end of ideologies," none of this is true. The worst of it all is precisely that there will be no end to anything, and all these things will continue to unfold slowly, tediously, recurrently, in that hysteresis of everything that, like nails and hair, continues to grow after death. Because, at bottom, all these things are already dead, and rather than to have a happy or tragic resolution, a destiny, we shall have a thwarted end, a homeopathic end, an end distilled into all the various metastases of the refusal of death. The metastases of all that resurfaces as history goes back over its own tracks in a compulsive desire for rehabilitation, as though with regard to some crime or other (a crime committed by us, but in spite of ourselves, a crime of the species against itself, by a process that is quickening with contemporary history, a crime of which universal waste, universal repentance, and universal *ressentiment* are, today, the surest signs), a crime on which the file has to be reopened, which necessarily involves going back into the past, right back to origins if necessary, where, for want of being able to find a resolution of our destiny in the future, we seek a retrospective absolution. We absolutely have to know what went wrong at a certain point and, hence, explore all the vestiges of the path we have traveled, root through the dustbins of history, revive both the best and the worst in the vain hope of separating good from evil. To return to Canetti's hypothesis: we have to get back beyond a fateful demarcation line that, in history too, might separate the human from the inhuman, a line that we might be said to have thoughtlessly crossed, in the dizzying whirl of some liberation of the species or other. It seems as though, caught up in a collective panic over this blind spot at which we passed out of history and its ends (but what were those ends? all we know is that we passed beyond them without noticing), we are hurriedly trying to get into reverse, in order to escape this state of empty simulation. Trying to relocate the zone of reference, the earlier scene, the Euclidean space of history. Thus, the events in Eastern Europe claimed to set in train the onward march of peoples once more and the democratic process. And the Gulf War sought to reopen the space of war, the space of a violence that could establish a new world order.

This is, in every case, a failure. This revival of vanished—or vanishing—forms, this attempt to escape the apocalypse of the virtual, is a utopian desire, the last of our utopian desires. The more we seek to rediscover the real and the referential, the more we sink into simulation, in this case a shameful and, at any event, hopeless simulation.

By analogy with illnesses, which are perhaps merely the reactivation of previous states (cancer, for example, reproducing the undifferentiated proliferation of the first living cells, or viral pathology, which causes the earlier states of the biogenetic substance to resurface in moments when the body is weak and its immune defenses low), can we not imagine that, in history itself, previous states have never disappeared but present themselves again in succession, as it were, taking advantage of the weakness or excessive complexity of the present structures?

However, these earlier forms never resurface as they were; they never escape the destiny of extreme modernity. Their resurrection is itself hyper-real. The resuscitated values are themselves fluid, unstable, subject to the same fluctuations as fashion or stock-exchange capital. The rehabilitation of the old frontiers, the old structures, the old elites, will therefore never have the same meaning. If, one day, the aristocracy or the royalty recover their old position, they will, nonetheless, be "postmodern." None of the "retro" scenarios that are being got up have any historical significance: they are occurring wholly on the surface of *our* age, as though all images were being superimposed one upon another, but with no change to the actual course of the film. Relapsed events: defrosted democracy, *trompe-l'oeil* freedoms, the New World Order cellophane-wrapped, and ecology in mothballs, with its immune-deficient human rights. None of these will make any difference to the *present* melancholy of the century, which we shall never get right through, since it will, in the meantime, have swung around and headed off in the opposite direction.

This is all, at bottom, a triumph for Walt Disney, that inspired precursor of a universe where all past or present forms meet in a playful promiscuity, where all cultures recur in a mosaic (including the cultures of the future, which are themselves already recurrent). For a long time we thought this was all imaginary, that is, derivative and decorative, puerile and marginal. But we are going to see that it was something like a prefiguration of the real trend of things—Disney World opening up for us the bewildering perspective of passing through all the earlier stages, as in a film, with those stages hypostasized in a definitive juvenility, frozen like Disney himself in liquid nitrogen: Magic Country, Future World, Gothic, Hollywood itself reconstituted fifty years on in Florida, the whole of the past and the future revisited as living simulation. Walt Disney is the true hero of deep freezing, with his utopian hope of awakening one day in the future, in a better world. But that is where the irony bites: he did not foresee that reality and history would turn right around. And he who expected to wake up in the year 2100 might well, following out his own fairytale scenario, awaken in 1730 or the world of the Pharaohs or any one of his many primal scenes.

We wondered what the point of this coming fin de siècle might be. Here we have it: the sale of the century. History is being sold off, as is the end of history. Communism is being sold off, as is the end of communism. Communism will have had no historical end; it will have been sold off, knocked down like useless stock. Just like the Russian army, sold off at the four corners of the earth —an unprecedented event relegated to the status of a banal market operation. All Western ideologies are knocked down too; they can be had at bargain prices in all latitudes.

The sales used to come after the feast days, but now they precede them. It is the same with our century: we are anticipating the end—everything must go, everything has to be sold off. We learn, for example, that, alongside the great Red Army stock clearance, the industrial laboratories are currently "selling off" the human genome, which they are copyrighting and commercializing sequence by sequence. Here again, everything must go, even if we do not know what these genes are for. Things must not be allowed to reach their natural term. They have first to be cryogenized, in order to ensure them a virtual, derisory immortality.

Messianic hope was based on the *reality* of the Apocalypse. But this latter has no more reality than the original Big Bang. We shall never be allowed this dramatic illumination. Even the idea of putting an end to our planet by an atomic clash is futile and superfluous. If it has no meaning for anyone, God or man, then what is the point? Our Apocalypse is not real, it is *virtual*. And it is not in the future, it is *here and now*. Our orbital bombs, even if they did not mean a natural end, were at least manufactured by us, designed, as it seems, the better to end it all. But in actual fact, that is not how it was: they were made *the better to be rid of the end*. We have now put that end into satellite form, like all those finalities that, once transcendent, have now become purely and simply orbital.

It circles around us and will continue to do so tirelessly. We are encircled by our own end and incapable of getting it to land, of bringing it back to earth. This is like the parable of the Russian cosmonaut forgotten in space, with no one to welcome him, no one to bring him back—the sole particle of Soviet territory ironically overflying a deterritorialized Russia. Whereas on earth everything has changed, he becomes practically immortal and continues to circle like the gods, like the stars, like nuclear waste. Like so many events, of which he is the perfect illustration, that continue to circle in the empty space of news (*l'information*), without anyone being able or willing to bring them back into historical space. A perfect image of all those things that continue their uncompromising performance in orbit but have lost their identity along the way. Our history, for example, has also been lost along the way and revolves around us like an artificial satellite.

Nostalgia for the lost object? Not even that. Nostalgia had beauty because it retained within it the presentiment of what has taken place and could take place

again. It was as beautiful as utopia, of which it is the inverted mirror. It was beautiful for never being satisfied, as was utopia for never being achieved. The sublime reference to the origin in nostalgia is as beautiful as the reference to the end in utopia.
It is something else again to be confronted with *the literal manifestness of the end*
(of which we can no longer dream as end) and the literal manifestness of the origin
(of which we can no longer dream as origin). Now, we have the means today to put
into play both our origins and our end. We exhume our origins in archaeology,
reshape our original capital through genetics, and operationalize our dreams and the
wildest utopias by means of science and technology. We appease our nostalgia and
our utopian desires in situ and in vitro.

We are, then, unable to dream of a past or future state of things. Things are in a
state that is literally definitive—neither finished, nor infinite, nor definite, but definitive that is, deprived of its end. Now, the feeling that goes with a definitive state,
even a paradisiac one—is melancholic. Whereas, with mourning, things come to an
end and therefore enjoy a possibility of returning, with melancholia we are not even
left with the presentiment of an end or of a return, but only with *ressentiment* at
their disappearance. The crepuscular profile of the fin de siècle is more or less of this
order, combining the features of a linear order of progress and a regression, itself
also linear, of ends and values.

Against this general movement, there remains the completely improbable and, no
doubt, unverifiable hypothesis of a *poetic reversibility of events,* more or less the
only evidence for which is the existence of the same possibility in language.

The poetic form is not far removed from the chaotic form. Both flout the law of
cause and effect. If in chaos theory, for sensitivity to initial conditions we substitute
sensitivity to final conditions, we are in the form of predestination, which is the form
of fate *(le destin)*. Poetic language also lives with predestination, with the imminence
of its own ending and of reversibility between the ending and the beginning. It is predestined in this sense—it is an unconditional event, without meaning and consequence, which draws its whole being from the dizzying whirl of final resolution.

It is certainly not the form of our present history, and yet there is an affinity
between the immanence of poetic development and the immanence of the chaotic
development that is ours today, the unfolding of events that are themselves also
without meaning and consequence and in which—with effects substituting themselves for causes—there are no longer any causes, *but only effects.* The world is
there, *effectively.* There is no reason for this, and God is dead.

If nothing exists now but effects, we are in a state of total illusion (which is also
that of poetic language). If the effect is in the cause or the beginning in the end, then
the catastrophe is behind us. This reversing of the sign of catastrophe is the exceptional privilege of our age. It liberates us from any future catastrophe and from any
responsibility in that regard. The end of all anticipatory psychoses, all panic, all
remorse! The lost object is behind us. We are free of the Last Judgment.

What this brings us to, more or less, is a poetic, ironic analysis of events. Against
the simulation of a linear history "in progress," we have to accord a privileged status to these backfires, these malign deviations, these lightweight catastrophes that

cripple an empire much more effectively than any great upheavals. We have to accord a privileged status to all that has to do with nonlinearity, reversibility, all that is of the order not of an unfolding or an evolution, but of a winding back, a reversion in time. Anastrophe versus catastrophe. Perhaps, deep down, history has never unfolded in a linear fashion; perhaps language has never unfolded in a linear fashion. Everything moves in loops, tropes, inversions of meaning, except in numerical and artificial languages, which, for that very reason, *no longer are* languages. Everything occurs through effects that short-circuit their (metaleptic) causes, through the *Witze* of events, perverse events, ironic turnabouts, except within a rectified history, which, for just that reason, *is not* a history.

Might we not transpose language games onto social and historical phenomena: anagrams, acrostics, spoonerisms, rhyme, strophe and catastrophe? Not only the major figures of metaphor and metonymy, but the instant, puerile, formalistic games, the heteroclite tropes that are the delight of a vulgar imagination? Are there social spoonerisms, or an anagrammatic history (where meaning is dismembered and scattered to the winds, like the name of God in the anagram), rhyming forms of political action or events that can be read in either direction? In these times of a retroversion of history, the palindrome, that poetic, rigorous form of pal mode, could serve as a *grille de lecture* (might it not perhaps be necessary to replace Paul Viriho's dromology with a palmdromology?). And the anagram, that detailed process of unraveling, that sort of poetic and nonlinear convulsion of language—is there a chance that history lends itself to such a poetic convulsion, to such a subtle form of return and anaphora that, like the anagram, would—beyond meaning—allow the pure materiality of language to show through, and—beyond historical meaning—allow the pure materiality of time to show through?

Such would be the enchanted alternative to the linearity of history, the poetic alternative to the disenchanted confusion, the chaotic profusion of present events.

In this very way, we enter, beyond history, upon pure fiction, upon the illusion of the world. The illusion of our history opens onto *the greatly more radical illusion of the world*. Now that we have closed the eyelids of the Revolution, closed our eyes on the Revolution, now that we have broken down the Wall of Shame, now that the lips of protest are closed (with the sugar of history that melts on the tongue), now that Europe—and memories—are no longer haunted by the specter of communism, nor even by that of power, now that the aristocratic illusion of the origin and the democratic illusion of the end are increasingly receding, we no longer have the choice of advancing, of persevering in the present destruction, or of retreating, but only of facing up to this radical illusion.

NOTE

1. The French is retained here, since to translate this by the English term "dark trace screen" would be to forfeit the desired connection with the idea of absorption.

Chapter Twenty-Two

The Impending Computer Crisis of the Year 2000

Sandra Schanzer

"Catastrophe," "crisis," "disaster," "time bomb"—these words are being used in consumer and trade journalism to describe the potential trouble that awaits computer systems throughout the world as they begin to deal with the year 2000 and beyond. At worst, the 00 in the year 2000 will spell doom for many computer systems. At the very least, companies and computer users will have to spend an estimated $300 billion to $600 billion worldwide to make their systems able to handle the next millennium. The cost to the federal government alone may be as much as $30 billion. A report prepared by Software Productivity Research on the global economic impact of the year 2000 states, "The cost of fixing the Year 2000 problem . . . appears to constitute the most expensive single problem in human history."[1]

The nature of this horrendous year 2000 (or Y2K) problem is conceptually simple: the majority of older computer systems, as well as many newer ones, assume that all dates are in the twentieth century. They have been designed to store the year as two digits, that is, the year without the century. These computers and the programs that run on them will not be able to distinguish between years in the twentieth century and those in the twenty-first. Dates after December 31, 1999, either will not be allowed or will be handled incorrectly. And some computers systems have been programmed to see a year ending in 00 as a sign to stop processing. These problems will occur not only in computers but also in devices that depend on computer chips, such as phone and security systems and elevators.

What will we see as a result? Calculations that use dates will be incorrect. The meaning of dates will also be ambiguous. For example, computers will not be able to tell whether 02/15/01 is 1901 or 2001. A date like 02/15/01 (where it is supposed to mean February 15, 2001) may be summarily rejected as too early (if the computer sees it as 1901) or accepted and kept in the computer as February 15, 1901. Some systems may stop working altogether. Companies that produce off-the-shelf software will incur enormous costs to fix and distribute new versions of their software. Some of the smaller vendors may conclude that it is too expensive to make the changes and will decide to go out of business, stranding their customers with software that is no longer usable. Examples of the potential for trouble abound. Some problems will not crop up until just before or after the beginning of the year 2000, but many have already surfaced.

In inventory systems, for example, products often have a defined shelf life, after which they are discarded. Systems calculate the expiration date by taking the manufacturing date, adding the number of years of shelf life, and comparing the resulting year with the current year. If the resulting year is earlier than the current year, the item is outdated and is discarded. If, for example, the item has a five-year shelf life and was manufactured in 1993, the expiration year is 1998. In 1999 this item will be outdated, since 1998, the expiration year, is earlier than 1999. If the computer system stores only the two-digit year, because 98 is less than 99 the item is discarded correctly. And in 1997, 97 is not less than 98 so the item is kept, again correctly. But consider what happens to an item manufactured in 1996 if the system keeps only the two-digit year. The real expiration date is 2001. However, in 1997, when the computer compares the two-digit expiration year of 01 with 97, 01 is less than 97, so the item will be discarded incorrectly years before its true expiration date.

For some companies, banks that issue long-term loans, for example, the nature of their business means at least some of their systems have always had to recognize the century. For others, problems of the year 2000 surfaced in the mid-1990s, and these organizations have had to deal with them half a decade before the next millennium. Credit card expirations, insurance policies, and forecasting systems have already been affected, since they use future dates. Some of these companies, unable to handle dates after 1999, have had to change their business practices, for example by issuing shorter-term policies, to avoid having to process later dates. Most businesses, however, have not yet felt the full impact of the coming millennium.

By 1999 all systems that calculate a future date will be affected. Accounts receivable and accounts payable systems will confront major problems as due dates and payable dates roll into the new century. In the year 2000, dates that are calculated backward will also be affected. Take, for example, an open invoice from the year 1999 that the system is aging in the year 2000. If the year is only two digits long, the system cannot tell that the current year is 2000 and not 1900. The aging calculation will show an invoice that is ninety-nine years old. And since that is certainly uncollectible, the system will write it off as a bad debt. In this way large amounts of receivables will be written off and companies will have severely restricted cash flow. Interest calculations on loans will be similarly mishandled, since a system with the Y2K problem will show that interest is due, not for the past year, but for the past −99 (00–99) years. Systems that generate bad-debt reports for credit bureaus will report large numbers of loans and their customers as bad risks.

In September 1996 Senator Daniel Patrick Moynihan proposed legislation to set up a national commission to examine the problem as it affects federal and state agencies and to provide recommendations on resolving it. Among the concerns to be addressed are the consequences if the corrections are not made on time: What agencies are at risk of not being able to perform basic services? and What happens to the United States economy if the problem is not resolved by mid-1999?

There are three causes of the year 2000 problem: historical, psychological, and managerial.

The Historical Reason

The problem has its roots in the early days of business computing, in the 1960s, when data was entered into the computer from punched cards. Each card could hold eighty characters of data. The cards were time-consuming to punch and awkward to handle, so the fewer cards used the better. Since the year 2000 was so far away, its existence was basically unimaginable. Clearly, the century of interest to business in almost every case was the twentieth; therefore, 19 did not have to be punched. In fact, with clever manipulation, a six-character date could be expressed in three characters, saving even more space.

Computer memory was also extremely limited. Memory is used to store both the programs as they are being executed and the data being worked on. In the 1960s major processing systems were run on computers that sometimes had as few as twenty-four thousand characters of memory. (In contrast, today's PCs have at least one hundred times as much memory). Again, space was at a premium. Data was stored on tapes, and these were inherently slow to use. Even when disks began to replace tapes, disk capacity was limited. All these factors meant that the fewer characters that had to be stored and processed, the more efficient the systems. This was true even when punched cards were replaced by data-entry terminals. An obvious way to save on storage was to eliminate the century, so it continued to be excluded. The practice continued even when memory, disk storage capacity, and processing speed increased. Dates without the century became the standard in all levels of computer design: in hardware, software, reports, and screens. We are now going to pay for that history.

The Psychological Reason

We are not accustomed to writing the century as part of dates. Forms we fill out and, of course, computer screens, present the date as mm/dd/yy, and that feels comfortable and natural. If there is any ambiguity in the date shown in this way, we can resolve the problem mentally. *Computers have no ability to deal with ambiguity,* yet the use of the two-digit date did not take this difference into account.

The upcoming millennium has always been seen as a distant, almost unreal event, too indistinct to think about and plan for. Because it was so far away, there would be time, in some undefined future, to resolve the problem. Furthermore, because the computer world changes so extensively and so quickly, there has also been a conviction that any computer system at risk would be replaced by a newer one sometime before the year 2000, and so it was not worth thinking about the problem now—whenever *now* was. When the time came, the problems would be resolved somehow. Computer systems have, however, proven to be far more long-lasting than expected. Of course, systems were set up that could handle the next century, but the fact that vast numbers of systems could not testifies to the pervasiveness of this feeling. For example, as late as 1995, personal computers whose internal calendars did not change correctly from December 1999 to January 2000 were still being shipped, and basic operating software for some of the most widely used large computers was still not completely able to handle the new century.

It was not until September 1996 that Senator Moynihan introduced his proposal for a national commission on Y2K. The commission was to report by the end of 1997, with the goal of making all agencies Y2K compliant by January 1999.

Much of Europe and the Far East seems to be even less Y2K aware than the United States. A Danish participant on an Internet discussion of Y2K wondered if this was just an American problem, not because Danish systems were all Y2K compliant, but merely because the United States was somehow in a special situation. He was assured that this was indeed a worldwide issue.

The Managerial Reason

Finally, the nature and management of the computer environment (information technology or IT) have been responsible for making the other two factors a reality. From the beginning of the computer revolution in the 1960s, computer departments have been under enormous pressure. They have been faced with ever-changing and ever more complex hardware, constant demands for new and enhanced computer systems, and overworked staff. A report in *Computerworld*,[2] a major trade journal, describes the frantic working conditions in many computer departments, where the staff routinely works fifty and more hours a week to keep up with company and market demands. In addition, budgets to support the continuing high costs for hardware and a highly skilled technical staff, and for training and support are not easy to justify to upper management. Most important, although computers themselves are precise, mechanical, and scientific, computer systems and programs are extremely complicated, somewhat exotic, and unpredictable.

Management of computer projects and departments, therefore, has always been a difficult task. With an overburdened and highly stressed staff, facing budgetary pressures, deadlines, and the threat that components of systems will fail, the goal of IT departments has been to deal with current priorities and problems and to meet upper management's expectations. Until recently, when the actuality of Y2K came to the fore, setting standards to handle the year 2000, making sure hardware and software could store a four-digit date, and retrofitting existing systems to make them year 2000 compliant have not been of immediate importance and so have been generally ignored. It is only in the past few years that management has started to think seriously about the implications of the new millennium for their systems. As late as 1996 many companies were first establishing task forces to analyze and deal with the Y2K, and others have not yet taken that first step.

In the computer world the nature of the year 2000 problem is unique. The deadline is absolutely fixed. It is not within anybody's control and does not allow slippage. Most computer departments and organizations have never had to deal with such a situation. Even a major company such as Microsoft is often late in getting its products to market. Computer departments are notorious for missing deadlines, often by months or even years. To meet these deadlines, the features of a system are often simplified and quality sacrificed. A colleague has described a computer department whose upgrade to an accounting system was months late and which had been given an absolutely final extension to a date that was six months later than the original. The design was scaled back to eliminate all functions that could not be finished on time. Project management was told in confidence to ignore good programming and design techniques if they would increase the time the project would take. The only goal was to deliver some semblance of a system by the new deadline.

Obviously, the year 2000 is different. The time frame cannot be changed, and components cannot be eliminated because they are inconvenient. In fact, there is a series of deadlines, each determined by the nature of the dates involved, as discussed earlier. Because of the complex nature of computer systems and their management, and sometimes because of poor management, computer departments do not have a good track record in handling such situations.

The Y2K problem will challenge even the finest management. For every computer program that is not definitively known to be year 2000 compliant, *every* date has to be found and examined. Once a problem date has been found, some way has to be devised to fix it. The date must be held and interpreted correctly within the computer. Every screen and every report that shows a date must also be checked and fixed. Millions of computer programs and hundreds of millions, even billions, of lines of computer code are involved. The effort will be enormous in terms of person-hours and cost. For example, in 1995 the Union Pacific Railroad estimated that it would take two hundred thousand person-hours or *one hundred person-years* just to modify its mainframe systems.[3]

Dates are everywhere in computer systems, and it is not always clear when something is a date. If you look at a list of items and you see one labeled "Birthdate" or "Expiration_Date" or it looks like 10/22/95 or Oct. 22, 95 you can assume you are looking at a date. But if something is called "StopIt" or "b" or appears as 952210 or as JV5 (J is the tenth letter of the alphabet and stands for October, V is the twenty-second letter of the alphabet, and 5 is the last character of 95), it is not so apparent that it also represents a date. Yet each must be identified.

These dates are used on computers that may not be able to handle the four-digit date without major changes in their basic operating systems (which underlie all programs and processing), or on computers that are no longer made. They are in computer files that may have vast numbers of records and are used in computer programs that are written in hundreds of computer languages. The vast majority of programs are written in common programming languages such as COBOL and Basic, but some are in languages that are known by only a few people or are so old that almost no one can program in them anymore.

The code that a programmer writes in these languages is called the source code. It is translated for the computer into machine language called object code. A person familiar with the language can read the source code, understand it, and change it, but without the source code it is extraordinarily difficult, and often impossible, to change a program. Since the computer runs on the object code, however, the source code is not necessary for the program to operate; in some cases the source code for programs that are still being used has been lost. In most cases the source code is available. However, documentation that is essential to understand the program, the steps within it, and its relations to other programs is more likely to have been lost or to be outdated.

Because of the complexity of the computing environment in large corporations, computer departments often do not have complete catalogs or knowledge of their own systems. Some programs and systems may run without anyone understanding exactly what they do or how they interact with and impact other systems. A knowledgeable staff can compensate for some of these deficiencies. Normal staff turnover naturally means that this information becomes attenuated as time passes, but the recent surge of company layoffs and mergers has exacerbated the problem by accelerating the loss of experienced staff.

Large corporations have substantial computer departments, and their primary responsibility and interest traditionally lies with their large, mainframe systems. However, since personal computers have become widespread, these organizations often have many smaller systems that have been created by the end users themselves. These can be of major importance to the business and are even less controlled than the mainframe systems. They are likely to have been created by people who are no longer with the company or by outside sources. They too are written in many languages and are often less sophisticated in their use of standards, documentation, and good design than the mainframe programs. The managers of these departments, who are business people rather than computer people, do not understand the computer aspects of their systems either. People interviewed for this essay who are responsible for year 2000 projects and who work for large organizations frequently stated that they had given little thought to the smaller systems in their companies.

The same scenario is found in smaller organizations, which usually employ few or no computer professionals. Individuals are affected as well. Both small companies and individuals generally rely on products purchased from software vendors or designed by users and consultants. They have little understanding of the complexities of their hardware and software. Yet, their systems are as much affected by Y2K as are the larger ones. Since there is no technically trained computer staff and little money to hire consultants, their problems will loom ever larger as the new millennium approaches.

So what do we have? Huge numbers of data files and lines of source code that have to be found, evaluated, and modified by an unalterable deadline, even when the computers and languages are obscure and source code and documentation are out of date or missing. All this must be done while normal computer work continues.

To accomplish this, people, software, and additional computer capacity are needed. This translates into the very high costs already mentioned. Computer departments have always had an insatiable need for more money and have always had to fight for adequate budgets. Government computer budgets have been even more inadequate, and the current trend to downsizing government spending is decreasing computer budgets as well. Yet the demand is for even more money, *for which the organization will see no tangible return.* The only promise is that the money will enable computer systems to continue to operate as they do now. A confidential source, a person who works in a large, sophisticated organization, reported that the IT staff was told to plan to deal with the year 2000 without any additional money or personnel, to fit it in along with their other tasks. Yet, time and energy are not infinitely expandable; sometime before the new millennium begins, some things will have to be left undone.

In addition, once changes are made to computer programs and systems, they must be thoroughly tested, to assure both that they still work as they did before and that the changes do what they are supposed to do. One estimate is that for every three thousand lines of code that are changed, one error is introduced into the program or system. Testing programs and systems is inexact, extremely time-consuming, and difficult. It has been so since the beginning. One author contended a number of years ago that a program cannot ever be tested completely and that the best one could do was to set up methodical tests that would catch the majority of errors.[4] The difficulty has not lessened since then, and it is exacerbated by the fact that, even under optimum conditions, there is never enough time to test adequately.

An interesting illustration of the difficulty of testing completely was provided by a problem with Italian bank automatic teller machines in 1990. The machines had been performing correctly until then, and there was no reason to suspect that 1990 would be any different. However, at the beginning of 1990 an error, a bug, surfaced. Although the machines would still dispense money, they no longer debited the customer's account for the amount of the withdrawal. It seems that the software could interpret years only up to 1989, so it read 1990 as 198-A and then did not know how to process the transactions properly.

Besides effort and time, testing requires computers on which to run the tests. Few companies have much computer capacity to spare. If they have to make a copy of a system in order to test it, they must have additional storage capacity to hold the data. And they may need extra computers on which to run the tests. Finally, they need people to execute the tests and verify the results.

Where are these resources to come from? Companies can have their staff work even longer hours, with the result that work that needs clear and logical thinking will be done by ever more tired and overworked people. Organizations can also postpone normal work while dealing with the year 2000, thus reducing their ability to respond to current needs or managerial demands. They can hire additional staff or contract the work to outside vendors. However, experienced personnel may not be available. They will certainly be expensive as the competition for their services increases. The staffing problem may be even worse for governments, since salaries for computer-related jobs are usually lower there than in private industry. Staff will be harder to keep as organizations raid each other for experienced Y2K personnel. Training novices to do some of the work is possible, but companies would then be relying on inexperienced people to carry out tasks crucial to the business.

Organizations can purchase software that has been developed recently to help find and, perhaps, fix noncompliant dates, though automated fixes will be incomplete. This assumes that the diagnostic software itself has been thoroughly tested. Even this software will not be able to find all dates, leaving open the really difficult and important question of which ones they missed.

In 1996, denial regarding Y2K began to lessen. Technical conferences, journals, consulting firms, and diagnostic software for the Y2K began to proliferate. Corporations and governments started to pay increased attention to the problem, though their focus is on their large-scale systems. Some began the actual Y2K work. Even more at least established task forces to provide direction to those responsible for making the changes. Yet, in October 1996 four major California agencies, including the Department of Transportation, had just hired a consulting firm to do "initial assessment and planning for Year 2000."[5]

As organizations tackle the year 2000 problem, they are formulating strategies. They must first assess the scope of their date problem, which means not only examining their programs but also understanding what the programs and systems really do. They must also make staffing decisions: hire additional people (who may not be needed once the problem is resolved), contract with consultants to provide additional personnel, or turn the job over to the consulting firms that have expanded or been established specifically for Y2K. Often, they are not waiting for the assessment phase to be complete, but instead, to save time, are tackling the critical systems as soon as possible. And they are making budget proposals.

Few of these task forces are dealing with systems created by end users or with personal computers. When asked, task force members often say they have not thought about this aspect of the problem. In some cases internal newsletters and meetings have begun to mention Y2K, but little support and guidance is being given to the users.

As organizations proceed, they have to choose how to handle each system. Each alternative has risks and will require testing, with all the problems inherent in the testing process. If there is enough time and enough staff they can leave a system basically intact but change it to be year 2000 compliant. If the changes affect structural aspects of the system, especially the data files, testing will have to be extremely comprehensive. Alternatively, they can rewrite the system, perhaps in a newer language and on state-of-the art hardware, and make the design year 2000 compliant. Some companies had planned to rewrite their systems anyway because of other business needs, and by insisting that the new versions be Y2K compliant they are, in effect, getting their "fix" for nothing. Yet, these are in essence new systems and require as extensive testing as if they were totally new. In addition, the rewritten systems need a shakedown period before they run smoothly, as operators and users get familiar with the processes and results. If an organization rewrites many of its systems within a short time, say between 1996 and 1999, it may be faced with an additional problem, that of having to manage too many new areas at once.

As pressures increase and the beginning of the new millennium nears, organizations may resort to drastic, triage-like measures, such as fixing critical parts of a system but discarding functions that seem less important. This tactic may simplify the Y2K fix, but it introduces its own complexity: discarding parts of a system means that the reduced system will have to tested to see not only that the changes are correct but also that the absence of the sections that were eliminated does not have an adverse effect on remaining areas. They may also discard a system entirely because it is judged unnecessary or too difficult to change in a cost-efficient and timely manner. It is likely that this tactic will also create its own problems, since some of the discarded systems will turn out to have been needed.

Small companies, except those that are already affected by the year 2000, are generally not doing anything at all. For all the current publicity, they have only a vague idea of how the problem will affect them and what they will have to do to solve it. When they finally have to face the year 2000, their lack of time, technical expertise, and money will profoundly affect the stability of their businesses.

There are many ways in which the problem can fail to be resolved. Some have already been mentioned, but it is worthwhile repeating them here.

The process can fail because an organization's efforts fail, for example,

- some dates are not identified
- programming changes do not work
- rewritten systems have too many bugs, do not work well, or do not match the functionality of the old ones
- testing is inadequate and does not catch the errors
- training is inadequate, so people do not use the new/changed systems correctly
- computer departments and users are unable to deal with too many changes at one time
- small systems are not fixed
- Time runs out

Or because the Y2K efforts at other organizations with which an organization does business or on which it relies for computer services fail, for example,

- vendors of software packages do not change their software, do not have the ability to distribute it, or do not provide a way to upgrade older versions of the software to the new version
- consultants responsible for an organization's software do not make the changes
- suppliers or customers fail to become year 2000 compliant, so they cannot provide materiel or cannot pay their bills, or they go out of business
- governments or multinational corporations fail to complete the process on time (it is sobering to remember that government projects are notorious for poor management and missed deadlines)

In the event of failure, what will we see? Companies will go out of business or have sharply reduced earnings. In addition, they may face severe legal liability for not having resolved the year 2000 problem on time. Government agencies will not be able to function properly. In the worst-case scenario, the effects of Y2K failures will propagate throughout the global economy and everyone will be harmed.

If the year 2000 problem is solved successfully worldwide, the beginning of that new year will be a cause for celebration, and our lives will not be adversely affected.

If, however, as is far more likely, the problem has not been fixed, the impact on our business and personal lives will be profound. The odds that all significant components of this highly intricate problem will be corrected on time are low. As the year 2000 deadline draws nearer (this will generally be no later than sometime in

1999, since most systems deal at some point with dates that are one year in the future), organizations will try to devote increasing resources to the problem. But as Frederick Brooks, Jr., wrote in *The Mythical Man-Month*, you cannot always shorten the time a project takes by adding resources to it. "The bearing of a child takes nine months, no matter how many women are assigned.[6]" And, he continued, adding people to a late project makes it later, since you have to take people who are already involved with the project away from their work to train the newcomers and you have also increased the number of lines of communication within the project.[7]

Despite the skepticism of many people who are actively involved in the Y2K problem, it is possible that the obstacles will be overcome and the year 2000 problem will be, for the most part, just a momentary, if expensive, concern. However, no matter how thoroughly and effectively the year 2000 challenge is met, some problems will surely arise. All systems, and computer systems especially, are subject to unforeseen outcomes. In *Systemantics*, John Gall pointed out that when systems do not perform as they were designed, they usually perform in worse, not better, ways.[8] One of his examples was the huge hangar at Cape Canaveral that was designed to protect NASA's rockets from the weather. Unfortunately, that building was so large that it generated its own weather, so that it would rain and be cloudy inside while it was dry and clear outside. So also with computer systems: they often do not perform as designed, but the actual performance is rarely an improvement.

Even more important in the world of computers is Murphy's Law, which says that if anything can go wrong, it will, and at the worst possible time. In other words, jbread always falls jelly side down. As computer systems struggle to meet the challenge of the new millennium, we can be sure that Murphy will be there, trying his best to push the bread off the table.

NOTES

1. "The Global Economic Impact of the Year 2000 Software Problem," report, Software Productivity Research, Burlington, Mass., 1996.

2. *Computerworld*, October 21, 1996.

3. *Datamation*, January 1, 1996, 39.

4. Glenford Myers, *The Art of Software Testing*. (New York: John Wiley, 1979).

5. *Computerworld*, October 21, 1996, 2.

6. Frederick P. Brooks, Jr., *The Mythical Man-Month: Essays on Software Engineering*, anniv. ed. (Chapel Hill: University of North Carolina Press, 1995), 17.

7. Ibid., 275.

8. John Gall, *Systemantics: How Systems Really Work and Why They Fail* (Ann Arbor, Mich.: General Systemantics Press, 1977).

Chapter Twenty-Three

Millennium, Texas

Michael Erard

In the bigger cities of Texas, as in other metropolitan areas of America, the rhetoric of the end of the millennium is raining down. But in the quiet, small town of Alpine, no one reads the bold vision of fashion pullouts from the Sunday *New York Times:*

> Wars are fought by e-mail. Handguns are only in museums. All sex is safe. America is back on its feet. The year is 2020.

In the newspaper in Alpine, perched in the vast, rocky, inhospitable Chihuahuan desert of West Texas, there are no career opportunity ads, as in an Austin, Texas, newspaper:

> In the New Millennium we are all explorers. It's just that some of us are bolder. As the world turns toward the new millennium, you'll find that S——— is already there. Our hands-on role in semiconductor technologies continues to redefine global strategies into the next century.

In Alpine, one can't go to the Café Armageddon, an Austin restaurant that is "open every day until the end of the world." And walking on the streets of Alpine, one finds no flyers saying,

> As we approach the end of the millennium, Christians are awaiting the Christ, Jews— the Messiah, Hindus—Lord Krishna, Buddhists—Maitreya Buddha or the 5th Buddha, and Moslems are expecting the Iman Mahdi or the Messiah.

One does, however, hear opinions like this:

> I hope the world ends long after I'm dead, because I'm gonna be really *pissed off* if the Four Horsemen come riding down the street and all that shit's true. If that happens I'm gonna desperately search for the Dalai Lama and say, "YOU LIED!" [More quietly] I like the Dalai Lama. But Tibetan Buddhism is quite a bit different than Christianity and its outlook on what happens to you after you die.

Alpine, Texas, population 5,637, is a county seat and a hub of commerce, transport, and law enforcement in the southwestern area of the state called the Big Bend. When I lived in Alpine during the summer of 1995, I found a quiet, traditional, and insular town, but one neither closed nor insulated. There is one one-screen movie theater, a radio station, two video rental places, and a weekly newspaper, the *Avalanche*; in order to watch television, you have to have cable. Residents are aware of events and trends in the world, but they do not see themselves participating in that world, because they consider Alpine to be a special place, in the world yet not of it. The ethnic composition is more or less evenly divided between Anglos and Hispanics, and tensions used to run high between them but relations now are mostly peaceful. The people are friendly and helpful, more realistic and practical than simply conservative. Because of the state university there, the town is accustomed to the presence of temporary residents from other places; the economy relies on tourism as well as a robust trucking industry and the railroad, so the residents of Alpine are open to passers-through too, and in fact many residents are not natives— the clean air, the mountains, the climate, and a certain undefinable, almost geological, quality of stability have encouraged retirees, artists, and loners to become permanent residents. These immigrants have not imposed their ways on the town, but they have enriched it culturally.

When I talked to the residents of Alpine about the meanings of the year 2000, they did talk about Jesus, Ross Perot and the One World Government, floating cars, cities without streets, computers that control houses, and living on the moon. But they also talked about local events, personal fears, and concrete experiences. In fact, I found multiple attitudes, feelings, and beliefs about the year 2000 in Alpine, a diversity that is worthy of comment and analysis. As Charles Strozier cautioned about the study of apocalyptic sensibilities, "To note only the eternal aspects of endism may prevent an appreciation for its more specific historical manifestations, compromising in the process specific moral and psychological insights."[1] Similarly, I would argue that one locates American voices solely within the rhetoric of overarching fictions, visions, images, and promises at the risk of ignoring other facets of the end of the millennium.

One important consideration is the possibility of outright resistance to ideas about the year 2000. The anarchist Hakim Bey wrote in a broadsheet entitled "The End of the World":

> The A.O.A [Association of Ontological Anarchists] declares itself officially *bored* with the End of the World. . . . Are these dreary ballads not simply mirror-images of all those lies & platitudes about Progress & the Future, beamed from every loudspeaker, zapped like paranoid brain-waves from every schoolbook & the TV in the world of the Consensus? The thanatosis of the Hip Millenarians extrudes itself like pus from the false *health* of the Consumers' & Workers' Paradises.[2]

Colorful, at times rhetorically extreme, and rare, Bey's opinions are a reminder that it is possible to question our fascination with 2000.

The year 2000 is now close, and conceivably so. That fact, I will argue, influences how people think and talk about the end of the millennium, and it is the reason why, as 2000 approaches, the various fevers and fervors will cool, not intensify.

Compared to widely held views of the end of the world, local events point more directly toward people's fears and are accessible and debatable within local frameworks of meaning. Consider, for instance, the significance of the 5.8 earthquake that rattled the Big Bend in April of 1995. Damage to buildings was slight. But seismic activity had not been a major threat in the Big Bend—not a threat at all, in local minds—and the earthquake unsettled a lot of people. In Alpine, end-of-the-millennium talk never subsumed the earthquake; rather, many residents brought up the earthquake when I asked them about their end-time feelings. April Rivera, fifteen years old, said, "The first time I ever thought the world was gonna end was when the earthquake hit. That's when I thought we were all gonna die. I thought it was just gonna keep on going and going on and wouldn't stop." Her friend, Jesse Torino, also 15, was in the shower. "It was badass," he said with a half-grin. "I always wanted to be in an earthquake, tornado, something like that. I ran outside with no clothes on. I didn't think I was gonna die. To me, it was pretty cool." Local events were rarely fit into an end-time–apocalyptic framework without first being related to other local events. Lucy Escovedo, age twenty-six, has a sister who belongs to the Apostolic church in town. "Like we never used to have earthquakes here," Escovedo told me. "My sister says, see, there are so many signs about the world ending." Escovedo, an off-and-on Catholic, said, "I know myself too that it's changing, things are happening that never used to happen that much, like tornadoes. A tornado by Alpine. There was never tornadoes around here! I think a tornado would definitely destroy this town, big time. Cause we're surrounded by mountains." To her, the world at large is implicitly destroyed when Alpine is destroyed. Some residents questioned how the earthquake was used as a sign for the end. Lauren Sharp, age forty-three, has worked at the *Avalanche* for four years as a layout editor and reporter. She mock-reported one woman's response to the earthquake. "After the earthquake, she called her daughter up, who wasn't home, because she was at a prayer meeting. When she talked to the daughter, the daughter said, 'I wondered if it was the end of the world, if it was the Reckoning, and Jesus was coming—but then I realized, I didn't hear any trumpets.' And *this woman was serious.*"

Furthermore, some recent technological developments in Alpine have already happened in other parts of the country. In 1995, three cellular phone businesses opened, and the ranch pickups now sport car phones as they drive through town. Despite these recent advances, some fear that Alpine is unable to prepare its children for the world. "I feel like our little area of Texas is behind. And I really want these kids to jump forth," said Sherrie Eppenauer, a kindergarten teacher. On the other hand, the university's new computerized catalog system is supposedly one of the most advanced. (Citizens are baffled, though. Eppenauer reported that she couldn't find the card catalog one day. "I asked, 'Where'd y'all put the card catalog?' And the librarian looked at me and she goes, 'Well there's the computer!'")

A more urban reality has been introduced, too. When I first visited the town, an elderly docent at the Museum of the Big Bend proudly crowed, "Alpine's got zee-roww crime!" At the end of May 1995, an altercation between two men started with fists and ended with gunfire and was called "Alpine's first drive-by shooting." Whether or not it was a "real" drive-by was debated all summer, but the incident introduced the possibility that the placid town had more in common with urban areas than its boosterism about its low crime rate would admit.

Finally, increased licit traffic from Mexico as a result of the North American Free Trade Agreement (NAFTA), as well as a constant stream of illicit traffic in drugs and illegal aliens, has made Alpine's residents increasingly aware of border issues. A proposed north-south interstate highway fifteen miles west of the town has waked them up to a world creeping inexorably in upon what many of them perceive as a paradise. The end of Alpine *is* the end of the world. Thus the potential effects of change, the uncertainty of the future, and the question of Alpine's future are on everyone's minds.

I went to Alpine to ask the following question: What does the year 2000 mean in a small West Texas town? The variety of answers made me conclude that the end of the second millennium and the beginning of the third evokes an impressively dispersed set of feelings and meanings, more loosely held than I had previously thought. I didn't hear everyone in Alpine, so the real scope of feelings and meanings is even more wide-ranging than I can discuss here. For people that I spoke with, the year 2000 is indeed a meaningful saeculum, an arbitrary chronological division invested with deep significance and feelings. But it is less successfully a cultural commodity used to package certain political, ideological, and commercial products. I myself had particular ideas about the year 2000 and expected that these were shared by others. What I found in Alpine in 1995 is that the end of the millennium and the sense of the future are both also continually reinvented personal understandings based on the content of everyday life and individuals' experiences of moving through time.

In Alpine I found people negotiating millennial issues through their lived lives. This knot of the abstract and the concrete appeared many times. A young woman who is afraid of the end of the world gets married and has children. A paradox? A minister questions apocalyptic thinking. Unorthodoxy? Someone sees through the saeculum's contingency, yet attributes social consequences to its approach. A contradiction? A professor notes that fin de siècle malaise is a privilege of the elite. Revolutionary, cynical? I would argue not. Rather, people are ambivalent about a future laid out before them like a glittering city, for the simple fact that they know there was yesterday, there is today, and there is likely to be a tomorrow, and that the future is nothing more than a string of todays sandwiched between what is known and what is not.

A police scanner, what Paul Kime would call his connection to "the insidious activities of the State," sits on a shelf in his art and curio gallery. The scanner is always on, frequently interrupting conversation with blasts of static and police transmissions. Kime is fifty-four years old, stocky, white-haired, often dressed in a cowboy shirt and boots. His gallery is stocked with his paintings of white buffalo on the horizon, cloud formations in the shape of a stampeding herd of longhorn cattle, a lone Indian in a forest clearing, and other scenes from a mythologized and commercialized West. I had been visiting his gallery, the Rusty Spur, for weeks. Finally he agreed to put up the CLOSED sign for half an hour. As we talked, I was surprised to hear how sympathetic he was toward the antifederalism that had motivated Tim McVeigh and Terry Nichols allegedly to explode a bomb in Oklahoma City five months earlier. Kime blamed the federal government for the deaths of innocent civilians in the blast. "Why was the daycare center there?" he asked. "Why . . . was this little organization of government . . . tucked in the middle of all these, like they're hidin' behind women's skirts or something?"

Kime was frustrated with the way he perceived the federal government to be growing.

> If you'll look into the housing industries and the building industry and all, and every-thing is having its problems mainly because of government interference. It's just all pointin' at government control. It has never worked in any other country, and it won't work here except for the downfall of the country. It's just like any other government in China or Japan or Germany where people have no freedom. They're getting more into our pockets all the time. It just scares me more and more every day. It's just like a creep-ing amoeba or something, like a giant amoeba coming up on us.

He has seen many attempts to change civic life in Alpine, and he has been left bitter and cynical by their failure. Sometime in the near future, he plans to retreat to a piece of desert property, the location of which he would not disclose. He dreamed the dream of self-sufficiency.

> If you're gonna have any law of protection you have to have yer own perimeter and say, "This is mine, stay out. I run it like I want to. Don't come in. Don't even open my gate, don't come up here." They can't freeze you out by saying, "We won't feed you then, we won't let you have food," well, you raise your own food. Or, "We'll cut off yer elec-tricity." Fine, cut it off. I got my own electricity. I got my own water. I'm just trying to protect me and mine. I'm not tryin' to mind anybody else's business, or takin' anything away from anybody or anything that I don't feel is mine and my family's deserve here on this earth. We deserve this kind of life and unbothered and unmolested by govern-ment officials that want to tear into people, and we're the kind of people they like to prey on.

As soon as he can find this piece of land, his gate will be closed, Kime said. If he can do it, before 2000.

Around the corner and down the street from Kime's store is the Presbyterian church, where Ed Waddill, sixty-four years old, is the minister, like his father before him. When I arrive at the church office, he is outside smoking one of the few ciga-rettes that he allows himself. "I would hope that smoking is not a part of my future," he said, laughing. "It looks like it is receding, and it makes me really happy." He gets his sense of the future not from his religious beliefs but from a technological dream, what the American space program once was:

> One of the things that greatly interested me about the whole space thing: it's not just a matter of sending people to the moon, or sending them up in the shuttle. Because what is increasing is all of this vast knowledge and ability to discover new medicine. To dis-cover new ways of feeding people. There's so many spinoffs in terms of other tech-nologies and other things that are so everlastingly beneficial to human beings. You're constantly running into products and news of products of various kinds that have come about because of the whole space technology. Everything. Computers, laser technolo-gy, everything right down to freeze-dried trail mix.

Unfortunately this vision ended for him with the explosion of the space shuttle Challenger. "All of a sudden, I thought, man, somebody's gotten way off the track here. This is not going well." Waddill was emotionally devastated. "Up to that time, I had seen the whole space program as a beam of shining light. Something that everybody can feel proud of and hopeful about. I saw the inception of that era as being absolutely packed full of promise." And then the accident. "I just felt . . . I felt the whole program might crash and burn. I thought they never would quit showing it on television. It just about killed me every time I watched it."

An amateur historian, Waddill disputed the notion that eras could be meaningfully divided with one date. It is possible, he argued, that the nineteenth century did not end until 1917; but the twentieth century was well introduced in the 1880s. To him, eras and chronological divisions were distinct. "I think the twenty-first century holds out a tremendous amount of promise. I definitely am excited for whoever is around to live," he said. Does 2000 usher in this age of promise? No.

Lucy Escovedo, twenty-five years old and a part-time receptionist at the Chamber of Commerce, imagines a future populated by labor-saving devices: a folding electric car easy to park in urban spaces, a smart refrigerator that tells the homeowner what she needs to buy, an energy efficient house that stays at the "perfect temperature." She was sure that these items would be in production, "maybe a few years before the year 2000." She added: "I think they'll be affordable. That's how I see it. I hope they're not that expensive." "Because you'd want one?" I asked. "Yes," she said bashfully. Such machines would reduce her domestic responsibilities after a hard day at the office. "That's why we don't even make food at home anymore," she said. "I like things fast. Easy. I like simple ways. There's no sense in killing yourself over hard work if you can do it an easier way, you know. Get it over and done with. And move to something else."

Escovedo is caught. She wants to join the American mainstream and get a computer, but she is also pulled to meet traditional Mexican-American obligations such as taking care of her older relatives. The result is a compromise: she will participate in the technological future only as it helps her to help her family, particularly her uncle and her grandmother. "I know my uncle forgets things, he'll buy stuff from the grocery that he already has there." If he had a smart refrigerator, "he could just go the refrigerator, get the stuff out, you know, and maybe he can focus on other little things." Already, machines more mundane than smart houses and talking appliances have had an impact on her relationships:

> I found it hard to leave my house in the same lot, because my grandmother is there, my mom is there, and I have to keep them both together so that I can know what they're both doing. And it was very hard when I moved from my house just a few feet to the new trailer we had gotten, when I got married. I thought, well, I'm just moving a few feet away, but we were so in touch, my grandmother and I, that I got depressed for like two weeks. I almost moved back. Now we have intercoms, to each house, and we have different phone numbers in each house so we can call each other.

The Alpine phone book lists eleven churches; at least four more by my count should be added to it. In each assembly, diverse meanings about the year 2000, the Second Coming of Jesus Christ, and the end of the world are taught and preached. At Linda Garcia's Apostolic church, the year 2000 is not the date for the end of the world. "Biblically," she said, "There is not a day, or an exact date, as such, for when God is coming. So we don't know. We walk by faith." She is Lucy Escovedo's sister, twenty-four years old; like her sister, she is married, has a child, is bilingual, and works at the Chamber of Commerce. "No one knows the time or the day when God is coming," she said. "You just have to be prepared. You have to live your life godly, 'cause biblically it says without holiness, no man shall see God. So we just believe in living right, till the day he comes." Living right is believing in the Bible's literal word and keeping the physical body holy in preparation for a heavenly transformation. From Garcia's own description, her adolescence was a tumult of truancy, drugs, alcohol, and sex, and now in the strict boundaries of her church—there is no smoking, drinking, dancing, or immodesty, and women always wear dresses and do not cut their hair—she seems to find comfort.

In her belief, the year 2000 is not a date for the Second Coming, though it marks the nearing of the end time. Unlike her fellow townspeople whom I interviewed, Garcia reads the signs of the coming end in the media she consumes. "Thousands of five year old girls get raped. . . . you hear about it constantly in the newspaper, if you just look, constantly you're seeing them being raped," she asserted. Other signs of the end are crime, immodesty, welfare fraud, violence against women, illegal immigration. She said, "Every year there has been an increase on everything: murder, rape, suicides. Social workers haven't helped. Things are getting worse." On the other hand, change can be local, day-by-day, focused on individuals. She believes that "if you do something for one person, it's better than you not doing anything. If you could change one person to believe that there is a God, to believe that you can live a better life . . . so if it's just one that'll change, I mean, that's better than none."

The Presbyterian minister, Ed Waddill, has no problem avoiding ideas like Garcia's; they depress him. He thought it sad that people would decide that their only solution was to hope for an end. He said, "I figure that God created me to live and work and be concerned about life on the earth. And where Jesus comes down, in so many words, is to say, 'Don't worry about this thing. There's no way you can know that. God knows. So forget it.'"

I found secular apocalyptic sensibilities to be more prevalent than religious ones. One kind of end was a national decline, a kind of chronic moral rot that Paul Kime described and that others feared as well. "I've always thought of America as a very strong, united country, and I am worried about this U.N. and this one government situation developing," said Sherrie Eppenauer, forty-eight, who has taught kindergarten for twenty years in a nearby town and who has dozens of alarming stories about her changing student body. Based on her experiences, her outlook for the future is largely pessimistic. "I'm already worried about what the world will be like when my daughter has children. I worry what my grandchildren will face. And I feel like America's losing its footholds so fast, I think I will be alive when our situation will have changed greatly." Eppenauer does not believe that it will happen in 2000.

Almost diametrically opposed to Eppenauer's and Garcia's positions was the outlook of Jennifer Rhodes, twenty-one years old, a cheerful young woman who works at the Railroad Blues, a respectable and easygoing rock and roll bar where patrons often bring their children. One Saturday night, she and I talked by the swimming pool of my apartment complex, stopping only once to marvel at a spider climbing up its web to an electric line twenty feet overhead. "It's a metaphor for our lives," Jennifer said. "Maybe you could work that into your essay somehow." One wouldn't have thought she was afraid of the end of the world until she described a movie about a nuclear war that ended the world, *Miracle Mile*. "The movie scared me," she said. "It all sounds so distorted and weird when you talk about it, but in the movie it makes some kind of scary sense." But she's outgrown her fear; she knows she'll die someday but doesn't need to link her individual mortality to that of the world. As for the year 2000, she said, "I don't know how everybody thinks it's gonna be something dramatic. You know, something dramatic could happen tomorrow. Just because it's gonna be the year 2000. I don't see why it's gonna make such a huge difference." Her dismantling of the saeculum was one of the most astute I encountered.

> If you look at the way we measure time, that's all to do with our culture and civilization. Just because the way we measure time hits certain points doesn't mean everything is going to go to hell in a handbasket, there's just no logic in it at all. I think it's kind of arrogant, because we made the calendar. We're saying, so this is when we say everything starts over? I mean, don't you think that's so . . . so . . . human?

In her mind it is an absolute principle that the end of the millennium has no absolute meaning. This doesn't mean, however, that people will not act on their opinions or beliefs. According to her, many people will commit suicide in the year 2000 because they have fears they aren't talking about. "[The end of the world] isn't a restaurant or bar conversation like it used to be," she said. "Now it's like people are getting afraid of it, so they don't want to talk about it, because it's coming closer."

Likewise, April Rivera. Bright and articulate, the teenager, who has a local reputation for speaking her mind to her peers and even to adults, reminded me that the population of the stretch of time beyond our own lifetimes is unknown to us, though we assume they will be connected to us through genetics or memory. Rivera reminded me that we don't know who lives in the future. Her other answers were mostly typical. "I think there's gonna be good things in the future," she said, such as on the TV series *Star Trek* and the movie *Back to the Future*. "I think they're gonna just take this spoonful of this, and you ain't gonna have cancer no more, and take two of these and you're gonna have it easy tomorrow. I think science does everything. They think of new things to cure this, and cure that, and make the future better."

Rivera was comfortable talking about herself and her opinions. As we were finishing, she asked if the people in the future were going to read what we had talked about. I explained what I was planning to do with our tape: I'd transcribe it and then I'd keep it, and perhaps someone in the future would want to put the tape in an archive or library in order to save the voices of people talking about the future. She replied:

> I'm like, I'm thinking of the tape as you're listening to it. Then you show it to people in the future and they're gonna be like, "God, they were thinking that, oh sure!! we don't have this, and flying cars?? all right!! Computers, what??!! What they didn't have flying cars in those days, or goll-ee, what did they do? Without computers, what?" That'd be weird. I'd be thinking about it in the future like, "God how can we live without flying cars, and driving on the street, what's a street?" Grandkids think, "Street? Street,

grandma?" They don't have to work in the future. I guess computers do everything, make the food, or whatever, and people, they don't have to work, they just eat, and are free. Grandkids go, "Grandma, what's *work?*"

She knew, in a way, that she could have said anything she wanted to about the future, but she also wanted to be excused if her predictions were wrong. "I don't know anything!" she cried. "It's only 1995, it's not two thousand and something! Please don't think I'm weird."

One thing became clear from my discussions in Alpine: what is mainstream, metropolitan, and "eternal" about the millennial saeculum differs considerably from how people try to find ways to talk about the same chronological limit. Why?

One answer would look at Alpine's population, its geographical isolation, and the number of media outlets there and conclude that residents do not participate in mainstream visions of the year 2000 because they do not have access to the mainstream. But why then did many of the people I spoke with cite television shows, movies, books, and news media? The answer cannot lie solely in Alpine's location on the periphery.

A better possibility is that the meanings of 2000 are negotiable because people know that life continues, moment by moment, sometimes sweeping by and sometimes chopped up and stuttering. When they attempt to relate abstract ideological systems to their everyday lives, they reach for evidence from what they know best, the content of their own lives.

It was impossible to talk about 2000 without discussing the future—who lives there, what it will consist of, when it will come, how long it will last. What people said about 2000 depended on where they located the future. In all cases, 2000, while still a chronological and historical limit, no longer constituted "the future" for people living in 1995, because it was too close, too visible, to wear well with their hopes and fears. The year 2000, around the corner, falls inside the range of plans for individual lives. It is just another kind of tomorrow, in its more quotidian sense as a unit of the absolutely unknowable. In such a view, a mere tomorrow is indistinguishable from 2000 and announces the future.

When does the future begin? I received a diversity of answers. (Not a single person mentioned, as a date, the year 2000.) Some interviewees suggested ten years from now. Others mentioned a later time. Lucy Escovedo said that the future was here when she was dead. The future, said April Rivera, belongs to people we can never know and who will never know us. Paul Kime said that the future was now.

> We're living in last year's future already. And we're constantly living in it. Actually, the way it looks to me is, we're living in the time when five year ago we were talking about. And four years ago we're living in the time, you know—it keeps getting a narrower gap, in other words. Before long, we're going to be living, day by day, the future.

Rivera questioned the notion of the future altogether. "I guess there isn't a future," she said:

> You say it's gonna be like the year 2000, something is gonna be the future to us for right now, but when we get there, like 2100 is gonna be the future for them and then on and

on. I guess there is no future, it's just—the present. Like they say, there's no tomorrow cause tomorrow never comes. . . . Tomorrow happens, but it's today.

When people in Alpine talked about "tomorrow," their anxieties surfaced. The human mind is profane, limited. Human life is short, and institutions and their visions can't fully prepare people for that fact. Ed Waddill told a joke about the preacher who, in the middle of a heated sermon, tells everyone in the church who wants to go to heaven to stand up. The congregation leaps to their feet. Meanwhile, the preacher sees an old man sitting down in the back of the church. He goes down and asks the old man, "Don't you want to go to heaven?" "Sure I do," the old man says. "I was just afraid that you were getting up a load right now."

I am pointing to a balance between an abstract and a concrete entity, between what is real and what is imagined, which has appeared in another era of American history. In a famous essay titled *The Significance of the Frontier in American History*, Frederick Jackson Turner derived the "frontier hypothesis" of American history. Turner called the frontier "the meeting point between savagery and civilization . . . [lying] at the hither edge of free land."[3] The census report that Turner treated in his essay is stricter in its definition: "as the margin of that settlement which has a density of two or more to the square mile."[4] Turner noted how this line—as both symbolic and geographical boundary—proceeded in stages westward, from the Atlantic coast to the Alleghenies, then to the Great Plains and the Rockies, and finally to the Pacific Coast. Each frontier provided new challenges; at each frontier, the civilizing forces of the previous frontier were adopted and adapted to these new conditions. "American social development has been continually beginning over again on the frontier," he wrote. As an abstract entity, a spatial saeculum, the frontier was powerful too. This power became apparent when the 1890 census announced that the frontier was closed. "At present the unsettled area has been so broken into by isolated bodies of settlement that there can hardly be said to be a frontier line."[5] Though there was still plenty of land to settle on, the frontier's promise as a symbol of hope and renewal was checked—not eradicated, however, for "he would be a rash prophet who should assert that the expansive character of American life has now entirely ceased."[6] Turner hypothesized that the demands of the frontier, combined with "this perennial rebirth, this fluidity of American life, this expansion westward with its new opportunities, its continuous touch with the simplicity of primitive society"[7] had created a uniquely American character.

The same is true of the contents of the saeculum of 2000. Whereas the frontier organized space, 2000 has organized time; both, as abstract and concrete limits, have constituted the boundary of the unknown and the inevitable destination of the known. I want to suggest that at any time before 2000, we can only write the history of the meanings of the year 2000. This does not mean that we don't have a lot to say about the year 2000, but rather that only part of what we can say includes the construction over many hundreds of years of the meanings, the visions, and the rhetoric of the second millennium. That other part—which was some of what I heard in Alpine—involves personal experiences, individual lives, local meanings. Approaching this frontier means that we have to try to refashion the civilization of the past for the wilderness of the future, where we will become unknown, even to ourselves.

NOTES

I would like to thank the following Alpine residents: Sherrie Eppenauer, Lucy Escovedo, Linda Garcia, Paul Kime, Jennifer Rhodes, April Rivera, Lauren Sharp, Jesse Torino, and Ed Waddill.

1. Charles B. Strozier, *Apocalypse: On The Psychology of Fundamentalism in America* (Boston: Beacon Press, 1994), 158.

2. Hakim Bey, *T.A.Z.: The Temporary Autonomous Zone, ontological anarchy, poetic terrorism* (Brooklyn, N.Y.: Autonomedia, 1991), 33–34.

3. Frederick Jackson Turner, *The Significance of the Frontier in American History* (1893; reprint, New York: Frederick Ungar, 1963), 28–29.

4. Ibid., 29.

5. Ibid., 27.

6. Ibid., 57.

7. Ibid., 28.

Chapter Twenty-Four

After Armageddon: Apocalyptic Art since the Seventies
Tactics of Survival in a Postnuclear Planet

Peter von Ziegesar

> Wild, dark times are rumbling towards us, and the prophet who wishes to write a new apocalypse will have to invent entirely new beasts, and beasts so terrible that the ancient animal symbols of Saint John will seem like cooing doves and cupids in comparison.
>
> —Heinrich Heine

Apocalyptic imagery is a fundamental, though by no means majority, strain in contemporary art in the last quarter of the twentieth century. A stroll through New York's Soho gallery district might show more artists concerned with the challenging of sexual mores or formalist conventions than with endist or apocalyptic musings, but such a glance would not represent the influence the subject has had and continues to have on the artistic consciousness in the past twenty years. An uncontrolled yearning for the end has been at the heart of at least one influential recent movement, the East Village art scene of the late seventies and early eighties, and has been the sole or main subject matter of many important individual artists since.

Although they hold in common themes of nuclear extinction, one can easily distinguish the more excessive imagery of the newer generation from the protest art of the sixties, which sought to deflect an avoidable human extinction. The most notable difference is that the contemporary artist often takes an ironic stance of acceptance toward nuclear and other potential holocausts, feigning to embrace them because they will spell the end of a boring and pointless bourgeois world. Of course, as has been pointed out many times, the possibilities of extinction have multiplied many times since the inception of the atom bomb, and we now can contemplate with grim imaginings destruction through a variety of causes: viral, environmental meltdown, economic catastrophe, extraterrestrial invasion, even the glancing blow of a stray comet. Yet artists since the late seventies have seldom visualized a complete end to human existence. Catastrophic mutations, yes; wholesale biological adaptation to new and completely alien environments, maybe; but not the blank, nuclear end that was commonly found in sixties antiwar art.

We might say that the thematic material of many of the resulting artworks, in contemporary art terms, was summed up in a much earlier work, a short film directed by Jean-Luc Godard in the 1960s. In this visionary film, part of a feature-length compilation called *RoGoPag,* a nuclear bomb ignites over Paris and is seen by everyone looking up as a bright, surrealistic flash of light. Yet, life seems to go on pretty much as before, with a few exceptions: all of the people now carry long knives at their belts, and they walk around saying things like, "I *ex*-love you." The Bomb, in other words, has not destroyed the planet, it has simply set up an alternate universe, in which a few fundamental things, such as the expression of love between two people, are unalterably changed.

Thus, if one imagines the cataclysm that will end the world as a looking glass through which we may pass, as in Lewis Carroll's famous fantasy, then a great deal of time and energy expended by the contemporary art world in the last quarter of this century has gone toward imagining what new beings, what strange differences exist on the other side.

The East Village art scene in the early eighties was an anarchic, multifaceted movement of New York writers, artists, and musicians arising out of the working-class Punk music scene in London. It should be remembered that this was the height of the cold war, when the scary, nuclear-fringed rhetoric of the Reagan years was turned full volume, like an apocalyptic radio program that could not be shut off— the "Evil Empire" talk, the initiation of grandiose "Star Wars" defense systems, the government's scornful, open disparagement of environmental concerns and of America's increasingly desperate urban poor. The East Village artists were suburban, middle-class white kids, for the most part, with degrees from well-established colleges of art, but circumstances had forced them to live in grimy, small, decaying tenement hovels east of Third Avenue. There they came in contact with an alien street culture that infected them with an exhilarating sense of impending urban violence and social-technological breakdown. Their heroes were the Puerto Rican and black street youths—some considered them geniuses!—who spray painted elaborate murals on the sides of subway trains: tightly drawn cartoons of vivid colors, weird slogans, and insane typography that seemed to rival and beat anything the art students had come across in a hundred thousand collective hours of art history class.

Out of this fertile cultural cross-pollination soon emerged a cadre of young "graffiti," "New Wave" or "No Wave" artists (as the art world variously dubbed them), whose work seemed to summarize the apocalyptic visions and vivid anarchic political beliefs of a desperate, dead-end culture. Within a few years the names of these artists began to resound internationally: the wall-poster polemicists Jenny Holzer and Barbara Kruger and the "graffiti artists" Keith Haring, Kenny Scharf, and Jean-Michel Basquiat, among many others in miscellaneous or shifting categories, such as David Wojnarowicz and the performance artist Ann Magnuson. The East Village artists were obsessed with mutation and decay but generally seemed to be in good humor. As artists they made no effort to create permanent works, but scribbled on crumbling urban walls, giant sheets of cheap paper, and subway poster stock, rather than durable artist's canvas, because "atomic blasts destroy canvas just as fast as paper."[1]

The world that these young artists mourned (or celebrated!) as passing was often not the human world of flesh, family, and relationships, but the pop culture they had grown to know and perhaps love better. A curious substitution had occurred. It was Betty Boop, Popeye, Beaver Cleaver, George Jetson, Mickey Mouse, and Bambi who received the stings of nuclear jelly in the art of the early eighties, rather than the village children of Cambodia. The scrim of images thrown at these Baby Boomers from television over the course of the past several decades had proved incredibly durable, perhaps more durable than their own dwindling resources and downsized employment opportunities. It was no wonder that young artists projected their fears and hopes upon the immortal characters of sitcoms and daytime cartoon shows, rather than on their flawed selves or people they barely could say they knew.

Their artwork looked ahead "through the looking glass," past the nuclear-techno-enviro-politico-viral conflagration that seemed just ahead, and tried to imagine just what was in store for everyone. The human species would survive—anything else seemed unimaginable—but how, and as what? A twenty-year-old art student from Pittsburgh, Keith Haring, wrote in his journal that he and his friends felt as if they were midwife to a holocaust about which they were extremely ambivalent:

> The silicon chip has become the new life form. Eventually the only worth of man will be to service and serve the computer. . . .
> And what is the role of an artist?
> Should the situation be resisted or accepted?
> It appears to me that human beings have reached an end in the evolutionary process. We will, if we continue on the same path, eventually destroy ourselves. . . .
> I agree to an extent, that if human beings are incapable of evolving further, we should evolve in the form of creating a new life form that can survive the human condition and transcend it. The question that I have trouble with is: Should the new life form be completely oblivious to the aesthetics of human beings? Is it forced, because of its very nature, to be a new life form with no traits of the human beings? Have we created a life form "in our own image" or is it a completely different form?
> This is the question that the artist of our times has to ask, because it is we who will have to lead the fight against a machine aesthetic or prepare people for it. . . .
> This for me is the question that will decide my position in the arts. . . .
> How do you help the human race realize its predicament? And if you do not see it as a predicament, how do you help prepare humankind for the reality of a machine-aesthetic world? . . .
> The destruction of this planet, this solar system, by human beings would not be an end to life. It would go on without us.
> We have a choice, whether we wish to continue evolution on this planet or not.
> I vote "yes."[2]

Haring's most arresting image, and one he drew over and over thousands of times, on dusty car windows and empty subway posters, was of an irradiated baby with cartoon ray-lines coming out of its torso. Born in a mushroom cloud, it was a figure of both innocence and ambivalent sexuality, as it was usually depicted on its hands and knees, being mounted by another "baby." "These poor little characters wiggling out from the radioactive communications they are bombarded with are superslick icons of turmoil and confusion," wrote Rene Ricard in a defining 1981 *Artforum* article. "They are without will, without protection from impulses of

24.1. As the HIV virus took command of his body, Keith Haring often depicted the human figure crucified upside down. Untitled, June 3, 1984. © The Estate of Keith Haring.

mysterious source. We can laugh at their involuntary couplings and tiny horrified runnings around because we see them as we cannot see, as the fish cannot see the water, ourselves."[3]

Locked together in protocubist edges, Haring's glowing angels, his humanoids mutated so that their extended parts could easily penetrate one another, his barking dogs and porpoises gathered to receive blessings from hovering spacecraft—all existed in a mutant world that was, essentially, happy to be changed: by computers, by atomic blast, by contact with extraterrestrial aliens. Later, as the HIV virus took command of his own body (he died of AIDS in 1989), Haring often depicted the human figure—his irradiated baby, grown up—crucified upside down (fig. 24.1). In one of his last canvases, he portrayed the virus that was killing him as a thousand miniature human figures dripping from an open wound while, ironically, a set of immense artist brushes impaled and mortally wounded our bright blue planet.

Haring's art school friend Scharf also put the best face on the coming annihilation. His was the hedonist approach to the end—if we're all to be grilled on a nuclear fire, then we might as well bring marshmallows! With sardonic humor the graffiti painter invented the faux philosophy of *Jetsonism*—that things will be much more fun after the bomb, when we will all be allowed to fuse genetically with our favorite television characters. His quickly sketched, Day-Glo wall murals contained a veritable pantheon of Hannah Barbara television characters—Fred and Wilma Flintstone and so on—with devolved limbs and caterpillar torsos, shown wiggling against a humorous backdrop of vortexes and giggling ghosts.

Andy Warhol had left his handprints all over the downtown art arena; his influence—grown benign and godmotherly in those years—was obvious in the way the New Wave artists dressed, the imagery they used (warmed-over Pop Art, some said), their black leather jackets, and even the kinds of drugs they ingested. But the true patron saint of the East Village art scene was the old Beat writer and prophesier of doom, William S. Burroughs, still writing novels, still addicted to heroin off and on, and still hovering over the stinking streets of Alphabetville like some ancient stalled meteor. Burroughs's first novel, *Naked Lunch,* published in 1959, had set the stage for the East Village party. There was almost nothing in the East Village program that you couldn't find in the novel: the artistic experimentation; the paranoia; the obsessions with aliens, viruses, government control, and addiction; the homosexuality, the gleeful dancing on the bones of the old doomed superstructure of the American success story. In further novels Burroughs had methodically gone about destroying the very structure of the English language with "cut-up" writings in which sentences were torn into strips and scraps and recombined at random. The "cut-ups" could be seen anew in the antic collages of the graffiti artists, who took such disjunction as a metaphor for the breakdown of the social order.

Burroughs was honored by a week-long "Nova Convention" in 1978 in an East Village church. He was writing pastoral novels in which outlaws rode through apocalyptic Western landscapes, shooting, riding, and mating with one another. In interviews he was advocating space travel and rapid biological transformation as a way to escape an evolutionary dead end: "Only way to go is up. We've got no place else, having burned down this planet!"[4] Burroughs met Haring and pronounced him the "real thing," commending him for his "weird mutations, weird figures . . . just jumping with vitality and life."[5] Haring admitted, for his part, "The major influence, although it is not the sole influence, has been the work of William S. Burroughs."[6]

Burroughs also met with Jean-Michel Basquiat in 1986. Basquiat was one of the few black artists to come out of the East Village scene, though his incendiary success burned out quickly—like Haring, he did not survive the eighties, but died of a drug overdose at the age of twenty-seven in 1988. Basquiat and Burroughs shared an addiction to heroin and an obsession with the power of language. Perhaps emulating Burroughs's ominous novels, Basquiat filled his faux-naive canvases with a ferocious, almost incomprehensible machine-gun staccato of words, phrases, advertising slogans, Christian and voodoo icons, street scenes, death's heads, and diseased pictures from a culture whose very cell walls seem to be dissolving before one's eyes. Basquiat's *Riding with Death,* painted just before his death, was an apocalyptic scene that seemed to fuse the religious and chemical in one simple arresting image, of a black man riding upon a white skeleton of a horse-man. The "horse" is certainly a reference to heroin, the drug both Burroughs and Basquiat were fascinated with, but it points more openly to the disturbing rider of Revelation that appears just before the world's end: "And I looked, and behold a pale horse: and his name that sat on him was Death, and Hell followed with him" (Rev. 6:8, AV). Conceivably, Basquiat, whose ears were exquisitely tuned to America's airwaves, may have intended to exploit white racist fears of a black uprising (or "race war") that was supposed to come as a signal just before Armageddon.

The East Village artists could be characterized as iconoclasts and innovators; their purpose was to succeed outside of normal art channels, indeed, as outsiders to the culture. But the East Village scene was not alone in dealing with the unfaceable truths proposed at the end of our century. On both sides of the Atlantic, the eighties also spawned a number of "conventional" painters who were employing realistic, "old master" styles of the past in their work, perhaps hoping that the use of such mannerisms would succeed ritualistically to ward off grim uncertainties that nevertheless crept into their subject matter.

The Norwegian painter Odd Nerdrum was (and still remains) the most curious and disquieting of these. Employing a meticulous style that owed a great deal to Rembrandt and Caravaggio, Nerdrum painted scenes of devolved Nordic warriors, dressed in furs but carrying modern weapons, who hunted and enacted strange rites against a twilight wasteland. The frames with which Nerdrum bound his canvases were grim, heavy, and oaken, like those a future Viking chieftain might chose to decorate his hall at the cold sunset of civilization. In these frames, too, angel-haired triads of blind women screamed tributes toward an invisible but still burning apocalypse, and the very clouds spelled out messages in a portentous and incomprehensible calligraphy. Although in interviews Nerdrum denied that his paintings depicted a postnuclear planet—the landscape was one he experienced on a trip to Iceland, and the rituals represented the myths of his forbears—nevertheless, his paintings received an extra fillip from their dangerous subtext, for if they told the truth, the future belonged not to the yellow, red, or brown races, as demographers and racists have tried to say, but to Hitler's Master Race.

On our side of the Atlantic, a brooding new realism had popped up in the work of a loose collection of mostly Philadelphia-based painters, headed by veteran artist Sidney Goodman and including the younger painters Bo Bartlett and Vincent Desiderio. The painters of this group were more than capable of mounding piles of corpses and gruesomely detailed war scenes within their postmodern tableaux, all composed in a luxuriant style that stemmed from Thomas Eakins (also of Philadelphia). In Bartlett's apocalyptic, mural-sized canvases, for example, the familiar sentimental truths of American rural life were turned upside down, yet the artist's detailed manner perversely recalled Norman Rockwell. Bartlett's inhabitants were frozen in cinematic flashforwards of hunters posing with their rifles and trucks while their prey, the deer, watched without fear. The artist's hyper-American protagonists often appeared shell-shocked, obsessed by rituals of death and sexuality, their eyes

24.2. Bo Bartlett's mural-sized Hiroshima imagines the Japanese city at the pristine moment before the nuclear bomb fell. Such "escapism" has a hard and brilliant edge. Hiroshima (134" x 204"), 1996. Courtesy PPOW Gallery, New York.

staring out into a landscape that was always lit by an end-of-the-world glow. The typical Bartlett background, a rolling prairie, had been erased of all human details except for distant plumes of smoke that spoke of continuing environmental destruction.

Unnervingly, it was often difficult to tell whether the past or the future was being invoked in Bartlett's pastoral landscapes; often there was a disquieting commingling that invoked a kind of postnuclear, *Road Warrior* feeling. As the critic and historian Arnold Hauser once noted, about the paintings of a different time and place: "The escape to the past is only one form of the romantic unreality and illusionism—there is also an escape into the future, into utopia. What the romantic clings to is, in the final analyses, of no consequence; the essential thing is his fear of the present and of the end of the world."[7]

Bartlett's work, continuing into the nineties, does not appear to invoke such yearnings, however, as much as to exploit and comment upon their strange needs. Like Nerdrum, his canvases are populated by deracinated whites, endlessly repeating small dramas of fear, lust, and narcissism. A mural-size painting from the recent, still unfinished "War Series" is perhaps the most "escapist" of all: it attempts to put the spirits of evil back into Pandora's box by depicting the Japanese city of Hiroshima at the pristine moment just seconds before the nuclear bomb fell (fig. 24.2). Such escapism has a hard and brilliant edge, however.

Also in the 1980s, a number of artists began to assume ironic "survival" strategies toward the world's perceived end. One was Ashley Bickerton, an artist born on the island of Barbados, who fabricated sculptural rafts of rubber, steel cables, sheet metal, and other bright industrial materials. These Bickerton

24.3. Richard Notkin had reinvented the apocalypse as a collectible. Cube Skull Teapot (Variation #6), Yixing Series, 1985. Collection of Everson Museum of Art, Syracuse, N.Y., Robert and Dorothy Riester Ceramic Fund.

"Arks" carried precious seed samples, organic materials, and survival tools such as shovels and mountaineering gear. The artist thus invited his audience to imagine him as a kind of water-borne Robinson Crusoe cum Johnny Appleseed, pushing his life raft from island to island within a catastrophically degraded oceanic future. The fetishistic construction of Bickerton's rafts seemed to carry with it the beginnings of a new cycle of technological self-destruction, as well.

The documentary photographer Richard Misrach returned to the sites of atom bomb testing in the American West, searching for human traces, and came back with pictures of a devastation that equaled the most apocalyptic imaginings of his fellow painters, all the more so because the pictures were "documentary" in approach. He photographed graffiti on the walls of abandoned army huts and the grim accretions of so-called dead animal pits, for cattle that die of mysterious causes, possibly radiation. Even more telling were the closeup images of *Playboy* magazines used for rifle target practice on a nuclear test site in Nevada. The advertising fragments, torn flesh-tones, and pictures of a crucified Sylvester Stallone, or a bullet-riddled Andy Warhol, made for juxtapositions as jarring as any found in an East Village storefront gallery. But the Armageddon depicted in Misrach's photographs had already arrived and could be photographed by anyone with an amateur camera.

Certain craft artists discovered that there could be a fine irony in presenting an object of exquisite beauty that is also a communicator of almost unbearable horror. For example, Richard Notkin became a master of the exquisite craft of the *yixing,* a form of decorative teapot that is made to look (for example) exactly like a small squash or some other vegetable, with a stem for a spout. In Notkin's diabolical twist, however, the lid's handle became a gemlike reproduction of a nuclear mushroom cloud, and the base of the pot was a human skull that rested on a set of perfectly modeled gaming dice (fig. 24.3). Notkin had reinvented the apocalypse as a collectible.

After the early eighties, and more so after the lessening of nuclear anxieties at the end of the cold war, the apocalyptic fears of the art world turned to AIDS. This was not a retreat, but an expansion of endist concerns to a wider field of play. The monolithic, incurable disease had taken its first baby steps in the process of wiping out much of the New York art community; now it threatened to destroy the entire human component of the planet. The art world's major preoccupations were thus transmuted from the macrocosmic to the microscopic: from the instant conflagration of the nuclear blast to the slow, subcellular depredations of the tiny HIV organism. One result was a new, almost obsessive focus on the human body, its mounded, vulnerable, fleshy permutations, its distillations and liquids, its wasting forms. In the new AIDS-haunted context, the older artist Bruce Nauman's neon signs of hanged men with huge erections, his decapitated heads with protruding tongues and mutant dog sculptures seemed right on target, even prescient. Following in his wake, Kiki Smith and Robert Gober began to show disemboweled or completely flayed rubbery human body forms, hanging from hooks or emerging from the walls, sometimes with tiny hairs still attached. Cindy Sherman's photographs in the eighties had been cool and self-possessed representations of herself as a minor movie actress or as a participant in draped romantic or classical poses, but she now began to add preposterous fleshy prosthetics, gleaned from sex shops, to her body. The artist finally replaced herself completely in her photographs with frightening, smooth-skinned hobby models and mannequins that swirled in a creamy vortex and coupled in robotic motion, seemingly controlled by diabolic radio signals from beyond.

Artists were aware that the Christian Right had characterized AIDS as a scourge to rid the planet of their kind, and they reacted ironically and forcibly with the tools they had at hand. Andres Serrano photographed a crucifix in a jar of human urine; the resulting *Piss Christ* earned gales of satisfying condemnation from the Christians and their political proxies, such as Jesse Helms. Serrano's *Morgue Series* then contemplated the inert weight and cold pallor of death with hugely enlarged and richly hued photographs of corpses from New York's back alleys and tenements, labeled only by their cause of death (*AIDS, Rat Poison,* etc.), often showing the cuts of the autopsy knife, which resembled the stigmata of Christ. Taken as a whole, Serrano's stylish "looking glass" imagery, the Klan members, the street royalty (i.e., homeless schizophrenic black men), interposed with such religious icons as a chocolate "Last Supper" immersed in some form of liquid, seemed to be setting the stage for the final wars to be staged between

24.4. Robert Mapplethorpe: Such a display seemed deliberately calculated to bring down God's fiery wrath. Self Portrait, 1983. © Estate of Robert Mapplethorpe. Used by permission.

opposing forces on the fields of Armageddon. Deliberately, Serrano has chosen to align himself with the dark side and has set about to provoke a fight with those who consider themselves in the "light," that is, the Christian right wing.

In wrapping himself in the cape of the diabolical, however, Serrano was merely following in the footsteps of the master, Robert Mapplethorpe. Mapplethorpe had sprung from the East Village art scene and then risen far above its crumbling sidewalks. His lushly textured, classically composed black and white photographs perversely combined Roman Catholic and black magic symbolism with graphic homosexuality, sadism, female body builders, nude black men and their (usually giant) sexually excited genitalia, cross-dressers, body excrescences, death's-heads, weaponry, and torture instruments of all kinds. Zeroing in on all levels of society, Mapplethorpe also shot a series of cool, cold portraits of the rich, the deranged, and the celebrated from the American Babylon (fig. 24.4). Such a display seemed deliberately calculated to bring down God's fiery wrath, and of course, it eventually did— Mapplethorpe died of AIDS in 1989, a result of what one might euphemistically call a "risky" lifestyle (as his essayist Arthur C. Danto daintily put it, Mapplethorpe "frequented the wilder precincts of sexual expression").[8] But not before provoking a national firestorm of debate on artistic freedom and censorship, with the religious Right leading the way to have Mapplethorpe's retrospective show in Washington, D.C., shut down (it was). Senator Helms is said to have remarked that, knowing his wife had looked through a catalog of Mapplethorpe's work, he was for a long time afterward ashamed to gaze upon her face.

Mapplethorpe placed himself in the Devil's corner. The guiltless universe of pain-turned-to-pleasure and ugly-truth-turned-to-classical-beauty depicted in the photographs was so hermetically sealed off from "normal" middle-class values and pleasures that it offered little opening for understanding or compromise. Hieronymus Bosch's *Garden of Earthly Delights* did not more surely and completely exclude ordinary notions of decorum from its realm. For Mapplethorpe this had a calculated effect: in the richly detailed antiplanet that the artist created through his photography, the normal, decent folk of America would certainly lose their way and perish, but the elect, those who already had become inured to a Bohemian existence, would learn to thrive. It was a curious reversal of the Christian theme of an elect of righteous ones who outlast God's final wrath. By thoroughly excluding from his photographs everything he did not wish to persist, Mapplethorpe had created his own cleansing Armageddon.

The 1987 Wall Street crash and the subsequent implosion of the New York art market burst the fin-de-siècle bubble a little before its time. The capitalist system had allowed greed to get the upper hand, and it had let down the art world, which had hoped to develop a relationship with Wall Street's princes somewhat like that of the artists of the Renaissance with their Medici patrons. In the sedate early 1990s, the art world continued to limp along. An artist no longer carried a license to debauch, however, and obsessions with sex, death, and oblivion seemed to lessen somewhat. Appearances could be deceiving, though. The "machine age" agonized about by Haring in his journal had overtaken us in fact, and many of the artists operating in middecade were cyber-centaurs, cantering around on digital hooves.

The hot-button issues of the eighties had been absorbed effortlessly into the culture of a new digitally aware generation—gender blending, genetic manipulation, body alteration, designer drugs, thorough viral penetration were the norm—and the universal discos of Alphabet City throbbed until dawn with the sound of computerized mutant dance music created without the aid of instruments or musicians. One might say that in the last decade of the twentieth century the most dire visions of William Burroughs had arrived as fully modeled realities, and in many cases they had proven to be startlingly beautiful. It was against this new cultural background of artificial pleasures, cataclysmic possibilities, and continuing urban neglect that young artists of the 1990s were moved to create psychologically coherent narrative chunks out of the disparities of the Information Age.

John G. Hanhardt, curator of film and video for the Whitney Museum of American Art, has attempted, with some success, to place the work of contemporary

24.5. In Matthew Barney's feature-length video, Cremaster 4, sexually ambiguous aliens wear their hair in hilarious sendoffs of Mickey Mouse ears. Matthew Barney, Cremaster 4, 1994. Photograph by Peter Streitmann. Courtesy Barbara Gladstone Gallery.

artists within a continuum of resistance to the norms of an aging and uncaring capitalist culture. In an essay he wrote for the 1995 Whitney Biennial Exhibition, he began with an apt quote from the historian Fredric Jameson.

> It seems to be easier for us today to imagine the thoroughgoing deterioration of the earth and of nature than the breakdown of late capitalism; perhaps that is due to some weakness in our imaginations.[9]

And Hanhardt continued:

> Like a sedated *noir* potboiler, the business journals tell their tales of corporate intrigue and personal ambition hidden behind the myth of corporate responsibility. . . .
>
> A large number of artists now working in film and media are motivated by a desire to rip through the veil of a self-satisfied Western bourgeois world order and expose the interstices of global avarice and individual greed. This is achieved in both metaphorical and literal ways, through an abstract logic of non-narrative design and through a new narrative impulse fueled by stories that reveal the psyche of desire. . . .
>
> They resist late capitalism's economy of images through a radical poetics that recasts the lost avant-garde and avoids a longing for the new, forging styles and impulses that disrupt the skin and sheen of bodies and corporate facades; trademarks become wounds that do not heal.[10]

There is some irony in the anticorporate rhetoric that pervades Hanhardt's essay, since the 1995 Whitney Biennial was sponsored by Philip Morris, one of the least responsible of America's corporate entities. Because the corporate world has become the only globally pertinent entity—the unstable, media-driven environment in which we all swim—the disruption of its "sheen and skin" is in itself an apocalyptic act. The point is that many of these young, urban-dwelling artists, like their East Village predecessors, are gazing ahead to a shared future that is *on the other side* of that featureless fireball, global oil spill, corporate-ordered political crackdown, or ozone-layer burnout toward which "late-capitalism" seems to be hurtling us. In essence they have already made the leap. Exuberant survivors, they reach out a hand (or fin or tentacle) from the other side of the apocalyptic "looking glass" and dreamily urge us to join the fun.

Matthew Barney's slickly produced videotape, *Cremaster 4,* was an example of the new aesthetic (it was the hit of the 1995 Whitney Biennial). Unusual for its tart vision and full-length production, *Cremaster 4* depicted a wholly artificial, depopulated planet in which fetishistic desires were catered to by sexually ambiguous aliens who wore their candy-bright red hair in hilarious sendoffs of Mickey Mouse ears (fig. 24.5). The tactics of *Cremaster 4* are familiar; as an ironic satire of bourgeois culture, every value of respectability is substituted for its bohemian, camp, or homosexual opposite. It provocatively posits a future world in which the things middle-class America formerly considered with horror are now held up as examples of pleasure. Yet, in *Cremaster 4* the complications and trenchant problems of contemporary culture also seem to vanish, to be replaced by a new world of smoother lines, new rules, and unfamiliar but rather handsome fashion. Once again, the artist has leapfrogged, or ignored, the present and transported us gleefully beyond the "looking-glass" to a place of safety that is also full of distant yearnings and strange sensations.

Some young artists of the nineties are so exuberant in their use of wires and electronic gadgets that it is difficult to tell whether they are unabashedly protechnology or, as the extremes of artificiality employed seem to hint, rather wary. In Andrew McCaslin's 1994 installation, *Bloomers,* for example, a set of gorgeous fast-motion video images of flowers bloomed and faded over and over, as if trapped in a life cycle inside their television monitors. Clusters of yellow work lights and vine-like coils of metal added to an overall sense that the artist had created a synthetic biological prototype. The artwork exists for a future time, perhaps, when radiation has destroyed all natural plant life and synthetic prototypes of a garden are needed to replace the real ones.

Just as artificially, Oliver Wasow's computer-altered, pseudodocumentary photographs of an interplanetary war set in rural America are seamlessly mixed and appropriated from stock photo material, rather than sampled from that imaginary kingdom we call "real life." Playing with our expectations of naturalism and landscape, his appealingly lurid scenes recall the technicolor movies of drive-ins and past decades. The juxtaposition of futuristic weapons of destruction with an idyllic rural landscape is a jarring hallmark of Wasow's series, which blends the past and the future in a heady, postapocalyptic cocktail.

In recent years artists have displayed a sophisticated sense of historical irony that was not available to confreres during the urgencies of an earlier decade. Jeff Aeling's 1996 installation, *A Layman's Guide to the Passage of the Millennium,* exhibited in

Kansas City, Missouri, was a multifaceted work that examined the various millennialist beliefs held by late-twentieth-century Americans (not surprisingly, the artist was strongly influenced by readings from Charles Strozier and other millennial thinkers). Aeling ingeniously conflated nineteenth- and twentieth-century technologies, in order to underline the perennial (or cyclical) aspect of endist thinking. The exhibit contained, for example, a beautifully crafted, Biedermeier-style stereopticon display cabinet that held a nuclear blast model that one pushed an electric button to operate. In another piece, *The Fearful Vortex,* a miniature railroad train rattled on spiral tracks endlessly into a pit; it was analogous to Dante's inferno, whose bottom depths could not be seen by viewers.

A 1993 work by Chris Burden (famous for his conceptual performances of self-mutilation in the sixties and seventies) also dealt with the historical truth that endist terrors are a human constant. Similar in physical presence to Aeling's *Vortex, Medusa's Head* was a five-ton, fourteen-foot-diameter model of an environmentally debased planet that one could see was in the process of being strangled by tightening bands of diminutive railroad tracks. The sculpture was inspired by a period in the last century when Western farmers issued dire warnings that the rapidly multiplying railroad lines that were cutting through their vast holdings would imminently destroy the world. That particular mechanistic (and naively nineteenth-century) forecast never materialized, but Burden's work left open the thought that planetary extinction might much more easily arrive through the forms of technology available in our own present time.

Although an apocalypse is only one of several alternative universes that appear plausible in the post–cold war era, the collective image of a scorched planet beset by radiological mutations and fought over by roving bands of high-tech (or sometimes extremely primitive) thugs is one that simply won't go away. We should wonder why so many artists continue, usually with a painstaking realism that is in itself anachronistic, to sketch scenes of a blasted future/Jeffersonian dystopia and why those same scenes are so familiar to the rest of us that they seem to have occurred not in the future, but in our collective past.

NOTES

1. Keith Haring, *The Keith Haring Journals* (New York: Viking Penguin, 1996), 16.

2. Ibid., 17–19. So rigid and persistent are the New York art world taboos against verbalizing content that only a few pages of the artist's journal, written at the very beginning of his career, contain any discussion of the apocalyptic underpinnings of his work.

3. Rene Ricard, "The Radiant Child," *Artforum,* December 1981.

4. Peter von Ziegesar, "Mapping the Cosmic Currents; An Interview with William Burroughs," *New Letters* 53, no. 1 (fall 1986): 61.

5. Ibid., 65.

6. Haring, *Keith Haring Journals,* 31.

7. Arnold Hauser, *The Social History of Art,* trans. Stanley Godman in collaboration with the author (New York: Knopf, 1951), quoted in Eleanor Heartney, "Apocalyptic Visions, Arcadian Dreams," *ARTnews* 85 (January 1986): 92.

8. Arthur C. Danto, "Playing with the Edge," in *Mapplethorpe* (New York: Random House, 1992), 311.

9. Fredric Jameson, *The Seeds of Time* (New York: Columbia University Press, 1994), xii, quoted in John G. Hanhardt, "A Mediated Utopics: Film and Video in the Age of New Technology," in *1995 Biennial Exhibition* (New York: Whitney Museum of American Art, 1995), 53.

10. Hanhardt, "A Mediated Utopics," 53–54.

Chapter Twenty-Five

Theater at 2000
A Witnessing Project

Karen Malpede

An alternative to apocalyptic thinking is the *witnessing imagination*.[1] Here is a way of looking at the world that contains within itself no discernible or desirable utopian or dystopic end, no revelatory utter certainty, no climactic, violent event separating "saved" from "damned," "us" from "them." The witnessing imagination supposes no definitive boundary between epochs but rather a slow unfolding, a porous leakage into the new millennium of the desire born, even as the bloodiest century of them all was born, to look within the human psyche, there to discover, also, how history is made.

No one escapes millennial fatalism, try as one might, especially not those whose consciousness was formed by the atomic cloud that split the century in two and hangs suspended in the collective unconscious, threatening as the century ends a perfect symmetry of mass death. The approach of 2000 adds renewed urgency to the effort to understand our own resilience in the face of our own destructive urge. The century littered with corpses has produced human beings capable of struggling to bear witness to this shameful sorrow. Charlotte Soloman was murdered at Auschwitz, but not before she created a brilliant series of paintings, *Leben oder Theatre,* which looked back over her family history of female suicides and documented her fierce will to live. Soloman's mentor, and lover, was a singing teacher whose radical theories of human voice production came to him when, as the lone survivor of a World War I mass execution, he crawled his way up through a body pile and seemed to hear how the human spirit sang still in the throats of the dying.[2] Listening to the victims of the century's rage produces a new way of seeing, called *witnessing,* compelled by an unflinching ability (the opposite of psychic numbing) to face the enormity of genocidal suffering and from within this terrible knowledge to somehow offer up surprising new, unsentimental affirmations of the human spirit.

I discuss here the witnessing imagination as it manifests itself in the art form that I practice, theater. The theater is a useful place to look because theater is precisely about that which we are seeking: a discernible intersection between individual psyche and social life. Drama requires a reach into the unconscious; inside the inner life is where the energy resides that propels character into action. Aristotle called our attention to the fact that moral quality is revealed by action.[3] We come to know or think we know or, anyway, try to know the inner lives of others by watching what they do and by feeling in our own selves the impact of their actions. The theater demonstrates how through their actions the inner life of individuals becomes the social life of groups.

Transitional epochs produce a dominant dramatic action that defines the essential human struggle of the time. The Greeks were obsessed with the psychic cost of becoming the heroic individual, the Elizabethans with the rule of untamed ambition in a suddenly fluid social system, the late-nineteenth-century realists with sexual guilt and social responsibility, and 2000 with images of collective genocidal death. In response, *witnessing* becomes the new dramatic action. Such theater matures from the conjunction of the personal with the extremities of the twentieth century. It reflects post-Freudian insights and strategies gained from testimony psychotherapies and trauma work with survivors of atrocity. This is a new ritual and poetic theater whose substance is the inner life as it is lived in the presence of historical trauma—a form, moreover, that by becoming cognizant of the extremity of twentieth-century violence poses the question, What does it take to be human in such an age as this?

There are precursors to what I am calling a theater of witness. Ironically, the most ancient might be the most relevant. Greek tragedy presents us with the closest formal antecedent to theater of witness. From my vantage point as a playwright, it is fifth-century Athens (not the dawn of the Christian era) that begins the epoch whose millennial evolution we now face. Greek tragedy marked the nexus of two wildly oppositional psychic worlds, which, simply put, were those of mother- and father-right. The emergence of the individual seemed to require that a rigid duality be established between the archaic world of nature/instinct/mother-centered tribe and the new world of culture/mind/and friend-centered, homogenous, male *demos*. Ever since the Greeks, humans have been conquering nature and subduing other groups, while trying to know themselves. Twenty-five hundred years later, we arrive at another nexus of wildly different worldviews. This time we are asking ourselves to go beyond the mother-father split, equally refusing ideas of matriarchy and patriarchy while nevertheless reinfusing the feminine into psychic and social life. Our millennial nexus proposes a worldwide extension of democracy to embrace all those who traditionally have been excluded from the privileges of governing themselves. In the face of overwhelming scientific and instinctual evidence that body and mind, conscious and unconscious, self and other, nature and culture are mutually interdependent, evolutionary parts of one another, this millennial nexus challenges us to replace dualistic, exclusionary thinking with an understanding of selfhood that is more expansive, porous, creative, inclusive, and relational. There is, of course, a serious backlash, a desperate wish to resolve the difficulty of our dilemma. Fundamentalism offers one such easy resolution; so does intellectualism. To quote Hélène Cixous:

> Now the fashionable code, these days, holds subjectivity, which is confused (unwittingly or not) with individualism, in suspicion: there is confusion—and this is a pity for everyone—between the infinite domain of the human subject, which is, of course, the primary

territory of every artist and every creature blessed with the difficult happiness of being alive, and stupid, egotistic, restrictive, exclusive behavior which excludes the other.[4]

Selfhood at the millennium depends upon recognizing the selfhood of the other.

Greek tragedy dramatized the lives of the makers of history, kings and the families of kings. Theater of witness dramatizes the lives of those who, as Camus said, "suffer history."[5] This is Arthur Miller's "tragedy of the common man," and these are Beckett's existentially disempowered tramps and clowns, but with further implications. Theater of witness holds that the stories of those who suffer history contain within them the understandings required to reshape and remake history. Hence, like the tragic kings, the modern sufferers are, at the same time, empowered agents. We are interested in their suffering because what they feel in extremity and the actions they take are consequential. It is not because they hold power over others, but because they have the ability to bear their pain and to see into its afflictions that they also hold the power to create. Whereas the tragic figures in Greek drama are what we might call perpetrators, the central characters in theater of witness are often trauma victims. The violence of the twentieth century has impacted on their bodies and their psyches; henceforth, they carry the memories of this violence within themselves, literally bearing history's burden for the rest of us.

The tragic hero is an isolated figure; he creates himself by cutting himself off from (and often killing someone in his) family and tribe. The characters in theater of witness are engaged in a process of reconnection. We see how the victim becomes part of the social group again and how the social group reforms around the victim and is changed. Tragedy shows us the consequences of the too-quick rush to judgment, of the inability to listen, and the impossibility of accepting insights or help from others (especially from those who are "weaker," women, or sons). The tragic character is both terribly alone and in the grip of terrifying certainty. The central characters in theater of witness live lives closely intertwined with others, and they dwell in uncertainty. Their very ability not to need false certainty is enhanced by their close connections with others who help them bear what is known and what remains unknown about past traumas. Though the past obsesses characters in tragedy, they are stuck in amnesia, false idealization, or wrong blame.[6] Characters in theater of witness determine to search through their pasts precisely to undo amnesia, false idealization, and wrong blame. Because they are not alone, but take someone, their witness, with them on this psychic journey, they are also better able to withstand the difficulties of traumatic memory. Theater of witness dramatizes the complexities of telling and listening; the slow growth of trust among characters; the decisions, which can be made only in the presence of another, to reclaim the past, to refrain from a rush to judgment and to cease blaming the self. In theater of witness, characters feel their way toward one another. They begin to sense that what they say is capable of being understood, that their memories have impact not only on their own bodies but also on the bodies of their listeners. Their challenge is to be able to remain uncertain, to dwell in ambiguities, to seek truth while knowing they will never know its whole, to tolerate complexity. Theater of witness dramatizes moments of speaking the unspeakable, hearing the unbearable, being seen in one's totality of suffering and striving; these are activities that can take place only between and among characters who acknowledge and respect each other's right to be.

Theater of witness is about reparation: it suggests that character can be repaired and that social connections, once ruptured by extremity, might be reforged. In theater of witness, both the authors and the characters take a firm stand against violence and name the crimes of *rape* and *genocide,* which are no longer seen (as they are throughout Greek tragedy) as unpunishable acts of the healthy warrior, the heroic man. Theater of witness recognizes rape and genocide as human rights abuses, as violations of life, and as unendurable by democratic societies.

Theater of witness offers the *hope* of resistance in place of the *fear* of misfortune; it emphasizes *compassion* (an interactive stance) over (isolating) *pity.* Instead of catharsis as purgation, theater of witness offers a passage through an intense experience in order to arrive at a state of integration of previously disorienting, fragmented memories. As the psychiatrist Judith Herman writes, "the goal of recounting the trauma story is integration, not exorcism."[7] After twenty-five hundred years, Greek tragedy is still sublime and meaningful; experiencing these plays is still an intensely humanizing act. The theater of witness is also humanizing, and it is arguably more necessary to us today.

Theater of witness begins to find its form in plays written in response to the Holocaust. Nellie Sachs won the Nobel Prize in 1966 for her poetry of the Holocaust. Her only play, the verse drama *Eli,* was written in 1943: "This mystery play was the outcome of a terrible experience at the height of the smoke and flame of Hitler's reign, and was written in a few nights after my flight to Sweden."[8]

The series of catastrophic extremities that are twentieth-century history leave no time for emotion recollected in tranquillity; now atrocity and urgency fuel the poet's imagination. The playwright of witness often must write from within the historical crisis, without distance, reflection, or actual knowledge of how the events he or she writes about will end.[9] Sachs writes a "mystery play" in the middle of the Holocaust in which she imagines the return of shtetl Jews to their ruined village after the Holocaust is over. The return she envisions never happened, so thorough was the continuing extermination, yet this does not invalidate her vision. Sachs is concerned already with remembering, memorializing, and asking how and whether communal life can reform itself around the knowledge of annihilation that it must now hold. In the thick of the *Shoah,* her questions are, and remain forever after the event, the essential ones. To ask them, Sachs, a secular, assimilated Jew, turns to Jewish mystical tradition:

> Through mime and the rhythm of the words, the performer must make the Hasidic mystical fervor *visible*—an encounter with divine radiance which accompanies each of our everyday words. The play is designed to raise the unutterable to a transcendental level, so as to make it bearable, and in this night of nights, to give a hint of the holy darkness in which both quiver and arrow are hidden. (Emphasis added)[10]

A dominant stylistic precursor to witnessing lies in the political engagement with tyranny so evident in playwrights as varied as Bertolt Brecht, Jean Genet, Vaclav Havel, and Harold Pinter, to whom Ariel Dorfman dedicates *Death and the Maiden.* Like Sachs's drama, Dorfman's is a mystery play. Marketed on Broadway, to quote

Frank Rich, then theater critic for the *New York Times,* as "a thriller that is full of action . . . as slam bang in its desired effects as *Wait until Dark* or *Deathtrap* or even *Fatal Attraction,*"[11] the script of the play is less a "who done it" than a series of profound and meditative questions about the nature of torture and survival. The distortions of this excellent play on Broadway and in film reveal the difficulties of realizing the witnessing imagination with old aesthetic methods, another discussion altogether; but I am referring now only to the script. Dorfman's interest is only partially with whether Dr. Roberto Miranda raped Paulina Salas fifteen years ago during the Pinochet dictatorship in Chile. Paulina is convinced from the moment she hears his voice that he did, and when she gets close enough to smell his body she is absolutely certain. Though the play leaves a bit of room for doubt, Dorfman and the audience come to believe along with the victim that this urbane doctor was once her torturer. The play's mystery, and it is a peculiarly twentieth-century unknown, is, What does the victim do when the perpetrator, returned to ordinary civilian life, arrives on her doorstep? (He actually has performed a "good deed"; he has driven Paulina's husband home.) What about revenge? forgiveness? justice? Are any of these desirable, or even possible? How does a human being seek reparation once she has been so badly brutalized? Furthermore, how can civil society reemerge after it has been brutalized by a totalitarian regime? Can victims and perpetrators live side by side?

Dorfman knew his play was "risky." He lacked "historical distance"; he was in danger of "succumbing to a 'documentary' or overly realistic approach." This is an immensely important concern because the intent of the witnessing writer, though working with historical fact, is precisely *not* to become a documentarian but rather to be the one who mobilizes the imagination in the face of extremity, arriving at the vision that has not happened yet. Hence, Dorfman feared he would be "savagely criticized . . . for 'rocking the boat.'" Nevertheless, he chose to remind "everyone of the long-term effects of terror and violence on people," by focusing on the victim and her reactions and needs.[12] In Chile *everyone* meant just that: neighbors, friends, professionals, officials, citizens, all of whom were either perpetrators of totalitarian violence or its victims and their potential witnesses. Yet, as the nation prepared to face its past, there was officially to be no naming of perpetrators' names, no punishment, and no investigation of crimes against the living, but only of those that resulted in death. Responsive to this particular historical moment, even impossible to conceive without it, the play extends historical possibility by rendering witnessing in far greater complexity than Chile's fragile new democracy was able to allow. Dorfman shows us it is possible for individuals to leap beyond the restraints of political caution. By dramatizing the inner lives of characters caught up in history, he provides insights into the truth and ramifications of events available to society only through the poet's imagination. The dilemmas of his characters act to extend our awareness of our own possibilities for choice and action.

The AIDS plays of Larry Kramer, Tony Kushner, and others also present examples of a new and engaged theater of witness emerging in the shadow of 2000. For both Kramer and Kushner the central question becomes love in the midst of death. The AIDS sufferers require the compassionate ones to accompany them on their spiritual journey through a particular life-threatening illness. In *The Normal Heart* Kramer weaves a personal love story, ending with a symbolic marriage at a deathbed, with the public history of his founding of the Gay Men's Health Crisis Center and subsequent expulsion from a leadership role in it. Kushner connects a panoramic account of the twentieth-century American historical shame of the McCarthy era, the "outing" of "Communists" by right-wing fanatics like the closeted homosexual Roy Cohen and the execution of the Rosenbergs, with questions of contemporary fundamentalist religious dogma, personal responsibility, loyalty, and difficult problems of self-knowledge in the age of AIDS. In his play the inescapable confrontation with brutal illness brings honesty and compassion, not without struggle, and a new spirit (the "angel in America") is released throughout the land.

My own plays for the past decade have been a conscious approach to a witnessing aesthetic from both a woman's and a politically engaged nonviolent perspective. Because I was born at the end of World War II in the shadow of the mushroom cloud, my childhood was punctuated by air raid drills, hands over the head, chin between the knees—futile exercises, as we children knew, all the more terrifying for their ultimate display of how completely out of its right mind was the adult world. The elementary school air raid image came back to haunt in a play called *Us*. Here the historical shame resonates with a tale of domestic abuse about a battered mother and a daughter subjected to incest. A man spurned by a wife who momentarily has found some comfort in an illicit love affair takes his young daughter to the movies. She confesses her fear of atomic war to him, and in her moment of vulnerability, he comforts himself by crooning to her and feeling her up.

Us is written to be performed by two actors who play themselves and their parents as lovers in a series of eleven scenes of twentieth-century psychosexual life. Not only the bomb, but memories of the Holocaust, the postwar anticolonialist movement represented by the French Algerian war, the dislocation of immigration, and the conflicts of intermarriage set the historical frame. Not only their violent pasts of war, abuse, and incest, but also the enormous power of an Eros freed by the sixties sexual revolution tie the young lovers to one another. The play's language is explicit, moving from the brutal tongue of the abusive and anti-Semitic father (married to a Jewess he loves and hates) to the song of bodily merging in which the lovers are entrapped. Written in 1986 and premiered in 1987, the play has been anthologized[13] and is frequently taught and staged in adventurous small theaters here and abroad.

In a different tone is *Better People*.[14] Premiered in 1990, this is a surreal comedy about the ethical dilemmas of genetic and reproductive engineering and the connections between pure research, pharmaceutical companies, and the defense industry. One of the characters, the world's oldest living geneticist, Haila Gudenschmartzer, was a recruit and a rebel from the Nazi euthanasia project. Set in the near future, when the human genome has been mapped, and told through scenes that alternate among the driven, competitive daily lives of four high-powered geneticists with their far-out, disturbing, revelatory dreams, the play turns on a (dream?) visit to the laboratories by a rare beast. Gudenschmartzer's half-Jewish son, who is the scientist charged with cloning this animal, is swallowed by the creature; inside the belly of the beast, he is reborn an ecologist.

I was writing a play about a group of poor artists living in East Village when the buildup to the Gulf War began. The war inserted itself into the play, which became a story about the struggle to maintain empathy in a country gone forcibly hard and cold. Television became an actor. The first act ends on the night of January 16, 1991, with the hush of humanity watching the "smart" bombs fall on Baghdad. The second act is a fever dream of the forty-two days of the war, during which the main characters, a performance artist–painter, Aria, and Herbie, the eccentric Hermes-like proprietor of the cafe in whose back room she lives, try to get (in their imaginations) to the Middle East, to be with the civilian victims and so maintain their own civility. I had a physical experience while writing *Going to Iraq*, which was emblematic of the reality of empathy I am trying to address. I was in the shower in my health club after a swim when all of a sudden I smelled the horrible odor of burning flesh rising up in the steam off my own body. I got out of the shower, turned on the Walkman, and learned that the bunker in the suburb of Baghdad had been bombed, burning to death more than four hundred women, children, and noncombatant men. I went home and, while the radio played the official justifications for this murderous act, I wrote the Baghdad bunker speech, which became the center point of the play.

The Beekeeper's Daughter, written in 1993 and premiered in Italy in 1994, is my play about a Bosnian Muslim victim of genocidal rape and her healing encounter with an eccentric American family. I was staying with friends in Greece and Italy in 1993, but all the while I seemed to feel "ethnic cleansing" as if its shock waves traveled across the Adriatic Sea, through the earth, and kept rupturing our Mediterranean paradise. The distinction I am making is between being aware that historical events are happening (reading newspapers and articles, attending meetings) and feeling the impress of those same events at odd moments when one is not consciously thinking about them, as if a hand reaches up through the earth to grab the inside of the guts. At an ancient castle where we often stay in Umbria, I walked the dirt roads to the cypress grove and plotted out a play in response to this repulsive new twist on genocide. Serbian nationalists who rape Muslim women do so in order to destroy the fabric of Bosnian society by creating female outcasts who give birth to "Serbian babies." Women who have given birth as a result of genocidal rape routinely attempt suicide, often successfully.[15] This play, written at the height of "ethnic cleansing," shows how the ability to bear witness challenges the patriarchal idea of power over women's wombs that leads to the actual rapes being planned, ordered, and carried out. In the play both the Bosnian woman and the child she bears are cared for by a group living outside the reality of genocidal war; but what has happened in Admira's body brings the terror home to them. The depth of their responses to the crisis in her body helps her to endure.

I had been thinking about a contemporary reworking of the *Hippolytus/Phaedra* themes and wondering what would happen if a daughter fell in love with her father's young lover and then whether the forbidden, once acted out, might be forgiven. I had intended to write this play of familial erotic conflict, except that the Bosnian genocide kept rising through the earth and entering my flesh. Finally, the play became the union of the family story of sexual transgression—between a poet-father; his bisexual male, Dionysian lover, a literary critic; and his daughter, still recovering from her mother's suicide—and the historical imperative. The poet's daughter, a human rights worker determined, since she could not save her mother, to save others, brings home from the war a pregnant victim of genocidal rape. The two plots twine around each other; the family love triangle becomes the ground against which the imperative to bear witness to genocidal rape is played out. Inexplicable, amazing Eros asserts itself even in the face of violence. When I returned to Brooklyn, in eight weeks of a sort of possessed and feverish writing, the play was mainly done.

The Mediterranean island paradise where the poet lives, enjoying a late-life blooming of increased creativity and passion for a lovely young man, is abruptly ruptured by the arrival of his daughter and her pregnant charge. Thus, the heaven of late-twentieth-century sexual and creative liberalism is broken by the intrusion of two women who have seen the worst of late-twentieth-century nationalist fanaticism. The women come to the island in search of the beekeeper, Rachel's strange, clairvoyant aunt Sybil, who might be able to help Admira bear the child and who has, Rachel knows, a violent secret past of domestic sexual abuse and death, the sharing of which might also help Admira heal her broken life. *The Beekeeper's Daughter* presents a series of witnessing encounters. Absent from this play is an actual confrontation with the perpetrators. Unlike Paulina Salas in Dorfman's play, Admira Ismic never confronts her young Serbian nationalist torturers. Instead, *The Beekeeper's Daughter* shows how her torturers have "crawled inside her flesh"; the play dramatizes the ways in which genocidal violence bleeds into and infects the inner lives not only of its victims, but of all those who attempt to hear and heal. Each character in *Beekeeper* comes face to face with inner demons who seem to have been strengthened by contact with the external evil force. Admira can defeat her torturers only by entering and facing down her own suicidal and infanticidal urge. Rachel integrates her mother's suicide only when she lets go of her need to control Admira's healing process and opens herself to the unknown in the presence of Dionysian Eros.

When the poet, Robert Blaze, assumes the role of caretaking parent to the newborn child of rape, he experiences the intoxication of a witnessing dynamic that has its source in the healthy parent/infant dyad: "I can't take my eyes off him. It's the most astonishing feeling. When I look into this baby's eyes I can see him seeing himself being seen. I feel as though I am giving birth to him as a person, as a human being. I am giving birth to him by my act of looking."[16] The characters in *The Beekeeper's Daughter* defy "ethnic cleansing" by sheltering a Muslim woman; by naming the child born of rape as theirs, they give her the time she needs in order to acknowledge the child as hers. This cyclical drama, in which Admira seems to get "better" only to relapse further into her own terror, involves everyone in her or his own cyclical journey of self-confrontation. The play asks how those outside a war might respond to refugees from a current genocide—and what it means to us, in human terms, if we choose to respond. Within the play's series of witnessing encounters, not only Admira, but all the others as well, find the way to live lives that more fully integrate their pasts.

In a scene deep in a pine forest, Admira finally begins to tell the story of her torture to Sybil. This happens in a duologue, in which the two women alternate their tales. Admira can speak only because Sybil dares to reveal that long before, desperate and unable to flee an abusive husband, she killed her own child in an automobile crash that she accidentally survived. A Bosnian refugee, herself the mother of three children she saved from the war, told me, "All Bosnian women should see this play because it proves to her that the child is hers no matter where it came from." More than a year later, when we spoke together on a panel, she explained why she cried when she first saw a rehearsal of this play. In order to have the courage to flee Bosnia, my friend had carried a gun because she knew she had to be ready to kill her own three children if necessary to protect them from torture. Sybil's story allowed my friend to give voice to her own internal nightmare.

To live on in the face of twentieth-century genocides, while recognizing the fullness of our implication in them—this is the action theater of witness imparts. To live on, consciously, feelingly, daring to know—resisting violence even as the largeness of its impact on the psyche becomes understood by us—is the event this theater lets us share. Like Greek drama, theater of witness communalizes the essential action of its age. If well done it is likely to produce a profound and lasting, unforgettable effect on audiences who have partaken collectively in a necessary passage. Our private fears too often find a voice only in end-time visions of apocalypse; theater of witness provides another sort of public image of our future. The witnessing action in the plays transmutes our fears. Here we find out how we might accompany one another on a journey into the darkest reaches of what violence can do/has done and how we might emerge more completely vulnerable, yet vital, more resilient, honest, and alive. Theater of witness helps us imagine ourselves through the traumatic violence of the twentieth century into what would truly be a new millennium.

NOTES

1. The idea of a witnessing imagination has been worked out during several years of conversation with Dr. Stevan Weine, a psychiatrist who is codirector of the Project on Psychiatry, Genocide, and Witnessing at the University of Illinois, Chicago, and who has been the dramaturg for two productions of *The Beekeeper's Daughter.*

2. Charlotte Soloman, *Charlotte: Life or Theater?* trans. Leila Vennewitz (New York: Viking, 1981).

3. Aristotle, *The Poetics,* book 6.

4. Hélène Cixous, *The Hélène Cixous Reader,* ed. Susan Sellers (London: Routledge, 1994), xvii.

5. Shoshana Felman and Dori Laub, *Testimony: Crises of Witnessing in Literature, Psychoanalysis, and History* (New York: Routledge, 1992), 53.

6. Jocasta, Orestes, and Electra are amnesiac, and they falsely idealize the past. Oedipus, once he learns the truth, lays false blame, against himself; Theseus idealizes his wife and rushes to curse his son to death, etc., etc.

7. Judith Herman, *Trauma and Recovery* (New York: Basic Books, 1992), 181.

8. Ellie Fuchs, ed. *Plays of the Holocaust* (New York: Theatre Communications Group, 1987), 52.

9. There are many examples of witnessing plays written virtually in the moment: Camus's underrated *State of Siege* (about World War II); Genet's *The Screens* (about the French

Algerian War); Larry Kramer's *The Normal Heart* and Tony Kushner's *Angels in America* (about AIDS); Slobodan Snajder's *Snakeskin* (about Bosnia), and others. The other sort of witnessing drama, which has its own strengths and pitfalls, is written from history and/or memory: Lillian Atlan's *Mr. Fugue* and many other Holocaust plays, Emily Mann's *Still Life* (though the documentary form makes it problematic in terms of witnessing), and Hélène Cixous's *Portrait of Dora,* for example.

10. Fuchs, *Plays of the Holocaust,* 52.

11. Ariel Dorfman, *Death and the Maiden* (London: Penguin, 1971), book jacket.

12. Ibid.

13. Rosette C. Lamont, ed., *Women on the Verge: Seven Avant-Garde Plays* (New York: Applause, 1993), 113–56.

14. Susan Hawthorne and Renata Klein, eds., *Angels of Power and Other Reproductive Creations* (West Melbourne, Aust.: Spinifex, 1991), 159–227.

15. Personal conversation with Dr. Stevan Weine, August 15, 1995.

16. Karen Malpede, *The Beekeeper's Daughter,* unpublished manuscript. The play was produced in Italy, Austria, and in New York in 1995 and 1997, and is currently in development as a film.

Chapter Twenty-Six

Economics of the Millennium

Hillel Schwartz

1. The Time By Which

Late last century, the French artist Albert Robida prepared a set of scenes of life in the year 2000. Among these was "*Un quartier embrouillé*" (fig. 26.1), which featured a woman under a Toulouse-Lautrec hat offering her card to a concierge while a chauffeur negotiates her airship through a welter of telephone wires and tall buildings. In this "embroiled" quarter of Paris, the people of the year 2000 are tangled in an explosion of lines of communication and flights of fancy transport, but the bank is still the bank and the economic classes remain distinct. The artist could magnify and transport, but he could not project a fully transformed world, a new economics.

At the same time, in 1897, writing *Forecasts of the Coming Century,* English Fabians, feminists, union leaders, and assorted socialists did attempt to project a new economics, but the editor, Edward Carpenter, could do no better for a frontispiece (fig. 26.2) than a languid sibyl dreamily holding a quill pen and looking out toward an unenlightening horizon.

The artist and the sybil had lost their prophetic powers to another figure of century's end, The Vision Seeing Medium (fig. 26.3), who appeared in Allan Pinkerton's *The Detective and the Somnambulist* in 1875. Here was no ethereal Spiritualist, no Gypsy fortune-teller, no stage magician; his stance, gesture, apparel, and countenance all bespoke a forceful advance man, an agent, an engaged capitalist. He who looked into the future was he who acted as if he already held the future in his hands.[1]

And so it has come to be: economics has supplanted art and faith as the main arena of public contestation, and economists, businessmen, and CEOs, masculine and commanding, have supplanted the more feminine artists and sibyls as the ones to whom we look for our weightier predictions. The year 2000 has become so newly formidable a number and presence because economists, corporate boards of directors, and planning commissions across the last half-century have set their and our sights upon 2000 as The Time By Which.

If, as "realists" say, the year 2000 is a mere trick of numerology, it is now in good measure a trick of twentieth-century numerology, compounded primarily of economic indicators and extrapolations. If it is an accident of a peculiar calendar, as "pragmatists" say, it is an accident of a peculiarly twentieth-century calendar, hedged each minute with time-and-motion studies, each hour with minimum wages,

UN QUARTIER EMBROUILLÉ.

Figure 26.1

each day with time and overtime, each week with deductions and days off, each season with quarterly reports and paid holidays, each year with taxes and dividends, each decade with secular trends in the market, interest rates, inflation, unemployment, and the GNP. The books of Daniel and Revelation may have laid out the initial arithmetic for a climactic year 1999, but the polls, statistics, calculations, and projections that mount up to our year 2000 and into the third millennium are preponderantly economists' numbers.

Figure 26.2

2. Scarcity

Economics presumes a mortal population that must consume to survive. The population must not only be individually and physically mortal; it must anticipate that mortality.[2]

If, as we are often taught, economics is about scarcity, it is first about scarcity of time, later about scarcity of goods. Had I all the time in the world to satisfy every hunger and thirst, the relative distribution of resources would fade as an issue. Had I no anxiety about suffering or dying were my hunger and thirst attended to later rather than sooner, I would hardly qualify as someone with needs. Needs are, at root, urgencies.

Must economics therefore also presume a population that cannot know everything? A prescient, omniscient population, one that knows the future as fully as it knows the world, might never experience urgency.

A VISION SEEING MEDIUM.

Figure 26.3

Of this I am unsure. In the past, human claims to forms of prescience or omniscience (second sight, the reading of thoughts, the discovery of an overarching historical pattern, the estimate of remaining planetary resources) have rarely been staked without an accompanying and usually aggravated sense of urgency.

More or less unknowing, mortal populations must deal directly with the scarcity of time, which makes all other kinds of scarcity prickle. Our sense of the finitude of land, food, fresh water, or the overall variety of things is dependent upon how our time is felt to be taken up.

Indeed, in a world where resources are (or are considered) completely sufficient but scattered hither and thither, the very scatter may be interpreted as scarcity according to the shortness of the time and the consequent urgency.

3. Redemption

Ill-will, dis-ease, anger, or diffuse anguish may explain the tenor of religious, psychiatric, and political rhetoric, but from urgency itself arises our embrace of one or another economy of redemption, each of which manages the scarcity of time in a different way:

- By remaking death in the image of life (the eternities of heaven and hell)
- By withdrawing life from time (meditative or hallucinatory timelessness)
- By dividing out and then conflating life and afterlife (anthropological misrepresentations of "aboriginal Dreamtime" and Neoplatonic images of a transtemporal progress toward a World Soul)
- By enlarging, freezing, or fuzzying time (science and science fiction, primitivism and tourism, advertising and fantasy)
- By declaring oases of relaxed time within a highly ordered routine (sabbaths, holy days, festivals of renewal)
- By recycling the dead into another life (metempsychosis or reincarnation)

Restoring by cosmological hook or shepherd's crook the full sufficiency of time often entails an expectation of release from every other sort of insufficiency. Wherefrom, the confusion of the Good with goods, of resumption with consumption, of resourcefulness with infinite resources and instantaneous change.[3]

4. Exchange

I am saying nothing here about *exchange*. The wealthiest or most knowing of mortal populations might well have ceremonies of gift-giving and elaborate exchanges of ideas or services. Human systems of exchange are not invariably prompted by scarcity; they may have to do with commensality, connubiality, or similar expressions of pairing and community. Systems of exchange must be considered aside from the sense of urgency, although the two on occasion may dramatically coincide, as in Cargo Cults.[4]

5. Forgetting

What is invariably prompted by urgency is memory. This is not so paradoxical. The more limited the time and the more pressing the anxiety, the more recourse is had to memory. Through memory we reassure ourselves by calling to mind a primitive, mythic moment when time was, or seemed, infinite, and there was no urgency.

This century we have exalted the act of remembering, but only as a remembrance of pain past; memory is now indissoluble from personal and communal (and strangely prideful) accounts of suffering, violence, and martyrdom.

Within each economy of redemption, memory is ritualistic, but pain has no monopoly over memory. The recall of trauma is offset by stories of transfiguration. Forgetting, however, is what keeps every economy of redemption fluid, so that time does not compress so quickly as to redouble urgency. Although each economy of redemption exalts certain notable anniversaries and commemorates archetypal events, in the process of exaltation and commemoration the quotidian moment-to-moment loss of time is overpassed, forgotten.[5]

6. History

As a thousand-year interval of peace, purity, and personal fulfillment, or more broadly as the blessed end to human anxiety and suffering, the Millennium promises forgetfulness no less than it promises to relieve us of the scarcity of time. Orthodox Jewish, Evangelical Christian, Shi'ite, and Mahayana Buddhist passages that speak of the arrival of a messianic figure and a millennial era in "the fullness of time" are promises of an end to urgency, to remembering, and to history.

Since the 1970s and especially since 1989, it has been said that we are living in a posthistorical era. Does this mean that we now abide in the Millennium? If so, how can there still be such ennui?

Lutz Niethammer has shown that the terms and meanings of "posthistory" have themselves been historically conditioned and reconditioned since the time of Hegel, but insofar as we can generalize, posthistory refers to that last, indefinite period during which there are no longer any fundamental contests over the direction humanity will take. The invoking of posthistory, then, is either a victor's creed or a loser's screed, according to whether the uncontested direction is seen to be heavenward or hellish.[6]

For those who understand posthistory to mean the once-and-for-all victory of capitalism over communism, democracy over fascism, and free markets over centrally planned economies, this turn-of-the-millennium is presented, verily, as prelude to the capital M, good-feeling, Millennium.[7]

For those who take posthistory to mean the abandonment of the class struggle, the subtle defeat of truly universal democratic processes, and the dominance of a monopoly capitalism that feeds worldwide desires to consume, this turn-of-the-millennium enjoins a capital M, good-feeling, Millennium only for the Elect. For everyone else it will precipitate violent upheaval and a catastrophic denouement.[8]

7. Modernity

But we are also supposed to be living in that denouement called postmodernity, when there are no master narratives, when all is merrily and summarily contested—wealth, gender, ethnicity, consanguinity, community, nationality, memory, history, the boundary between the living and the dead. Is postmodernity therefore anti-millennial? Quite the opposite. Postmodernity has become a master narrative all by its lonesome, and what the postmodernist narrative celebrates is suspiciously millenni-al: a world of unending variety, a world globally aware and sensitive, a world of transitive and playful identities, a world unencumbered by traditional demarcations of space or normative experiences of time. All happening now, willy-nilly, on the approach of 2000 A.D. or C.E. or just plain Year 2000.[9]

The difference between posthistory and postmodernity appears to be consider-able but is actually negligible: in the first case, only one vital thing remains to be con-tested, market share; in the second case, everything must be contested. Yet in both cases contestation is the motor of behavior and the stimulus of social and intellec-tual energies. In both cases, pain and suffering are subordinated to larger visions of distribution and reinvestment or redistribution and re-creation. In both cases, the scarcity of time is dismissed if not relieved; either it is swept away by global postin-dustrial electronic downlinks and just-in-time inventories, or it is challenged as yet another questionable element of "hegemonic" discourse.

The difference between latter-day millenarians and those who smile as they pro-claim posthistory is that millenarians need human history to go in one (dread) direc-tion while they go off in another (happy) direction. Given the economic position and political predilections of those who smile as they proclaim posthistory, this is not a great difference.

The difference between latter-day millenarians and those who smile as they embrace postmodernity is that millenarians cannot, ever, enjoy the Millennium.

8. Discernment

How do we know we are postmodern, posthistorical, or on the verge of the Millennium? At this fin de siècle, the signs for all three are the same, and they are economic. Of course, one could always saddle the Four Horsemen of the Apocalypse—War, Plague, Famine, and Premature Death—with underlying eco-nomic causes, but I have reason to be more literal.

I am paging through *Awake!* for June 22, 1995. Average printing 12,990,000 (topped only by *TV Guide*?), published in seventy-five languages by the Watch Tower Society, *Awake!* "builds confidence in the Creator's promise of a peaceful and secure new world before the generation that saw the events of 1914 passes away." Better hurry.

The cover page asks, "False Predictions or True Prophecy: How Can You Tell the Difference?" On page 9 the editors admit with unusual candor that many Jehovah's Witnesses believed Christ's millennial reign would start in 1975, at the beginning of what was calculated to be the seventh millennium of human history from the instant that Adam appeared. These Witnesses were wrong, but "The wrong conclusions were due, not to malice or to unfaithfulness to Christ, but to a fervent desire to realize the fulfillment of God's promises in their own time," and anyway, they were not so far off or far out. Last December ('94), after all, a mainline academic, "Charles B. Strozier, a New York psychoanalyst and professor of history, said, 'We no longer need poets to tell us it could all end with a bang, or a whimper, or in the agony of AIDS.' In fact, he added: 'It now takes an active imagination *not* to think about human endings.'" Selah.

Look around you, wrote the editors, for clear and cogent evidence that the world will end shortly, within your lifetime: see the wars, the plagues, the earthquakes, the rising crime rates, the devastating food shortages everywhere. The Four Horsemen and more: a feature on teen "Stealing—Why Not?" (because [1 Cor. 6:10] "thieves will not inherit God's kingdom"); articles on aging (loss of respect after sixty) and extinction (the Tasmanian wolf, lost in 1936). Down the back-page column, "Watching the World," I read snippets on "parents who abandon their children to gamble" in Australia; on runaway children who may turn to crime and become homeless adults; on water shortages in South Africa; on noise pollution in Brazil— "The human ear was not made to tolerate the noises made by civilization"; on over-fishing around the world. The inside back cover, full color, informs me about the honesty of Jehovah's Witnesses in Nigeria, where a lost five-naira note, pinned to a tree awaiting its owner, remained unclaimed for many a day until at last it was put in the Society's contribution box.

The thrust of the entire issue of *Awake!*, unlike those of most millennial tracts a century ago, is economic. The focus is far less upon examples of spiritual and moral decline, far more upon the telling consequences of a spreading economic disorder. Time is scarce, and the global breakdown in our economic system is the best (most revealing) bad news. Earthquakes and wars are refractory; they may be haphazardly stickpinned to any historical endtime in any eschatology, so "ridiculers" have little trouble dismissing them. Economic indices and industrial circumstances, on the other hand, are more time-specific and have truly shifted. "The fact is," insist the Watch Tower editors, "*things have changed*. Bible prophecies *are* being fulfilled. The evidence that the end is near is overwhelming." The economic evidence.

Doomful prophecies of the end now summon up, in preference to instances of moral depravity and faithlessness, a series of economic conflicts and fiscal horrors: an impending global war between the developed and the underdeveloped countries (First World against Third World); gang wars everywhere to control the incessant, enormously profitable traffic in drugs; massive migrations of the poor and starving from South to North, with grief along all borders; the Antichrist arising from the midst of the governors of the European Economic Community or the World Bank; an Armageddon battle over oil and water, which will never mix until the Second Coming; aliens arriving from a neighboring country or galaxy to use up all our resources; industries worldwide disrupted by rioting displaced workers, countries jeopardized by dangerously decaying infrastructures, the planet falling apart, its inhabitants crowded, hungry, sickly, hopeless. Everything that falls must converge. Around the year 2000.[10]

Isn't it incredible how, at this bleak or bloated economic juncture, posthistory has come so swiftly to the fore as a credible though controversial category? Posthistory represents the ultimate in convergences social, political and, to be sure, economic. For posthistorians, the sudden end to the Cold War, the breakup of the Soviet Union, and the apparent victory of postindustrial capitalism over communism means that nothing more is devoutly to be wished for, or wished away. Posthistory has arrived, if it has arrived, because there is no visible remaining economic narrative to compete with that of capitalism, and therefore no underlying to-and-fro by which to make history a sensible drama. The King Is Dead; let the comedy go on.

Postmodernity also owes its origin and much of its momentum to economics. We know we are postmodern when we observe that the free market economy has lost that monolithic structure imputed to it during its battles with so-called centrally planned economies. The endless variations now played over and across the baseline of capitalism, electronic tickers, and Dow Jones averages are exact metonyms for the riffs of postmodernity. Posthistorians find capitalism resurgent and dominant; postmodernists, finding capitalism multiplex and metamorphic, help posthistorians explain how capitalism triumphed. Capitalism triumphed because it had taken on so many different forms that it was, for all essential purposes, the very model of postmodernity. From each according to his manner of reinvestment, to each according to his (yes, *his*) needs.

9. 1999 Plus Tax

In Classical Greece, "economy" referred to the household management of resources and expenses; women often took care of these or shared in their oversight. Modern "economics" refers to larger entities—industries, cities, provinces, nations—usually (still) commanded by men. Realizing this, educated women at the turn of the last century engendered the science of Household or Home Economics, believing that the transfer of commercial and industrial techniques into the home could free up a woman's time and redeem her from the drudgery of a badly run household. The picture of a perfectly run household, like hagiographical portraits of perfectly run corporations, was completely millennial: everything done on the dot, so no anxiety about the scarcity of time; everything ordered and accumulated ahead of time, so no anxiety about the scarcity of goods; everything properly proportioned, so no anxiety about taste or equity; everything done with spirit and personality, so no anxiety about a gradual loss of variety; everything in place and clean, so no anxiety about illness or impurity; every visitor, guest, boarder, suitor, and new baby accounted for, so no anxiety about losing track of the world; every emergency anticipated, so no anxiety about disorder and change. In short, a quiet, efficient, foresightful, peaceful, prosperous, happy, healthful, halcyon home.

This picture, reconfigured for multinational corporations and for different-sized nation-states, has supplanted most other visions of the Millennium in the twentieth century and for the millennial year 2000.

Should this vision of the Millennium appear at once too vague and too good to be humanly true, that's not my fault. The avenues of approach to a Millennium are always sketched out in more detail than the state of life within a Millennium, which is after all posthistorical, relieved of the scarcity of time and the urgency of needs.

Strictly, then, millenarianism is about avenues of approach to the Millennium, not about the Millennium per se, which will take care of itself and us in the best of all possible ways as the best of all impossible worlds. This may explain why the year 2000 is regularly appointed The Time By Which, rarely The Time In Which.

It follows that this anthology of essays on 2000 cannot be about the year 2000. It must be about 1999 plus.

On 1999 have been pinned most of the cataclysmic apocalyptic visions that have accumulated since the sixteenth century. 1999 is the well-limned End to which 2000 is a celebrated but obscure successor. 1999 clamps the horizon shut. Only then can 2000 come, as it must, out of the blue (something like the monolith of *2001*).

Millennial countdowns, like most millennial arithmetics and economics, are concurrently count-ups. They share that millennial inclination of twentieth-century popular economics to confound multiplication with division: the more things are multiplied, the more easily they can be divided (and distributed). Is this regressive or progressive?

Here are three options for 1999's "plus tax":

A *sales tax*. Everyone who buys into the notion of a Millennium at the turn of the millennium pays for it, the poor disproportionately. As an economic strategy and as a theoretical construct, this is regressive. It puts a particularly unfair burden upon the poor and the struggling, and it lays an onus of superstition, irrationality, or sentimentalism upon them.

A *capital gains tax*. Everyone who is already getting a return on selling or investing in the millennium as a capital *M* Millennium (advertising agencies, satellite launching companies, multimedia corporations, Microsoft and web crawling systems, MCI, Sprint, Pat Robertson, pentecostal and Survivalist publishing houses) is assessed a percentage of all gains. This has been vaunted as progressive, since it puts the burden and the blame upon the rich and powerful, who know what they are doing—but it also assumes that the rest of us are easily and perpetually duped.

A *tariff*. Anyone who wants to enter the millennium as a Millennium must pay to enter and then take whatever risks may be involved in making the millennium into a Millennium. This is protectionist, for it defends the year 2000 and the first years of the twenty-first century from all cynics, sceptics, agnostics, and interlopers.

10. *Thieves of Time*

In medieval Europe the crime of usurers was explained as a theft of time.[11] To extend credit at interest was to bank on the sheer passage of time to increase one's own coffers. Ultimately, usurers were pretending to trade in what was God's alone to manage: the passage of time, through to eternity. (Those who sold indulgences that relieved a Christian believer or a dead relative of so many years in purgatory were accused by Protestant reformers of being, in essence, usurers. Luther blew red in the face every time he spoke of usury.) Since the sixteenth century, when notaries, financiers, and businessmen began to craft more complex instruments of credit for emerging nation-states and quasi-national corporations, Western society has come to embrace credit as a moral, healthy, adventurous means of promoting industrial and commercial development. Instead of fearing the scarcity of time, investors and investment brokers have profited both from others' fears and from the scarcity itself.

Now, however, backed up against the years 1999 and 2000, at a fin de siècle in which, like other '90s, people have come to be terrified about the prospects for their children in the next century, usury has once again been seized upon as a mortal and cultural sin. Usury . . . in the sense of the wasting of resources: stealing some of the time we might have had left in which to remedy what has gone wrong. Usury . . . in the sense of short-term profit-taking: stealing the time we might have had to invest in a sustainable future. Usury . . . in the sense of selfish shortsightedness: stealing the time we might otherwise have had available to us to assure the basic security of the lives of our children. Usury . . . in the sense of believing that things will always go on pretty much as they have always gone on: the hubris of believing that one has a private handle on all of time, scarce as it may be.

I am struck by one further and increasingly common accusation of usury: usury in the sense of fear-mongering, of stealing our time by overplaying the urgency and seducing us into replaying old scenarios whose comfort is illusive and, eventually, inhuman.

Philip Gourevitch, reviewing Lawrence Keeley's *War before Civilization*, Benjamin R. Barber's *Jihad vs. McWorld,* and Robert D. Kaplan's *The Ends of the Earth: A Journey at the Dawn of the Twenty-First Century,* accuses them all of usury: "These books serve merely as symptoms of the age they propose to diagnose; they are selling fear more than understanding. . . . Catastrophe surrounds us, and there is no reason to expect an end to it. But isn't this very endlessness the quality that makes the woeful human condition so stubbornly interesting?" We have been told, writes Gourevitch, "that we are living in a condition called postmodern, in an era called post–Cold War, and these labels convey a floaty mood of hangover. On any given day, the newspapers announce that humanity is going global *and* that it is splintering into fragments." Keeley, Barber, Kaplan each hopes to have written the commanding new global narrative for the next century, a century that otherwise threatens to disintegrate into fratricide, genocide, and famine, but they press their individual cases by collapsing our opportunities and stealing our time. Doomsdays do that.[12]

11. Once upon a Time

Isn't doom useful? What would an economist say about the value of doom? A Benthamite utilitarian might say that if the promise of inexorable doom bludgeons the majority of people into acting for the common good, then doom is to some extent valuable. A liberal, Christian, French free-trader like Frédéric Bastiat, writing "Of Value," would argue that doom is counterproductive: "What makes these laws [of Providence] harmonious and not discordant is, that all principles, all motives, all springs of action, all interests, co-operate towards a grand final result, which humanity will never reach by reason of its native *imperfection,* but to which it will always approximate more and more by reason of its unlimited *capability of improvement.*" Doom would cut action and improvement short, and "If you take away Liberty from man, he becomes nothing else than a rude and wretched machine."[13] English mechanician and mathematician Charles Babbage observed in 1832 that one of the most useful of the employments of machinery was "extending the time of action of forces"; in this context, an economist might conceive of doom as a machine to drive people to act in concert more continually and reliably than usual.[14]

Peculiar question and peculiar answers, but not frivolous. From one prospect or another, the contributors to this anthology have had to ask themselves about the value of doom. Is it more valuable when it appears antique and we can see what lies behind it? Is it more valuable when it is closer and we can understand those parts of our psyches it sets off? Is its value geared to a calendar and the time remaining? Is its value upset if it is only contingent or not total or not unique? As the epitome of the scarcity of time, is doom a human *need*? Will we no longer have any use for doom once we have cleared the millennial divide of the year 2000 and entered safely into the third millennium?

In the Prelude to *Joseph and His Brothers,* Thomas Mann suggested that each generation updates and conflates its memories of *the* Deluge, which was always more than one Deluge, but which must always be, in our minds, *the* Deluge. "What concerns us here," he writes, "is not calculable time. Rather it is time's abrogation and dissolution in the alternation of tradition and prophecy, which lends to the phrase 'once upon a time' its double sense of past and future, and therewith its burden of potential present."[15]

Is doom a necessary anchor, past and future, to our being temporal creatures? Is doom integral to our "once upon a time" tales of survival? Can we do without doom?

12. Buried Treasure

"Though it's late in the twentieth century," writes a contemporary poet, Deborah Digges,

> if you watch closely,
> you can make out a man, above the tide-line,
> sweeping the sand with a contraption
> that listens for buried treasure,
> coins like the ones in the new airports'
> or shopping malls' terrariumed, sky-lit tile fountains
> which buy a midnight janitor
> his cigarettes and coffee.
>
> As for the wishes the coins are proof of,
> they seem sometimes to hover

and that hovering may become something of a blessing, a "self-blessing."[16]

What is it about a search for coins, the sweeping of the sand with a metal detector and headphones, that is so evocative of the end and turn of a millennium? Not, surely, the cliché of the tide coming in and going out.

Some years ago, early on a Saturday morning, I met an older man walking just above the tide-line, sweeping the sand patiently with his matte-finish long-handled metal detector. What was he looking for, I asked. Nothing in particular, he said, removing his headphones. He showed me the loot in the bag tied to his waist: dimes, a quarter, a rare half-dollar, two segments of a dental brace, a hairpin, a dimestore bracelet. Some people find Spanish doubloons, valuable coins, he said, but he personally wasn't looking to get rich. He liked the calm, the ocean air, and the listening. On the quiet beach he could tell one kind of metal from another by the tone in his 'phones, and he could guess what he would be sifting through, scooping up. He wasn't looking for much; he was listening.

He was listening, I would say now, for loss: lost wishes (pennies tossed), lost opportunities (engagement rings), broken promises (discarded wedding rings).

We have yet some things to learn about retrieval and about listening. The economics of the millennium has to do with the scarcity of time, and so with memory and forgetting, but also, surely, with listening.

13. Burning Man

On the silent sands of Black Rock Desert, happening even as I write, is Burning Man 1996. Last year too, in 1995, in the blazing heat, Burning Man took place on that same four-hundred-square-mile alkaline slab in northern Nevada. The Church of Warm Noise was there, and the Harpo Marx Memorial Croquet Society, and big four-wheelers with 2000-amp loudspeakers, and pyromaniacs with exotic fireworks. The huge Burning Man, destined to burn, burned. This year, the Inferno: "a rendering of Hell in our Postmodern Age . . . a place where every sin and folly of our age is catalogued, held up for public view, and punished." Pilgrims journeying through Hell will arrive at the City of Dis, whose towers will collapse in flames as all fin de siècle demons are destroyed. And then the Burning Man, destined to burn, must burn.[17]

Next year, too.

As the French theorists might say, there is an anti-economics to every millennium. Jacques Derrida has proposed that counterfeit money is a mechanism for making things happen;[18] and, no doubt, counterfeit doom.

14. The Number of Lines in a Sonnet

There is nothing in Scripture or natural science or the structure of European languages that requires a stanza to be fourteen lines long. The fourteen is arbitrary, and for some poets, magical, nay, transcendental. There are different rhyme schemes to Petrarchan, Spenserian, Shakespearean, Miltonic, tailed, and curtailed sonnets, and modern poets have worked the sonnet with a bewildering variety of metrics, but every true sonnet comes to an end with its fourteenth line. The fourteen lines tend to demand language that is spare, metaphorical, and conclusive; room for maneuver is nearly infinite, but on the last word of the fourteenth line every true sonnet decisively *ends*. Period. You may return to a sonnet time and again, learn it by heart, recite it on apt occasions, quote it, perhaps misremember it. No matter: you can always be sure it has fourteen lines and when you reach its last word you have come to the end of a thought, a feeling, an insight.

There may well be something in Scripture, natural science, and the structure of European languages that requires us to lay out our eras by centuries and millennia, though the habit of tens and epochs is neither inveterately ancient nor inviolable. The lesson of the sonnet is that numbers, arbitrary or no, must command respect, in much the same way that economists respect them: as signs of human activity and as prompts to further engagement. Numbers are part of us, but we make them add up. When we cannot seem to make them add up, we play with them until they do.[19]

The economics of the millennium is, all told, about the casting out of nines, the roundness of numbers, and the roundedness of narrative: a 000-sum game.

NOTES

1. For the fin de siècle context of another prophetic medium, the Dow Jones Index, see my *Century's End: A Cultural History of the Fin de Siècle from the 990s through the 1990s* (New York: Doubleday, 1990), 174–75.

2. One of the few works that takes seriously the connection between mortality and millenarian thought is Stephen D. O'Leary, *Arguing the Apocalypse: A Theory of Millennial Rhetoric* (New York: Oxford University Press, 1994), chap. 2. I have also taken into consideration here Alden E. Wessman and Bernard S. Gorman, eds., *The Personal Experience of Time* (New York: Plenum, 1977).

3. In Christian theological vocabularies, the economy of redemption refers to the orderly plan of salvation adopted by God (Roman Catholic); to the divine government of the world through a series of dispensations (Protestant); to the tactful presentation of doctrine (post-Reformation). Of the few scholars who have thoughtfully considered the economics of redemption with regard to millenarian behavior, the most perceptive is Kenelm Burridge, *New Heaven New Earth: A Study of Millenarian Activities* (New York: Schocken, 1969), esp. 4–7, 143–49. On goods and consumption, see Mary Douglas with Baron Isherwood, *The World of Goods* (New York: Basic, 1979); Georges Bataille, *The Accursed Share,* vol. 1, *Consumption,* trans. Robert Hurley (New York: Zone, 1988). I do not intend in this essay to produce an analysis of economic policies that may be so wrong as to be apocalyptic, although some policies do appear to encourage a frighteningly catastrophic disregard for the human polity. Nor will I produce a set of critiques about the origins of millenarian movements in poverty or economic oppression, although such a critique still needs to be made more strongly than I have made it in the past. Nor do I have the space in which to draw out in elaborate detail the analogies between modern economic thought and calculation and millennial thought and calculations, although such an elaborated analogy would likely prove to be strong and illuminating.

4. On exchange in particular relation to Cargo Cults, see especially I. C. Jarvie, *The Revolution in Anthropology* (Chicago: Henry Regnery, 1967); Peter Worsley, *The Trumpet Shall Sound: A Study of "Cargo" Cults in Melanesia,* 2d ed. (New York: Schocken, 1968); Andrew Strathern, "Cargo and Inflation in Mount Hagen," *Oceania* 41 (1971): 255–65. It is worth noting here that the greater the millennial urgency, the greater the likelihood that recycling will become a conscious, public, and widely-bespoken principle, in the processing of materials as of souls. Recycling will be decried on the right because it implies a set of resources that is contained and apparently finite. Recycling will be decried on the far left because its mild successes may temporarily lead to the suspension or reduction of that sense of urgency which stimulates sociopolitical change.

5. It is no coincidence that, in these 1990s, attempting at once to recall an entire millennium and to forget it, we have come to doubt the truthfulness of any memory not externally documented and have lost any scientific conviction that we know how human memory works. We look therefore to computers, instant replay, and perpetual reenactment to assure ourselves

of a common past, even as we become ever more suspicious of elicited or solicited memories of child abuse, alien abduction, satanism, or other trauma. See my *Culture of the Copy: Striking Likenesses, Unreasonable Facsimiles* (New York: Zone, 1996), chap. 7. On rehearsing a thousand years, see especially Felipe Fernández-Armesto, *Millennium: A History of the Last Thousand Years* (New York: Scribner, 1995). His last sentence: "No earlier age had access to awareness of such comprehensive menace, or of such an awesome chance." Memory, and forgetting.

6. Lutz Niethammer, with Dirk van Laak, *Posthistoire: Has History Come to an End?* trans. Patrick Camiller (London: Verso, 1992).

7. See the seminal article by Francis Fukayama, "The End of History?" *The National Interest* 16 (summer 1989): 3–18, with responses following—and now a book by the same title.

8. See Chris Brown, "The End of History," in *Fin de Siècle: The Meaning of the Twentieth Century,* ed. Alex Danchev (New York: Tauris, 1995), 1–19; "Epistème and Entropy at the Fin de Siècle," special section of the *International Journal of Politics, Culture & Society* 8 (fall 1994), 105–92.

9. Contrast Albert Borgmann, *Crossing the Postmodern Divide* (Chicago: University of Chicago Press, 1992), and Fredric Jameson, *Postmodernism, or, the Cultural Logic of Late Capitalism* (Durham: Duke University Press, 1990).

10. See, for example, Robert O'Driscoll, ed. [and author], *The New World Order Observed: A Trilogy,* vol. 1, *The New World Order and the Throne of the AntiChrist;* vol. 2, *The New World Order in North America: Mechanism in Place for a Police State;* vol. 3, *New World Order Corruption in Canada* (Toronto: Saigon Press, 1993–94).

11. Jacques Le Goff, *Your Money or Your Life: Economy and Religion in the Middle Ages,* trans. Patricia Ranum (New York: Zone, 1988), esp. 33–46.

12. Philip Gourevitch, "Misfortune Tellers," *The New Yorker* (April 8, 1996), 96–100.

13. Frédéric Bastiat, *Harmonies of Political Economy,* trans. P. J. Sterling (London, 1860), vol. 1, pp. 32, 105.

14. Charles Babbage, *On the Economy of Machinery and Manufactures,* 2d ed. (London, 1832), chap. 5.

15. Thomas Mann, *Joseph and His Brothers,* trans. H. T. Lowe-Porter (New York: Knopf, 1934), 18.

16. Deborah Digges, "For the Second Millennium," in her *Late in the Millennium* (New York: Knopf, 1989), 4.

17. Erik Davis, "Terminal Beach Party," *Building* (spring 1996): 1–2, excerpted from the *Village Voice,* October 31, 1995; see also the rest of the spring 1996 issue of *Building.*

18. Jacques Derrida, *Given Time: I. Counterfeit Money,* trans. Peggy Kamuf (Chicago: University of Chicago Press, 1992), 96.

19. See the acute psychological connection drawn between statistics and apocalyptic thought by novelist Robert Coover, *The Universal Baseball Association, Inc., J. Henry Waugh, Prop.* (New York: New American Library, 1968).

Contributors

Marie L. Baird, an assistant professor of theology at Duquesne University, has published articles in the field of spiritual theology. Her current research projects include the development of a model of spiritual theology that is capable of addressing the realities of life in extremity, a spirituality of the self, an ethics-based inquiry into Eric Voegelin's conception of order and history, and an examination of twelfth-century French depictions of female saints as ethical subjects.

Michael Barkun is professor of political science in the Maxwell School at Syracuse University. His books on millennialism include *Religion and the Racist Right* (rev. ed., 1997), *Crucible of the Millennium* (1986), and *Disaster and the Millennium* (1974). Barkun edits the Religion and Politics Series for Syracuse University Press. His current research includes a study of the influence of New World Order conspiracy theories.

Jean Baudrillard is professor of sociology at the University of Nanterre, France, and author of *The Illusion of the End* (1995) and *Looking Back on the End of the World* (1988).

Norman Cohn, now professor emeritus, previously held the titles professorial fellow, director of the Centre for the Study of Persecution and Genocide, and Astor-Wolfson Professor of History, all at the University of Sussex, England. A Fellow of the British Academy, he has written *The Pursuit of the Millennium* (1957), *Warrant for Genocide* (1967), *Europe's Inner Demons* (1975), *Cosmos, Chaos, and the World to Come* (1993), and *Noah's Flood* (1996).

Sara Diamond holds a doctorate in sociology from the University of California, Berkeley. She is the author of *Spiritual Warfare: The Politics of the Christian Right* (1989), *Roads to Dominion: Right-Wing Movements and Political Power in the United States* (1995), and *Facing the Wrath: Confronting the Right in Dangerous Times* (1996).

Jean Bethke Elshtain is the Laura Spelman Rockefeller Professor of Social and Political Ethics at the University of Chicago and author most recently of *Augustine and the Limits of Politics* (1996).

Michael Erard is a Ph.D. candidate in the Department of English at the University of Texas at Austin.

Richard Falk is Albert G. Milbank Professor of International Law and Practice at Princeton University. He has written *On Humane Governance: Toward a New Global Politics* (1995) and, with Robert Jay Lifton, *Indefensible Weapons: The Political and Psychological Case against Nuclearism* (1992).

J. William Gibson teaches sociology at California State University, Long Beach. Gibson is the author of *Warrior Dreams: Paramilitary Culture in Post-Vietnam America* (1994), and *The Perfect War: Technowar in Vietnam* (1986). He is currently studying ecological conflicts along the coast of southern California.

Catherine Keller is associate professor of theology at Drew University and author of *From a Broken Web: Sexism, Separation, and Self* (1986) and *Apocalypse Now and Then: A Feminist Guide to the End of the World* (1996).

Richard A. Landes is associate professor of history and codirector of the Center for Millennial Studies at Boston University. He is the author of *The Peace of God: Social Violence and Religious Response in France around the Year 1000* (1993) and *Relics, Apocalypse, and the Deceits of History: Ademar of Chabannes, 989–1034* (1995).

Robert Jay Lifton is Distinguished Professor of Psychiatry and Psychology at John Jay College and the Graduate Center, City University of New York. He has written more than twenty books, including *Thought Reform and the Psychology of Totalism: A Study of "Brainwashing" in China* (1961), *Death in Life: Survivors of Hiroshima* (1968), *The Nazi Doctors: Medicalized Killing and the Psychology of Genocide* (1985), and (with Greg Mitchell) *Hiroshima in America: Fifty Years of Denial* (1995). He is currently writing a book on Aum Shinrikyo.

Lois Ann Lorentzen is associate professor of social ethics at the University of San Francisco. She is the coeditor of *The Gendered New World Order: Militarism, the Environment and Development* (1996) and *Liberation Theologies, Postmodernity, and the Americas* (forthcoming). Lorentzen is also an experienced wilderness guide and climbs mountains.

Phillip Charles Lucas teaches American religion at Stetson University. He has published articles on sectarian and new religious movements in the *Journal of Contemporary Religion, Public Culture,* and *SYZYGY: Journal of Alternative Religion and Culture* and has contributed to such books as *America's Alternative Religions, Perspectives on the New Age,* and *From the Ashes: Making Sense of Waco.* His monograph *The Odyssey of a New Religion: The Holy Order of MANS from New Age to Orthodoxy* was published in 1995. Lucas is currently general editor of *Nova Religio: The Journal of Alternative and Emergent Religions.*

Karen Malpede is the author of eleven plays, including *The Beekeeper's Daughter, Better People, Going to Iraq,* and *Us,* that have been produced across the United States and in Europe and Australia. She is author of *A Monster Has Stolen the Sun and Other Plays* and *Women in Theater: Compassion and Hope.* Her plays are anthologized in *Women on the Verge* (1993), *Angels of Power and Other Reproductive Creations* (1991), and *A Century of Plays by American Women* (1979). In 1995 she was awarded the National Jerome McKnight Fellowship in Playwriting.

Bernard McGinn is the Naomi Shenstone Donnelley Professor at the Divinity School of the University of Chicago. Trained in theology and in medieval history, he has written primarily in the areas of the history of Western apocalyptic traditions and Christian spirituality and mysticism. His current project is a five-volume history of Christian mysticism, *The Presence of God.*

Lee Quinby is professor of English and American studies at Hobart and William Smith Colleges. She is the author of *Anti-Apocalypse* (1994) and *Freedom, Foucault, and the Subject of America* (1991), editor of *Genealogy and Literature* (1995), and coeditor of *Feminism and Foucault* (1988).

Sandra Schanzer has worked in the computer industry since the 1960s, as a systems analyst and programmer and as a manager in information technology departments. Since 1986 she has headed her own company, Dorset Consulting of Teaneck, New Jersey, which provides computer services to corporate and not-for-profit organizations.

Hillel Schwartz is an independent scholar and senior fellow at the Millennium Institute, Arlington, Virginia. He has written, among other books, *Century's End: A Cultural History of the Fin de Siècle from the 990s through the 1990s* (1990) and *The Culture of the Copy: Striking Likenesses, Unreasonable Facsimiles* (1996).

Margaret Thaler Singer is professor emeritus of psychology at the University of California, Berkeley, and author of *Cults in Our Midst* (1995).

Clarence Taylor is associate professor of history and African New World studies at Florida International University and author of *Black Churches in Brooklyn* (1994) and *Knocking at Our Own Door: Milton A. Galamison and the Struggle for School Integration in New York City* (forthcoming).

Peter von Ziegesar is a writer and filmmaker living in New York City. He writes regularly for *Art in America* and the on-line magazine *Artnet.*

Index

About the Editors

Charles B. Strozier is professor of history and codirector of the Center on Violence and Human Survival, John Jay College and the Graduate Center, City University of New York, and a training and supervising psychoanalyst at the Training and Research Institute in Self Psychology (TRISP) in New York City. He trained at Harvard, the University of Chicago, the Chicago Institute for Psychoanalysis, and TRISP. He is the author of *Apocalypse: On the Psychology of Fundamentalism in America* (1994) and *Lincoln's Quest for Union: Public and Private Meanings* (l982); he is the editor (with Michael Flynn) of *Genocide, War, and Human Survival* and *Trauma, Broken Connections, and the Self* (both 1996); other books edited by him include *Heinz Kohut, Self Psychology and the Humanities: Reflections on a New Psychoanalytic Approach* (1985); *The Leader: Psychohistorical Studies* (1984) (with Daniel Offer); and *The Public and Private Lincoln: Contemporary Perspectives* (1979) (with Cullom Davis, Rebecca Veach, and Geoffrey Ward). Strozier founded the *Psychohistory Review,* continued as editor for fourteen years, and is now associate editor, often contributing articles. He is currently writing a biography of Heinz Kohut.

Michael Flynn is lecturer in psychology at York College and associate director of the Center on Violence and Human Survival, John Jay College, City University of New York. He is coeditor of *Genocide, War, and Human Survival* and *Trauma, Broken Connections, and the Self* (1996). Flynn is a clinical psychologist in private practice in New York City, specializing in the treatment of victims and perpetrators of physical and sexual violence.